CW00734924

Negotiating Freedom in tl Circum-Caribbean

Bringing together Jamaican Maroons and indigenous communities into one framework—for the first time—McKee compares and contrasts how these non-white, semi-autonomous communities were ultimately reduced by Anglophone colonists. In particular, questions are asked about Maroon and Creek interaction with Anglophone communities, slave-catching, slave ownership, land conflict and dispute resolution to conclude that, while important divergences occurred, commonalities can be drawn between Maroon history and Native American history and that, therefore, we should do more to draw Maroon communities into debates of indigenous issues.

Helen M. McKee completed her Ph.D. at Newcastle University. She is the author of "From Violence to Alliance: Maroons and White Settlers in Jamaica, 1739–1795," published in *Slavery & Abolition*.

Routledge Studies in the History of the Americas

Memory of the Argentina Disappearances
The Political History of Nunca Más
Emilio Crenzel

Projections of Power in the Americas
Edited by Niels Bjerre-Poulsen, Helene Balslev Clausen, and Jan Gustafsson

Mexico, 1848–1853
Los Años Olvidados
Edited by Pedro Santoni and Will Fowler

Tuberculosis in the Americas, 1870–1945
Beneath the Anguish in Philadelphia and Buenos Aires
Vera Blinn Reber

Negotiating Freedom in the Circum-Caribbean
The Jamaican Maroons and Creek Nation Compared
Helen M. McKee

For more information about this series, please visit: www.routledge.com/ Routledge-Studies-in-the-History-of-the-Americas/book-series/RSHAM

Negotiating Freedom in the Circum-Caribbean

The Jamaican Maroons
and Creek Nation Compared

Helen M. McKee

Routledge
Taylor & Francis Group

NEW YORK AND LONDON

First published 2019
by Routledge
52 Vanderbilt Avenue, New York, NY 10017

and by Routledge
2 Park Square, Milton Park, Abingdon, Oxon OX14 4RN

First issued in paperback 2020

Routledge is an imprint of the Taylor & Francis Group, an informa business

© 2019 Taylor & Francis

Library of Congress Cataloging-in-Publication Data
Names: McKee, Helen M., author.
Title: Negotiating freedom in the circum-Caribbean : the Jamaican
    Maroons and Creek Nation compared / by Helen M. McKee.
Description: New York : Routledge, 2019. | Series: Routledge studies in
    the history of the Americas ; 5 | Includes bibliographical references
    and index. |
Identifiers: LCCN 2018051042 (print) | LCCN 2018056146 (ebook) |
    ISBN 9780429024702 () | ISBN 9780367110833
Subjects: LCSH: Maroons—Jamaica—History—18th century. |
    Maroons—Jamaica—History—19th century. | Creek Indians—
    History—18th century. | Creek Indians—History—19th century. |
    Maroons—Jamaica—Ethnic identity. | Jamaica—Race relations.
Classification: LCC F1896.N4 (ebook) | LCC F1896.N4 M38 2019
    (print) | DDC 972.92/00497385—dc23
LC record available at https://lccn.loc.gov/2018051042

ISBN 13: 978-0-367-66189-2 (pbk)
ISBN 13: 978-0-367-11083-3 (hbk)

Typeset in Goudy
by Apex CoVantage, LLC

Printed in the United Kingdom
by Henry Ling Limited

To Mummy and Daddy

Contents

Figures

Acknowledgements

My greatest academic debt is to my Ph.D. supervisor, Diana Paton, who has been a constant source of knowledge and constructive criticism, and whose endless support enabled my confidence to grow enough to start, never mind complete, a Ph.D. I would also like to thank my second supervisor, Ben Houston, for his continual feedback on my writing and his invaluable input during meetings.

This book would not have been possible without the help of people who care for the records that this manuscript is based upon. I have relied heavily on the advice of those who work at the British Library, the U.K. National Archives, the British Library, the U.S. National Archives, the Library of Congress, the Georgia Department of Archives and History, the Georgia Historical Society, the Alabama Department of Archives and History, the National Library of Jamaica, the Jamaican National Archives, the P.K. Yonge Library of Florida History and Florida State University Library.

I have been privileged enough to have received generous financial support from the Arts and Humanities Research Council in the form of a doctoral award, without which I could not have undertaken this research. I have also received kind bursaries to attend conferences and overseas research from the AHRC Overseas Research Fund and the David Nicholls Memorial Trust. The majority of the Creek sections of this book were written during my six-month fellowship at the Library of Congress, supported by the AHRC. My thanks go to the many people there who made my visit so memorable: Jon, Chris, Jenny, Jamie, Mike, Alex, Mary-Lou and JoAnn.

Aspects of this manuscript have been presented at several conference and workshops in the United Kingdom, the United States and Jamaica and beyond. I am incredibly grateful for the feedback and comments I received from colleagues at The Kluge Center, Library of Congress, Washington, D.C.; the Institute of Historical Research, London; the International Maroon Conference, Charles Town, Jamaica; the Society of Caribbean Research, Germany; and the Resistance and Empire Conference, Lisbon. I am also indebted to all those at Routledge for their hard work in bringing this work to publication, in particular Max Novick, Jennifer Morrow and Brindha Thirumoorthy, as well as the endeavours of all of the reviewers who have infinitely improved this book.

Without the support of my family, friends and colleagues, the researching and writing of this manuscript would have been impossible. Firstly I would like to thank my parents, Bill and Anne, who have supported me unconditionally throughout the entire process. I owe them more than I could ever repay. Thank you to Babsi for the unparalleled encouragement, the inspiring discussions and the unwavering belief in me over the last six years. I would also like to thank the rest of my family and friends who have helped me through some of the most trying of times; in particular, Ben, James and Jeanie, Aunty Judy and Uncle Brian, Suzie, Phil, Zoe and Jen. Thank you to my friends who have let me stay with them on research trips, Phil for the countless late-night travel stories after trips to the British Library and Gylfi for providing the best homemade mojitos during my research stays. Zaineb and Muneeb in Georgia, and Barbara and Nicoletta in Jamaica, have made my international trips so memorable. This work would never have made the transition from thesis to manuscript without my current support network in Germany, in particular Jean-Philippe, Marc, Angela, Anke and James, who have always been ready to listen to my rants and frustrations with a smile and a beer. I also could not have completed this book without my friends in Kassel, especially Katja, Alex and Steve. I would also like to remember some of those who are not here to see my work finished: Pev, Aunty Fran, Aunty Kath, Aunty Eva, Uncle John and my deeply missed Grandad. Finally, I would like to dedicate this book to my beloved father who passed away during the final stages of re-writing. He proofread everything I have ever written and I know he would have done the same for me with this manuscript. I love you, Daddy.

Introduction

In March 1736, as the First Maroon War raged in Jamaica, a proposal intending to bring about the defeat of "those rebellious negroes" was put forward to the House of Assembly. Bloody battles with the Maroons had plagued the colonists, and every attempt to resolve the conflict had so far failed. The colonial government knew that it would be unable to establish the type of colony that it desired while still at war with the Maroons. Moreover, the vast expense of such warfare was crippling the Jamaican economy. Previous efforts to defeat the Maroons had been "ineffectual and attended with very considerable expense." The colonial government needed a solution, or the potential goldmine of Jamaica would be lost to the British Empire. Therefore, after long discussions, it was recommended that two hundred Creek Indians who "inhabit a country as rocky and mountainous as any part of Jamaica" be deployed against the Maroons. The proposal justified the choice of Creeks by drawing similarities between the two communities, saying "They are a hardy warlike people, exceedingly good marksmen, nimble and expert in finding out and following tracts, accustomed to mountains, bush fighting, and ambushing. They are also inured to hardships and the extremities of weather."[1] Similarities between Maroons and Creeks, however, did not end with those of physical attributes. Comparisons extended beyond their competence in warfare to commonalities in political interactions with governments, social relationships with slaves and settlers, and disputes over land. The Act did not end up being passed by the Assembly, but it serves to show how, even in 1736, parallels were being drawn between Maroon and indigenous communities.

This comparison of 1736 raises questions that have yet to be answered about non-white communities who signed peace treaties with European or European-descended governments. Despite the similarities being so obvious to contemporaries, no study has brought Maroons and Creeks together to assess how they negotiated new roles with the societies that surrounded them. Indeed, the Maroon experience is rarely related to that of any indigenous community in the Americas. However, much can be learned if Maroons are considered within such a framework. Rather than continuing the colonial undertaking of classifying Maroons as merely "runaway slaves," comparing them with an established, indigenous confederation surrounded by a society which also promoted slave-driven capitalism, we can further see the complexities of the Maroon experience. Issues important to Creeks were also critical to Maroons: land disputes, judicial reform, economics and relations with the enslaved population, to name but a few.

That is not to say, of course, that no differences existed between the origins of Maroons and Creek communities. It is worth briefly introducing each community now to aid the later comparison. Maroons were typically escapees from the plantations prior to 1739. Bev Carey has argued that these early runaways fled these English-owned estates and joined with indigenous Taíno communities in the mountainous interior of the island.[2] As time passed and the indigenous population significantly decreased, Maroons became even more reliant on the influx of runaways from the plantations to bolster their number.[3] Once escaped, Maroons maintained close ties with enslaved people on the plantations who often acted as spies.[4] Apart from depending on these plantation rebels to feed them information, Maroons were also indebted to them for supplying arms, ammunition and certain food provisions.[5] In turn, Maroons were instrumental in physically instigating and psychologically inspiring uprisings on the plantations, such as the slave revolt in St. Ann's Parish in 1673.[6] Thus, what became manifest before 1739 was an island-wide revolutionary network of Maroons and slaves; a cooperation between enslaved rebels and Maroons steeped in an inherent desire for freedom.

In the years preceding the treaties, Maroons amassed control over a substantial amount of territory. Most of the land that they acquired was situated along the slopes of the mountain chain that runs through the central part of the island. Apart from this location, Barbara Kopytoff stresses that the western central part of the island was also an important region in which Maroons settled.[7] These natural enclaves worked as protective fortresses that British colonists found difficult to penetrate.[8] Such topography was central to the Maroon offensive campaigns against settlers, and their war strategy successfully curtailed the rise of European civilisation in Jamaica. Only three major colonial towns were built during this period, all in close proximity to each other: Kingston, Port Royal and Spanish Town.[9] Along with these towns, there was limited development of pens, small farms and sugar plantations in the areas primarily adjoining the coast.[10] In contrast, Maroons established numerous settlements, with those in the west becoming known as the Leeward Maroons, and those in the east as the Windward Maroons.

The rapid pace at which Maroons advanced in the pre-treaty years towards cementing their rule over a sizable proportion of the Jamaican landscape exasperated the British colonists.[11] Without firm control of the island, there was a strong possibility that the colonists' worst fear would materialise: relinquishing Jamaica to the black population.[12] Whites were in a precarious position during this uncertain period and the situation was a pressing concern. Not only was the pride of white colonists at stake, but the future of establishing Jamaica as a valuable and profitable colony in the British Empire was being jeopardised. Colonists invested enormous sums of money in the early eighteenth century to counter black attempts to gain freedom in Jamaica. Edward Long, the eighteenth-century Jamaican planter-historian, estimated that at least £240,000 was spent over eighty years in efforts to suppress the resistance of the Maroons.[13] Over two centuries later, Barbara Kopytoff suggested the figure exceeded Edward Long's estimate and stated that such an expense dealt a serious blow to colonial coffers.[14] The military campaigns that the British government funded were not only costly but also largely unsuccessful.

What confronted the colonists was far more complex than Maroons as individuals or, indeed, as a community. For colonists, the real threat was the act of marronage itself and its implications for the development of the island's economy. With an increase in the number of runaways in the years leading up to 1739, colonists were aware that, even if they managed to wipe out the existing Maroons, new groups would be ready to replace them. Colonists faced established networks between plantation rebels and Maroons, an increase in the number of African runaways and the large acreage of "idle" land in the interior.[15] The war of this period was thus against a much larger enemy than the Maroons. Many colonists increasingly came to support the view that it would be more sensible to win over some Maroons by entering into treaties with them, than to persist with the impossible task of exterminating them. With this in mind, the colonial government began overtures to bring the Maroons to peace. In the west, the Maroon leader Cudjoe was known to have a firmer control over his people than the Maroons in the east of the island, so the British first approached him. Successful negotiation led to a peace treaty being declared with these Leeward Maroons. The colonial government then turned to the Windwards in the east. The Windwards took longer to agree on terms, and there are claims they did so only because they feared Cudjoe would ally the Leeward Maroons with the colonists to defeat the Windwards.[16] Nevertheless, peace with the Windwards was shortly declared. Therefore, the five major Maroon towns after the peace treaties were the Leeward communities of Trelawny Town and Accompong in the west, and the Windward communities of Scotts Hall, Moore Town and Charles Town (also known as Crawford Town) in the east. Nanny Town had been abandoned during the skirmishes with the British (see Figure I.1).

In the years of the peace treaties, Jamaica was still an under-developed colony. Some areas had large numbers of white people living in them, particularly around Kingston, Spanish Town and Port Royal, and mass African importation had begun. However, large areas of the island lay untouched by development, predominantly in the northeast in parishes such as Portland, largely because of the hostile Maroon presence. A British-appointed Governor led the colonial government in Jamaica, the most prominent part of which was the House of Assembly, full of white planters from around the island. Absentee owners possessed significant amounts of land, and this situation would worsen in the years to come as their fortunes grew and they returned to the metropole.[17]

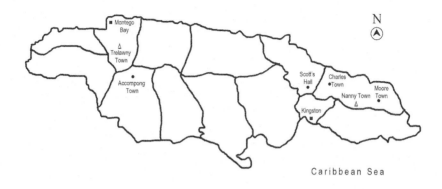

Figure I.1 Map of Jamaica showing parish boundaries and locations of the major Maroon settlements. This map was provided to the author by Professor Jada Benn Torres of Vanderbilt University.

With the signing of the peace treaties, a great deal changed, and yet much remained on the same path since the 1730s. Tracts of land were opened up to cultivation, but it was for cultivation that would consolidate the trade in Africans and their use as slave labour, rather than as an antithesis to slavery. Planters continued to dominate the political and economic arenas and seemed more in control than ever but they were still troubled by frequent slave rebellions and the threat of invasion from other European powers, and, of course, they were always wary of the intentions of the Maroons themselves. Despite this, the period under study is concurrent with the "golden age" of Jamaican slavery, at least for the slaveholders, where planter power was at its highest. This was particularly true following the end of the Seven Years' War from which Britain emerged as the world's leading colonial power.[18] The situation was to last until the eve of the nineteenth century. Abolitionist voices were rising, and economically Jamaican planters were beginning to be hurt by the competition of colonies such as Cuba. However, any attempt to view these processes as linear and one-dimensional obscures the complexity of both Jamaican history and the history of the circum-Caribbean.

Whilst Maroons were descended from runaway slaves, and to some extent from the indigenous population of Jamaica, members of the Creek Nation were almost exclusively indigenous and native to what is now the United States.[19] Hernando de Soto, the Spanish explorer, led the first expedition into the interior of North America in the sixteenth century. As a result of this expedition, infection spread, leading to the collapse of the Mississippian culture and the rise of the Creek confederacy.[20] The people who became known as the Creeks, located in present-day Georgia and Alabama, were actually a confederation of tribes such as the Hitichi, the Alabama and the Coosa, who had been incorporated into the wider umbrella term of "Creek" as generations passed. The term "Creek" referred to the fork of a trading path from Charleston and was first used by the British to describe the Native Americans who lived in the area around this creek.[21] Tribes were brought into the confederation either through negotiation or as a result of incorporation after being defeated by the larger confederation in wars. The basic Creek social unit was the town, or *talwa*. Abihka, Coosa, Cusseta and Coweta formed the four "mother" towns of the confederacy. Creeks were also often split into the "Lower Creeks" and the "Upper Creeks," with each side often showing allegiance to differing European powers. The Lower Towns were located along the Chattahoochee, Flint and Apalachicola rivers, as well as the Ocmulgee and Oconee rivers; some of the major towns being Coweta, Cusseta, Hitichi and Oconee. The Upper Towns were located on the Coosa, Tallapoosa and Alabama rivers; major towns included Tuckabatchee, Coosa and Hilibi (see Figure I.2).[22]

Figure I.2 Map of major towns and rivers in the south-eastern United States. Robert H. Labberton, *New Historical Atlas and General History* (New York: Townsend MacCoun, 1886) Plate LXVIII.

As most Creeks felt a stronger allegiance to their town than to the confederacy as a whole, the most important leader in Creek society was the village chief, or *micco*. Far from being dictators, *miccos* were negotiators who could only attempt to persuade members of their villages to support their plans. *Miccos* ruled with the assistance of lesser chiefs, or *micalgi*, who held posts such as medicine men, warriors and village elders. However, what outranked even a Creek's allegiance to their town was their allegiance to their clan. The authority of the *miccos* was, therefore, limited by a Creek's reverence to their clan leader, who was often a woman, as Creek society was matrilineal. The Wind clan is considered the most influential with numerous powerful Creeks, such as Alexander McGillivray, belonging to that clan. Other clans include the Bear, the Potato and the Beaver.[23]

As the Creek confederacy grew, so too did the European presence in what is now the south-eastern United States. Britain, France and Spain all established colonies in the region following Hernando de Soto's initial exploration. Trade and war were features of interactions between indigenous communities and all the European nations present in the region. With the end of the Seven Years' War in 1763, France lost its North American empire and British settlers moved inland towards Creek territory. Many settlers increasingly felt that the British government favoured the Native American deerskin trade over their own needs and began to join the Sons of Liberty.[24] Fears of these land-hungry settlers, and the Creek need for European manufactured goods such as guns, led many Creeks to side with the British once the American Revolution broke out.[25] However, different Creeks sided with different armies as a result of the complex social structure of the *talwa*, the clan and the personal situation of each individual Creek. In general, Upper Creeks tended to side with the British and Lower Creeks attempted to remain neutral although many towns eventually joined the Loyalist cause. Despite this support, when the war ended in 1783, the Creek confederacy learned that Britain had ceded their lands to the new republic.

At the end of the American Revolution, the south-eastern United States as a place was not entirely different from 1730s Jamaica. A bloody war had ravaged the country, killing thousands and sending the cost of the war spiralling, much like the First Maroon War did with Jamaica. There were developed parts of the area that were under plantation cultivation, but there were also vast amounts of lands open for development, both indigenous-owned and not. Much like in Jamaica, there were large concentrations of white people living in coastal regions, centred on the coastal zones such as Charleston, South Carolina, and Savannah, Georgia. A newly formed federal government, based first in New York City and then subsequently Philadelphia and Washington, D.C., included representatives from the states, and each state itself had its own government.

When negotiating the first of many peace treaties with the Creek Nation, the federal government had to come to terms with the fact that many Creeks had actually fought alongside the Loyalists and were, in the eyes of some

Americans, the defeated enemy. The confederation was now dealing with a young country rather than an empire: a country that wanted land to pay off the war costs and to grow into a more powerful force to protect itself from the European empires that surrounded it. Despite this, as with Jamaica, continuities occurred both internal and external to the Creeks. For example, despite the trading company of Panton, Leslie & Co. being Loyalist and moving to be based in Spanish Florida, it was allowed to continue trading with Creeks. In a more national context, there was no sudden change to the path that the United States was on. The same crops were cultivated and the emphasis was on growth of wealth; it was simply now in the context of a new country rather than as colonies of the British Empire. In contrast to the period under consideration in Jamaica, this was not the "golden age" for the United States. There were good times, for the contemporary white population at least, of mass expansion and escape from metropolitan control; but it was also a young republic, torn on the issue of how best to move forward and bring the thirteen colonies together into one nation. It was a time of political turmoil and uncertainty, yet eventually, and especially following the defeat of the Western Confederacy, it seemed that nothing could stop the expansion of the United States.

Within this book, therefore, I compare two semi-autonomous communities with a corporate identity. But it begs the question, why Maroons and Creeks, given their differing backgrounds? It is precisely because of those different backgrounds, however, that the commonalities which emerge become all the more interesting. I am, of course, not arguing that their experiences were strictly uniform but merely that commonalities did occur and, therefore, we can learn a great deal by considering Maroons in the framework of an indigenous community. Too often is Jamaica dealt with as a binary society of black/white, African/European, or slave/free. Indeed, even the titles of the seminal works of Richard Price and Richard Hart explicitly reduce Maroon communities to the slave heritage of some, but not all, Maroons.[26] By conducting a sustained comparison with an indigenous community, we can move beyond the view of Maroons as ex-slaves and relate their experiences to those of other free communities in the Americas. Maroons and Creeks in the time period under examination had a different understanding of race, and we should not be bound by colonial pigeon-holing when it comes to the analysis of non-white, autonomous communities in the Americas. Further, there is a growing desire in contemporary Maroon communities to gain recognition as indigenous because of their shared heritage with the Taíno people of Jamaica. A comparison between Maroons and an indigenous community from another English-speaking, plantation-based slave society is, therefore, long overdue.

This comparison, consequently, investigates the cultural, social and political role of Maroons and Creeks in the circum-Caribbean region during roughly the century that saw the consolidation, and for Jamaica at least, the beginnings of the decline of slavery, that is, from 1739 until 1813. Both communities are analysed in an inter-war period to assess how they negotiated new roles with their former enemies. I examine the Maroons from the end of the First Maroon War in 1739 until the outbreak of the Second Maroon War in 1795. I analyse the Creeks in a slightly later period—from the end of the American Revolution in 1783 until the Creek War of 1813, also known as the Redstick War. I have chosen these timeframes for several reasons. Maroons are considered over a longer period of time because they signed only two significant sets of peace treaties with the British, and it is that time between the treaties that is under consideration. In addition to this, the archival evidence for the Maroons is much more limited than that regarding the Creeks and, therefore, the timeframe had to be extended in order to provide more access to archival evidence and a more viable comparison. The reverse is true for Creeks; the archival evidence can be, at times, overwhelming, and one way to limit the sheer volume of documents is to examine a shorter time period. Additionally, beginning with the end of the American Revolution enables this study to focus on how the newly formed United States dealt with Creeks, avoiding over-complicating the situation by bringing British policies into the study which, while fascinating, would simply not be possible for a study of this length. Taking the Creek War of 1813 as the end-point also allows the study a suitable end-point in terms of another significant treaty, the Treaty of Fort Jackson, being signed. This permits an analysis of how both the communities, and their negotiations of new relationships outside of their own societies, changed in an inter-war period.

Having two slightly different timelines does present some challenges, however. First, it means that Maroons are considered in a colonial context, whereas Creeks are not.[27] Second, the geo-political context of the two studies is different—for example, the French and Spanish represent a significant threat in the region during the Maroon period, whereas, following the Haitian Revolution and the Louisiana Purchase, the French threat is removed in the Creek period. Third, contemporary theories of the day, such as those regarding slaves and slavery, are different depending on which time period is in question. However, whilst these are important issues, I have chosen the time periods because I believe they make the most pertinent comparison. It allows an examination which begins with significant treaties, following the end of significant wars, and traces the impact of those treaties until the outbreak of other significant wars.

It is also important to briefly clarify here some of the terms that are used throughout the book. In this manuscript, the term "circum-Caribbean" applies to a geographic region in the Americas. Coming from the Latin word "circum," meaning around, the term has typically referred to the Caribbean Sea, its islands and the surrounding coasts.[28] However, I extend that definition to include parts of Georgia and Alabama that are situated further away from the coast. The "circum-Caribbean" region refers to an area in which ideas, people and products were exchanged in many directions. It was a fluid world, in a similar manner to that of the Atlantic World. I argue that large areas of Georgia and Alabama, if not the entire states, had more in common with the Caribbean islands than they did with the northern U.S. states which bordered

Canada. The societies in Georgia and Alabama, which were plantation-driven, slave-based and peopled by African slaves, free communities and Euro-descended colonists, had clear similarities with islands such as Jamaica and Barbados. Therefore, I have broadened the definition of the "circum-Caribbean" to include them.

There are also issues with both the terms "Maroon" and "Creek." Whilst "Maroon" is a British construct, having previously used the terms "wild negroes" and "bush negroes" among others, I have chosen to use "Maroon" because it is the word that current communities use to define themselves. Where possible, I differentiate between which community a Maroon belonged to, but this is sometimes impossible given the British habit of reducing all communities to "Maroon." "Creek" is even more problematic. Initially used to refer to the communities which lived along the Ochese Creek, it, too, is a European construct. A popular term is "Muskogee," which is currently used in many discussions. However, not all Creeks were Muskogees. Therefore, in order to simplify the matter, I will use the term "Creek" while acknowledging its limitations. Where possible, I also refer to the particular tribe, but American-produced sources tend to be no more accurate in this regard than British-produced ones.

The structure of this manuscript lends itself to its comparative framework. Following this short introduction, two chapters lay out the chronological narrative of Maroon and Creek history in order to build a tentative model of how colonial and federal governments attempted to control these non-white, semi-autonomous communities once peace had been negotiated. Following this, the remaining chapters take on a much more comparative approach, moving back and forth between Maroon and Creek examples. Chapter 3 examines the act of slave-catching and suppression of rebellions, whilst Chapter 4 addresses the notion of slave ownership and personal relationships with enslaved peoples in both communities. Chapter 5 analyses the land disputes that plagued Maroons and Creeks. Finally, Chapter 6 delves into interpersonal interactions between Maroons and Creeks on the one hand, and colonists and settlers on the other.

This study of race, free communities, the circum-Caribbean region and, of course, the Maroons and Creeks themselves would not be possible without the scholarly work that has gone before. Creek history has received much previous attention, spanning many different aspects. The early history focused on notable Creek leaders and general histories which were particularly U.S.-centric.[29] Out of these publications grew works which aimed to critically analyse events such as the Redstick War,[30] the civilisation plan and mass acquisition by the United States of indigenous lands.[31] Other scholars have widened the investigation of the land issue to include the effects of the U.S. roads built through Creek territory in the early nineteenth century.[32] In the 1960s, the influence of the Civil Rights Movement and the growing interest in African American history resulted in a shift of focus towards the relationship between African Americans and Creeks, as well as debating the extent to which Creeks owned African American slaves.[33] Current scholarship continues to widen the scope of Creek history and incorporates it into the history of the United States.[34]

In contrast to the scholarship on Creeks, relatively little has been written on the Jamaican Maroons. The first publications were aimed towards a more popular audience and often focused on the folkloric history of the Maroons.[35] A publication in the same popular vein as those works is Bev Carey's *Maroon Story*, which I reference frequently given the Maroon heritage of the author and her insights into Maroon history not found elsewhere.[36] Following these more popular publications came several more academic texts, largely from historians, which delved into the archives to tell the complex history of the Maroons.[37] Building on such archival work, subsequent scholars moved to utilise oral traditions in their discussion of Maroon communities.[38] Not stopping with oral traditions, Kenneth Bilby also introduced cultural studies of the Kromanti dance of the Windward Maroons, as well as Maroon spirit possession, to try to comprehend Maroon culture.[39]

In recent years, comparative history has appeared in the histories of both communities. These, however, have tended to treat each community within the framework of African-descended history for Maroons, and an indigenous framework for Creeks.[40] Rebecca Bateman has gone beyond most studies by comparing the Black Caribs and Black Seminoles.[41] Her work does begin to bring together "Africans and Indians," albeit by comparing two communities that were largely of the same race. It is upon such work that this manuscript is built.

Taking a wider scope, earlier works of non-white, semi-autonomous communities focused on white societies and their political machinations when dealing with enslaved populations, free communities and other empires. Subsequently, there has been a move away from this focus to concentrate on the internal politics of non-white societies in the Americas.[42] My work builds on both of these approaches. The primary focus is on the Maroons and Creeks but includes extensive examination of their interaction with white and black societies. In some ways, it is an attempt to weave together all of these stories that have been told individually, to build a picture of the complex, frequently changing interactions between the different sectors of society. The book, when taken together, highlights how Maroon communities can be considered within an indigenous framework.

Overall, this study examines how Maroons and Creeks forged new identities out of interactions with Anglophone communities, how they negotiated new roles for themselves in a post-war world and how both communities were ultimately reduced by Anglo-colonialism. As I will show, those who encountered European societies faced largely similar problems but often arrived at different solutions. The paths taken in the quest to resist European encroachment frequently diverged but resulted in the same outcome—war and loss of territory.

Notes

1. *Journals of the House of Assembly (JHA)*, 24th March 1736, Vol. III, National Archives of Jamaica (NAJ).
2. Bev Carey, *Maroon Story: The Authentic and Original History of the Maroons in the History of Jamaica, 1490–1880* (St. Andrew, Jamaica: Agouti Press, 1997), 51–52.

3. Barbara Klamon Kopytoff, 'The Early Political Development of Jamaican Maroon Societies,' *The William and Mary Quarterly*, 35, 2 (Apr., 1978), 289.
4. Orlando Patterson, 'Slavery and Slave Revolts: A Sociohistorical Analysis of the First Maroon War, 1655–1740,' in *Maroon Societies: Rebel Slave Communities in the Americas*, ed. Richard Price (Baltimore: Johns Hopkins University Press, 1996) 78–93.
5. Mavis Campbell, *The Maroons of Jamaica, 1655–1796: A History of Resistance, Collaboration & Betrayal* (Trentin: Africa World Press, 1990), 49.
6. *Ibid.*, 54.
7. Barbara Klamon Kopytoff, 'The Maroons of Jamaica; An Ethnohistorical Study of Incomplete Polities, 1655–1905' (Ph.D. diss., University of Pennsylvania Press, 1973), 3.
8. Alvin O. Thompson, *Flight to Freedom: African Runaways and Maroons in the Americas* (Kingston: University of West Indies Press, 2006).
9. Rhett Jones, *White Settlers, Black Rebels: Jamaica in the Era of the First Maroon War, 1655–1796* (Providence: Brown University, 1976).
10. For more on the history of Jamaica, see Kamau Brathwaite, *The Development of Creole Society in Jamaica, 1770–1820* (Kingston: Ian Randle, 2005); Verene A. Shepherd, *Livestock, Sugar and Slavery: Contested Terrain in Colonial Jamaica* (Miami: Ian Randle, 2009); Mary Turner, *Slaves and Missionaries: The Disintegration of Jamaican Slave Society, 1787–1834* (Urbana: University of Illinois Press, 1982); Christer Petley, *Slaveholders in Jamaica: Colonial Society and Culture During the Era of Abolition* (London: Pickering & Chatto, 2009).
11. Campbell, *The Maroons of Jamaica*, 57.
12. *Jamaican Courant*, Wednesday 20th June 1722, National Library of Jamaica (NLJ).
13. Edward Long, *The History of Jamaica: Or, General Survey of the Ancient and Modern State of that Island: With Reflections on its Situations, Settlements, Inhabitants, Climate, Products, Commerce, Laws, and Government*, Vol. II (London: F. Cass, 1970), 340. According to a conversion on the website www.measuringworth.com, that would equate to £36,390,000 in 2018's money.
14. Kopytoff, 'The Maroons of Jamaica,' 105.
15. Campbell, *The Maroons of Jamaica*, 55.
16. *Ibid.*, 21; Richard Hart, *Slaves Who Abolished Slavery* (Kingston: University of the West Indies, Institute of Social and Economic Research, 1985), 68.
17. The apparent high frequency of absentee owners in Jamaica has been disputed by Trevor Burnard, who claims that absenteeism has been exaggerated. For more on this debate, see Burnard, 'Passengers Only: The Extent and Significance of Absenteeism in Eighteenth-Century Jamaica,' *Atlantic Studies*, 1, 2 (2004), 178–195.
18. For more on the Seven Years' War, see Daniel Marston, *The Seven Years' War* (Oxford: Osprey Publishing, 2014); Rupert Furneaux, *The Seven Years War* (London: Hart-Davis, 1973); Mark H. Danley and Patrick J. Speelman, eds., *The Seven Years' War: Global Views* (Leiden: Biggleswade, 2012); Matt Schuman and Karl W. Schweizer, *The Seven Years War: A Transatlantic History* (London: Routledge, 2008); Warren R. Hofstra, ed., *Cultures in Conflict: The Seven Years' War in North America* (Lanham: Rowman & Littlefield Publishers, 2007); Fred Anderson, *Crucible of War: The Seven Years' War and the Fate of Empire in British North America, 1754–1766* (London: Faber & Faber, 2000); Daniel Baugh, *The Global Seven Years War, 1754–1763* (London: Pearson Press, 2011); Frank McLynn, *The Year Britain Became Master of the World* (London: Jonathan Cape, 2004).
19. Certain scholars, such as Richard Hart, assert that the Maroons were descendants of Taínos and escaped Africans in early Jamaica.
20. John Reed Swanton, *Early History of the Creek Indians and Their Neighbours* (Washington, DC: U.S. Govt. Print. Off., 1922).
21. Claudio Saunt, *A New Order of Things: Property, Power, and the Transformation of the Creek Indians, 1733–1816* (Cambridge: Cambridge University Press, 1999), 13.

22. Robbie Franklyn Ethridge, *Creek Country: The Creek Indians and Their World* (Chapel Hill: University of North Carolina Press, 2003), 21. For more on Creek social structure, see David W. Miller, *The Taking of American Indian Lands in the Southeast: A History of Territorial Cessions and Forced Relocation, 1607–1840* (Jefferson: McFarland, 2011).

23. For more on Creek clans, see Saunt, *A New Order of Things*, 19–21.

24. Walter S. Dunn, *Choosing Sides on the Frontier in the American Revolution* (Westport, CT: Praeger, 2007).

25. *Ibid.*

26. Hart, *Slaves Who Abolished Slavery*; Richard Price, ed., *Maroon Societies: Rebel Slave Communities in the Americas* (Baltimore: Johns Hopkins University Press, 1996).

27. The technique of comparing a community in a national context with one in a colonial context has been successfully implemented by Lisa Ford in her seminal work *Settler Sovereignty: Jurisdiction and Indigenous People in America and Australia, 1788–1836* (Cambridge, MA: Harvard University Press, 2010).

28. See, for example, Roberta Delson, *Readings in Caribbean History and Economics: An Introduction to the Region* (London: Taylor & Francis, 1981), xvi; Bonham C. Richardson, *The Caribbean in the Wider World, 1492–1992: A Regional Geography* (Cambridge: Cambridge University Press, 1992), 6; Kenneth R. Andrews, *The Spanish Caribbean: Trade and Plunder, 1530–1630* (New Haven and London: Yale University Press, 1978), 2, 253.

29. John Walton Caughey, *McGillivray of the Creeks* (Norman: University of Oklahoma Press, 1938); Angie Debo, *The Road to Disappearance* (Norman: University of Oklahoma Press, 1941).

30. Theron A. Nunez, 'Creek Nativism and the Creek War of 1813–1814,' *Ethnohistory*, 5, 1 (Winter, 1958), 1–47; See, for example, Frank L. Owsley, *Struggle for the Gulf Borderlands: The Creek War and the Battle of New Orleans, 1812–1815* (Gainesville: University Press of Florida, 1981).

31. James Leitch Wright, *Creeks and Seminoles: The Destruction and Regeneration of the Muscogulge People* (Lincoln: University of Nebraska Press, 1990), 152; Kathryn E. Holland Braund, *Deerskins and Duffels: The Creek Indian Trade with Anglo-America, 1685–1815* (Lincoln: University of Nebraska Press, 1996), 185; Angela Pulley Hudson, *Creek Paths and Federal Roads: Indians, Settlers, and Slaves and the Making of the American South* (Chapel Hill: University of North Carolina Press, 2010); Saunt, *A New Order of Things*; Ethridge, *Creek Country*.

32. Henry deLeon Southerland Jr. and Jerry Elijah Brown, *The Federal Road Through Georgia, the Creek Nation and Alabama, 1806–1836* (Tuscaloosa: University of Alabama Press, 1989).

33. William S. Willis, 'Divide and Rule: Red, White, and Black in the Southeast,' *The Journal of Negro History*, 48, 3 (July, 1963), 157–176; William G. McLoughlin, 'Red Indians, Black Slavery and White Racism: America's Slaveholding Indians,' *American Quarterly*, 26, 4 (Oct., 1974), 367–385; Daniel F. Littlefield Jr., *Africans and Creeks from the Colonial Period to the Civil War* (Westport, CT: Greenwood Press, 1979); Kathryn E. Holland Braund, 'The Creek Indians, Blacks and Slavery,' *The Journal of Southern History*, 57, 4 (Nov., 1991), 601–636; Claudio Saunt, '"The English Has Now a Mind to Make Slaves of Them All": Creeks, Seminoles and the Problem of Slavery,' *American Indian Quarterly*, 22, 1/2 (Winter–Spring, 1998), 157–180.

34. Hudson, *Creek Paths*; Miller, *The Taking of American Indian Lands*; Alan Gallay, *Formation of a Planter Elite: Jonathan Bryan and the Southern Colonial Frontier* (Athens: University of Georgia Press, 2007); William W. Winn, *The Triumph of the Ecunnau-Nuxulgee: Land Speculators, George M. Troup, State Rights, and the Removal of the Creek Indians from Georgia and Alabama, 1825–38* (Macon: Mercer University Press, 2015); Christopher D. Haveman, *Rivers of Sand: Creek Indian*

Emigration, Relocation, and Ethnic Cleansing in the American South (Lincoln: University of Nebraska Press, 2016); Katja May, *African Americans and Native Americans in the Creek and Cherokee Nations, 1830s–1920s* (London: Routledge, 2016); Michael P. Morris, *George Galphin and the Transformation of the Georgia-South Carolina Backcountry* (Lanham: Lexington Books, 2015); Kathryn E. Holland Braund, ed., *Tohopeka: Rethinking the Creek War and the War of 1812* (Tuscaloosa: University of Alabama Press, 2012); Robert Paulett, *An Empire of Small Places: Mapping the Southeastern Anglo-Indian Trade, 1732–1795* (Athens: University of Georgia Press, 2012).

35. Joseph J. Williams, *The Maroons of Jamaica* (Boston: Boston College Press, 1938); Carey Robinson, *The Fighting Maroons of Jamaica* (Kingston: William Collins & Sangster, 1969); Kamau Brathwaite, *Nanny, Sam Sharpe, and the Struggle for People's Liberation* (Kingston: Published by the API for the National Heritage Week Committee, 1977); Milton McFarlane, *Cudjoe, the Maroon* (London: Allison & Busby, 1977).

36. Carey, *Maroon Story*. Carey's exhaustive study of the Maroons is unparalleled. Unfortunately, her work does not utilise many footnotes. It is, however, clear that her work is based on extensive archival research because many of her references can be found in archival sources and in other published works. There continues to be references which I have not uncovered. These may stem from unidentified archival sources or from Carey's own Maroon background and I, therefore, have assumed empirical foundation of incidents in Carey's work and included them in my manuscript.

37. Campbell, *The Maroons of Jamaica*; Hart, *Slaves Who Abolished Slavery*; Kopytoff, 'The Maroons of Jamaica,' 1993. Kopytoff has published multiple articles related to her doctoral research including, but not limited to, 'The Early Political Development of Jamaican Maroon Societies,' *The William and Mary Quarterly*, 35, 2 (Apr., 1978); 'Colonial Treaty as Sacred Charter of the Jamaican Maroons,' *Ethnohistory*, 26, 1 (Winter, 1979), 45–64; 'The Development of Jamaican Maroon Ethnicity,' *Caribbean Quarterly*, 22, 2/3, Essays on Slavery (June–Sept., 1976), 33–50; 'Jamaican Maroon Political Organisation: The Effects of the Treaties,' *Social and Economic Studies*, 25, 2 (June, 1976), 87–105.

38. Richard Price, *First Time: The Historical Vision of an African American People* (Chicago: University of Chicago Press, 2002); Kenneth Bilby, *True Born Maroons* (Gainesville: University of Florida Press, 2005).

39. Kenneth Bilby, 'The Kromanti Dance of the Windward Maroons of Jamaica,' *Nieuwe West-Indische*, 55, 1/2 (1981), 52–101; Kenneth Bilby, 'Swearing by the Past, Swearing to the Future: Sacred Oaths, Alliances and Treaties Among the Guianese and Jamaican Maroons,' *Ethnohistory*, 44, 4 (Autumn, 1997), 655–689.

40. Michael Craton, ed., *Testing the Chains: Resistance to Slavery in the British West Indies* (Ithaca: Cornell University Press, 1982); Monica Schuler, 'Ethnic Slave Rebellions in the Caribbean and the Guianas,' *Journal of Social History*, 3, 4 (Summer, 1970), 374–385; Theda Perdue, *Nations Remembered: An Oral History of the Cherokees, Chickasaws, Choctaws, Creeks, and Seminoles in Oklahoma, 1865–1907* (Norman: University of Oklahoma Press, 1993).

41. Rebecca B. Bateman, 'Africans and Indians: A Comparative Study of the Black Carib and Black Seminole,' *Ethnohistory*, 37, 1 (Winter, 1990), 1–24.

42. Colin A. Palmer, *The First Passage: Blacks in the Americas, 1502–1617* (Oxford: Oxford University Press, 1995); Nancy Priscilla Naro, ed., *Blacks, Coloureds and National Identity in Nineteenth Century Latin America* (London: Institute of Latin American Studies, 2003); Frederick C. Knight, *Working the Diaspora: The Impact of African Labour on the Anglo-American World, 1650–1850* (New York: New York University Press, 2010).

Bibliography

Primary Sources

National Archives of Jamaica, Spanish Town, Jamaica

Journals of the House of Assembly, Vols. I–X.

Newspapers and Magazines

Jamaican Courant.

Ph.D. Sources

Kopytoff, Barbara Klamon, 'The Maroons of Jamaica: An Ethnohistorical Study of Incomplete Polities, 1655–1905' (Ph.D. diss., University of Pennsylvania Press, 1973).

Published Sources

Anderson, Fred, *Crucible of War: The Seven Years' War and the Fate of Empire in British North America, 1754–1766* (London: Faber & Faber, 2000).

Andrews, Kenneth R., *The Spanish Caribbean: Trade and Plunder, 1530–1630* (New Haven and London: Yale University Press, 1978).

Bateman, Rebecca B., 'Africans and Indians: A Comparative Study of the Black Carib and Black Seminole,' *Ethnohistory*, 37, 1 (Winter, 1990), 1–24.

Baugh, Daniel, *The Global Seven Years War, 1754–1763* (London: Pearson Press, 2011).

Bilby, Kenneth, 'The Kromanti Dance of the Windward Maroons of Jamaica,' *Nieuwe West-Indische*, 55, 1/2 (1981), 52–101.

Bilby, Kenneth, 'Swearing by the Past, Swearing to the Future: Sacred Oaths, Alliances and Treaties Among the Guianese and Jamaican Maroons,' *Ethnohistory*, 44, 4 (Autumn, 1997), 655–689.

Bilby, Kenneth, *True Born Maroons* (Gainesville: University of Florida Press, 2005).

Brathwaite, Kamau, *Nanny, Sam Sharpe, and the Struggle for People's Liberation* (Kingston: Published by the API for the National Heritage Week Committee, 1977).

Braund, Kathryn E. Holland, 'The Creek Indians, Blacks and Slavery,' *The Journal of Southern History*, 57, 4 (Nov., 1991), 601–636.

Braund, Kathryn E. Holland, *Deerskins and Duffels: The Creek Indian Trade with Anglo-America, 1685–1815* (Lincoln: University of Nebraska Press, 1996).

Braund, Kathryn E. Holland, ed., *Tohopeka: Rethinking the Creek War and the War of 1812* (Tuscaloosa: University of Alabama Press, 2012).

Burnard, Trevor, 'Passengers Only: The Extent and Significance of Absenteeism in Eighteenth-Century Jamaica,' *Atlantic Studies*, 1, 2 (2004), 178–195.

Campbell, Mavis, *The Maroons of Jamaica, 1655–1796: A History of Resistance, Collaboration & Betrayal* (Trentin: Africa World Press, 1990).

Carey, Bev, *Maroon Story: The Authentic and Original History of the Maroons in the History of Jamaica, 1490–1880* (St. Andrew, Jamaica: Agouti Press, 1997).

Caughey, John Walton, *McGillivray of the Creeks* (Norman: University of Oklahoma Press, 1938).

Craton, Michael, ed., *Testing the Chains: Resistance to Slavery in the British West Indies* (Ithaca: Cornell University Press, 1982).

Danley, Mark J., and Patrick J. Speelman, eds., *The Seven Years' War: Global Views* (Leiden: Biggleswade, 2012).

Debo, Angie, *The Road to Disappearance* (Norman: University of Oklahoma Press, 1941).

Delson, Roberta, *Readings in Caribbean History and Economics: An Introduction to the Region* (London: Taylor & Francis, 1981).

Dunn, Walter S., *Choosing Sides on the Frontier in the American Revolution* (Westport, CT: Praeger, 2007).

Ethridge, Robbie Franklyn, *Creek Country: The Creek Indians and Their World* (Chapel Hill: University of North Carolina Press, 2003).

Ford, Lisa, *Settler Sovereignty: Jurisdiction and Indigenous People in America and Australia, 1788–1836* (Cambridge, MA: Harvard University Press, 2010).

Furneaux, Rupert, *The Seven Years War* (London: Hart-Davis, 1973).

Gallay, Alan, *Formation of a Planter Elite: Jonathan Bryan and the Southern Colonial Frontier* (Athens: University of Georgia Press, 2007).

Hart, Richard, *Slaves Who Abolished Slavery* (Kingston: University of the West Indies, Institute of Social and Economic Research, 1985).

Haveman, Christopher D., *Rivers of Sand: Creek Indian Emigration, Relocation, and Ethnic Cleansing in the American South* (Lincoln: University of Nebraska Press, 2016).

Hofstra, Warren R., ed., *Cultures in Conflict: The Seven Years' War in North America* (Lanham: Rowman & Littlefield Publishers, 2007).

Hudson, Angela Pulley, *Creek Paths and Federal Roads: Indians, Settlers, and Slaves and the Making of the American South* (Chapel Hill: University of North Carolina Press, 2010).

Jones, Rhett, *White Settlers, Black Rebels: Jamaica in the Era of the First Maroon War, 1655–1796* (Providence: Brown University, 1976).

Knight, Frederick C., *Working the Diaspora: The Impact of African Labour on the Anglo-American World, 1650–1850* (New York: New York University Press, 2010).

Kopytoff, Barbara Klamon, 'Jamaican Maroon Political Organisation: The Effects of the Treaties,' *Social and Economic Studies*, 25, 2 (June, 1976), 87–105.

Kopytoff, Barbara Klamon, 'The Development of Jamaican Maroon Ethnicity,' *Caribbean Quarterly*, 22, 2/3, Essays on Slavery (June–Sept., 1976), 33–50.

Kopytoff, Barbara Klamon, 'The Early Political Development of Jamaican Maroon Societies,' *The William and Mary Quarterly*, 35, 2 (Apr., 1978), 287–307.

Labberton, Robert H., *New Historical Atlas and General History* (New York: Townsend MacCoun, 1886).

Littlefield, Daniel F., Jr., *Africans and Creeks from the Colonial Period to the Civil War* (Westport, CT: Greenwood Press, 1979).

Long, Edward, *The History of Jamaica; or, General Survey of the Ancient and Modern State of That Island: With Reflections on Its Situations, Settlements, Inhabitants, Climate, Products, Commerce, Laws, and Government*, Vol. II (London: F. Cass, 1970).

Marston, Daniel, *The Seven Years' War* (Oxford: Osprey Publishing, 2014).

May, Katja, *African Americans and Native Americans in the Creek and Cherokee Nations, 1830s–1920s* (London: Routledge, 2016).

McFarlane, Milton, *Cudjoe, the Maroon* (London: Allison & Busby, 1977).

McLoughlin, William G., 'Red Indians, Black Slavery and White Racism: America's Slaveholding Indians,' *American Quarterly*, 26, 4 (Oct., 1974), 367–385.

McLynn, Frank, *The Year Britain Became Master of the World* (London: Jonathan Cape, 2004).

Miller, David W., *The Taking of American Indian Lands in the Southeast: A History of Territorial Cessions and Forced Relocation, 1607–1840* (Jefferson, NC: McFarland, 2011).

Morris, Michael P., *George Galphin and the Transformation of the Georgia-South Carolina Backcountry* (Lanham: Lexington Books, 2015).

Naro, Nancy Priscilla, ed., *Blacks, Coloureds and National Identity in Nineteenth Century Latin America* (London: Institute of Latin American Studies, 2003).

Nunez, Theron A., 'Creek Nativism and the Creek War of 1813–1814,' *Ethnohistory*, 5, 1 (Winter, 1958), 1–47.

Owsley, Frank L., 'Fort Mims Massacre,' *The Alabama Review*, 24 (Jan., 1971), 192–204.

Palmer, Colin A., *The First Passage: Blacks in the Americas, 1502–1617* (Oxford: Oxford University Press, 1995).

Patterson, Orlando, 'Slavery and Slave Revolts: A Socio-Historical Analysis of the First Maroon War, 1655–1740,' *Social and Economic Studies*, 19, 3 (Sept., 1970), 289–325.

Paulett, Robert, *An Empire of Small Places: Mapping the Southeastern Anglo-Indian Trade, 1732–1795* (Athens: University of Georgia Press, 2012).

Perdue, Theda, *Nations Remembered: An Oral History of the Cherokees, Chickasaws, Choctaws, Creeks, and Seminoles in Oklahoma, 1865–1907* (Norman: University of Oklahoma Press, 1993).

Petley, Christer, *Slaveholders in Jamaica: Colonial Society and Culture During the Era of Abolition* (London: Pickering & Chatto, 2009).

Price, Richard, ed., *Maroon Societies: Rebel Slave Communities in the Americas* (Baltimore: Johns Hopkins University Press, 1996).

Price, Richard, *First Time: The Historical Vision of an African American People* (Chicago: University of Chicago Press, 2002).

Richardson, Bonham C., *The Caribbean in the Wider World, 1492–1992: A Regional Geography* (Cambridge: Cambridge University Press, 1992).

Robinson, Carey, *The Fighting Maroons of Jamaica* (Kingston: William Collins & Sangster, 1969).

Saunt, Claudio, "'The English Has Now a Mind to Make Slaves of Them All': Creeks, Seminoles and the Problem of Slavery," *American Indian Quarterly*, 22, 1/2 (Winter–Spring, 1998), 157–180.

Saunt, Claudio, *A New Order of Things: Property, Power, and the Transformation of the Creek Indians, 1733–1816* (Cambridge: Cambridge University Press, 1999).

Schuler, Monica, 'Ethnic Slave Rebellions in the Caribbean and the Guianas,' *Journal of Social History*, 3, 4 (Summer, 1970), 374–385.

Schuman, Matt, and Karl W. Schweizer, *The Seven Years War: A Transatlantic History* (London: Routledge, 2008).

Shepherd, Verene A., *Livestock, Sugar and Slavery: Contested Terrain in Colonial Jamaica* (Miami: Ian Randle, 2009).

Southerland, Henry deLeon, Jr., and Jerry Elijah Brown, *The Federal Road Through Georgia, the Creek Nation and Alabama, 1806–1836* (Tuscaloosa: University of Alabama Press, 1989).

Swanton, John Reed, *Early History of the Creek Indians and Their Neighbours* (Washington, DC: U.S. Govt. Print. Off., 1922).

Thompson, Alvin O., *Flight to Freedom: African Runaways and Maroons in the Americas*, (Kingston: University of West Indies Press, 2006).

Turner, Mary, *Slaves and Missionaries: The Disintegration of Jamaican Slave Society, 1787–1834* (Urbana: University of Illinois Press, 1982).

Williams, Joseph J., *The Maroons of Jamaica* (Boston: Boston College Press, 1938).

Willis, William S., 'Divide and Rule: Red, White, and Black in the Southeast,' *The Journal of Negro History*, 48, 3 (July, 1963), 157–176.

Winn, William W., *The Triumph of the Ecunnau-Nuxulgee: Land Speculators, George M. Troup, State Rights, and the Removal of the Creek Indians from Georgia and Alabama, 1825–38* (Macon, GA: Mercer University Press, 2015).

Wright, James Leitch, *Creeks and Seminoles: The Destruction and Regeneration of the Muscogulge People* (Lincoln: University of Nebraska Press, 1990).

1 The Relationship Develops

Maroons and Creeks in the Early Post-Treaty Years

In early 1739, after the colonial government had decided that negotiation, rather than war, was the only way to defeat the Maroons, a detachment of soldiers was sent to parlay with Cudjoe and his followers. Once the Leeward Maroons in the west of the island were located, a series of shouted exchanges led to a short conference between the Maroon leaders and the colonists. On 1st March 1739, negotiations concluded and the Leeward treaty was signed by Captain Cudjoe and Colonel John Guthrie.[1] Buoyed by this success, the British set out to treat with the Windward Maroons in the east. The British hailed them with a trumpet and told them they had "come to agree, not to fight." Philip Thicknesse, one of the British soldiers present, declared that the Governor had "given Cudjoes people freedom, and that the same terms were upon to them."[2] Once again, negotiations were held, which resulted in Quao's treaty, named after the Windward leader, being signed on 23rd June 1739. These two treaties brought to an end the decades of fighting between colonists and Maroons. Many of the clauses, and their effects, are discussed in subsequent chapters; I will begin here with those directly relevant to the new alliance to be formed with the colonial government.

The most important clauses of the treaties attempted to secure the alliance of Maroons in returning runaways and/or rebellious slaves. In Cudjoe's treaty, Clause Six required the Leewards to "use their best endeavors to take, kill, suppress, or destroy" all of the "rebels wheresoever they be throughout the island"[3] This clause rather vaguely refers to "rebels" without explicitly stating that the "rebels" were, most frequently, runaway slaves. In Quao's treaty, it became more precise. Clause Four stated, "that the said captain Quao, and his people shall be ready" on the command of the Governor "to suppress and destroy all other party or parties of rebellious negroes" that may gather or settle in any part of the island and "shall bring in such other negroes as shall from time to time runaway from their respective owners."[4] Quao's treaty, therefore, not only stated that the "rebels" are runaway slaves but also required the Windwards to treat them as "rebels" as soon as they ran away from their masters.

A further requirement of both treaties was to provide aid when the island was under external threat. Clause Seven of the Leeward treaty stated, "that in case this island is invaded by any foreign enemy," Captain Cudjoe and his successors should "immediately repair to any place the governor . . . shall appoint" in order to "repel the said invaders with his or their utmost force." During these skirmishes, the Leewards were to be under the orders of the commander-in-chief.[5] Similarly, Quao's men were required, in their Clause Five, to be ready to assist the Governor "in case of any invasion" and to put themselves "under the command of the general or commander of such forces, appointed by his excellency to defend the island from the said invasion."[6]

Subordinance to the Governor was also demanded in yearly meetings. Cudjoe's Clause Eleven stated that, "captain Cudjoe, and his successors, shall wait on his excellency, or the commander in chief for the time being, once every year if thereunto required."[7] Likewise, Clause Six of Quao's treaty required him "and all his people" to be in "subjection to his excellency the Governor for the time being; and the said captain Quao shall, once every year, or oftener, appear before the Governor, if thereunto required."[8] Details of these meetings, and their consequences, will be discussed later in this chapter.

Finally, both treaties also laid out the line of succession of both the Leewards and the Windwards. Clause Fifteen of Cudjoe's treaty stated "that captain Cudjoe shall, during his life, be chief commander in Trelawny-Town" and, after his death, the command was to be passed to Accompong, then Johnny, Cuffee and finally Quaco. After all of their demises, it was decreed that the "governor, or commander in chief for the time being shall appoint, from time to time, whom he thinks fit for that command."[9] The line of succession in Quao's treaty was to be Quao, then captain Thomboy, Apong, Blackwell and, finally, Clash, after which the Governor or commander-in-chief was to appoint "whom he thinks proper."[10] Therefore, the Maroon-determined line of succession was, at best, to last a little over a generation. After that, it was to be the preserve of the colonists to decide on a leader. Quite how they expected to do this is unclear.

Kathleen Wilson argues that these treaties constituted a pivotal moment in British-Maroon relations, the differing interpretations of which had lasting repercussions for both sides.[11] Carey Robinson agrees, stating that the treaties changed "the entire character of the Maroons and reverse their way of life."[12] There is no doubt that, on paper, the British gained more: peace, an internal police force and a psychological blow to the enslaved people left on the plantations. But Maroons also gained much: recognition of some of their territories, the ending of hostilities and an acceptance by the colonial government that they would not return to slavery. The treaties, however, also left both Maroons and the colonial population in a precarious position. Maroons lived in close proximity to a slave society, where their brethren were still in chains, and were now allied to their former enemies. The plantocracy also found itself in a difficult situation after the peace treaties. Its fear that Maroons might use peace to regroup and then join with the slaves in one great alliance to overthrow the slave system was not unreasonable. The colonists' horror of such an alliance would later be realised in neighbouring Saint Domingue.[13] However, the fear in Jamaica was soon dissipated, although never disappeared, when Maroons stuck faithfully to the clauses of treaties which obliged them to hunt and return runaway slaves. In fact, fourteen years after the signing of the treaties, Governor Charles Knowles of Jamaica said, "I verily believe the Maroons will prove of more service to the country, than they ever were of prejudice."[14] Despite this, Michael Mullin asserts that Maroon support was never taken for granted by the colonial government.[15] The Governor offered three explanations for this: the Maroons' "manner of life," their strategic location "in the heart of the country" and the "very high idea the slaves entertain of them."[16] In addition, it is doubtful that the terms of the treaties were acceptable to all Maroons. Alvin O. Thompson argues that some Maroons were hardliners who would have preferred to fight the colonists to the last man for both ideological and pragmatic reasons.[17] But how true were these statements? Had Governor Knowles interpreted the situation correctly, or had the colonial government made a grave error in treating with the Maroons? As a cautionary measure, the colonial government decided to search for an alternative defence force, as "they would likewise form a proper counter balance to the Maron [Maroon] negroes."[18] The colonial government, at this conjuncture, had no idea how Maroons would act following the signing of the treaties. Was it a trick? Was it a chance to regroup before attacking with renewed vigour? The colonial government could do little but wait, see and hope.

Despite this search for alternative forces, the immediate post-treaty relationship could not have started out any better for the colonial government. Upon hearing of the declaration of war against Spain in March 1740, Cudjoe sent one of his principal men to offer assistance to the British. Cudjoe's man enquired how best to "Dispose of his People for the Defense of the Island" and whether he "could otherwise be of Service."[19] Several of his men even sailed as volunteers on the British ship *Louisa*.[20] This first test of the alliance had proved successful.

The colonial government was quick to further trial the resolve of the Maroons. In April 1741, just a few months after it became generally known that the Maroon treaties had been ratified, the members of the Assembly heard that a considerable number of slaves had deserted from several plantations in the parishes of Clarendon and St. Elizabeth and formed themselves into groups to settle in the mountains of Clarendon and St. George. Advising the Governor, the Legislature requested him to "give proper direction to Captain Cudjoe and Captain Accompong to pursue, take and destroy those in Clarendon and St. Elizabeth and the commanding officer in Crawford Town to do the like in St. George."[21] A few days later, on 2nd May, the Assemblymen drew up a bill, which became Act Number Seven of 1741 to

> encourage Colonel Cudjoe and Captain Quao and the several negroes under them in Trelawny and Crawford Town and all other towns of the rebellious negroes who submitted to terms to pursue and take up runaway slaves and such negroes as continue in rebellion; and for remedying some inconveniences in the laws already made for that purpose.[22]

The bill was passed in one day and received the assent of the Governor within six days, on 8th May. Its success was almost immediate. Cudjoe instructed a group of Maroons to assist colonial troops, and the threat was quickly quelled.[23]

Cudjoe's response to the rumoured rebellion occasioned rapturous applause from the Assembly. Colonial officials poured gratitude on him and his actions, stating, "the use such an example must be of in preventing other negroes, for the future, from running away in bodies in hopes of being protected by them."[24] The Assembly followed up their lavish words with generous rewards. Reckoning that money was soon spent, and therefore forgotten, the colonists searched for a more long-lasting token of their appreciation. Learning that the Maroons were "desirous" of a few cattle, the committee recommended a reward of two cows each for the two Leeward leaders, Accompong and Cudjoe, and one each for each of the captains of the Leeward towns. They further awarded a clothing allowance of ten yards of cloth per annum for each officer and five yards per annum for every other Maroon—to a sum of £300 annually—and agreed to the cutting of roads from Sandler's estate to Trelawny Town, for which the government would pay. Finally, they agreed to the manumission of Molly, the daughter-in-law of a prominent Maroon called Captain Cranky.[25]

Despite these rather encouraging acts, at least in the eyes of the colonists, the government saw fit to propose a resolution in 1744 to recommend that the House appoint a committee to revise the laws relating to "the negroes in Trelawny Town, Crawford Town, Nanny Town and Accompong Town" and to consider the most proper methods to render "those negroes" useful and governable by encouraging them to engage in services to the public.[26] This resulted in the following:

1. An Act for raising companies in the several negro towns and encouraging them to reduce rebellious and runaway slaves.[27]
2. An Act for the better order and government of the negroes belonging to the several negro towns and for preventing them from purchasing slaves.[28]
3. An Act for suspending an Act entitled "an act to prevent the selling of gunpowder to the rebellious or any other negroes whatever."[29]
4. An Act "to regulate the selling of gunpowder and to prevent the selling of firearms to slaves."[30]

Rather than introducing these acts because of any Maroon action or inaction, it is more likely that they were a result of the declaration of martial law after Spanish threats to the island. Despite the actions of some Maroons in earlier skirmishes by Spain, it seems that some in the colonial government were still not assured of their alliance. Indeed, the act also outlined the need for more power to be placed in the hands of the superintendents in an attempt to increase the surveillance of the Maroons. This was despite the view that Edward Long, no friend of black Jamaicans, held—that many Maroons seemed to instantly take up their treaty obligations and began to hunt and return rebellious slaves.[31] Nevertheless, the colonial government was unwilling to take the apparent allegiance for granted.

Law-making was to become a common method in the effort to control Maroon communities. In 1746, a rebellion started in Kingston and soon spread to other areas. Almost immediately, a Colonel Bennett recruited forty mercenaries from Crawford Town who served in the suppression of that rebellion.[32] The actions of those few Maroons did not prevent the colonial government from distrusting the majority. In 1746, the government passed yet another law for the "better order and government of the negroes belonging to the several negro towns" and another for "raising companies in the several negro towns and encouraging them to 'reduce' rebellious and runaway slaves."[33] These Acts seemed to have had an effect on certain Maroons. For example, a bounty hunter named George Currie was subsequently rewarded with £100 for killing the "rebel slave," Quaco Venter, in 1752.[34] George Currie was an officer at Accompong Town and had many times gone out after Quaco Venter and his gang—capturing Beauty, one of Venter's wives, in February 1752. Shortly after, while he was at Lludias Vale, Currie set his party on the trail of Venter, and a fortnight later, Venter was shot dead by Currie's men. The committee of the House of Assembly considered the act "a very extraordinary service, as he was a dangerous rebel [who] killed many, and was a great terror in the area."[35]

In addition to the legislation to encourage slave-catching, the colonial government paid a salary for every day a Maroon was out on the hunt.[36] The treaties provided for few economic opportunities and hunting runaways, thus, became an important source of income for the Maroons. Therefore, Maroon observance of this particular clause of the treaties was most likely a result of economic need rather than devotion to the colonial government and their mutual agreement. Nevertheless, hunting runaways reassured the colonial government that it had a new formidable ally in its quest for dominance. A more in-depth exploration of this act can be found in Chapter 3.

Overall, in these early post-treaty years, the colonial government was impressed with Maroon adherence to their treaty obligations and rewarded them with gifts. Edward Long, the infamous Jamaican planter-historian, wrote: "They have been very serviceable, particularly the Leeward parties, in suppressing several insurrections. Their captains are distinguished with a silver chain and medal, inscribed with their names, they wear cockades, and are regularly commissioned by the Governor."[37] To further facilitate amicable relations, when the Governors gave an audience to the Maroon chiefs once a year, they would confer some mark of favour on Maroon leaders such as "an old laced coat or waistcoat, a hat, sword . . . or any articles of the like nature." Long states that, "They are pleased with these distinctions; and a trifling douceur of this sort bestowed annually, accompanied with expressions of favour, wins their hearts, and strengthens their dutiful attachment."[38] Gift-giving contributed to the pacification of these free communities and encouraged their attachment to the alliance. However, these gifts and audiences with the Governor had an ominous tone. The fact that Maroons were required to wait on the Governor every year hints at a darker relationship with the colonial government. As Carey Robinson asserts, no chief who was at the beck and call of another figure could retain his authority for long.[39] By arranging these annual meetings, the colonial government could claim to be extending the hand of friendship to the Maroons while at the same time attempt to undermine the power and authority of Maroon leaders. These meetings may also have served as a sinister way to deduce the power of the Maroons—particularly as meetings with the Governor were often accompanied by a martial display. On the other hand, Maroons may have also used the occasions to display their military prowess to colonial officials who a few years previously had been their enemies and to remind them of the consequences of a return to hostilities.

If Edward Long is to be believed, the Maroon leader Cudjoe saw the benefit of an alliance with the colonists and frequently sought meetings with the Governors. In the early years after the treaty, he stood before his men and "addressed His Excellency aloud, desiring the continuance of the great King George's favour and protection." He announced that the Governor would administer right and justice to the Maroons, according to "the happy treaty and agreement subsisting between them and the white people on the island."[40] The reciprocity of the relationship was then highlighted by the Governor, who stated that the Maroons "might depend on the favour and protection of the great King George." A dinner was ordered for the Maroons and a present of three cows given, after which they "were dismissed, and went away perfectly well satisfied."[41] These addresses are typical of the diplomatic language of the day and do not necessarily display Cudjoe's commitment to the alliance. However, throughout the archival record, the evidence suggests that it was Cudjoe and his men who took to the alliance more than the Maroons in the east of the island. For example, it was Cudjoe who sent his men to assist during the Spanish threat, Cudjoe who dealt with the 1742 rebellion, and Cudjoe who allegedly went so far as to have enforced the use of English to replace the several different African languages.[42] That is not to say that the Windward Maroons took no part in their treaty obligations, but that Cudjoe came to be synonymous with the alliance between Maroons and colonists.

These early, amicable, interactions led to the colonial government becoming involved in Maroon internal affairs just a little more than a decade after the treaties. In February 1754, a Maroon named Quao plotted to overthrow the government of Captain Ned Crawford at Crawford Town. He staged a coup in which Crawford was killed, closed the town and stopped all communication between the town and other settlements. News soon reached the Governor, and he responded by sending out a detachment of regular troops, accompanied by Maroons from all of the other towns. Under orders to capture or kill Quao, they went in pursuit and he was quickly extirpated. The New Nanny Town Maroons (later the Moore Town Maroons), who participated in putting down the coup, were awarded a part of the £1100 spent on subduing the rebellion.[43] It is not clear whether the Crawford Town Maroons petitioned for help from the colonial government or not; however, there is no record of any dissent from them following the government's intervention, suggesting assistance was perhaps not welcomed but tolerated. It is not surprising that the colonial government was willing to intervene. The terms of the treaty laid out the succession of Maroon leaders and, in the colonial government's view, killing the chief was tantamount to breaking the peace treaty.

This unrest brought another round of law-making with a view to further controlling the Maroon towns. In one 1751 law, it was claimed that several Maroons

> have frequently left their several Towns, and continued absent there from a considerable Time without the Leave of their Commanding-Officer, or, having had such Leave, have not returned back by the Time prescribed to them, but have rambled about in the several Parishes of this Island, and been harboured and concealed in divers Places.

The law decreed that if any Maroon absented himself from his town without leave of the commanding officer, or, if he obtained leave, continued to absent himself for seven days after the expiration of such leave, then, upon complaint made to any magistrate of the parish where the truant was found, he was to be sent to the jail of St. Jago de la Vega in order to be brought to trial. The trial would be conducted in the same form and manner as free blacks were tried, that is, before two justices and three freeholders. If convicted, even if the trial was before only one justice and one freeholder, then they were "required to deprive the said Offender of his Freedom, and order him or her to be transported off this Island by the receiver-general and sold."[44] This law was a clear attempt to confine Maroons to their territory, only to be allowed out when on slave-catching duties or when otherwise assisting the colonial government. Exactly how this law was to be enforced was not clear. If keeping to the mountainous interior, it is unlikely that a Maroon would be located, with or without permission to travel; and, if a Maroon headed to the coastal market towns, they would be able to blend in with the free black population or the slaves going to market.

A further law in 1751 brought Maroon courts under the jurisdiction of the superintendents. This law claimed that internal disorders were occurring "frequently" because of a "want of authority" in the chiefs and commanders. It was, therefore, recommended that "all Disorders, Tumults, and Disturbance" be suppressed as soon as they appeared, and the perpetrators be brought to "speedy Punishment." The list of crimes to be punished by the superintendent was vague and all-encompassing:

> every Negroe being resident in, or belonging to any of the Negroe Towns, who shall disobey . . . the Governor's Orders, or excite others to do the same; or shall excite, cause or join in any Disorder, Tumult, or Disturbance, tending to break the Peace and good Order of the said Towns or any of them shall be punished by "the white men residing in the Town to which

the Offender belongs, and Four of the Negroes of the said Town, of which the Chief or Commanding Offi cer shall be one, not extending to life."[45]

This marks a distinct change in Maroon jurisdiction. The peace treaties had allowed for the punishment of all crimes which occurred in Maroon territory, short of capital crimes, to be administered by the Maroons themselves. The 1751 law completely undermined this and placed the power to punish almost all crimes in the hands of the superintendents.

This law introduced even more pressure to the superintendent's already dif- ficult job. Superintendents were to send frequent reports to the Governors on the state of Maroon towns, as well as reports on all court proceedings within thirty days of the hearing, and were fined £20 for every failure to do so. They were to reside in the Maroon town and "on no pretence whatsoever, should he be absent therefrom for a longer time than a fortnight without the Gover- nor's permission."[46] Despite this demand, no provision was made at all to pay for this. On certain occasions, after lengthy and difficult efforts, the House would grant superintendents £50 as lodging money for the year. However, the grant was on an individual basis, and petitions had to be submitted every year. A positive response was far from guaranteed.[47] Bringing Maroons under the superintendents' jurisdiction might have seemed a good idea to colonial law-makers but, in practice, would have done very little. Superintendents were already stretched and, often relying on Maroon individuals to rent their houses, very much under the influence of Maroon leaders.

The 1750s also saw the colonial government finally addressing the disputed land grants of the 1739 treaties. In the treaty with the Leeward Maroons, it was not clear whether the 1500 acres awarded were to include Accompong Town or not. It was specific in that it reserved "all the lands situate and lying between Trelawny Town and the Cockpits . . . bearing North-west from the said Trelawny Town" for Cudjoe and his men; however, it did not specifically mention Accompong Town. As will be seen in Chapter 5, this led to numer- ous land disputes between the Leewards and local colonists. Therefore, the Assembly decided to formally investigate the issue in 1756. A committee was formed with the explicit aim of examining these land claims made by Maroons of Trelawny Town and Accompong Town. It is unclear from the archival record if such an investigation was requested by colonists, Maroons or both. Nevertheless, it was instructed: to analyse whether the 1500-acre land grant from Cudjoe's treaty had been surveyed; to determine whether Accom- pong Town was to be included in the original Trelawny Town grant; and to recommend measures necessary to prevent surveyors and other persons from disturbing both the Trelawny and Accompong Maroons.[48] This latter point does suggest that the complaints were brought by either Trelawny or Accom- pong Town as a result of encroachments by colonists.

The committee investigated and, the following month, submitted a report with the following findings: the original 1739 land grant had not yet been surveyed; the 1500 acres did not include Accompong Town; and Accompong

Town and its provision grounds comprised of 400 acres, and that Governor Knowles, before leaving Jamaica, had assured the town "of their having a quantity of land laid out," but so far this had not occurred.[49] The committee further stated that surveyors of other lands had been engaged in "running out lines" very close to Accompong Town, leading the Accompongs to be "uneasy and under great apprehension from the present uncertainty of their title." To prevent further trouble, the committee recommended that these surveyors of other land claims should cease their activities and that both the 1500-acre Trelawny grant and the 1000-acre Accompong grant should be immediately surveyed, at which point the other surveys could continue. The superintendents of Trelawny and Accompong Towns, the Maroons themselves, as well as nearby colonists, were advised to assist in this endeavour, and to help with "marking fair lines and corner trees according to law."[50] In other words, the Assembly recommended granting the Leeward Maroons additional lands *after* the peace treaties. At this point, the colonial government followed a policy of undermining Maroon independence by law-making rather than land cession, and seems to have recognised the benefit of additional land grants in an effort to reduce the possibility of long-running border disputes with local white settlers.

Two years later, in 1758, an act was declared to "ascertain and establish the boundaries of Trelawney Town, and to settle and allot one thousand acres of lands for Accompong's Town, and to ascertain the boundaries thereof."[51] Under this law, the land of Trelawny Town was declared to bind northerly on land unsurveyed; easterly and southerly on rocky mountains and cockpits and partly on unsurveyed land; south-westerly on or near land patented by Thomas Reid; and north-westerly on rocky mountain and cockpits.[52] The newly granted 1000 acres for Accompong Town was declared to bind easterly on lands patented by James Smith, and partly on land patented by George Raxtead, esquire; south-easterly on land patented by Edward and Francis Smith, now belonging to Mr. Samuel Smith; south on land patented by Alexander Stanhope, and partly on land laid out for George Currie; west and south-west on rocky mountain and cockpits.[53]

In a hint towards disputes which had been occurring between the western Maroons and local white settlers, Clause Three of the act stated that the Leeward Maroons were to "have and enjoy" the said parcels of land "peaceable and quietly." There was no determined end to the possession of the lands. Indeed, in a phrase which has led to difficulties which continue to this day, the land was granted to the Leewards "forever." The law, however, went further than simply ascribing the lands to the Maroons by providing a sort of protection from incursions. It stated that if any surveyors or "other persons" were to intrude in any way, or otherwise "molest or disturb" the Maroon towns, then that person, or those people, were to forfeit the sum of £500 for "each and every intrusion, molestation or disturbance of the enjoyment of the Maroons and their posterity."[54] This is an incredibly striking piece of legislation. To not only grant additional territory just a decade after the peace treaties, but protect that land with the punishment of a fine for any incursions, is a vast contrast to what occurred in many other similar contexts. As yet, there is no evidence that anyone was ever prosecuted under this law, but its mere existence stands the Maroon experience in opposition to that of many other non-white, semi-autonomous communities in the Americas.

After the fractious years of the 1750s, these land grants went a long way towards smoothing contact between Maroons and the colonial government. This was good news for the colonists and served them well when Tacky's Rebellion exploded in 1760. I will discuss this uprising in Chapter 3, so it is not necessary to go into great detail here. What is important to address, however, is the reaction of the colonial government to the Maroons' actions. According to Edward Long, admittedly not the most unbiased of chroniclers, Tacky and his followers "planned to murder all whites, enslave all negroes who would not join them and to partition the island into small principalities in the African mode." They were motivated by the unhampered life of Maroons, who, they observed, "had acquired many comfortable settlements and a life of freedom, easy by dint of their prowess."[55] Therefore, the Maroon actions in killing Tacky and quelling such a rebellion had two great advantages for the colonists—the significant danger of Tacky and his rebellion was nullified, and it showed that attempting to emulate the Maroons would result in capture, suicide or death. For this, Maroons were handsomely rewarded by the House of Assembly. On 11th October 1760, £450 were awarded to the Leeward Maroons for their actions.[56] Several individual payments were made to Charles Town (formerly Crawford Town) Maroons. For example, one captain was paid 2s. 6d. for forty-six days on party service and seven shotsmen were paid 7 1/2d. for those forty-six days.[57] This was exclusive of the special rewards paid for rebels killed and captured. As far as Tacky's Rebellion was concerned, colonial officials were thrilled with the actions of many Maroons.

Despite the handsome awards granted by the government, some colonists suspected that other Maroons did not contribute enough to hunting the rebels and, thus, their allegiance was questioned. Colonists told of how, in one skirmish, a body of Maroons and a detachment of the 74th regiment stationed at Down's Cove were attacked by Tacky's men. The Maroons apparently disappeared, and some eyewitnesses alleged that they had thrown themselves flat on the ground and stayed there until the rebels had been driven off.[58] Far from being cowardice, however, this tactic would be familiar to any adherents of guerrilla warfare.[59] Despite this, Maroons found themselves accused, from some quarters, of desertion.

These suspicions were not confined to Maroon action, or inaction, during Tacky's Rebellion. Indeed, certain rumours began to spread that Maroons were actively involved in slave revolts. In one instance, in 1761, it was alleged by some colonists that the rebellion was actually a revolt of the Maroons, who had become so numerous and strong that they now desired "no less than the extirpation of all the white men in the island."[60] However, Edward Long countered the claim by stating that "as far as we have any certain information,

[they] have always adhered to the treaty, and were the principal instruments employed in suppressing that very insurrection."[61] What neither view takes into account, however, is the possibility that Maroons were involved in both supporting and suppressing slave rebellions. Or, indeed, that some colonists saw the advantage of an alliance with Maroons, while others deplored it— leading to such conflicting reports. These differences in colonial opinion are explored further in Chapter 6.

As the century wore on, Maroons were less likely to be called upon to assist in putting down slave rebellions. One reason was the above-mentioned colonial resistance, but another was that some Maroons increasingly deemed the reward money insufficient for the task. For example, in 1761, the government received a report from a planter in Westmoreland saying that, during an earlier rebellion, he had sent up a message to Trelawny Town to request Maroon support for stopping riots which were occurring in his parish. However, Maroons had been reluctant to come out. He had, therefore, been obliged to offer them an additional incentive of one pound per slave head before they would leave Trelawny Town. They did eventually turn out, and twelve slaves were killed with a total of £115 awarded in reward money. Even when sufficient rewards were granted, however, Maroons often struggled to claim their pay from the colonial government. On one occasion, a year earlier, a group of Scotts Hall Maroons called upon to suppress the "Coromantee" rebellion would not act until their arrears had been cleared. It is apparent that Maroons were increasingly unwilling to trust payments to be made in a timely manner and demanded money up-front. These financial issues, whilst not unique to Maroons, led many to refrain from their treaty duties.

Despite the frictions over lack of pay, Maroons still greeted Governor Lyttelton on his Leeward tour in 1764. When the Governor passed through St. James, eighty-four Trelawny Town Maroons met him at Montego Bay. After the parish's white militia were reviewed, the men of the Maroon group drew up, impatient to show their military skill. Long describes how:

> They drew their swords; and, winding their horns again, they began, in wild and warlike capers, to advance towards His Excellency, endeavouring to throw as much savage fury into their looks as possible. On approaching near him, some, with a hurried circling flourish, waved their rusty blades over his head, then gently laid them upon it; whilst others clashed their arms together in horrid concert. They next brought their muskets, and piled them up in heaps at his feet, which some of them desired to kiss, and were permitted.[62]

Whilst the reliability of parts of Edward Long's description can be questioned, particularly the image of Maroon warriors desiring to kiss the Governor's feet, it is clear that Maroons took part in this military display. Such acts, however, do not mean that this was a show of allegiance. Kathleen Wilson argues that such a display not only demonstrated the martial skills of the Maroons, but also offered up suggestions as to the consequences of those skills being withdrawn.[63] Seeing Maroons exhibit such military prowess might serve as a timely reminder to the British that the Maroons continued to be a force to be reckoned with. Such demonstrations may have contributed to the colonial government's eventual decision to restrict Maroon freedom.

Maroon adherence to their treaty duties of having an audience with the Governor did not prevent further rumours of Maroon involvement in slave rebellions.[64] In 1765, in the same parts of St. Mary's in which Tacky's Rebellion had been quashed, plans were laid for another uprising. Several Coromantin headmen from plantations across the parish met to discuss details of an armed rebellion. Coromantin slaves on "no less than seventeen estates" were engaged in the alliance. The plans, however, were discovered early due to the hasty actions of some of the participants. According to W. J. Gardner, the premature rising at Whitehall plantation was a result of the actions of one Quamin, who would not wait for the appointed time to launch the attack.[65] This slip in the plans led the uprising to be quickly quashed. In the days after the attempted rebellion, some of the alleged participants "threw out insinuations" that Maroons were involved in the secret.[66] This, apparently, led to a "good deal of alarm" that Maroons had joined with the rebels to divide the country between them. It is indeed possible that Maroons were involved in some capacity, but we must not ignore the possibility that this information could have resulted from unintentional misinformation; a ploy by the captured slaves to deflect interest in them; or, indeed, the actions of some colonists to undermine reliance on the Maroons. Certainly, no evidence has emerged which implicates any Maroons in this rebellion. The mere rumours alone, however, were enough to cast Maroons in an untrustworthy light.

Just two years later, Maroons had the opportunity to again prove their allegiance. In 1766, a group of Coromantins had risen up in Westmoreland, killing several nearby planters and settlers and throwing the entire parish into chaos. Companies of colonists immediately formed to hunt down the Coromantins responsible and engage them in battle. But, at the first moment of opportunity, the Coromantins retreated into the forest. Then, seemingly from nowhere, a body of Maroons appeared who had heard of the fight while out hunting hogs. The Maroons attacked the Coromantins, and by sunset Maroons had killed or captured two-thirds of them while the others scattered. Thereafter, Maroons endeavoured to hunt down the majority of the escapees over the following days.[67] Events such as these demonstrate the difficulty in determining Maroon allegiance—some Maroons were apathetic to engaging in hostilities with slaves, whilst others were willing to do so in order to claim their much-needed reward money.

After these events in the 1760s, the then Governor Elletson took a more involved approach to the internal workings of the Maroon towns. In 1767, upon hearing that there had been "lately many quarrels and disturbances among the Maroon negroes at Moore Town," rather than turn a blind eye, Elletson investigated the causes. After hearing the reports, he concluded that the main cause was the refusal of the superintendent, Charles Swigle, to reside within the Maroon settlement.[68] He contended that this lack of residence was causing leadership problems in the town. During his investigation, one Maroon alleged that a Captain Clash had attempted to forcibly remove a Maroon called Sambo's personally engraved silver badge of office. Elletson involved himself in the dispute by requesting that Clash leave Moore Town and retire to his residence at Bath, so that Sambo's badge could be returned to its owner.[69] Similar interference happened with the Leeward Maroons. In the same year, Elletson instructed Superintendent James to appoint Ashamboy, Yanow, Appia and Appena as officers and demote Captains Cuffee and Tulappany, as well as to remove their badges.[70] Given such meddling by the colonial government, it is unsurprising that Maroons took to calling upon Governor Elletson, unannounced, at his home to discuss matters with him.[71] The Governor had apparently made a rod for his own back.

This involvement in internal affairs, seemingly without widespread dissent, led government officials to introduce further laws which were beneficial to colonial society. In 1769, for example, some modifications were made to the laws previously passed regarding the collection of runaways. The new Act "to remedy some inconveniences in the Laws already made" stated that after 1st March 1770,

> all runaways who shall be captured by the Maroons shall be taken to the magistrates of the parish within five days, who shall pay the Maroons mileage at the rate of seven pence half penny per mile, in addition to the sum of Two Pounds per slave.

This reduction of one pound from the payment of the Act of 1741 would affect cash earnings for Maroons. Further, having to return the runaway to a magistrate meant Maroon slave-hunters lost time when they could be out on the hunt earning more money. It was only upon handing over the runaway to the magistrate that the Maroon would receive a certificate confirming their actions. The Maroon then had to take the certificate to the owner of the slave, who would pay him the outstanding balance. To prevent fraud, payments to Maroons had to be witnessed by a white settler. Default was punishable by a fine of £10 per offence without the right of appeal.[72] These reduced rates did not inspire the British to call upon the Maroons during a short-lived uprising in Kingston in 1769.[73]

As the 1770s dawned, relations between Maroons and the colonial government were increasingly strained and, given the wider context of the on-coming American Revolution, distrust grew on both sides. This is demonstrated in the rather complex tale of Captain Davy and Sam Grant. In April 1774, Captain Davy, chief of the Scotts Hall Maroons, engaged in a runaway hunt in the Hellshire Hills in St. Catherine, accompanied by white rangers under Colonel Bennett. The group descended to the coast to search for slaves when they came upon twelve merchant ships lying at anchor. For unknown reasons, rumour spread among the Maroons that there was a plan to ship them away from Jamaica. Against this backdrop, Captain Davy approached a group of slaves and accused one of them of being a runaway. A fight broke out, and Davy chopped the man down before running away. In the melee that followed, a Charles Town Maroon named Sam Grant leapt from a house, fired and killed another slave. Grant then also tried to run away, but a young English sea captain attempted to prevent him from doing so. Grant apparently told the man to move, but when he did not do so, Grant killed him and ran off. He took refuge in Moore Town whilst the colonial government ordered the former superintendent of the Maroons, a man called Robert Brereton, to capture him. When Brereton arrived, the Moore Town Maroons "broke into open rebellion." The Maroons claimed they were being ill-used by the British, but Brereton eventually managed to calm the situation and persuade them to sign a written agreement saying that they would deliver Grant to the Governor, a promise which was never fulfilled. Brereton returned and captured Grant. He was tried for murder but acquitted because it was found that he had not intended to kill the sailor or the slave. Grant later became a major and chief commander at Charles Town.[74]

This tale reveals several insights into the Maroon-colonial government relationship. Firstly, Grant's story shows the distrust that some Maroons had of the colonists—believing as they did that the merchant ships were there to transport them from the island. Thus far, no evidence has been uncovered of any ploy, before the Second Maroon War, to do so. Secondly, Sam Grant was able to find shelter in Moore Town, despite being a Charles Town Maroon, and the colonial government was unable to immediately force his recovery. Thirdly, when he was eventually caught, Sam Grant was actually acquitted despite killing a white man. This was perhaps because the British feared the consequences that a guilty verdict might have had. Indeed; the Governor of the time, Sir Basil Keith, cautioned of the consequences of provoking a war. During Grant's trial, he wrote to the Earl of Dartmouth saying that he hoped his leniency would serve

> His Majesty better . . . than by directly sending Troops against them and making a body of people desperate, who might do us infinite Mischief in the Country, and who are living amoung us under the Sanction of a Treaty we found convenient to make after a very long War with them.[75]

Keith's comments display the very real fear that many white Jamaicans still had of the Maroons.

Following the incident with Sam Grant and Captain Davy, fears ramped up among the colonists. One speculated about the prospect of war with the Maroons, writing:

> "It would be a very unequal warfare . . . with a parcel of savages who have nothing to lose; and what might still be worse it is to be feared, that if we

had the fortune to extirpate them, our great wilderness which occupies the middle range of the Island, would soon be filled again by another set of Banditti more Savage than these."

The colonist concluded that the best solution would be a uniform adherence to justice in all our dealings with them.[76] Rather than attempting to reduce the Maroons by force, another round of law-making was introduced. A law banning Maroons from blowing the abeng between sunset and sunrise, except as a call to militia duty, was introduced. Further, their superintendent was asked to read to them on a quarterly basis all the laws under which they were governed and to counsel them to respect those laws. John James, the superintendent of Trelawny Town, sought to get a residence built in the town for himself and an armoury to lock away the Maroons' arms, to control their use. These restrictions, however, did not prevent Maroons from coming to the aid of the colonial government in times of external threat. For example, parties of Windward Maroons decamped into Kingston and were quartered at the theatre on Harbour Street for some months in 1779 during the American Revolution.[77] Thus, the initial decades after the peace treaties ended with increasing restraints on Maroon life but, at this conjecture, still also a reliance on Maroons for security.

In contrast to the under-developed state Jamaica found itself in following the First Maroon War, the newly created United States had seen centuries of progress and had previously had functioning colonial governments which represented an extension of the English government. Courts enforced the common law of England, the Governor's Council formed to advise the appointed royal Governor in each province and the legislative body was elected by enfranchised voters. The colonial population was nearly 2.5 million on the eve of the American Revolution, and growing. Infrastructure, whilst not fully developed, was progressing. The United States, therefore, began the inter-war period in a different position from that of 1730s Jamaica. The terms of the Treaty of Paris, which concluded the war, protected the situation. It set boundaries between the British Empire and the United States that were generous to the Americans and granted the United States access to key trade routes such as the Mississippi River. These enlarged boundaries were intended to benefit both the United States and Britain. The concession of the trans-Appalachian region was designed to facilitate the growth of the American population and to create lucrative markets for British merchants.[78]

When it came to Native Americans, however, the Treaty of Paris completely excluded them from negotiations and from mention in the official documents. Under the peace terms, Britain handed over all of its territory east of the Mississippi, south of the Great Lakes and north of Florida, even though much of that land was not British. The treaty referenced no protection of, or rights belonging to, Native Americans. According to the treaty, citizens of the new republic were free to act as they pleased with regards to the indigenous communities. Yet in the Confederation Congress Proclamation of 1783, dated 22nd September 1783, the federal government reserved all rights to extinguish indigenous land titles in the United States.[79] From that point of view, dealings with Creek communities were to be the sole preserve of federal representatives. But, despite the Articles of Confederation and the Constitution itself, citizens of states such as Georgia continued to regard Creeks as their wards.

The period immediately following the Treaty of Paris was to be dominated by two men, with two distinct views towards treaties with the United States— Alexander McGillivray and Hoboithle Micco. Alexander McGillivray was born in Creek country in 1750 to a Creek mother, Sehoy, and a Scots father, Lachlan. He was educated in Charleston whilst his father slowly became one of the largest landowners in the colony.[80] Alexander then went on to be apprenticed in two colonial trading companies, giving him experience in plantation management and Atlantic commerce. When the American Revolution broke out, Lachlan McGillivray was forced to flee to Scotland, and Alexander returned to the land of his mother.[81] Academic opinion about McGillivray and his role in Creek history has divided scholars, but it is undeniable that he had a prominent role in Creek society.[82] He, however, did not represent the entire Creek Nation—an oversight made by earlier historians, largely because of his literacy and, therefore, the subsequent availability of sources related to him. Indeed, many Creeks did not recognise his leadership and instead turned to Hoboithle Micco. A Creek chief also known as the Tame King, the Tallassee King or the Good Child King, Hoboithle Micco came to be the antithesis of Alexander McGillivray and, later, Benjamin Hawkins. Towards the end of 1783, he led a small number of Creeks, along with Neha Micco, the Fat King, to Augusta, where they ceded land bordering the Oconee and Apalachee rivers on one side, and the Ogeechee River on the other. This became known as the Treaty of Augusta. Two years later, seventeen Creeks, including once again Hoboithle Micco, confirmed this cession to Georgia in the Treaty of Galphinton and, in addition, ceded land east of a line drawn from the fork of the Ocmulgee and Oconee rivers to the source of the St. Marys River. Finally, in 1786, the Treaty of Shoulderbone was signed after Georgia used strong-arm tactics to intimidate and coerce several Creek leaders, including Hoboithle Micco and Neha Micco. This treaty confirmed the prior cessions and promised satisfaction for thefts and murders committed since those treaties. Upon hearing of these treaties, McGillivray was incensed and refused to recognise them—because they were signed without his permission, and because Georgia insisted that the agreements were binding for the whole nation. These treaties, and their concurrent acceptance and rejection by different sectors of Creek society, set the difficult scene that developed in the post-revolutionary period.

These early interactions with representatives of Georgia led many Creeks, including McGillivray, to be wary of the federal government and its motivations—despite differing state and federal interests. Indeed, McGillivray wrote to Governor Zéspedes of Spanish Pensacola that the United States had held forth the "most tempting baits" to his people to meet the commissioners of the states in Congress, "but being sensible of their insidious views I have hitherto prevented the Indians from complying with their wishes."[83] We must, however, always view McGillivray's statements with some suspicion—he often played off Spain and the United States against each other in order to secure a better deal for himself and his followers.[84] Therefore, his claim of rejecting American advances may have been to make Spain aware of those advances and counter with their own.

Indeed, some Creeks clearly had recognised the benefits of a friendly relationship with the federal government and were "desirous of establishing with them a permanent peace"[85] but McGillivray discouraged them from doing so. In 1785, the federal government sent representatives to the Creek Nation in order to negotiate a treaty. McGillivray was furious and forbade any person "from attending the place where the Americans desire to meet the Indians in treaty."[86] The representatives waited impatiently for the Creek delegation to arrive. However, only a few Creek chiefs, representing two towns, trickled into the meeting place. In keeping with the terms of the Confederation Congress Proclamation of 1783, the federal officials told the representatives of the two towns that a treaty could not be concluded with so few of them and promptly left Creek country. What happened next was to become typical of treaty and land negotiations. Smelling an opportunity, agents of Georgia raced to the meeting place and sought a treaty with the two Creek towns present. After lengthy negotiations with the Creek chiefs, the Georgians obtained a cession of all of the lands south of the Altamaha and eastward of a line southwest from the junction of the Oakmulgee and Oconee rivers, and northwest of the Oconee River.[87]

Georgians were to constantly undermine federal attempts to treat with the Creek Nation in the following years. On their part, federal commissioners constantly implored Creek leaders not to negotiate with individual states. In one letter, in 1789, federal representatives vehemently wrote to the entire Creek Nation requesting that they not hold any treaty with "an individual state or with individuals of any state."[88] The federal government's efforts were not lost on McGillivray, who subsequently wrote to Arturo O'Neill, then Governor of Spanish West Florida, that the federal government seemed much disposed to agree to "a fair and equal peace" and that he was increasingly "desirous to conclude one."[89] However, McGillivray was not ready to submit to just any terms—he reminded federal representatives of the incident at Muscle Shoals when a party of Americans arrived in three large boats, intending to settle the area. Creeks had attacked the boats, killing twenty-seven and wounding five. He warned that this was what the Americans could expect if they persisted in their schemes.[90] McGillivray was willing to urge Creeks to violently defend their interests if pushed to by any sector of American society.

As time passed, the federal government began to slowly make progress with McGillivray. William Panton, the owner of the trading company Panton,

Leslie & Co., declared that McGillivray did not want to deal with the Georgians because, he said, they had violated all treaties, but that he was willing to treat with Congress.[91] Nevertheless, McGillivray was still concerned that, if forced to choose, the federal government would support Georgia for the interests of the Union rather than side with the Creeks—even if the Georgians were guilty of the violation. McGillivray thought that the federal government would not compel the Georgians to restore stolen Creek lands and if "we take strong measures to obtain justice, the force of the Union will be employed to reduce us to accept of their own terms of peace."[92] Creek leaders were conscious of the fragility of the new Union and the need to unite against Native American threats. This knowledge constantly fed into Creek negotiations with federal representatives and bred a certain wariness of government actions. Indeed, McGillivray wrote that they frequently received the "flattering appellations of friends and brothers," in reply to their complaints over land but, while doing so, the Americans were "stripping [them] of their natural rights" by depriving Creeks of their inheritance which belonged to their ancestors. Creeks continually petitioned the federal government for intervention on the issue of land but were repeatedly ignored. On one occasion, after a petition for assistance against Georgia incursions, the federal government declared its "ignorance of the discontents of the nation."[93] Turning a blind eye to Georgian trespass on Creek lands was a convenient policy for the federal government to follow. Doing so allowed a claim of ignorance whilst slowly undermining Creek ownership of the land—more of this will be discussed in Chapter 5.

Such underhand actions led McGillivray to backtrack on his desire for treaties, and he became increasingly forthright in his dislike of the Americans. In a letter to William Panton, he told how he successfully blocked a treaty with the United States, stating

> In this do you not see my cause of triumph in bringing these conquerors of the old & masters of the new world as they called themselves, to bend & supplicate for peace at the feet of a people whom shortly before they despised and marked out for distruction [sic].[94]

McGillivray's continued refusal to deal with the United States worried the federal government, which quickly sent federal representatives to Creek country to communicate the new republic's desire for good relations. In these early talks, the federal government chose to approach Creeks with speeches more reminiscent of indigenous communication than of European. The U.S. commissioners stated:

> Friends and brothers of the Creek nation, we trust that the Great Master of Breath who has formed us all brothers whether white men or red men, has created this day to be the time for preventing our people and your people from taking away that breath which none but he can give or should take away.[95]

The commissioners continued, saying that they could not forget entirely the "calamities we suffered in the late war" with Great Britain, but that they had "buried all resentment" for the part which Creeks had played. They declared that the United States would guarantee and defend all the lands of the Creek Nation. The commissioners then attempted to entice the Creeks by the one method they had available so soon after the war—open ports for trade. They offered cheaper imports than any offered elsewhere, saying a "secure port for the Creeks in the U.S. will be much more convenient than in any other country," claiming that "both of us will be gainers by being friends. The promotion of our mutual interest will promote our mutual friendship. This will be found the only method to make a peace happy and lasting."[96]

This careful treatment of the Creek Nation was said to be a result of the efforts of one man in particular—George Washington. George Stiggins, a Creek mestizo, claimed that from the close of the Revolutionary War to 1794, the general attitude of Creeks towards the Americans had been "rancorous and undoubtedly very unfavourable." He continued, claiming that it was Washington's "humane request" for the leader McGillivray to visit Philadelphia, then the capital, that improved the relationship. When McGillivray took up the American offer, he and a delegation of Creeks travelled north from the southeast to meet with Washington.

Upon their arrival, the group were given a "kind reception" which, Stiggins claimed, was flattering because Creeks were unused to such treatment by white people.[97] According to John Pope, an American soldier who wrote of his experiences in the region, Alexander McGillivray was complimented during the visit with a selection of elegant gilt-bound books and also with a golden epaulette.[98] This event likely had a great impact upon the Creek delegation, because it followed the Creek practice of bestowing prestigious ceremonies upon visiting chiefs. It is still more feasible that Creeks, when they did align themselves with the United States, were convinced by the negotiations between the two sides rather than by flattering words. However, lavish ceremonies allowed those negotiations to build on a basis of respectful treatment. Subsequently, the Creek delegation returned to their territory and regaled their fellow Creeks with tales of how they had been received with kindness and hospitality by their "great Father Washington." This visit went a long way towards convincing certain Creek leaders to consider a formal treaty with the United States.

Such lavish ceremonies and gift-giving was one method which the federal government used to make inroads into Creek society during a time when they were determined to achieve their goals peacefully. In 1789, the Secretary of State, Henry Knox, wrote that the President was "exceedingly desirous" that a war should be avoided if it can be "effected consistently with the interest and dignity of the United States," in particular, because such a war would cost significant amounts in terms of money but also in the "embarrassment it would occasion to the Government."[99] Knox had estimated the year earlier that it would cost the government $450,000 to protect the Georgia frontier with a

2800-man army for nine months.[100] Quite simply, the federal government had more pressing areas in which to spend such amounts. In addition to the expense, the federal government could not risk the ire of their citizens by having a large standing army during times of peace to protect against Creek attacks. Indeed, one cause of the American Revolution had been the Patriots' dislike of the British standing army, so the federal government was keen to avoid making the same mistake and, therefore, kept their military relatively small.[101]

This small standing army did not mean the federal government would not defend their territory if pressed to do so. William Panton wrote to McGillivray in 1790, saying that if the Creeks struck, the United States must punish them. He reiterated that the United States was disposed to be favourable and friendly to the Creeks but could not "sacrifice their national dignity and justice."[102] Doing so would undermine its desired power in the region. In these early years of the republic, the United States could not afford to be seen as weak by their Native American neighbours, particularly in these years of the Western Confederacy. With its origins in the pan-tribal movements of the 1740s, this loose confederacy came together in an attempt to resist the expansion of the United States into the Northwest Territory after Great Britain ceded the region to the United States in the Treaty of Paris. Against this background, and in the face of other European empires looking to capitalise on any American false moves, the United States had to appear strong. McGillivray, who could be criticised in some areas, could not be accused of political naivety. He realised that the United States would have to strike if attacked. In a 1790 letter he noted that the new government was established on a basis which rendered it capable of making war on the Creeks "in a fashion that would assure them a complete success," in which case "the terms prescribed [to us] by the Americans would leave us very little or nothing."[103]

Such awareness led to many Creeks being increasingly mindful of the need to sign a peace treaty with the United States and formalise an alliance between the two nations. In 1789, the United States had approached representatives of the Creeks at Rock Landing, Georgia, to sign such a treaty. But McGillivray abruptly ended the negotiations, citing the United States' intended support of Georgia's land claims as the reason for the curtailment of talks.[104] George Washington once again had to intervene and sent a special emissary, Colonel Marinus Willett, to persuade McGillivray to come to New York, then the capital of the United States, to conduct a treaty with Washington and Henry Knox directly. McGillivray had little choice but to agree, given the Spanish had recently curtailed the flow of munitions and manufactures into Creek country and a new arrangement, even with the Americans, was increasingly necessary. McGillivray was keen not only to continue the flow of goods, but to be the one in control of that flow.[105]

In the hot summer months of 1790, McGillivray and a contingent of over thirty chiefs travelled to New York. The group had made a lengthy journey from the south and, at the encouragement of George Washington, had been feted by local officials at every stage. Upon arrival in New York, a special ship ferried them across the Hudson River while the Battery's guns roared. The chiefs were met by a detachment of soldiers and escorted to Henry Knox's residence to meet the Secretary of War, President Washington, and other officials. After several days of negotiation and talks, the Treaty of New York was formally signed on 7th August 1790. The treaty itself was crafted by Secretary of War Knox, but much of the text was proposed by McGillivray, an individual, rather than by the tribal council. This change highlighted the increasing precedence of an individual voice over a collective one.

The treaty included several notable articles which were to dictate the relationship between the Creek Nation and the United States. Article Two, for example, required the "undersigned Kings, Chiefs and Warriors" and all parts of the Creek Nation to be "under the protection of the United States of America" and of "no other sovereign whatsoever." It further stipulated that the Nation would not hold any treaty with any individual States.[106] Creeks were to be under the influence of the United States and would be subject to federal laws rather than Georgia state laws. Creeks in Florida remained subject to Spanish law, although this would change in 1795 with the ratification of Pinckney's Treaty.[107] Articles Four and Five laid out the boundary between the Creek Nation and the United States which, unsurprisingly, resulted in Creeks ceding significant amounts of their lands.[108] In a similar article to that found in the Maroon treaties, Article Eleven required Creeks to "give notice" to the United States of "any designs, which they may know or suspect to be formed in any neighbouring tribe," or by any other person, against the "peace and interests" of the United States.[109] Perhaps the most infamous article was Article Twelve, which first introduced the civilisation plan to the Creek Nation. In particular, it called for the Creeks to be "led to a greater degree of civilisation, and to become herdsmen and cultivators, instead of remaining in a state of hunters."[110] In return, Creeks were to be granted certain amounts of domestic animals, agricultural tools, up to four interpreters, and a free port where they could trade without duty.

Six additional articles were agreed, on a separate document, that were kept secret from the rest of the Creek chiefs. The first established new trade agreements between the United States and the Creek Nation, including shifting the traffic in trade goods away from Spanish ports to those in American territory. This article was particularly attractive to the Creek leaders, given that it seemed war could break out between Britain and Spain at any moment. The United States also agreed to pay select Creek chiefs a $100 yearly stipend and to commission McGillivray as a brigadier-general with annual pay of $1200. This last clause was agreed with the aim of encouraging McGillivray to promote American interests and policies among his fellow Creeks. A further clause aimed to secure the longer-term interests of the United States. This stated that the United States would educate "and clothe" up to four young Creeks at any one time. This favoured the children of prominent Creeks and ensured they became acquainted with American values and customs before bringing them back to Creek country to promote U.S. ideals.[111]

While McGillivray lauded the treaty as "the main foundation of the south-western frontier,"[112] the Georgians violently denounced it. According to E. Merton Coulter, "it was unthinkable to them that a government of civilised white people would definitely hand over to savages for permanent occupation all of Georgia excepting a small eastern strip."[113] Dissatisfaction was not just within the American ranks; not all Creeks accepted the treaty and McGillivray's leadership, either. There were suspicions that McGillivray, using his literacy, had negotiated articles beneficial to his interests rather than the wider interests of the Nation. Indeed, McGillivray could easily have misled his fellow chiefs in New York. Given their limited knowledge of English, it is unlikely that they were present during the informal English-language negotiations between McGillivray and Secretary of War Knox. Further, they would have been unable to read the written treaty as they were all illiterate—as demonstrated by the marks they gave instead of signatures on the final version.[114] At the signing ceremony, Washington read the articles aloud, "which address was communicated sentence after sentence, by Mr. Cornell, sworn interpreter, to all of which the Creeks gave an audible assent."[115] It is not, however, beyond the realm of possibility that Cornell deliberately misinterpreted the treaty. It does seem that in one clause, Cornell replaced the word "Apalachee" with "north fork of the Oconee," in order to make it more agreeable to Creek leaders.[116] This exchange led to violent disputes in later years. Cornell was known to be a close ally of McGillivray, and deceit by him was not impossible to imagine given his assent to the secret articles which made him a brigadier general in the U.S. Army and established potential commercial ties between American traders and Creeks.[117].

The Treaty of New York also initiated a new method of control—the annuity system. In the early years of federal Native American policy, no monetary compensation was offered for land cessions. Instead, in a similar way to the British system, provision was made for "gifts" to smooth negotiations. Increasingly, however, federal and state officials began to "purchase" land through annuities. Under this system, the United States agreed to pay a yearly stipend to whichever Native American community it was negotiating with. In the initial treaties, these stipends were to be paid "in perpetuity"; but, in later treaties, the U.S. Senate insisted that stipends were to be for a set number of years only, and a lump sum was to be paid upon the signing of the treaty.[118] On the surface, the annuity system seems to have been beneficial to Native Americans, since they were to receive payment for any lands lost. In reality, however, the system undermined Native American sovereignty and turned land into a commodity. The gifts given in previous treaties were never considered as payment for the lands; rather, they were seen as a critical part of diplomacy. This changed with the Treaty of New York.

In practice, however, the annuity system was rife with problems. In a move similar to the withholding of payments to Maroons, the federal government constantly delayed payments due to the Nation or gave only partial payments. This was the case in the 1796, 1797 and 1798 stipends[119]—eventually being paid in December 1799.[120] Further, payments due to chiefs under the secret articles of the Treaty of New York were not made until 1802.[121] These tardy payments remained characteristic into the early nineteenth century. In 1816, Benjamin Hawkins, the federal Indian agent, complained to the War Department that Creeks were still due back annuities for every year between 1812 and 1816, in total about $64,000.[122] The federal government never explained to the Creeks why their payments were not forthcoming.[123] Creeks, for their part, suspected the federal government of foul play and believed "there was a deliberate plan in operation on the part of the United States."[124] All the blame, however, cannot be placed with the federal government. The annuities were increasingly entangled with the Creek Factory finances, the civilisation plan, trade affairs and reparations for damages and thefts committed on the Georgian frontier. Further, the Creeks themselves had a complicated way of distributing the annuity money and goods. Regardless of these explanations, it cannot be denied that payments promised to the Creek Nation for lands ceded were infrequently paid—a clear violation of the treaties and a subtle method of reducing the economic power of the Creek Nation.

Following the apparent success of the Treaty of New York, subsequent meetings strengthened the relationship between the federal government and the Creek Nation. Federal representatives were often sent to Creek territory to speak with Creeks and promise further favourable conditions. William Johnson, a federal politician, wrote in 1792 that the President "out of his great goodness, and friendship for you and your people" had been pleased to "concert means for effectually punishing all who dare attempt to disturb Creek peace."[125] McGillivray suggested that the federal government tried to further reduce tensions by being lenient with Creeks and apparently turning a blind eye to Creek attacks on the frontier. McGillivray told groups of Creeks that they had nothing to fear from the Americans as he had assurance from General Washington that the "killing of a few people, and stealing of horses, even to the number of forty or fifty of either, from Georgia, would not cause them to send any force against them."[126] Rather than such a stance being a result of a genuine alliance, it is more likely that the federal government was aware of the advances made by the Western Confederacy of indigenous communities, which had continued into the 1790s and contributed to the subtle handling of the Creek Nation. Any overt action may have forced the Creeks into the arms of their northern counterparts.

However, as the tide of the struggle with the Western Confederacy turned in favour of the United States, federal officials could afford to be more assertive in their speeches regarding the Creeks. In 1793, Andrew Pickens, a member of the House of Representatives, stressed to the Secretary of War that demonstrating the ability of the United States to punish Creeks was the only measure that would secure "from their cruel depredations the inhabitants of the southwest frontiers."[127] Fortuitously for the United States, it was at this point that certain sections of the Creek Nation petitioned the federal government for assistance to settle an internal dispute. In May of that year, a consortium of

Creeks called for an army to destroy the Cowetas, Broken Arrow, a part of the Uchees, Usuchees, Big Tallassee and a part of the Chehaws. The petitioning Creeks desired this "as, without doing so, there can be no hope of peace."[128] Those involved in the request may not have viewed themselves as the subordinate partner asking for help, but merely saw it as an opportunity to defeat their internal enemies. Nevertheless, the petition gave the Americans the perfect excuse to enter into Creek internal affairs.

The loose confederation of the Creek Nation was ideally suited for the United States to interfere in the internal workings of the Nation. It promoted internal disputes between different power blocs vying for supremacy, many of which were willing to call on assistance from the United States to improve their chances of success. Interference occurred again in 1793, when a group of Creek chiefs dispatched warriors to murder the prominent Creek John Galphin and five other Lower Creeks. The attempt having failed, they called on the United States for assistance. "No other step can be taken to bring them to their sense, but for you to come amongst them and subdue them," Tustanagee Thlucco told General John Twiggs.[129] He supplied the officer with detailed directions to the towns of Coweta, Chiaja and Usiche and concluded by asking to be notified before the troops arrived, promising to keep the information secret from the hostile towns.[130] At the time, this may have seemed a purely military exercise, but it set a dangerous precedent for the years to come. U.S. forces ultimately burned down the town of Hothlitaiga. Using the excuse of being requested to intervene, the United States became embroiled in Creek internal affairs.

In 1794, the federal government decided to consolidate its foothold in Creek country by offering a new trade deal to the Nation. William Eustis, a congressman from Massachusetts, reminded the Creeks that George Washington had provided bread for their starving "squaws and children" and wanted nothing in return. Yet, "You have not returned our prisoners, nor restored our property, or acted as friends." He went on to state that, if Creeks returned the requested American prisoners and property and restrained their "bad men" from stealing American horses, "all will be peace, and General Washington will open a trade to your land, when you may have goods for one fourth less than you now give Mr. Panton for them, and get more for your skins and furs."[131] As discussed later, this was the first deceitful step of using debt as a method to gain Creek lands.

However, at this point, it was the government of Georgia that resorted more frequently to underhanded methods. Allegations surfaced that claimed the Georgians wished to provoke war as an excuse to strip the Creeks of their lands. James Durouseaux, a settler who lived in the vicinity, wrote in 1796 that:

> It is the wish of the Georgians to commence a war with the Indians in hoere [here] to incorach [encroach] on more of thaer [their] land, as they could not aptain [obtain] a grant for it the laitt [late] treitty [treaty], they would wish to taeke [take] it by force of arms.[132]

Earlier in the spring, the Georgians had murdered a Coweta Indian who, Durouseaux claimed, was innocently present at one of the Georgians' houses. The Cowetas demanded satisfaction and eventually went to take it.[133] The Creek policy of blood revenge was being used by the Georgians as a cynical ploy to launch a war in order to justify incursions into Creek territory.[134]

Alongside Georgian actions, however, the federal government also implemented its new plan to gain a foothold in Creek country. Starting in 1795, the federal government decided to open trading posts for Creeks to take their produce to. In theory, this was to guarantee the best prices, but in practice, it was yet another way to attempt to control the Creeks. These American-owned stores, or factories, provided Creeks with fixed exchange rates and ample supplies of goods so Creeks were quick to utilise them. Most transactions were carried out by barter, but certain persons were allowed goods in advance of payment and, as a result, chiefs, captains, interpreters and traders fell into increasing debt to the factories.[135] Once in debt, the Americans had a stronger hand at the negotiating table and accepted land cessions in return for a reduction of the debt.

Jean Chaudhuri argues that Thomas Jefferson, the infamous American President, first instigated this method of writing off debt in return for a cession of lands. He hoped that the factories and trading posts would engage in trade in such a way that Creeks and other southern Indians would be so deeply in debt they would be forced to cede their lands in order to cover their arrears.[136] The archival evidence supports this claim. In 1803, Jefferson wrote to the American military officer, William Henry Harrison, that he would be "glad to see the good and influential individuals among them run into debt, because we observe that when these debts get beyond what the individual can pay, they become willing to lop them off by a cession of lands."[137] Forcing Creeks into debt had become a federal policy, and this policy exacerbated the economic woes felt by non-payment of the annuity and the decreasing deerskin trade. Soon the non-payment of the annuity became explicitly tied to land cession. The federal government explained that it would withhold the stipend as payment for debts incurred at the federal trading posts. Creeks were given the option of ceding their lands in payment of those debts rather than paying with their stipend. This policy marked the beginning of a new push to reduce the Creek Nation.

It was against this backdrop that Benjamin Hawkins entered Creek country. Born in 1754, Hawkins was a delegate to the Continental Congress and a U.S. Senator for North Carolina before being appointed by George Washington as General Superintendent for Indian Affairs in 1796. In his role, he was responsible for all Native American groups south of the Ohio River and was principal agent to the Creek Nation. His main role was to act as the intermediary between the United States and the Creek Nation, but his focus was always on his infamous "civilisation plan" which was authorised by President Jefferson. In this plan, it was intended that Creeks would turn to Euro American agricultural practices, towards animal husbandry and pastoral farming and away from hunting. This would not only prevent Creeks from honing their warrior skills on the hunt but would also mean they needed less land to live on. Imperative to this was reshaping of gender roles in Creek country. He encouraged men to abandon the chase in favour of ranching and planting, and women to vacate their farms for the production of "household manufactures." In addition, the Indian agent urged men to take control of family property and to assume command over their wives and daughters.[138]

Hawkins's arrival in Creek country coincided with the period when cotton was replacing deerskins as the most valuable commodity in the region. Eli Whitney had invented the cotton gin in 1793. Before that, cotton growing had been confined to coastal areas where wealthy tobacco and sugar planters had the land and labour available for growing cotton. With Whitney's invention, however, cotton seeds could be removed relatively quickly rather than the slow and arduous process of removing them by hand.[139] Cotton subsequently became an extremely profitable enterprise, and land quickly developed into the most in-demand natural resource. With this change in the global economy, Creeks not only were unnecessary but represented an impediment to the spread of the system. By assimilating Creeks into American society, as the civilisation plan intended, their land would become available for growing cotton. Indeed, according to government reasoning, the civilisation plan was so "that the U.S. may be saved the pain and expense of expelling or destroying them [the Native Americans] from their lands."[140]

Despite his ulterior motives, Hawkins began life in Creek country relatively well. In 1797, he wrote to a friend, "I visit them [the Creeks], take them by the hand and talk kindly to them, and I eat with them frequently." He went on, "and this day I had four Indian women to dine with me with some Chiefs and white men, a thing they tell me unknown before to either of them."[141] Indeed, Native American women stated that he was the first Indian agent who "thought it worth while to examine into the situation of the women."[142] This was not lost on Creek men, who often viewed Hawkins's policies with trepidation. Creek masculinity was heavily based on the warriors' activities of hunting, which Hawkins actively sought to discourage.[143] It was not just their masculine skills which were under threat. According to Hawkins, Creek men were "apprehensive . . . that if their women could clothe and feed themselves," an explicit goal of the civilisation plan, then they would become "independent of the degrading state of connexion between them."[144]

Hawkins did not stop at addressing gender roles and agricultural production. On assuming his post, he immediately began drawing up plans for a National Council composed of representatives from each Creek town and led by a speaker. It was to meet annually to draft and enforce laws "for the welfare of the nation." Hawkins wrote to the Secretary of War that "An establishment of this sort appears to me indispensable to enable the nation to fulfill its engagements with us."[145] The idea of meeting to discuss important matters was not new in Creek country but had previously occurred only when specific issues arose on an irregular basis. Representatives from every town were rarely, if ever, present.[146] Hawkins was determined to change this. It was, after all, easier to impose the will of the United States on a small group of men rather than on a loose confederation of distant towns. Still, despite all the grand statements about the power of the National Council, any decrees had to be made by consensus rather than force—limiting the Council's influence.[147] With the powers of the National Council constrained, Hawkins moved to introduce another form of control—the "lawmenders." This coercive group of warriors was to force the will of the National Council, and therefore the United States, on Creeks who committed transgressions.[148] More on this new style of justice is found in Chapter 6.

Hawkins's policies were an assault on the very identity of Creeks; therefore, it comes as no surprise that factions threatened his life on several occasions. In the spring of 1798, some Coweta headmen roused Hawkins from his sleep and instructed him to flee because a group of warriors were en route to slay him. Hawkins refused to leave, and Coweta women and warriors had to guard him through the night.[149] In 1799, after Hawkins had insisted on punishing some Creek horse thieves, the thieves openly threatened Hawkins's life.[150] That same year, British adventurer William Augustus Bowles, who was campaigning among the Seminoles and Creeks to garner British allies to oust the Americans from the South, issued a death warrant for Hawkins.[151] Hawkins again refused to leave even though he was advised to do so; in his words, "I am not sensible of danger, in other words, when I am resolved in doing what I conceive to be my duty, I never calculate on the dangers."[152] Hawkins's answer was to cultivate the allegiance of a number of warriors by drawing on the annuity to reward Creeks who "assisted the agency."[153] For example, in 1798, Tussekiah Micco received $50 for his "faithful and persevering exertions in the service of his country," and Tustanagee Hopoy and Tuskegee Tustanagee each earned $12.50 for their "faithful service" and "fidelity."[154] All three actively helped Hawkins implement the civilisation plan.[155] The same year, George Cornell, a "chief of Tuckabatche," received $100 for "the use of the chiefs of the Creek nation."[156] The need to reward loyal Creeks was a direct result of the massive changes taking place in Creek country at the instigation of federal policies, rendering Hawkins a target for this anger. It was against this backdrop that the century drew to a close. Tentative negotiations in the immediate post-war period had led to the United States portraying itself as the protector against Georgian incursions. Such a stance encouraged some Creeks to become favourable towards the federal government—a situation enhanced by the trade benefits offered by the United States. Hooked on trade, Creeks became vulnerable to the more overt methods of reduction which were to follow in the nineteenth century.

This chapter has shown the early years of formal agreements that European or European-descended governments formed with Maroons and Creeks. From the ashes of war new alliances had to be negotiated. Peace treaties were lauded by both the federal and colonial government as the first step to gaining such alliance. Indeed, not just the act of concluding treaties itself was the same;

the clauses within those treaties were strikingly similar. For example, Maroons and Creeks were both required to assist if Jamaica or the United States came under external threat, both were to return runaway slaves, and both were to have governmental representatives within their territories. In other words, Maroons and Creeks were expected to begin the post-war periods in a remarkably similar manner. Colonial and federal officials wanted the same thing from these treaties—to secure a military alliance, to prevent Maroon and Creek territory from being a haven of subversiveness and to gradually undermine the autonomy of the communities.

This analysis of the early relationships between, on the one hand, Maroons and the Jamaican colonial government and, on the other, Creeks and the U.S. federal government allows us to construct a tentative model of European strategies to control semi-autonomous communities. As stated, the first stage in both cases was to sign treaties. These treaties represent the initial step in undermining the communities and were the first opportunity to introduce restrictions. For example, both communities lost land by signing the treaties with Jamaica and the United States. The Maroon peace treaties included a "land grant" which masks the true state of affairs in which Maroons lost control of almost the entire interior of the island. Similarly, the Creek treaties with Georgia and the federal government ceded millions of acres of territory to the United States. This loss of land weakened both communities and forced them into smaller plots, thus increasing reliance on external communities for trade, sustenance and employment.

Another provision in both sets of treaties was the requirement to provide "assistance" in times of external threat. Clearly, this was an attempt to prevent any future potential alliances with enemies of either Jamaica or the United States whilst, at the same time, boosting the military forces at the disposal of each government. Such a requirement also served to undermine the independence of these communities. Indeed, in the Maroon treaties, it was explicitly stated that when coming to the assistance of the colonial government, Maroon fighters would be under the command of the British forces. This was not the case with Creeks, although they were expected to "give notice of any designs" by outsiders against the United States—thus, indirectly allying the Creek Nation with the United States against these potential enemies and preventing any potential neutrality that Creeks may have wished to enact.

Both communities were also obliged to allow government representatives to live within their communities. This was no doubt construed as the governments wishing to keep communication open and for these men to act in an almost ambassadorial capacity; but, in reality, this was yet another step in undermining independence. As the years passed, the superintendents in Jamaica, as well as Indian agents like Benjamin Hawkins, took on more and more roles which limited the autonomy of Maroons and Creeks. From jurisdiction to movement in and out of Maroon and Creek country, these men increasingly dictated the lifestyles of Maroons and Creeks.

The inclusion of clauses which demanded the return of runaways aimed to draw divisions between these semi-autonomous communities and the enslaved population, more of which will be discussed in Chapter 3. In addition, however, these clauses also served to extend European control over Maroons and Creeks. When called upon to hunt slaves, these Maroons and Creeks would seem to be acting on the orders of Europeans. Further, the financial recompense that was provided helped to deepen the financial reliance on the white societies of Jamaica and the United States.

Once the peace treaties were signed, the governments of both Jamaica and the United States set about consolidating the dependence of the Maroon and Creek communities on European societies. Some of the methods were strikingly similar, whilst others took on more of a local flavour. The first method, present in both cases, was gift-giving. On the surface, gift-giving enabled government officials to smooth relations with Maroon and Creek leaders as well as to consolidate the alliances forged in the peace treaties. With Maroons, the colonial government decided a gift which kept on giving, as opposed to monetary reward for service, would be the best way to ensure continuing friendship between the two groups. Therefore, colonists gifted such things as cattle to the Maroons. In a similar vein, the federal government decided against one-off payments to Creeks for their lands, or for their alliance, and agreed upon annuities which would continue to be given in subsequent years. The immediate benefits of such decisions are not hard to see. On a deeper level, gift-giving consolidated the dependence of both communities on the colonial and federal governments. Take, for example, the cows presented to Maroon leaders in the 1740s. These cows and their potential offspring would last a lot longer than the British military jackets sometimes gifted to loyal Maroons. The cows, their milk, their meat and their offspring would sustain the communities and "remind" the Maroons of the benefits of an alliance with the British. Further, gifting cattle to the Maroons, rather than cash, meant that Maroons had to turn to other methods of earning money, methods which increasingly drew the Maroons into colonial society, thus intertwining them with the fate of the British. Giving cash would most likely have led to fewer Maroons partaking in the act of slave-catching because an alternative, more stable source of income would surely have been preferred to the erratic lifestyle of the slave-catcher. Gifting cattle would not represent such an obstacle. Likewise, monetary gifts encouraged Creeks to become dependent on a ready supply of cash which could be used in the U.S. factory stores popping up across their territory. By pushing the American system of finance, the federal government encouraged Creeks to become acquainted with cash and credit and, when the cash income or credit decreased, it left Creeks in debt and more willing to cede lands in payment of that debt.

Another form of control was the demand for both Maroons and Creeks to meet with government leaders on a frequent basis—for the Maroons, this was to be the Governor, and for the Creeks, this was to be either official representatives of the federal government or the President himself. Once again, these meetings were billed as opportunities to display martial skills, cultural occasions or political negotiations, but it is noteworthy that none of these meetings took place in Maroon or Creek country. In other words, Maroons and Creeks were expected to undertake often arduous journeys to wait upon European officials. This expectation was a subtle method of billing Maroons and Creeks as subservient players in the new alliance.

As the years progressed, more overt, although still not explicit, methods of control were introduced by the governments. In Jamaica, these measures took the form of legislation; whereas, in the United States, further treaties were negotiated and agreed upon. The primary reason for these different approaches was that the Creek Nation was a sovereign nation on which the federal government could not simply impose its will. On the other hand, the colonial government had earlier passed several laws which had benefited Maroons, particularly those that granted more lands and raised the payment of hunting runaways, and, therefore, a precedent had been set. The legislation introduced later in Jamaica was, in theory, intended to protect Maroons from abuses by colonists. But, in reality, it was yet another way of exerting control. If the colonial government could, for example, restrict opportunities for financial betterment, then Maroons would become more reliant on the alliance with the colonists. Likewise, the treaties signed with the Creek Nation increased dependence through trade and land loss. Land loss led to a decreasing ability to hunt deer for deerskins, the Creeks' primary source of income, and led to an increased trade with U.S. trading stores. Loss of land also meant less land to supply the Creek towns with provisions, rendering an increased reliance on the United States.

The federal and colonial governments perhaps felt invigorated to introduce such increasingly restrictive measures because of the invitations they had received to become involved in Maroon and Creek internal affairs. Whilst most likely neither the Maroons nor Creeks realised what extending such a request would ultimately mean, doing so gave both governments the footholds they desired in Maroon and Creek country. Once precedent was set, neither government was willing to give it up. When the Crawford uprising broke out in Crawford Town in 1754, it is no surprise that the town turned to the colonial government for assistance given the years of quiet undermining of Maroon authority. Similarly, in 1793, when the consortium of Creeks that called for an army to destroy the Cowetas, Broken Arrow, Uchees, Usuchees, Big Tallassee and a part of the Chehaws, they claimed that without U.S. intervention, "there can be no hope of peace."[157] Indeed, such invitations made sense from a militaristic point of view. Once, however, the governments had been asked to intervene in internal affairs, there was no turning back. The entire structure of the communities would be altered by the colonial and federal governments.

To increase reliance on the governments, both communities had further opportunities for trade and employment severely reduced. In Jamaica, Maroon communities had been, by treaty, allowed to grow every crop except sugar but, through legislation, saw their opportunities to move easily around the island, and therefore to market, curtailed. Opportunities for employment through slave-catching were also on the downturn following Tacky's Rebellion and the success of Britain in the Seven Years' War. Any Maroons who did find themselves called upon to hunt runaways often found their payments delayed by months or even years. Whilst such tardy payment was not unusual for the Jamaican government—indeed, surveyors employed to mark boundaries struggled to secure their pay, too—it did contribute to an increasing reliance on colonial society. Pushing communities into financial difficulty was also a tactic used by the federal government. Payments due under the annuity system were delayed, whilst at the same time U.S. traders allowed Creeks to use credit to buy provisions, thus forcing them further into debt. Financial dependency was, therefore, a tool utilised by both the Jamaican and American governments to achieve the mutual goal of reduction of these semi-autonomous communities. Once a certain level of dependency was established, it became easier for government officials to try to change the fundamental structure of Maroon and Creek society, thus rendering them more pliable for control.

Therefore, as we have seen, both governments initially utilised more subtle forms of control in these early years. The necessity of such subtle methods was a result of the vulnerability of both Jamaican and American societies in the period immediately after the peace treaties. Neither the colonial government of Jamaica nor the federal government of the United States was in a position to overtly impose its will on these free communities. Economically, Jamaica and the United States needed peace and stability after years of war and bloodshed. Jamaica was under-developed in the 1730s, the sugar boom was yet to happen and the coastal settlements were under threat of invasion.[158] Likewise, in the 1780s, the federal government faced years of political wrangling to even form a coherent government which served the needs of the new republic.[159] A resounding defeat by the Western Confederacy in 1791 highlighted the vulnerabilities of the young country. The last thing it needed was war with a formidable enemy like the Creek Nation. Therefore, initially at least, these subtle methods of control were necessary to initiate a creeping influence over the free communities.

Overall, therefore, we can trace similar patterns in both cases. Both governments used the peace treaties as the first step in undermining the authority of Maroon and Creek leaders, their independence and their identity. Once this step had been negotiated, both moved on to consolidate the new alliances by bestowing gifts upon the free communities and through meetings with government leaders. These steps led to government officials being used as mediators in internal disputes, strengthening the European position within the semi-autonomous communities. Once they had become involved in internal affairs, slightly more overt methods could be deployed. These included alterations to trade patterns and influence over jurisdiction, to name but two. These subtle methods of control were necessary in the initial years after the peace treaties. Anything more explicit would have re-ignited war in the regions. However, once the subtle methods took hold, more overt methods of control could begin to be implemented by both the colonial and federal governments.

Notes

1. The treaties are dated 1738/9 because dates before 1752 (when Britain adopted the modern Gregorian calendar) appear in the Julian calendar format, in which the year starts on 25th March. The treaty was signed before March, thus meaning the date given is often 1738/9. I will refer to the year as 1739.
2. Philip Thicknesse, *Memoirs and Ancedotes of Philip Thicknesse, Late Lieutenant Governor of Land Guard Fort, and Unfortunately Father to George Touchet, Baron Audley* (Dublin: Printed by Graisberry and Campbell for William Jones, 1790), 75–76.
3. *Journals of the House of Assembly of Jamaica (JHA)*, 1st March 1739, Vol. III, National Archives of Jamaica, Spanish Town, Jamaica (NAJ).
4. *JHA*, 23rd June 1739, Vol. III, NAJ.
5. *JHA*, 1st March 1739, Vol. III, NAJ.
6. *JHA*, 23rd June 1739, Vol. III, NAJ.
7. *JHA*, 1st March 1739, Vol. III, NAJ.
8. *JHA*, 23rd June 1739, Vol. III, NAJ.
9. *JHA*, 1st March 1739, Vol. III, NAJ.
10. *JHA*, 23rd June 1739, Vol. III, NAJ.
11. Kathleen Wilson, 'The Performance of Freedom: Maroons and the Colonial Order in Eighteenth-Century Jamaica and the Atlantic Sound,' *The William and Mary Quarterly*, 3rd Series, LXVI (Jan., 2009), 59.
12. Carey Robinson, *The Iron Thorn: The Defeat of the British by the Jamaican Maroons* (Kingston: Kingston Publishers Limited, 1993), 51.
13. For more on the Haitian Revolution, see David P. Geggus, Rosemary Brana-Shute and Randy J. Sparks, eds., *The Impact of the Haitian Revolution in the Atlantic World* (Columbia: University of South Carolina, 2001); Nick Nesbitt, *Universal Emancipation: The Haitian Revolution and the Radical Enlightenment* (Charlottesville: University of Virginia Press, 2008); Maurice Jackson and Jacqueline Bacon, eds., *African Americans and the Haitian Revolution: Selected Essays and Historical Documents* (London: Routledge, 2010); Laurent DuBois, *Avengers of the New World: The Story of the Haitian Revolution* (Cambridge, MA: Belknap, 2004); David Patrick Geggus and Norman Fiering, eds., *The World of the Haitian Revolution* (Bloomington: Indiana University Press, 2009); Jeremy D. Popkin, *A Concise History of the Haitian Revolution* (Malden: Wiley-Blackwell, 2012); Malick W. Ghachem, *The Old Regime and the Haitian Revolution* (Cambridge: Cambridge University Press, 2012); Jeremy D. Popkin, *You Are All Free: The Haitian Revolution and the Abolition of Slavery* (Cambridge: Cambridge University Press, 2010); Doris L. Garraway, *Tree of Liberty: Cultural Legacies of the Haitian Revolution in the Atlantic World* (Charlottesville: University of Virginia Press, 2008).
14. Mavis Campbell, *The Maroons of Jamaica, 1655–1796: A History of Resistance, Collaboration & Betrayal* (Trentin: Africa World Press, 1990), 149.
15. Michael Mullin, *Africa in America: Slave Acculturation and Resistance in the American South and the British Caribbean, 1736–1831* (Urbana: University of Illinois Press, 1994), 49.
16. Keith to Germaine, 24th December 1778, CO 137/73, National Archives, Kew, England (NA).
17. Alvin O. Thompson, *Flight to Freedom: African Runaways and Maroons in the Americas* (Kingston: University of West Indies Press, 2006), 304.
18. Edward Long, *The History of Jamaica; or, General Survey of the Ancient and Modern State of That Island: With Reflections on its Situations, Settlements, Inhabitants, Climate, Products, Commerce, Laws, and Government* (London: F. Cass, 1970), 334.
19. Edward Long Papers, BM: Ad. Ms. 12431, British Library (BL).
20. William Beckford to James Knight, 11th October 1740, Edward Long Manuscripts, Add. Ms. 12431, BL.

21. *JHA*, 29th April 1741, Vol. III, NAJ.
22. *JHA*, 8th May 1741, Vol. III, NAJ.
23. It is notable that, in the above bill, Cudjoe was referred to as "colonel" rather than "captain" as he had previously been called. Perhaps his men's endeavours against the Spanish in 1740 had encouraged a new relationship between him and colonial officials.
24. *JHA*, 23rd June 1741, Vol. III, NAJ.
25. *Ibid.*
26. *JHA*, 12th April 1744, Vol. III, NAJ.
27. Anno 17 George II, 1744, *The Laws of Jamaica: 1760–1792* (London: A. Aikman Printer's to the King's Most Excellent Majesty, 1811), Chapter 3.
28. *Ibid.*, Chapter 4.
29. *Ibid.*, Chapter 14.
30. *Ibid.*, Chapter 17.
31. Edward Long, Edward Long Manuscript, Add. Ms. 12431, BL.
32. *JHA*, 2nd April 1746, Vol. IV, NAJ.
33. Anno 19 George 2, 1746, *Laws of Jamaica*, Chapters 9 and 10.
34. *JHA*, 22nd February 1752, Vol. IV, NAJ.
35. Robinson, *The Iron Thorn*, 131.
36. Richard Hart, *Slaves Who Abolished Slavery: Blacks in Rebellion* (Kingston: University of the West Indies Press, 2002), 137.
37. Long, *History of Jamaica*, 347.
38. *Ibid.*
39. Robinson, *The Iron Thorn*, 121.
40. Long, *History of Jamaica*, 348.
41. *Ibid.*
42. Edward Long Manuscripts, Add. Ms. 12431, BL.
43. *JHA*, 27th October 1751, Vol. IV, NAJ.
44. Acts of Assembly Passed in the Island of Jamaica from 1681 to 1733 Inclusive (BL), CSF., 154/4, 332–333.
45. *Acts* (BL), CSF., 154/4, 332.
46. *Acts* (BL), CSF., 154/7, 474–481; *ibid.*, CSF., 167/2, 200–4.
47. *JHA*, 14th November 1793, Vol. IX, NAJ.
48. *JHA*, 24th September 1756, Vol. IV, NAJ.
49. *JHA*, 26th October 1756, Vol. IV, NAJ.
50. *Ibid.*
51. *JHA*, 2nd March 1758, Vol. V, NAJ.
52. Bev Carey, *Maroon Story: The Authentic and Original History of the Maroons in the History of Jamaica, 1490–1880* (St. Andrew, Jamaica: Agouti Press, 1997), 422.
53. *Ibid.*, 423.
54. *Ibid.*
55. Long, *History of Jamaica*, 428.
56. *JHA*, 11th October 1760, Vol. V, NAJ.
57. *JHA*, 27th October 1760, Vol. V, NAJ.
58. *Ibid.*, 135.
59. For more on guerrilla warfare, see Max Boot, *Invisible Armies: An Epic History of Guerilla Warfare from Ancient Times to the Present* (New York: Liveright, 2013); Sam C. Sarkesian, ed., *Revolutionary Guerilla Warfare: Theories, Doctrines, and Contexts* (Somerset: Transaction, 2010); Michael L. Gross, *The Ethics of Insurgency: A Critical Guide to Just Guerilla Warfare* (New York: Cambridge University Press, 2015); Anthony Clayton, *Warfare in Woods and Forests* (Bloomington: Indiana University Press, 2012).
60. Long, *History of Jamaica*, 445.
61. *Ibid.*

62. *Ibid.*, 347–348.
63. Wilson, 'The Performance of Freedom,' 47.
64. *Ibid.*, 64.
65. W. J. Gardner, *The History of Jamaica from Its Discovery . . . to the Year 1872* (1st edition 1873), new edition (London: T. Fisher Unwin, 1909), 141–142.
66. Long, *History of Jamaica*, Vol. II, 465–468.
67. Robinson, *The Iron Thorn*, 134–135.
68. 16th March 1767, Roger Hope Elletson Letter Book, 1766–1770, NLJ.
69. Carey, *Maroon Story*, 448.
70. 3rd August 1767, Roger Hope Elletson Letter Book, 1766–1770, NLJ.
71. 21st September 1768, Roger Hope Elletson Letter Book, 1766–1770, NLJ.
72. Anno 10 George III, 1769, *Laws of Jamaica*, Chapter 5.
73. Gardner, *The History of Jamaica*, 14.
74. Bryan Edwards to Mark Davis of Bristol, 18th April 1774, Add. Ms. 12431, BL; Keith to Dartmouth, 22nd April 1774, CO 137/69, NA.
75. Keith to Dartmouth, 22nd April 1774, CO137/69, NA.
76. Edward Long Papers, Add. Ms. 12431, BL.
77. Wilson, 'The Performance of Freedom,' 64.
78. Charles R. Ritcheson, 'The Earl of Shelbourne and Peace with America, 1782–1783: Vision and Reality,' *International History Review* (1983), 325.
79. 25 *Journals of the Continental Congress, 1744–1789*, at 602 (22nd Sept., 1783) (Washington, DC: U.S. Govt. Print. Off., 1904–37).
80. Edward J. Cashin, *Lachlan McGillivray, Indian Trader: The Shaping of the Southern Colonial Frontier* (Athens: University of Georgia Press, 1992), 210, 252, 258–259.
81. *Ibid.*, 258, 263.
82. For more on Alexander McGillivray, see Arthur Ormont, *Diplomat in Warpaint: Chief Alexander McGillivray of the Creeks* (Glasgow: Aberlard-Schuman, 1968); Cashin, *Lachlan McGillivray*; John Walton Caughey, *McGillivray of the Creeks* (Norman: University of Oklahoma Press, 1938); Michael D. Green, 'Alexander McGillivray,' in *American Indian Leaders: Studies in Diversity*, ed. R. David Edmunds (Lincoln: University of Nebraska Press, 1980), 41–63; Lawrence Kinnaird, 'International Rivalry in the Creek Country, Part I, The Ascendancy of Alexander McGillivray,' *Florida Historical Quarterly*, 10 (1931), 59–85; J. M. O'Donnell, 'Alexander McGillivray: Training for Leadership, 1777–1783,' *Georgia Historical Quarterly*, 49 (1965), 172–183; Thomas D. Watson, 'Strivings for Sovereignty: Alexander McGillivray, Creek Warfare, and Diplomacy, 1783–1790,' *Florida Historical Quarterly*, 58 (1980), 400–414; Arthur P. Whitaker, 'Alexander McGillivray, 1783–1789,' *North Carolina Historical Review*, 5 (1928), 181–203, and 'Alexander McGillivray, 1789–1793,' *North Carolina Historical Review*, 5 (1928), 289–309; J. Leitch Wright, 'Creek-American Treaty of 1790: Alexander McGillivray and the Diplomacy of the Old Southwest,' *Georgia Historical Quarterly*, 51 (1967), 379–400.
83. Alexander McGillivray to Governor Zéspedes, 22nd August 1785, Reel 2, Archivo Nacional de Cuba (ANC), Library of Congress, Washington, D.C., United States (LOC).
84. Andrew K. Frank, 'Taking the State Out: Seminoles and Creeks in Late Eighteenth Century Florida,' *The Florida Historical Quarterly*, 84, 1, Special H-Florida Issue: Florida History from Transnational Perspectives (Summer, 2005), 10–27.
85. Hawkins, Pickins, Martin and McIntosh to Charles Thomson, 17th November 1785, Reel 3, ANC, LOC.
86. Alexander McGillivray to Arturo O'Neill, 26th October 1785, Reel 3, ANC, LOC.
87. Hawkins, Pickins, Martin and McIntosh to Charles Thomson, 17th November 1785, Reel 3, ANC, LOC.
88. United States Commissioners to the Creek Nation, 25th September 1789, Reel 8, ANC, LOC.

89. Alexander McGillivray to Arturo O'Neill, 8th May 1790, Reel 6, ANC, LOC.

90. *Ibid.*

91. Man of Augusta to Another at Charleston, 26th September 1786, Reel 5, ANC, LOC.

92. Alexander McGillivray to Esteban Miró, 12th August 1788, Reel 6, ANC, LOC.

93. Alexander McGillivray to John Habersham, 18th September 1786, Reel 3, ANC, LOC.

94. Alexander McGillivray to William Panton, 10th August 1789, Papeles Procedentes de Cuba, Archivo de Indias, Seville, Spain (microfilm leg. 203, 1022, reel 282A, P. K. Yonge Library of Florida History, University of Florida, Gainesville (PKY).

95. U.S. Commissioners to the Creek Nation, 15th September 1789 (ANC), MSS17376, LOC.

96. Thomas C. Cochran, ed., *The New American State Papers, 1789–1860* (Wilmington: Scholarly Resources, 1972–81), 73.

97. George Stiggins, *Creek Indian History: A Historical Narrative of the Genealogy, Traditions, and Downfall of the Ispocoga or Creek Indian Tribe of Indians* (Birmingham: Birmingham Public Library Press, 1989), 64–65.

98. John Pope, *A Tour Through the Southern and Western Territories of the United States of North-America; the Spanish Dominions on the River Mississippi, and the Floridas; the Countries of the Creek Nations; and Many Uninhabited Parts* (Richmond: Printed by John Dixon, 1792), 51.

99. Henry Knox to the Governor of Georgia, 24th November 1789, South-eastern Native American Documents, 1730–1842, Special Collections available online at Galileo Digital Library of Georgia.

100. J. Leitch Wright, *Creeks and Seminoles: The Destruction and Regeneration of the Muscogulge People* (Lincoln: University of Nebraska Press, 1990), 133.

101. Mary E. Young, 'Conflict Resolution on the Indian Frontier,' *Journal of the Early Republic*, 16, 1 (Spring, 1996), 1.

102. Benjamin Hawkins to Alexander McGillivray, 6th March 1790, *McGillivray of the Creeks*, 257–258.

103. Alexander McGillivray to Howard, 11th August 1790, Reel 6, ANC, LOC.

104. McGillivray to Panton, 8th October 1789, in Caughey, *McGillivray of the Creeks*, 252–254.

105. Kinnaird, 'International Rivalry in the Creek Country,' 67.

106. Treaty of New York, August 1790, Entry No. 108, RG11, NA.

107. For more on Pinckney's Treaty, see Samuel Flagg Bemis, *Pinckney's Treaty: A Study of America's Advantage from Europe's Distress, 1783–1800* (Baltimore: The John Hopkins Press,1926); Ethan Grant, 'The Treaty of San Lorenzo and Manifest Destiny,' *Gulf Coast Historical Review*, 12, 2 (Spring, 1997), 44–57; Raymond A. Young, 'Pinckney's Treaty: A New Perspective,' *Hispanic American Historical Review*, 43, 4 (Nov., 1963), 526–539.

108. Treaty of New York, August 1790, Entry No. 108, RG11, NA.

109. *Ibid.*

110. *Ibid.*

111. Henry Knox to George Washington, rough copy, August 1790, Vol. 26, p. 122, Henry Knox Papers, Gilder Lehrman Collection, Pierpoint Morgan Library (PML), New York.

112. Washington to Senate, 11th August 1790, in *The Writings of George Washington from the Original Manuscript Sources, 1745–1799*, ed. John C. Fitzpatrick (Government Printing Office: Washington, DC, 1931–1944), XXXI, 88.

113. Ellis Merton Coulter, *A Short History of Georgia* (Chapel Hill: University of North Carolina Press, 1933), 183.

114. James F. Doster, *Creek Indians and Their Florida Lands, 1740–1823* (New York: Gardland Publishers, 1974), 107.

115. Extract from the *Pennsylvania Packet and Daily Advertiser*, 18th August 1791, No. 147, in *McGillivray of the Creeks*, ed. John Walton Caughey (Norman: University of Oklahoma Press, 1938).

116. Oath of Joseph Cornell, 7th August 1790, Vol. 26, 126, Henry Knox Papers, Gilder Lehrman Collection, PML.

117. Henry Knox to George Washington, rough copy, August 1790, Vol. 36, 122, Henry Knox Papers, Gilder Lehman Collection, PML.

118. Commissioners of Indian Affairs, *Treaties Between the United States of America and the Several Indian Tribes from 1778 to 1837* (1837) Reprint (Millwood: Kraus, 1975), 62.

119. Benjamin Hawkins to Edward Wright, 20th October 1799, Entry No. 42, RG 75, National Archives and Record Office of the United States, Washington, D.C., United States (NORA).

120. Benjamin Hawkins to Edward Wright, 5th December 1799, Entry No. 42, RG 75, NORA

121. Benjamin Hawkins, *Letters of Benjamin Hawkins, 1796–1806* (Savannah: Published by the Georgia Historical Society, 1916), Vol. II, 411.

122. Hawkins, *Letters*, Vol. II, 751, 775.

123. *Ibid.*, 635.

124. *Ibid.*, 525.

125. James Seagrove to the Creek Nation, 24th February 1792, Reel 12, ANC, LOC.

126. James Leonard to James Seagrove, 24th July 1792, Reel 12, ANC, LOC.

127. Andrew Pickens to the Secretary of War, 24th July 1793, Reel 14, ANC, LOC.

128. James Seagrove to the Secretary of War, 24th May 1793, Reel 10, ANC, LOC.

129. Timothy Barnard to (James Seagrove), 20th June 1793, Lockey Collection (LC), PKY; Timothy Barnard to James Jackson, 20th June 1793, Unpublished Letters of Timothy Barnard, 1784–1820 (LTB), 171, edited by Louise F. Hays, Typescript in Georgia Department of Archives and History (GDAH); Timothy Barnard to Henry Gaither, 21st June 1793, *American State Papers, Class II: Indian Affairs*, Vol. I (Washington, DC, 1832), 422–423.

130. Copy of talk from Big Warrior to General Twiggs, 1793, LTB, 160, GDAH.

131. J. Merriweather to the Headmen and Warriors of the Creek Nation, 11th August 1794, Reel 10, ANC, LOC

132. James Durouseaux to Caron, 28th October 1796, Reel 9, ANC, LOC.

133. *Ibid.*

134. This is discussed in greater detail in Chapter 5.

135. Daniel H. Usner, 'American Indians on the Cotton Frontier: Changing Economic Relations with Citizens and Slaves in the Mississippi Territory,' *The Journal of American History*, 72, 2 (Sep., 1985), 299–300.

136. Jean Chaudhuri, *A Sacred Path: The Way of the Muscogee Creeks* (Los Angeles: UCLA American Indian Studies Center, 2001), 143.

137. Jefferson, "Hints on the Subject of Indian Boundaries. . .," in *The Writings of Thomas Jefferson*, eds. Andrew A. Lipscomb and Albert E. Bergh (Washington, DC: Thomas Jefferson Memorial Association, 1903–4), 374.

138. For more on this, see Claudio Saunt, *A New Order of Things: Property, Power and the Transformation of the Creek Indians, 1733–1816* (Cambridge: Cambridge University Press, 1999).

139. Ulrich Bonnell Phillips, *Life and Labour in the Old South* (Columbia: University of South Carolina Press, 2007), 21–29.

140. Hawkins, *Letters*, Vol. I, 402.

141. Benjamin Hawkins to Elizabeth House Trist, 25th November 1797, *Letters*, Vol. I, 1664–165.

142. Journal of Benjamin Hawkins, 2nd December 1796, *Letters*, 21–22.

143. James Durouzeaux to Vicente Folch, 27th May 1798, Papeles Procedentes de Cuba, Archivo de Indias, Seville, Spain (PC), leg. 208A, 592, reel 286, PKY.

144. Benjamin Hawkins to James McHenry, 9th January 1799, *Letters*, Vol. I, 238.

145. Benjamin Hawkins, "A Sketch of the Creek Country in the years 1798 and 1799," *Letters*, Vol. I, 316–317; Benjamin Hawkins to James McHenry, 6th January 1797, *Letters*, Vol. I, 63.

146. Daniel Pepper to Governor Lyttleton, 18th November 1756, *Documents Relating to Indian Affairs, Colonial Records of South Carolina*, Vol. II, ed. William L. McDowell Jr. (Columbia: South Carolina Archives Department, 1958), 255.

147. Duane Champagne, *Social Order and Political Change: Constitutional Governments Among the Cherokee, the Choctaw, the Chickasaw and the Creek* (Stanford: Stanford University Press, 1992), 113–114. In contrast, Saunt, *A New Order of Things*, 1, 164–185, argues that the National Council could exert its control over every Creek Person.

148. Affidavit of Jeremiah Oates, 10th April 1797, "Indian Depredations, 1787–1825," 3: 77, GDAH; Benjamin Hawkins to James Jackson, 11th July 1798, *Letters*, Vol. I, 211; Benjamin Hawkins to Timothy Barnard, 13th July 1797, *Letters*, Vol. I, 120.

149. Hawkins, *Letters*, Vol. I, 193.

150. *Ibid.*, 269.

151. *Ibid.*, 269, 279, 281, Vol. II, 454. For more on Bowles, see Gilbert C. Din, 'William Augustus Bowles on the Georgia Frontier: A Reexaminaton of the Spanish Surrender of Fort San Marcos de Apalache in 1800,' *Georgia Historical Quarterly*, 88, 3 (2004), 305–337; Gilbert C. Din, *War on the Gulf Coast: The Spanish Fight Against William Augustus Bowles* (Gainesville: University Press of Florida, 2012); Joseph Millard, *Incredible William Bowles* (Philadelphia: Chilton Books, 1966); James Leitch Wright, *William Augustus Bowles, Director General of the Creek Nation* (Athens: University of Georgia Press, 1967).

152. Hawkins to Edward Price, 8th January 1801, Entry No. 42, RG75, NA.

153. See the various orders on the stipend in Hawkins, *Letters*, Vol. I, 324–339.

154. Creek Stipend for 1798, *Letters*, Vol. I, 331.

155. Journal of Richard Thomas, 30th July 1798, *Letters*, Vol. I, 490–492; Benjamin Hawkins, "A Sketch of the Creek Country in the years 1798 and 1799," *Letters*, Vol. I, 306; and "Journal of Benjamin Hawkins," 30th June 1804, *Letters*, Vol. II, 472.

156. Creek Stipend for 1798, *Letters*, Vol. I, 330.

157. James Seagrove to the Secretary of War, 24th May 1793, Reel 10, ANC, LOC.

158. Richard B. Sheridan, 'The Wealth of Jamaica in the Eighteenth Century,' *The Economic History Review*, 18, 2 (1962), 297.

159. Rosemarie Zagarri, *The Politics of Size: Representation in the United States, 1776–1850* (Ithaca: Cornell University Press, 1987), 2.

Bibliography

Primary Sources

British Library, London, United Kingdom

Acts of Assembly Passed in the Island of Jamaica from 1681 to 1733 Inclusive.
Edward Long Manuscripts.

Galileo Online Digital Library of Georgia (website)

South-eastern Native American Documents, 1730–1842.

Georgia Department of Archives and History, Morrow, Georgia, United States

"Creek Indian Letters, Talks, and Treaties, 1705–1839."
"Indian Treaties: Cessions of Land in Georgia, 1705–1837."

"Letters of Benjamin Hawkins, 1797–1815."
South-eastern Native American Documents Database.
Unpublished Letters of Timothy Barnard, 1784–1820.

Library of Congress, Washington, D.C., United States

Archivo Nacional de Cuba Collection (microfilm).

National Archives, Kew, United Kingdom

CO 137/32	CO 137/40	CO 137/42
CO 137/56	CO 137/69	CO 137/73
CO 137/90	CO 137/91	CO 137/92
CO 137/94	CO 137/95	CO 137/96
CO 137/97	CO 137/98	

National Archives of Jamaica, Spanish Town, Jamaica

Inventories.
Journals of the House of Assembly, Vols. I–X.

National Archives and Records Office, Washington, D.C., United States

Foreign Letters of the Continental Congress and the Department of State.
Records of the Bureau of Indian Affairs.

National Library of Jamaica, Kingston, Jamaica

Roger Hope Elletson Letter Book, 1766–1770.

P. K. Yonge Library, University of Florida, Gainesville, United States

Archivo General de Indias (microfilm).
Lockey Collection.
Papeles Procedentes de Cuba (microfilm).

Pierpoint Morgan Library, New York, United States

Henry Knox Papers.

Special Collections, University of Georgia, Athens, United States

Southeastern Native American Documents, 1730–1842.

Newspapers and Magazines

Cornwall Chronicle.
Nova Scotia Magazine.

Published Sources

Boot, Max, *Invisible Armies: An Epic History of Guerilla Warfare from Ancient Times to the Present* (New York: Liveright, 2013).

Campbell, Mavis, *The Maroons of Jamaica, 1655–1796: A History of Resistance, Collaboration & Betrayal* (Trentin: Africa World Press, 1990).

Carey, Bev, *Maroon Story: The Authentic and Original History of the Maroons in the History of Jamaica, 1490–1880* (St. Andrew, Jamaica: Agouti Press, 1997).

Cashin, Edward J., *Lachlan McGillivray, Indian Trader: The Shaping of the Southern Colonial Frontier* (Athens: University of Georgia Press, 1992).

Caughey, John Walton, *McGillivray of the Creeks* (Norman: University of Oklahoma Press, 1938).

Champagne, Duane, *Social Order and Political Change: Constitutional Governments Among the Cherokee, the Choctaw, the Chickasaw and the Creek* (Stanford: Stanford University Press, 1992).

Chaudhuri, Jean, *A Sacred Path: The Way of the Muscogee Creeks* (Los Angeles: UCLA American Indian Studies Center, 2001).

Clayton, Anthony, *Warfare in Woods and Forests* (Bloomington: Indiana University Press, 2012).

Cochran, Thomas C., ed., *The New American State Papers, 1789–1860* (Wilmington: Scholarly Resources, 1972–81).

Commissioners of Indian Affairs, *Treaties Between the United States of America and the Several Indian Tribes from 1778–1837* (1837) Reprint (Millwood: Kraus, 1975).

Coulter, Ellis Merton, *A Short History of Georgia* (Chapel Hill: University of North Carolina Press, 1933).

Din, Gilbert C., 'William Augustus Bowles on the Georgia Frontier: A Reexaminaton of the Spanish Surrender of Fort San Marcos de Apalache in 1800,' *Georgia Historical Quarterly*, 88, 3 (2004), 305–337.

Din, Gilbert C., *War on the Gulf Coast: The Spanish Fight Against William Augustus Bowles* (Gainesville: University Press of Florida, 2012).

Doster, James F., *Creek Indians and Their Florida Lands, 1740–1823* (New York: Garland Publishers, 1974).

DuBois, Laurent, *Avengers of the New World: The Story of the Haitian Revolution* (Cambridge, MA: Belknap, 2004).

Edmunds, R. David, and Russell David, *Tecumseh and the Quest for Indian Leadership* (Boston: Little Brown, and Company, 1984).

Fitzpatrick, John C., ed., *The Writings of George Washington from the Original Manuscript Sources, 1745–1799* (Washington: Government Printing Office, 1931–1944).

Flagg Bemis, Samuel, *Pinckney's Treaty: A Study of America's Advantage from Europe's Distress, 1783–1800* (Baltimore: The John Hopkins Press, 1926).

Frank, Andrew, *Creeks & Southerners: Biculturalism on the Early American Frontier* (Lincoln: University of Nebraska Press, 2005).

Gardner, W. J., *The History of Jamaica from Its Discovery . . . to the Year 1872* (1st edition 1873), new edition (London: T. Fisher Unwin, 1909).

Garraway, Doris L., *Tree of Liberty: Cultural Legacies of the Haitian Revolution in the Atlantic World* (Charlottesville: University of Virginia Press, 2008).

Geggus, David P., Rosemary Brana-Shute and Randy J. Sparks, eds., *The Impact of the Haitian Revolution in the Atlantic World* (Columbia: University of South Carolina, 2001).

Geggus, David Patrick, and Norman Fiering, eds., *The World of the Haitian Revolution* (Bloomington: Indiana University Press, 2009).

Ghachem, Malick W., *The Old Regime and the Haitian Revolution* (Cambridge: Cambridge University Press, 2012).

Grant, Ethan, 'The Treaty of San Lorenzo and Manifest Destiny,' *Gulf Coast Historical Review*, 12, 2 (Spring, 1997), 44–57.

Green, Michael D., 'Alexander McGillivray.,' In *American Indian Leaders: Studies in Diversity*, ed. R. David Edmunds, 41–63 (Lincoln: University of Nebraska Press, 1980).

Gross, Michael L., *The Ethics of Insurgency: A Critical Guide to Just Guerilla Warfare* (New York: Cambridge University Press, 2015).

Hart, Richard, *Slaves Who Abolished Slavery* (Kingston: University of the West Indies, Institute of Social and Economic Research, 1985).

Hawkins, Benjamin, *Letters of Benjamin Hawkins, 1796–1806* (Savannah: Published by the Georgia Historical Society, 1916).

Jackson, Maurice, and Jacqueline Bacon, eds., *African Americans and the Haitian Revolution: Selected Essays and Historical Documents* (London: Routledge, 2010).

Jamaica, *The Laws of Jamaica: 1760–1792* (London: A. Aikman Printer's to the King's Most Excellent Majesty, 1811).

Journals of the Continental Congress, 1744–1789, at 602 (22nd Sept., 1783) (Washington, DC: U.S. Govt. Print. Off., 1904–37).

Kinnaird, Lawrence, 'International Rivalry in the Creek Country, Part I, The Ascendancy of Alexander McGillivray,' *Florida Historical Quarterly*, 10 (1931), 59–85.

Long, Edward, *The History of Jamaica; or, General Survey of the Ancient and Modern State of That Island: With Reflections on its Situations, Settlements, Inhabitants, Climate, Products, Commerce, Laws, and Government*, Vol. II (London: F. Cass, 1970).

McDowell, William L., ed., *Documents Relating to Indian Affairs, Colonial Records of South Carolina*, Vol. II (Columbia: South Carolina Archives Department, 1958).

Millard, Joseph, *Incredible William Bowles* (Philadelphia: Chilton Books, 1966).

Mullin, Michael, *Africa in America: Slave Acculturation and Resistance in the American South and the British Caribbean, 1736–1831* (Urbana: University of Illinois Press, 1994).

Nesbitt, Nick, *Universal Emancipation: The Haitian Revolution and the Radical Enlightenment* (Charlottesville: University of Virginia Press, 2008).

O'Donnell, J. M., 'Alexander McGillivray: Training for Leadership, 1777–1783,' *Georgia Historical Quarterly*, 49 (1965), 172–183.

Ormont, Arthur, *Diplomat in Warpaint: Chief Alexander McGillivray of the Creeks* (Glasgow: Aberlard-Schuman, 1968).

Phillips, Ulrich Bonnell, *Life and Labour in the Old South* (Columbia: University of South Carolina Press, 2007).

Pope, John, *A Tour Through the Southern and Western Territories of the United States of North-America; the Spanish Dominions on the River Mississippi, and the Floridas; the Countries of the Creek Nations; and Many Uninhabited Parts* (Richmond: Printed by John Dixon, 1792).

Popkin, Jeremy D., *You Are All Free: The Haitian Revolution and the Abolition of Slavery* (Cambridge: Cambridge University Press, 2010).

Popkin, Jeremy D., *A Concise History of the Haitian Revolution* (Malden: Wiley-Blackwell, 2012).

Ritcheson, Charles R., 'The Earl of Shelbourne and Peace with America, 1782–1783: Vision and Reality,' *International History Review* (1983), 322–345.

Robinson, Carey, *The Iron Thorn: The Defeat of the British by the Jamaican Maroons* (Kingston: Kingston Publishers Limited, 1993).

Sarkesian, Sam C., ed., *Revolutionary Guerilla Warfare: Theories, Doctrines, and Contexts* (Somerset: Transaction, 2010).

Saunt, Claudio, *A New Order of Things: Property, Power, and the Transformation of the Creek Indians, 1733–1816* (Cambridge: Cambridge University Press, 1999).

Sheridan, Richard B., 'The Wealth of Jamaica in the Eighteenth Century,' *The Economic History Review*, 18, 2 (1962), 292–311.

Stiggins, George, *Creek Indian History: A Historical Narrative of the Genealogy, Traditions, and Downfall of the Ispocoga or Creek Indian Tribe of Indians* (Birmingham: Birmingham Public Library Press, 1989).

Thicknesse, Philip, *Memoirs and Anecdotes of Philip Thicknesse, Late Lieutenant Governor of Land Guard Fort, and Unfortunately Father to George Touchet, Baron Audley* (Dublin: Printed by Graisberry and Campbell for William Jones, 1790).

Thompson, Alvin O., *Flight to Freedom: African Runaways and Maroons in the Americas* (Kingston: University of West Indies Press, 2006).

Usner, Daniel H., 'American Indians on the Cotton Frontier: Changing Economic Relations with Citizens and Slaves in the Mississippi Territory,' *The Journal of American History*, 72, 2 (Sept., 1985), 297–317.

Watson, Thomas D., 'Strivings for Sovereignty: Alexander McGillivray, Creek Warfare, and Diplomacy, 1783–1790,' *Florida Historical Quarterly*, 58 (1980), 400–414.

Whitaker, Arthur P., 'Alexander McGillivray, 1783–1789,' *North Carolina Historical Review*, 5 (1928), 181–203.

Whitaker, Arthur P., 'Alexander McGillivray, 1789–1793,' *North Carolina Historical Review*, 5 (1928), 289–309.

Wilson, Kathleen, 'The Performance of Freedom: Maroons and the Colonial Order in Eighteenth-Century Jamaica and the Atlantic Sound,' *The William and Mary Quarterly*, 3rd Series, 66 (Jan., 2009), 45–86.

Wright, J. Leitch, 'Creek-American Treaty of 1790: Alexander McGillivray and the Diplomacy of the Old Southwest,' *Georgia Historical Quarterly*, 51 (1967), 379–400.

Wright, James Leitch, *William Augustus Bowles, Director General of the Creek Nation* (Athens: University of Georgia Press, 1967).

Wright, James Leitch, *Creeks and Seminoles: The Destruction and Regeneration of the Muscogulge People* (Lincoln: University of Nebraska Press, 1990).

Young, Mary E., 'Conflict Resolution on the Indian Frontier,' *Journal of the Early Republic*, 16, 1 (Spring, 1996), 1–19.

Young, Raymond A., 'Pinckney's Treaty: A New Perspective,' *Hispanic American Historical Review*, 43, 4 (Nov., 1963), 526–539.

Zagarri, Rosemarie, *The Politics of Size: Representation in the United States, 1776–1850* (Ithaca: Cornell University Press, 1987).

2   The Relationship Deteriorates
On the Road to War

As the 1780s dawned in Jamaica, the western coast of the island was ravaged by one of the worst hurricanes the area had ever experienced. Savanna-la-Mar was completely destroyed after the sea surged into the town and swept houses away. There were no buildings left standing in the town or in the area for thirty to forty miles around it. An earthquake followed, which almost totally demolished every building in the parishes of Westmoreland, Hanover, part of St. James and some parts of St. Elizabeth. It was against such devastation that the tense Maroon alliance with the colonial government continued. By this period, the opportunities for mercenary employment of Maroon companies were becoming increasingly rare, adding to the festering tensions. In 1781, the Scotts Hall and Moore Town Maroons complained that they had not been paid their additional £200 for killing Three Fingered Jack, the rebellious slave who had been at large in the St. Thomas area for around a year.[1] Whilst, as we have seen, it was not particularly unusual for the colonial government to be tardy when making such payments, the delay increased tensions which had been growing for decades and which became more threatening given that the Age of Revolutions had now broken out. Maroons had assembled to assist the colonial government in repelling the threatened French invasion under Count D'Estaing in 1779 and again in 1780, but were increasingly disinterested in aiding the government in the subsequent years.[2]

The increased tensions of the era led the colonial government to become stricter when it came to enforcing the requirement of superintendents living amongst the Maroons. Previously, many superintendents had responded to the lack of accommodation by simply living outside of the Maroon town. In other cases, superintendents had rented houses or rooms, usually from Maroon women. But, by being reliant on Maroons for living space, the superintendents' influence was markedly reduced. Therefore, in 1784, the House voted for £100 to be diverted to the building of superintendents' accommodation in both Moore Town and Trelawny Town.[3] Typically, however, there was little evidence of either of the houses being completed, or indeed, even started. The impasse of the 1770s was continuing into the new decade—the colonial government attempted to increase control over the Maroon communities but, through a lack of funds and an inability to force Maroons to conform to its wishes, little changed.

As a result, the colonial government moved away from offering Maroons high levels of employment and mobility around the island. The loss of the American colonies in the 1770s added to the growing tension felt across Jamaican society and an increase in the determination of the British to sub-due any potential threats to their Caribbean colonies. The continued refusal of Maroons to submit to these demands only exacerbated the situation. In contrast to Richard Hart's claim that the colonial government had "so much confidence" in the Maroons that it was indifferent as to whether the superin-tendents appointed to reside in the Maroon towns lived there or elsewhere, the colonial government actually implemented measures to increasingly restrict the Maroon lifestyle.[4] Once again, the primary method was law-making.

In 1791, the colonial government introduced the most stringent measures yet. By this time, the overall population of the Maroon communities had increased markedly and was still growing, posing a threat to the government because, as one official put it, "the lands granted to them will soon be unable to provide for their support and maintenance."[5] The Assembly, therefore, ruled

> That it shall be lawful for any maroon negro or negroes to appear in per-son before the justices of their precinct, . . . and there and then publicly and solemnly to declare, that he, she, or they, are desirous and willing to give up any right he, she, or they, may have to any part of the island, except in any of the maroon-towns.

Should they make such a declaration then they would be "entitled to every right and privilege of a free person of colour, and shall no longer be subject to the command or control of any superintendent or maroon officer in the island. . . ."[6] This rather grand declaration should be seen in the context of what "rights and privileges" a free black had, or rather did not have, in Jamaica at the time. Free blacks and mulattos were, within the slave system, incapacitated by numerous socio-legal, as well as economic, restrictions. For example, only a handful of free black people would have had access to land in the manner that Maroons did. Further, as a free black, these former Maroons would be subject to militia duty and to any tax the government might wish to impose.[7] As long as the slave system lasted, Maroons would actually be trading their relatively secure position to one of uncertainty and instability. It is unsurprising, therefore, to discover that very few Maroons took the colonial government up on its offer. In fact, the only records we have of any Maroons doing so date from after the outbreak of the Sec-ond Maroon War. On one occasion, ten Maroon women gave up the rights granted to them as Maroons. With them, ten mulatto children and four quadroon children relinquished their identity.[8] Mavis Campbell lists a fur-ther twenty-two people who surrendered their Maroon status in 1796. Of those twenty-two, all except seven women were mixed-race. Of those seven, three had liaised with white men and had produced mulatto children.[9]

Therefore, it was mainly the offspring of unions between European men and Maroon women who decided to relinquish their Maroon identity.

The colonial government did not stop at this one law. Another prevented Maroons from leaving their towns and staying out as long as they pleased. They had permission to leave, but if they stayed seven days beyond the time allowed, they could be seized and sent back to Maroon territory for trial. In addition, no party of Maroons participating in a hunt for runaways could be larger than twelve, including the leader. No party could be sent out without the written permission of the superintendent, or remain out longer than twenty days. Maroons could no longer be hired by Europeans without a written agreement, and any debts which they owed, or which were owed to them, had to be settled by two magistrates.[10] Finally, Maroons were required to obtain a licence from a magistrate to sell their surplus goods—thus entrenching the authority of the local government over Maroons, emphasising their restriction to settlements and curtailing their freedom.[11]

The House further instructed the Governor to issue orders "forthwith" to the superintendents of the Maroons

> not to permit or suffer on any pretence whatever, the Maroons, or any of them, in their several departments, to fire guns or any fire arms, or to blow horns, on any occasion, after sun-set till sun-rise, unless when actual duty may render their firing necessary.

The House also ruled that the superintendents should be ordered to muster the Maroons together, "in the most public place in such towns," once every three months, "and then and there to read openly to them, the articles of pacification concluded and agreed upon between Colonel John Guthrie, Lieutenant Francis Sadler, and Cudjoe, and the articles of pacification" between Bennett and Quao, as well as the laws subsequently passed with respect to the Maroons. They were also to explain succinctly and accurately all relevant articles and laws, instructing the Maroons to observe "all and every clause, article, matter and thing, therein contained, which to them relate."[12]

Finally, the 1791 laws addressed the punishment of Maroons under colonial jurisdiction. A Maroon may be sentenced to death "without benefit of clergy," to transportation, to public whipping, or to confinement with hard labour for a period up to twelve months.[13] These laws applied to Maroon men as well as women, although women with children were temporarily exempted from execution "until a reasonable time after delivery."[14] The laws even stipulated how the punishment was to be carried out, saying that the execution should

> be performed in a public part of the parish, and with due solemnity; and care shall be taken by the gaoler or deputy-marshal that the criminal is free from intoxication at the time of his trial, and from thense to and at the time of his execution, under penalty of £5; and the mode of such execution shall by hanging by the neck, and no other.[15]

In other words, Maroon jurisdiction over their own people, short of capital punishment, which had been enshrined in the treaties, was officially overturned in the 1791 laws, with no agreement from the Maroons themselves. Thus, as indicative of the whittling away of power in other areas of Maroon life, the ability to judge their own cases (at least officially) was gradually lost. First, the treaties had disallowed Maroon courts from passing sentences of death; then, the 1751 law handed over the complete jurisdiction of Maroon courts to the superintendents; and, finally, the 1791 law addressed the punishments that Maroons would suffer under colonial jurisdiction.

By placing more restrictions on Maroon behaviour, the 1791 laws also increased the workload of the superintendents. They were now required to submit reports to the Governor every three months, under oath, of the number of men residing in each town, with particular emphasis on "the Number of Men capable of bearing arms" as well as those unfit for duty, the number of women and children, the population increase and decrease, the condition of the superintendent's accommodation, the condition of the roads leading to the towns, and the frequency of slave-holding by Maroons. Superintendents, as well as Maroon chiefs, were to be tried if suspected of neglect of duty or of "improper favour or partiality towards the offender or offenders to be tried." In such cases, the Governor would convene a court martial and the punishment was up to six months imprisonment.[16] It seems that this plethora of laws was largely ignored, but it is of great significance that the colonial government passed them at all. Maroons refusing to follow these new rules only added to the increasing distrust of the colonial government.

Some of these laws, particularly those regarding being hired by Europeans, were supposedly meant to protect the Maroons since there, allegedly, had been exploitation by colonists. It is questionable whether this was actually the case or whether it was a ruse to whittle away the independence of the Maroons. Likewise, the laws preventing slave-hunting groups from staying out too long and those attempting to confine Maroons to their territories would inhibit the chances of slaves and Maroons being able to interact in the woods, away from the eyes of observing colonists—thus reducing the possibility for plots to be hatched. The evidence suggests that Carey Robinson was right to claim that the Maroons were increasingly being treated as a conquered race rather than as a people who had voluntarily agreed to make peace at the request of their antagonists.[17] Maroons did not just sit back and allow this to happen, however. The towns continued to petition the colonial government about issues which were unsatisfactory to them. In March 1792, for example, the Trelawny Town Maroons sent a petition to the Assembly claiming that most of their land was comprised of very high, rocky mountains, and the rest was exhausted because it had been cultivated continuously since 1739. Not only was this land unable to support their growing population, but it was also being trespassed upon. This petition was signed by notable Trelawny Town Maroons such as Montague James, John Jarrett and Zachary Bayley, and was certified by their superintendent, Major John James.[18] Trespass caused such a concern because land symbolised Maroon freedom and was what set them apart from other free blacks in Jamaica. Local settlers encroaching upon Maroon lands symbolised the wider encroachment of colonial society on Maroon freedoms.

The 1792 petition of the Trelawny Maroons was eventually investigated by the House. It declared that a committee should be sent to the "towns in Trelawny" to ascertain the extent of the claims. After investigation, the committee alleged that only the officers who had signed the petition were even aware of its existence. They did find, however, that most of the town generally supported the demand for more lands, but they decreed this should not be granted for several reasons. First, they claimed that much of the Trelawny land was still uncultivated and that they should cultivate first the lands they already had; second, rapid settlement was taking place in that part of the island, and lands should be made available for colonists; third, because, if so desired, Maroons could gain lands through the "late law" of 1791 which allowed Maroons to give up their identity and live as free blacks—the law explicitly permitted them "to acquire what land they want as private property on leaving the town"; and fourth, because they did not depend on cultivation for their supply of clothing or other necessaries that they required.[19]

This rebuffal of Maroon requests was indicative of the colonial government's move away from its conciliatory stance of the earlier eighteenth century. The rejection of the Trelawnys' petition is founded upon baseless statements such as the one which claimed Maroons would be able to amount their own private property if they gave up their Maroon identity. Former Maroons would not be eligible for land grants, given their non-white status, and even if they found someone willing to sell land to them, the prices most likely would have been out of their financial reach. Further, the claim that much of the Trelawny land was uncultivated could have been through either ignorance or deceit. Ignorance, because it may have been the Maroons were practising the African technique of allowing fields to lay fallow for some time before being replanted—a practice not always familiar to colonists. Deceit, because the committee may well have known that much of the Trelawny land was rocky and uncultivable and, thus, had nothing planted on it. In the eyes of the colonists, forcing Maroons to live on exhausted or uncultivable lands would render them easier to control.

At this conjecture, the colonial government was very pleased with itself. It proclaimed that "property has acquired a degree of security which it never heretofore had in this island" and was impressed with the effectiveness of the signing of the peace treaties with the Maroons.[20] It believed it had handled the Maroon question well, but more trouble was brewing. Just a few months later, the Governor declared that the Trelawny Town Maroons had been "very troublesome and insolent" because of a law the Legislature had passed two years earlier. The main cause of the discontent was a clause which allowed the evidence of slaves to be used against Maroons in "all cases of delinquency." The colonial government claimed that allowing such evidence was necessary because the Maroons' depredations were "fast increasing and were performed only in the view of slaves," although the government does not explicitly out-line what those depredations were.[21] This, as the colonial government was aware, would have irritated Maroons because, since the signing of the peace treaties, they had been pitted against the slaves and had been encouraged to view slaves as beneath them. That the colonial government was aware of this and still proceeded with implementing this clause is symbolic of the changing attitude towards the Maroons.

The most catastrophic development when it came to Maroons and the colonial government, however, was the arrival of the Earl of Balcarres as Lieutenant-Governor on the island. Born in 1752, Alexander Lindsay was the sixth Earl of Balcarres and, after joining the army at the age of 15, fought in European theatres as well as the American Revolution. In 1794, he was made Governor of Jamaica.[22] Almost immediately, he set about further increasing restrictions on Maroon autonomy. One of his first acts—and in hindsight, one of his most catastrophic—was to dismiss Major John James as superintendent because of his refusal to leave his estate and return to Trelawny Town. James was particularly popular with the Trelawny Maroons, and his termination was a grave error. Balcarres installed Thomas Craskell and James Merody to succeed James and considered the matter closed, writing to the Duke of Portland that the island seemed to be in a "State of perfect internal Tranquility."[23] Despite Balcarres's claims, the Trelawny Maroons were incensed. Craskell was utterly unsuited to life as a superintendent. They alleged he lacked the authority to settle disputes, instead hiding in his house when any quarrels broke out.[24]

By mid-1795, it was clear that Balcarres's assessment was fatefully flawed. The Trelawny Maroons in particular were in a state of extreme agitation, and it was in this context that two of them travelled to Montego Bay. After a few days in the town, the two Maroons were accused, and convicted, "by the evi-dence of two white people, of killing tame hogs." For their alleged crime, they were flogged in the common workhouse by a slave they had previously caught as a runaway. Unsurprisingly, the slaves present were delighted with the fate of the two Trelawnys. But to the Maroons, the depth of their humiliation knew no bounds. They left Montego Bay in a rage apparently being "laughed at, hissed, and hooted by the slaves" as they passed.[25] It is extraordinary, as Rich-ard Hart rightly states, that the magistrates decided to sentence the alleged offenders, rather than send them back to Trelawny Town to be dealt with there.[26] The decision to flog the Maroons, and particularly to use a former runaway to administer the punishment, was foolhardy at best and intentional provocation at worst. In a rage, the two Trelawnys returned to their town, complained of their treatment, and the scene was set for war. However, even at this stage, violence could have been avoided, had it not been for the actions of Balcarres.

The first to hear of the tensions were a group of magistrates from St. James, and eight of them wrote a letter to Balcarres expressing their alarm of the measures taken. Without going into details of their actions, which will be discussed in Chapter 6, suffice here to say that the magistrates went back and forth attempting to quiet the discontent. In response, the Trelawnys sent the following note:

> The Maroons wishes nothing else from the country but battle; and they desires not to see Mr. Craskell up here at all. So they are waiting every moment for the above on Monday.
>
> Colonel Montague, and all the rest. Mr. David Schaw will see you on Sunday morning, for an answer.
>
> They will wait till Monday, nine o'clock; and if they don't come up, they will come down themselves.[27]

According to R. C. Dallas, this note was dictated by "a few drunken Maroons" to a "poor ignorant white man" without the knowledge of their leader Montague James, or nine-tenths of the people.[28] Nevertheless, it is clear that the new superintendent, Thomas Craskell, was the problem. A few days later, his assistant, John Merody, sent another message from the Trelawnys, saying

> The Maroons inform you that they do not want anything, for they have got plenty of powder and ball; for it is too late to do anything, that is good. They have received an answer from the bay, by Mr. David Schaw [a local planter], and he has taken all the business upon himself . . . they do not want any more letters from you, except it is from the bay.[29]

The local planters once again convened to intervene. Perhaps with their actions alone, war could have been avoided. Unfortunately for the island, Balcarres was Governor, and he was not willing to let things rest.

Balcarres's approach was to take "every vigorous measure to reduce them by Force."[30] He wasted no time in acting and refused to wait for higher orders, explicitly stating, "It is not time for waiting for orders, I may be obliged to judge, decide, and execute in an Instant Should any disturbance happen in this Island it can only be saved by raising Negro Corps."[31] In his actions, Balcarres was spurred on by the claim, whether he truly believed it or not, that the Maroons were being stirred up by French brigands from Saint Domingue. The Trelawnys, however, were still open to dialogue. Their representatives sent a message to Balcarres saying that they wished to see him in person. Balcarres's response was to order them to appear before him on 31st July. News of this did not reach magistrate Samuel Vaughan until 28th July, and even if he was able to immediately inform the Trelawnys, it would have been impossible to march across half of the island to make the appointment. Nevertheless, four captains and two other Maroons set out for Spanish Town. Still unsure of the exact causes of the rebellion, Balcarres declared that, in his opinion, he should strike at Trelawny Town in order that the fibres of rebellion "be cut off."[32] By the next day, the council of war had concluded and military action was set.

As such, heartened by the "manly and energetic" advance of the Council not to negotiate with the Trelawnys, Balcarres declared martial law on

2nd August.[33] He recalled the ships which were heading to assist Sir Adam Williamson in Saint Domingue and set about raising companies of militia and black shot to counter the Trelawnys. He stationed himself at Vaughansfield, within a mile and a half of Trelawny Town, and summoned his troops. His force was impressive, consisting of approximately 1500 crack British troops and supported by "several thousand militia." On the Maroon side were just over 500 men, women and children, only 167 of whom were able to bear arms. According to Balcarres, only about thirty of them were "really stout boys."[34]

On 5th August, Balcarres arrived at St. Ann's Bay, finding the six envoys who had been arrested on their way to Spanish Town. Balcarres immediately demanded they be held in irons, despite being aware of the impossibility of his 31st July deadline. He then continued on to Montego Bay. On 8th August, Balcarres issued a proclamation demanding the Trelawnys surrender on or before 12th August and offering rewards for any Trelawny captured after this date. Any who surrendered would be spared their life, but nothing more was promised.[35] The proclamation stated:

> You have entered into a most unprovoked, ungrateful, and most dangerous Rebellion.
>
> You have driven away your Superintendent. . . —you have endeavoured to massacre him.
>
> You have put the Magistrates . . . and all the White People, at Defiance, You have challenged and offered them Battle. . .
>
> Martial Law . . . has been proclaimed. Every pass to your Town had been occupied . . . You are surrounded by thousands. . .
>
> I have issued a Proclamation offering a Reward for your Heads. That terrible Edict will not be put in Force before Thursday the Thirteenth Day of August.
>
> To avert those terrible Proceedings I . . . command every Maroon of Trelawny Town, capable of bearing Arms, to appear before me at Montego Bay, on . . . the Twelfth Day of August . . . and there submit themselves to his Majesty's Mercy.[36]

A proclamation issued on the same day offered a reward of £20 for every Maroon capable of bearing arms taken prisoner on or after 13th August.

In an age-old tradition, the Trelawnys split largely along generational lines. Many of the elders preferred to surrender, while the younger clamoured to take up arms. Montague James' response to this proclamation was to round up thirty-seven of his "best and ablest marksmen" and travel with them to submit to Balcarres.[37] They surrendered at Vaughansfield on 11th August and were immediately placed in chains by colonial troops.[38] Again, without Balcarres's provocative actions, perhaps war could have been avoided. As it was, the younger contingent of the Trelawnys, "the wild and impetuous young savages," in the words of Balcarres, were now even more determined to resist. They burnt both their old and new town and tried to head through the encirclement of colonial troops.[39] Balcarres responded by sending a strong company of mulattoes from the St. James' Regiment against them, inflicting a "considerable loss."[40] The Trelawnys retreated into their methods of guerrilla warfare, and it soon became a conflict of attrition with very little loss on the Maroon side.

Once such hostilities had broken out, the colonial government moved to secure the alliance of the other Maroon towns. The only Maroons who actively fought against the Trelawnys seem to have come from Accompong Town in the west. The Accompongs' fidelity to the government was immediately expressed, upon the outbreak of the war, in a formal agreement. And, in a symbolic move, the Accompongs held a solemn ceremony baptising all the younger Maroons. Accompong support did not just come in symbolic form, however. There are also mentions in the archival records of Accompong Maroons being killed whilst fighting alongside colonial forces. For example, when Colonel Fitch, who had taken over command over the forces, was killed, two Accompong Maroons also died, along with some privates from the 83rd regiment. The families of those who fell with Fitch, Captain Reid and Edward Badnedge were compensated for the loss and, in recognition of their service to the colonial government. The Assembly voted to award £500 for "providing for and rewarding the Accompong Town Maroons for their good conduct."[41] This split between Trelawny and Accompong Maroons grew out of a long dispute over the possession of the Leeward treaty. R. C. Dallas mentioned that the Trelawny Maroons "had long manifested their discontent against the Accompongs, for not yielding to them the original treaty made with Cudjoe, which they claimed the right of keeping."[42] If true, then this discontent had morphed into open violence during the Second Maroon War. According to Dallas, one Trelawny Town Maroon defected to the side of the government. This was Captain Thomas, not mentioned in any official documents. He fought under Colonel Sandford and was apparently offered protection and reward for his services, but he refused and was hurt that rewards should be thought necessary.[43] Other than that, there are no records of Trelawny defection to the colonial side.

In the Windward towns of the east, support was not forthcoming. Nor, however, did the towns seemingly deliver active support to the Trelawnys. Instead, the Windwards appeared to do as much as possible to keep out of the hostilities. In the first week of September, Balcarres ordered the Maroons of Portland to attend upon him in Spanish Town. Shortly afterwards, he wrote, "I rejoice to hear from Mr Atkinson that near fifty of the Charlestown Maroons have come in. I look upon this as of the very highest consequence during our present contest."[44] But, by the end of the month, rumours that the Scotts Hall Maroons had joined the Trelawnys rocked Balcarres. He wrote of his wishes that the gifts appropriated for the Charles Town Maroons would be collected by them or else "the rebellion may extend itself to windward."[45] On the same day, Balcarres wrote to the superintendent of Moore Town praising their "quiet and orderly behaviour." He conceded that the Moore Town Maroons may have been staying away from Spanish Town because of "their fears" and allowed them to stay away until those fears were past.[46] This more concilia-tory stance towards the Windwards seems to have grown out of the belief that those communities in the east were actually in a "state of rebellion." Balcarres did not wish to provoke the Windwards and believed that "if we do nothing against them, they will not for the present act against us."[47]

Elsewhere, skirmishes and guerrilla warfare characterised the subsequent period of battle. Despite being at a numerical disadvantage, the Trelawnys continued to take the fight to the colonists, and the British were no closer to defeating them as the days passed. The rewards offered for killing or capturing a Maroon began to increase, reflecting the severity of the situation. For each Trelawny Maroon carrying arms, the House of Assembly offered three hun-dred dollars.[48] The parish of St. James offered a further three hundred dollars, the parish of Trelawny two hundred, and the parish of Westmoreland twenty dollars—a total of 920 dollars per Maroon.[49] In the currency of the time, the Spanish silver dollar was 6s. 8d. so the reward stood at 326 pounds 13s 4d per head. The reward for killing or capturing a slave who had joined the Maroons was fixed by the Assembly at 150 dollars per head.[50]

This warfare may have dragged on for decades, as the First Maroon War had, if it were not for the introduction of Cuban bloodhounds. Shortly after the outbreak of the rebellion, Balcarres had sent W. D. Quarrel, a planter from Hanover, to Cuba to procure the dogs, which were used to hunt down runaways in the Spanish colony. He succeeded and "near 100" dogs and forty-three of their keepers, or *chasseurs*, arrived in Jamaica on 17th Decem-ber 1795.[51] The introduction of these bloodhounds turned the tide of the war. Balcarres delighted that "the negroe all over this Island has been struck with Horror at hearing of this measure, and these Doggs have most opportunely arrived." The ferocity of the dogs was clear to all. On one occasion, a black cook was attacked when one of the dogs wanted her meat; she struck it and was instantly killed by the bloodhound.[52]

News of the dogs' procurement had an immediate impact. Around this time, Balcarres received news of the Trelawnys desire to "treat" with the colonists.[53] Skirmishes continued, but there was a feeling, on both sides, that negotiation was preferable to continued fighting. Between bouts of fighting, overtures were made towards the Trelawnys. It was not until December, though, that General Walpole, the leader of the colonial forces, was able to report a favourable response. He wrote that, "Hull has agreed . . . to a sort of truce . . . I understand that they will surrender on their lives only, wishing for land to be allotted them to cultivate."[54] The Maroons were invited to send some of their cap-tains to meet with white officers but they declined, preferring instead to meet with Walpole himself.[55] Battles continued to flit back and forth across the island whilst the colonial government searched for a solution. One proposal, from three "gentleman" of the colony, suggested that the most "judicious" way of continuing the war would be to attempt to starve the Trelawnys.[56] The presence of the chasseurs, however, was enough, and proposals of peace were formally signed by General Walpole and Montague James on 21st December 1795, and ratified by Balcarres on the 28th. The terms were, that the Maroons would first, "on their knees," beg his pardon; second, they would go to the old Town, Montego Bay, or any other place that might be pointed out, and would settle on whatever lands the Governor, Council and Assembly might think proper to allot; third, that they would give up all runaways. Walpole had also agreed to a secret article, that he was "obliged to acceded on [his] oath . . . that they should not be sent off the island."[57] The date set for the Trelawnys to "come in" was 1st January at 10 o'clock.[58] However, when the day came, Walpole reported that only five had surrendered.[59] Balcarres raged, "the farce has ended as I expected," and he was ready to unleash the bloodhounds again.[60] The threat of the dogs soon had further impact. By 5th January, thirty Trelawnys had surrendered and was daily increasing. By 15th January, most of the Trelawnys had surrendered. Those who remained at large were eventually harried into surrendering by March.[61] On 16th March 1796, Balcarres wrote to the Duke of Portland,

> I have the gratification to inform your Grace of the termination of the Maroon War. Thus has ended the Nation of the Trelawny Maroons, a People which Historians assert, were not to be overcome, but would ultimately acquire the Dominion of this Island.[62]

Thus ended the Second Maroon War.

The Second Maroon War represents a dramatic break in the relationship between the Maroons and the colonial government. A major cause of this was the presence of Balcarres as Lieutenant-Governor in Jamaica. Another, however, was the outbreak of the Haitian Revolution in 1791. Balcarres was obsessed with the potential involvement of the French in Jamaica. Indeed, in 1795, he wrote that "much was to be apprehended" from a foreign enemy who was also aware of the tensions in Jamaica. In particular, he feared that a foreign enemy might "foment and keep up" a rebellion to "place us between two fires."[63] The willingness of the colonial government to accommodate the Maroons had expired. As far as the government was concerned, the island had been stabilised enough to strengthen colonial society, and it was time to reduce the power of the Maroons and avoid another Haiti. Therefore, the move from accommodation to warfare was complete. The combination of continued Maroon independence, the refusal of the Maroons to relinquish their unique identity and live as free blacks, the lurking presence of other imperial forces, the constant threat of an alliance between the Maroons and the slaves and, most importantly, this all taking place against the backdrop of the largest slave revolt the Americas had seen, meant that the colonial government followed the course of action it deemed most effective—unleashing the full force of the British army against the Maroons.

As the new century dawned in the United States, Benjamin Hawkins threw himself into further implementing the civilisation plan. In 1802, for example,

Hawkins proclaimed that the "philanthropist & the friend of humanity" would "rejoice" at the news that Creeks had appropriated $1000 for axes, grubbing hoes and salt—all necessary for the success of his plan.[64] Hoboithle Micco, a staunch opponent of Hawkins's programme, expressed a different view of such purchases—he thundered that he did not want a "Blacksmith in the nation or weavers to bring them into slavery, no plough or any plantation tools."[65] This tension between those Creeks who embraced Hawkins's plan and those who rejected it was to increase in the early years of the nineteenth century.

Despite this opposition, a group of Creek chiefs journeyed to Fort Wilkinson to negotiate a new treaty with the federal government in 1802. The result was the Treaty of Fort Wilkinson, which ceded two separate pieces of Creek land. One piece was a small strip to the west of the Oconee River, and the other was a piece along the Flint River on which a Creek agency was to be built to manage U.S.-Creek affairs. The treaty also allowed the United States to construct garrisons to "protect" its frontiers. For these concessions, the Creek Nation was to receive a yearly stipend of $3000 for a period of ten years, and the chiefs who were to oversee the finances were to share $1000 a year over the same period. How this annuity was to be divided was decided by the federal government and can be seen as no less than a bribe for those chiefs agreeable to the treaty and the civilisation plan. The speaker of the National Council received $150, the first three chiefs $70 each, and sixteen other chiefs $40 each. Presents totalling $10,000 were also distributed to those attending the treaty signing.[66] This treaty merely added to the discord in Creek country. Creeks unhappy with the agreement threatened to kill at least one of their representatives who was friendly to the Americans.[67]

Symptomatic of the growing strength of the United States, the federal government ignored this discontent and pushed ahead with further plans to infiltrate Creek country. The federal government coveted Creek land not only to turn into profitable plantations but also to provide better access across the region. This became particularly critical after 1803, when the federal government wanted to build a road joining the eastern territory of the United States to the newly acquired Louisiana Territory. In 1805, after years of attempted negotiations, a Creek delegation travelled to the American capital and relinquished title to two million acres, whilst also authorising the federal government to build a road through the country in return for a yearly annuity.[68] Creek negotiators also agreed to allow American citizens free passage through their remaining territory. Congress then appropriated a further $6400 to build a postal road through the Creek Nation that would link Athens, Georgia, to Fort Stoddert on the Tombigbee River north of Mobile. When completed, the post road would connect Washington, D.C., and New Orleans over a distance of some 1100 miles. Whilst some Creeks took advantage of the economic opportunities that the road presented, such as inn-keeping and running ferries, others angrily protested. Angela Pulley Hudson contends that this profusion of American roads through Creek country became a reason for many to take up arms.[69]

Encroachment of the United States into Creek country did not just take a physical form. The National Council, at the behest of Benjamin Hawkins, was urged to take a growing role in Creek society. In the early nineteenth century, however, the majority of the Creek Nation still had little to do with this newly formed centralised authority. By July 1803, two and a half years after the formation of the National Council, police had only executed two Indians and three blacks and publicly whipped twenty-four others.[70] Whilst these numbers are relatively low, they still represent how the National Council was beginning to implement U.S.-style punishments at the expense of traditional Creek justice. The National Council came to symbolise the creeping influence of the United States.

Discontent with the National Council ramped up following these punishments, which bulldozed over traditions sacred to many Creeks. This dissatisfaction led two Kasihtas to murder Hopoie Micco, the speaker of the National Council, during the winter of 1805.[71] In addition, Creeks removed William McIntosh and Tuskeneah Chapco (Long Lieutenant) from their positions as leaders for their role in approving the construction of the post road and for misuse of the stipend.[72] Control of the stipend had long caused feuds between factions of Creeks. One such feud, between Upper and Lower Creek leaders, prevented the appointment of a new speaker to replace the murdered Hopoy Micco. This dispute rumbled on with Benjamin Hawkins asserting that each leader was "intent on his own gain, regardless of the public."[73] He further retorted that "the great men" among the Upper Creeks contended for office wishing "to embezzle their stipend."[74] It took until 1810 for this particular power struggle to be won, when the Upper Creek leader Tustanagee Thlucco appointed himself as the new speaker of the National Council.[75] Thlucco was said to be "a lover of wealth" who entered office in order to further his own interests, and his own finances.[76]

Despite these often-violent disputes, Hawkins claimed he had intended to transform Creeks gradually and peacefully into respectable members of the new American republic. He explained in 1807,

> The plan I pursue is to lead the Indian from hunting to the pastoral life, to agriculture, household manufactures, a knowledge of weights and measures, money and figures, to be honest and true to themselves as well as to their neighbors, to protect innocence, to punish guilt, to fit them to be useful members of the planet they inhabit and lastly, letters.[77]

Whether he intended to or not, however, his civilisation plan had unleashed internal violence in the Creek Nation.

This growing involvement of the federal government in Creek life was set against the backdrop of a food crisis in the south-east. Beginning in 1804, a famine swept across Creek country, devastating both Upper and Lower Creek towns. Previous food catastrophes had hit the south-east; in 1756, for example, several people had "dyed for Want"[78] and, in 1760 and 1777, some had even been reduced to eating dogs and horses.[79] However, what made the food crisis of 1804 so disastrous was the recent emphasis on the individual over the community. In past famines, resources had been pooled to try to weather the worst of the disaster; in the 1804 crisis, however, some Creeks increasingly took an individualistic stance and protected their crops for themselves, leaving others to starve.

The famine ravaging the south-east did not prevent the march of the Americans, which seemed relentless and particularly cruel given the desperate situation of many Creeks. In 1805, Creek chiefs were invited to Washington, D.C., to negotiate yet another land cession. Six Muskogee leaders agreed to the meeting and travelled to the capital to meet with federal officials. The outcome of the encounter was the cession of the remaining Creek land between the Oconee and Ocmulgee rivers and, despite explicit instructions to the contrary from the National Council, permission for the construction of a post road across Creek lands from the Ocmulgee River to Mobile. This post road, like so many other issues, divided the Nation. More individualistic Creeks, such as Alexander Cornell and William McIntosh, attempted to influence events to their own advantage. Cornell supported the deal on the condition that the road would pass by his house just south of the Tallapoosa River so that he could open a lucrative tavern.[80] McIntosh had intended to do the same, but the swampy terrain of the area thwarted his plans. Instead, he intended to operate a ferry across the Chattahoochee River to provide better access to the road.[81] Whilst some Creeks starved, others were determined to use the entry of the United States into their lands to their benefit.

The food crisis which had entrenched itself in Creek country continued to aggravate inequalities in the Deep South which resulted from American encroachment. In July 1807, Hawkins reported, "We have had a greater scarcity of corn than was ever known in this country" leading it to be called "the hungry year."[82] Hawkins did not miss the opportunity to highlight the benefits of the civilisation plan when it came to surviving the famine. He claimed that Creeks who had livestock were able to live on "their beef and milk" whereas those who did not lived "by theft or on China briar root, by Potatoe, Blackberries and whortleberrys."[83] Creeks received a yearly cash payment of $16,000 from the federal government, which Hawkins believed could have alleviated the famine. Instead, he claimed, the "rich will not let their stipend go for wheat or anything else to accommodate [the poorer part of the Nation] nor anybody else who can get carts, wheels, etc. under the plan for their civilization."[84] It seems that those who had converted to Hawkins's vision blamed those who rejected the tools of civilisation for their own suffering.

In 1808, Creeks again experienced a poor harvest, and again the link between the civilisation plan and lack of hunger was highlighted. That year Micco Achulee wrote to Hawkins, "I am the first Chief who ploughed and adopted the plan of civilization and am clothed and fed by it"[85] whereas Hoboithle Micco, one of the great critics of Hawkins's plan, reported to Thomas Jefferson, "Such as have stocks of cattle and hogs can clothe themselves," but "others must and do go naked."[86] However, the link between traditional practices and starvation was not so simple. Always exacerbating the problem was the corrupt dealings of many of the Creek chiefs. In some years, the Creek chiefs insisted upon the annuity being paid in cash—a useful way to embezzle money.[87] Therefore, when the famine hit, there was no annuity money left to buy badly needed provisions. In 1811, representatives of seven Upper Creek settlements wrote to Hawkins explicitly blaming the greedy habits of the chiefs for their dire situation, saying "Our stipend being delivered by order of the Chiefs to certain Great Chiefs to share out and grow ritch out of it, we have received no part of it." In a remarkable admission of bribery, Hawkins replied that "you do not all attend to your affairs, and when you do not, those who attend will not attend to you." In other words, the stipend—supposed to be for the entire nation—was actually only accessible for those who adhered to American values.[88]

In an even more astonishing admission, Hawkins wrote to William Eustis, a federal official, that if the Creeks really were a poor people from "necessity and not from choice" then he would assist them. However, he believed that their stipend and lands were sufficient to cover the costs of feeding their people. He went on to claim that, if the Creeks had used their stipend to this end, then he would have applied to the President to help them.[89] As, however, they had spent their stipend on non-essential items, he would not provide assistance. There was no acknowledgement in Hawkins's claims of the corrupt actions of some Creek chiefs that had led to many in the villages becoming poor. Those who were willing to negotiate with the Americans, and give away their lands, received assistance and aid, while those who did not were left to starve. Such a stance contributed to the deep divisions within Creek country and led Hoboithle Micco, who had organised the resistance to McGillivray in the 1780s and 1790s, to explain that he looked on his Creek enemies "as people of the United States," even if their genetic backgrounds were in part Native American.[90]

Matters were further exacerbated by the expansion of the federal road through Creek country in September 1811. In that month, Hawkins attended a meeting with Creek chiefs in an attempt to convince them of the necessity of the road, arguing that "the white people must have roads" to market and for travelling where they choose. Of particular importance, he claimed, was the establishment of a road to connect Mobile to the people of Tennessee.[91] The resulting road was opened in November, 1811 and the entire course ran from Milledgeville, Georgia, to Fort Stoddert on the Mobile River and on to New Orleans. Against this backdrop of physical symbols of American expansion, the Shawnee warrior Tecumseh entered Creek country.[92] Tecumseh was a prophet who called for a pan-Indian movement to resist the encroachments of the United States. In 1805, his brother, Tenskwatawa, had a dream which led him to urge Native Americans to reject American culture and to stop poisoning themselves with American food and alcohol. Calling on indigenous communities across the United States, his message inspired Ottawas, Wynadots,

Potawatomis and, eventually, Creeks. In September 1811, a mixed group of Shawnees, Choctaws, Cherokees, and two or three unidentified groups, led by Tecumseh, met Creek leaders and warriors in the square ground of Tucka-batche on the Tallapoosa River. With Benjamin Hawkins present, Tecumseh preached peace between Native Americans and Euro Americans, saying he had followed the war pipe south to urge all to reject it in favour of peace.[93] But, when Hawkins had withdrawn from the scene, Tecumseh changed his stance, saying he carried a pipe "to unite all the red people in a war against the white people."[94] Tecumseh hoped to form a military alliance between the Creeks and Shawnees, Delawares and other Indians of the Old Northwest and claimed that such an alliance had the support of the British.[95] Creek leaders refused to join the alliance, though many young warriors were receptive to Tecumseh's overtures given his arrival during the hungry years.[96] Unsuccessful, the Shawnee leader moved on to meet with the Coweta and Kasihta on the Chattahoochee River. His message of unification spread across the south-east helped by natural intervention. At the time of his journey to the Creeks and beyond, a meteor blazed across the sky and a series of violent quakes, including a tremendous one centred at New Madrid, Missouri, shook the earth. Creeks took this as signs of the coming war.

Meanwhile, the violence within Creek country, often at the behest of the National Council, continued. In May 1812, for example, four of Hawkins's cattle were killed and forty-three warriors were sent in pursuit of the alleged perpetrators. As punishment, their noses and ears were cropped "in accord with Creek law for theft." However, punishments for theft of personal prop-erty, particularly when the act was carried out by a "police force," clashed with traditional views of the Creeks.[97] Such actions led some young Creeks to act on Tecumseh's call to resistance. A few days after the punishment, four Creeks murdered two Americans travelling through the Deep South to settle in Mississippi Territory, and others killed a third American riding on the post road.[98]

Around the same time, a party of Upper Creeks murdered two white fami-lies at the mouth of the Duck River on the Tennessee.[99] The site at Duck River is particularly significant, for it is situated on the path that Tecumseh had followed on his journey to the south-east.[100] Creek leaders responded with brutality. Lower Creek warriors representing the National Council promised to assist Upper Creek leaders in punishing those involved in the murders.[101] At a meeting of the Council in Tuckabatche, Creek leaders "unanimously agreed that satisfaction shall be given without delay for the murders com-mitted in our land" and appointed several parties to pursue the culprits.[102] By the end of July 1812, Creek police had executed six of the murderers.[103] One Creek warrior charged with murder fled to Tallassee, traditionally a "white" or "peace" town where accused Creeks could often find asylum.[104] Thinking he was in a place of safety, he took sanctuary on the honoured seat of Hoboithle Micco, but the leader of this new police force hunted him down and "shot him on the seat through the head and body."[105]

From this time onwards, divisions were insurmountable. There was, however, no clear line which divided those Creeks who became known as Redsticks and those who did not. Some were pro-American while others were anti, some split along religious lines, or the Upper/Lower Creek divide. There was also some distinction between Muskogee-speakers and non-Muskogee speakers. Redstick numbers included all clans, towns and kinship networks, and there were even divisions among these categories.[106] The war which erupted when hostilities boiled over became known as the Redstick War, or the Creek War of 1813, and embroiled the United States. The Redsticks, however, first turned on their own people. Their initial targets were pro-American chiefs and headmen, killing hogs, horses and other symbols of the civilisation plan.[107] After a number of such attacks, the Redsticks turned towards the Americans. In the spring of 1813, a group of Redsticks were returning from Pensacola and encountered the militia of the Mississippi Territory led by Creek mestizos. The militia attacked the Redsticks, took their supplies, and fled the scene. In retaliation, the Redsticks attacked Fort Mims on 30th August 1813 and decimated the Americans and their allies defending the fort.[108] In much the same way that Balcarres was itching to attack the Trelawny Maroons, the states of Tennessee and Georgia had been waiting for such an opportunity in order to fall on the Creek Nation.

The Americans, led by Andrew Jackson, who would later become President, retaliated with vigour. They immediately invaded Creek territory and engaged the Redsticks in battles across the south-east. Facing the might of the U.S. Army, Redsticks had little hope and were forced back to their stronghold of Tohopeka at the Horseshoe Bend on the Tallapoosa River. On 27th March 1814, Jackson attacked.[109] The battle was no less than a rout, with hundreds killed. Those remaining had no choice but to flee to the Seminoles in Florida. The Battle of Horseshoe Bend won the war for the United States. After the end of the Creek War of 1813, or the Redstick War, the Upper Towns were completely destroyed. Benjamin Hawkins lamented that there was "not a living thing in them."[110] Despite the Redstick War being instigated by select Creeks, the United States held the whole nation responsible. In August 1814, Creek chiefs were forced to meet with Andrew Jackson at Fort Jackson to negotiate peace under the threat of further hostilities.[111] The signers of the treaty, with one exception, had all remained loyal to the United States but were forced to cede more than half of all Creek territory.[112] Robbie Ethridge has placed the cession at two-thirds of Creek land.[113] In echoes of General Walpole's reaction to the treatment of the Trelawnys, Benjamin Hawkins was disgusted by the unfairness of the treaty[114] and resigned from his post little more than six months later.[115] By 1850, the remaining Creeks were forcibly removed west of the Mississippi, losing completely their lands in the south-east.

Once again, we can trace similar patterns in the next steps taken by the colonial and federal governments to reduce the Maroons and the Creeks. This second phase began with a new round of restrictive measures stronger than the last. Such a stance was possible because of the success of more subtle methods in the previous period. In addition, external events increased the strength of both Jamaica and the United States. In Jamaica, the successful conclusion of the Seven Years' War in 1763 saw the British head into the second half of the eighteenth century as the foremost colonial power. Such a strong position led many in Jamaica to believe they had the upper hand over the Maroons. In the 1770s, however, the British were shaken by the loss of the thirteen American colonies. The defeat led to the prioritising of keeping Jamaica at all costs.[116] To do so, stronger checks had to be placed on the Maroon communities. The importance of reducing the Maroons was re-emphasised following the outbreak of the Haitian Revolution in 1791. There, Maroons joined with the enslaved population in one of the many alliances forged during the uprising.[117] Colonists in Jamaica feared the island would dissolve into another Haiti— terrified for both their lives and their property. As a reaction, Balcarres and his supporters launched the Second Maroon War with the aim of removing the most belligerent Maroon communities to save the island. Indeed, it was explicitly remarked, when the Second Maroon War did break out, that "not a moment should be lost in apprizing the country of their danger." According to James Merody, the island was "on the very brink of destruction," and the British must "either strike at the Maroons and cut at the very root of rebellion or that this valuable colony was forever gone."[118] In Jamaica, Balcarres either suspected, or used as an excuse the presence of French people on the island to drum up support for war.[119] Had the Haitian Revolution not broken out, it is possible that the Second Maroon War may not also have. Colonial fears had ramped up the tensions already existing between Maroons and the British; the tension finally burst following the flogging of the two Trelawny Maroons.

Similarly, the federal government began this second period in a much stronger position than it had immediately after the American Revolution. A quarter of a century after the outbreak of the Revolution, the United States had continued consolidating as a new republic. Thomas Jefferson's vision of a nation of farmers had defeated the Hamiltonian demand for an industrialised nation. It had a small but highly competent army and was expanding rapidly in most sectors. The threat of France and Spain was decreasing, particularly in light of the Age of Revolutions, and the United States continued its rise towards establishing itself as a regional player. In Creek country, the efforts of Benjamin Hawkins had taken hold and deep changes were underway as the new century dawned. The defeat of the Western Confederacy in 1795 at the Battle of Fallen Timbers heralded this new age of Native American policy. In the United States, the end of the Haitian Revolution, and the threat of warfare with the British, led Napoleon, then First Consul of the French Republic, to sell the vast Louisiana Territory to the Americans. Initially, the United States sought only to purchase the port town of New Orleans and its adjacent coastlands but quickly accepted the bargain offer of the French for the whole territory.[120] Once the Louisiana Territory was incorporated into the United States, the westward push would never cease. The Creek Nation, not only desirable for its fertile agricultural lands, now stood in the way of the unification of the United States. In both cases, we can see the impact of the Haitian Revolution on government relations with these semi-autonomous communities.

These external factors led the colonial and federal governments to ramp up their efforts in removing the Maroons and Creeks as autonomous peoples—albeit in different ways. The first attempt to do so in Jamaica was the 1791 law which allowed Maroons to relinquish their Maroon identity and live as free blacks elsewhere on the island. In the United States, it was the continued use of the civilisation plan. In fact, the mass legislation of 1791 in Jamaica and the civilisation plan in the United States were remarkably similar. Both attempted to change the very fundamentals of Maroon and Creek life, and both, if successful, would lead to a loss of identity. They included policies which impacted trade, cultural behaviour and leadership. And both were used to achieve the shared goal of reduction of these semi-autonomous communities. If Maroons relinquished their unique identity to live as free blacks, their strength would immediately reduce. Dispersed around the island, away from their mountainous strongholds, they would become far less of a threat to the colony. Likewise, if the Creeks "civilised," they, too, would be dispersed across the region and would need less land, thus opening up more lands to American settlers and making westward expansion easier and faster.

Indeed, the land policies of the colonial and federal governments dovetailed more in this period than in the prior period. R. S. Cotterill has claimed that the federal Native American policy changed to one of removal with the coming of Jefferson to the presidency.[121] Likewise, the colonial government's stance changed from one of granting lands to refusing requests for land grants and, ultimately, removing the Trelawny Maroons from the island. An extreme shift in strategy had occurred in both cases as a result of the external factors outlined earlier, but also as a result of Maroon and Creek action or inaction. Their refusal to conform to government demands led to increased suspicion towards the communities. If they could not be removed as autonomous groups through the 1791 laws or the civilisation plan, then military action by the government became almost inevitable.

Before it reached that critical stage, however, both governments continued with efforts to weaken the independence of the two communities. As ever, this was through economic sanctions. In Jamaica, opportunities to earn rewards through slave-catching were reduced, and access to markets was restricted by the laws introduced in 1791. In the United States, economic sanctions came through the federal policy of pushing Creeks into debt at the federal trading stores. Both actions led to the Maroons and Creeks finding themselves in an economically dire situation. These situations were compounded by the exhausted lands of the Maroons and the famine the Creeks experienced. To an extent, both were natural disasters, but both were seized upon by the governments to weaken these communities. The colonial government not only refused to grant additional lands, or even trade lands of the same size, as

Maroons had done in previous years, but it also attempted to restrict Maroon trade at colonial markets. The federal government also refused to come to the aid of starving Creeks, blaming those who did not adapt to the civilisation plan for the state they found themselves in. Starving, weakened communities would, in the eyes of the government, be easier to convince to cede land or relinquish identity, and ultimately would become more malleable to control.

However, such a situation led many Maroons and Creeks to breaking point. Refusing to change their very way of life, the only answer was war. It is no surprise that the Trelawny Town Maroons who, just a few short years before had had a petition for extra lands refused, were the ones to take up arms against the colonial government. Nor is it a surprise that many Redsticks were the Creeks who refused to adopt the civilisation plan and become farmers and ranchers. The colonial and federal governments had hoped to remove these threats through subtle methods, legislation, federal policy, or starvation. None had worked. Therefore, these governments, too, were ready for war. With both Jamaica and the United States emerging victorious from the hostilities, the colonial and federal governments could implement the final step of their plans—removal and destruction.

Therefore, we can see another stage in the model for reduction of semi-autonomous communities. Once the more subtle methods to undermine Maroon and Creek authority had been successful, external events then led to more overt methods. Attacks on the very identity of the communities took place in an attempt to remove their threat without needing to resort to warfare. When environmental events, such as land exhaustion or famine, occurred, these were seized upon in the battle to reduce these communities' power. When unsuccessful, however, warfare was the final step.

Notes

1. Carey Robinson, *The Iron Thorn: The Defeat of the British by the Jamaican Maroons* (Kingston: Kingston Publishers Limited, 1993), 132. For more on Three Fingered Jack, see Frances R. Botkin, *Thieving Three-Fingered Jack: Transatlantic Tales of a Jamaican Outlaw, 1780–2015* (New Brunswick: Rutgers University Press, 2017).
2. *Ibid.*, 135.
3. *Journals of the House of Assembly of Jamaica (JHA)*, 17th December 1784, Vol. IV, National Archives of Jamaica, Spanish Town, Jamaica (NAJ).
4. Richard Hart, *Slaves Who Abolished Slavery: Blacks in Rebellion* (Kingston: University of the West Indies Press, 1985), 158.
5. *Acts of Assembly Passed in the Island of Jamaica from 1681 to 1733 Inclusive* (BL), CSF, 154/7, 482.
6. *Journals of the House of Assembly of Jamaica (JHA)*, 19th December 1791, Vol. V, National Archives of Jamaica, Spanish Town, Jamaica (NAJ).
7. For more on free blacks in Jamaica, and the wider Americas, see Jill E. Rowe, *Invisible in Plain Sight: Self-Determination Strategies of Free Blacks in the Old Northwest* (New York: Peter Lang, 2017); Bruce A. Glasrud and Milton S. Jordan, eds., *Free Blacks in Antebellum Texas* (Denton, TX: University of North Texas Press, 2015); Jane G. Landers, ed., *Against the Odds: Free Blacks in the Slave Societies of the Americas* (London: F. Cass, 1996); Michael L. Nicholls, 'Creating Identity: Free Blacks

and the Law,' *Slavery & Abolition*, 35, 2 (2014), 214–233; Paul Finkelman, ed., *Free Blacks in a Slave Society* (New York: Garland, 1989); K. O. Laurence, *The Settlement of Free Negroes in Trinidad Before Emancipation* (Diego Martin, Trinidad: John Hilton Hackshaw, 1999); R. Hoefte, 'Free Blacks and Coloureds in Plantation Suriname: The Struggle to Rise,' *Slavery and Abolition*, 17, 1 (1996), 102–129.

8. *Journal of the House of Assembly of Jamaica (JHA)*, 6th November 1795, Vol. VI; 24th February 1801, Vol. X, National Archives of Jamaica, Spanish Town, Jamaica (NAJ).

9. Mavis Campbell, *The Maroons of Jamaica, 1655–1796: A History of Resistance, Collaboration & Betrayal* (Trentin: Africa World Press, 1990), 186–187.

10. Anno 17 Geo. III, 1791, *The Laws of Jamaica: 1760–1792* (London: A. Aikman Printer's to the King's Most Excellent Majesty, 1811), Chapter Four; Alvin O. Thompson, *Flight to Freedom: African Runaways and Maroons in the Americas* (Kingston: University of West Indies Press, 2006), 132–133.

11. Bev Carey, *Maroon Story: The Authentic and Original History of the Maroons in the History of Jamaica, 1490–1880* (St Andrew, Jamaica: Agouti Press, 1997), 362.

12. *JHA*, 21st December 1774, Vol. VI, NAJ.

13. *Acts of Assembly Passed in the Island of Jamaica from 1681 to 1733 Inclusive* (BL), CSF., 154/7, 475–476.

14. *Ibid.*, 476.

15. *Ibid.*

16. *Ibid.*, 474–475.

17. Thompson, *Flight to Freedom*, 132–133.

18. *Ibid*, 140.

19. *JHA*, 9th December 1792, Vol. IX, NAJ.

20. Balcarres to the Duke of Portland, 30th January 1795, WO 1/92, National Archives, Kew, England (NA).

21. William Vaughan to the Right Honourable Henry Dundas, 26th October 1795, WO 1/92, NA.

22. For more on Balcarres, see Alexander Crawford Lindsay, *Lives of the Lindsays: Or a Memoir of the Houses of Crawford and Balcarres. . .* (Wigan: Privately Printed, 1840).

23. Balcarres to the Duke of Portland, 11th May 1795, CO137/94, NA.

24. *JHA*, 20th July 1795, Vol. IX, NAJ.

25. Robert C. Dallas, *The History of the Maroons: From Their Origin to the Establishment of Their Chief Tribe at Sierra Leone: Including the Expedition to Cuba, for the Purpose of Procuring Spanish Chasseurs; and the State of the Island of Jamaica for the Last Ten Years: With a Succinct History of the Island Previous to That Period* (London: Printed by A. Strahan . . . for T. N. Longman and O. Rees. . ., 1803), Vol. I, 145.

26. Hart, *Slaves Who Abolished Slavery*, 159.

27. Montego Bay Magistrates to Balcarres, 10th July 1795, CO 137/95, NA.

28. Dallas, *History of the Maroons*, Vol. I, 147–148.

29. Merody to Craskell, 11th July 1795, CO 137/95, NA; *JHA*, 19th July 1795, Vol. IX, NAJ.

30. Balcarres to Portland, 19th July 1795, CO 137/95, NA.

31. Balcarres to Portland, 21st July 1795, CO 137/95, NA.

32. Lindsay, *Lives of the Lindsays*, 46–48.

33. Balcarres to Portland, 11th August 1795, CO 137/95, NA.

34. Balcarres to Portland, 13th May 1795, CO 137/95, NA.

35. Proclamation, 8th August 1795, CO 137/95, NA.

36. *Ibid.*

37. G. W. Bridges, *The Annals of Jamaica* (London: John Murray, 1827), Vol. II, 228.

38. Balcarres to Portland, 14th August 1795, CO 137/95, NA.

39. *Ibid.*
40. *Ibid.*
41. *JHA*, 23rd and 30th September 1795, Vol. IX, NAJ; Balcarres to Portland, 25th August 1795, CO 137/95, NA.
42. Dallas, *History of the Maroons*, Vol. I, 146.
43. *Ibid.*, 186–187.
44. Alexander Lindsay, *Lives of the Lindsays* (London: John Murray, 1858), 23.
45. *Ibid.*
46. *Ibid.*, 46–48.
47. Balcarres to Walpole, 1st October 1795, CO 137/95, NA.
48. *JHA*, 27th September 1795, Vol. IX, NAJ.
49. Lindsay, *Lives of the Lindsays*, 23.
50. *JHA*, 27th November 1795, Vol. IX, NAJ.
51. Balcarres to Portland, 29th December 1795, CO 137/96, NA.
52. *Ibid.*; Balcarres to Portland, 3rd March 1796, CO 137/96, NA.
53. Lindsay, *Lives of the Lindsays*, 23.
54. *Ibid.*, 92–93.
55. Dallas, *History of the Maroons*, Vol. II, 137.
56. Lindsay, *Lives of the Lindsays*, 82–84.
57. Walpole to Attorney General, 26th December 1795, CO 137/96, NA; *JHA*, 20th December and 22th 1795, Vol. IX, NAJ.
58. *Ibid.*; *JHA*, 20th and 28th December 1795, Vol. IX, NAJ.
59. *Ibid.*; *JHA*, 20th, 25th and 30th December 1795, Vol. IX, NAJ, *JHA*, 1st January 1796, Vol. IX, NAJ.
60. Balcarres to Portland, 1st January 1796, CO 137/96, NA.
61. *JHA*, 14th, 15th and 16th January 1796, Vol. IX, NAJ.
62. Balcarres to Portland, 26th March 1796, CO 137/96, NA.
63. Balcarres to the Duke of Portland, 20th December 1796, WO 1/96, NA.
64. Benjamin Hawkins to Henry Dearborn, 17th July 1802, *Letters of Benjamin Hawkins* (Savannah: Published by the Georgia Historical Society, 1916), Vol. II, 448; Benjamin Hawkins, 'Journal of Occurrences in the Creek Agency from January to the Conclusion of the Conference and Treaty at Fort Wilkinson by the Agent for Indian Affairs,' *Letters*, Vol. II, 411.
65. James Durouzeaux to Vicente Folch, 5th October 1803, Papeles Procedentes de Cuba Archivo de Indias, Seville (PC), leg. 220A, 489, reel 307, PKY.
66. Treaty at Fort Wilkinson with the Creek Indians, 1802, "Indian Treaties: Cessions of Land in Georgia, 1705–1837," 336, GDAH.
67. Journal of Benjamin Hawkins, 30th June 1804, *Letters*, Vol. II, 472.
68. See William S. Coker and Thomas D. Watson, 'Indian Traders of the Southeastern Spanish Borderlands: Panton, Leslie & Company and John Forbes & Company, 1783–1847,' *Louisiana Historical Association*, 28, 1 (Winter, 1987), 243–272.
69. Angela Pulley Hudson, *Creek Paths and Federal Roads: Indians, Settlers, and Slaves and the Making of the American South* (Chapel Hill: University of North Carolina Press, 2010), 91.
70. Benjamin Hawkins to James Madison, 11th July 1803, *Letters*, Vol. II, 458.
71. Benjamin Hawkins to John Milledge, 9th June 1806, *Letters*, Vol. II, 505.
72. Benjamin Hawkins to David Meriwether, 1st October 1807, *Letters*, Vol. II, 526.
73. Benjamin Hawkins to Henry Dearborn, 16th September 1807, *Letters*, Vol. II, 524; Benjamin Hawkins to David Meriwether, 1st October 1807, *Letters*, Vol. II, 526.
74. Benjamin Hawkins to Reverend Christian Benzien, 7th October 1810, *Letters*, Vol. II, 569.
75. Benjamin Hawkins to William Eustis, 8th April 1810, *Letters*, Vol. II, 562.
76. Absalom Harris Chappell, *Miscellanies of Georgia; Historical, Biographical, Descriptive, Etc.* (Columbus, GA: Gilbert Printing Company, 1928), 72.

77. Carl Mauelshagen and Gerald H. Davis, eds., *Partners in the Lord's Work: The Diary of Two Moravian Missionaries in the Creek Indian Country, 1807–1813* (Atlanta: School of Arts and Sciences Research Papers, Georgia State College, 1969), 7.

78. Daniel Pepper to Governor Lyttelton, 18th November 1756, *Documents Relating to Indian Affairs, Colonial Records of South Carolina*, Vol. II, ed. William L. McDowell Jr. (Columbia: South Carolina Archives Department, 1958), 255.

79. David Taitt to Patrick Tonyn, 24th August 1777, enclosed in Tonyn to Germain, 18th September 1777, PRO 5/557, 699, reel 66C, PKY; Bernardo de Gálvez to Joseph de Gálvez, 13th October 1777, Stetson Collection (SC), bnd. 6614-A, 87–1–6/63, SD, 2596, PKY.

80. Henry deLeon Southerland Jr. and Jerry Elijah Brown, *The Federal Road Through Georgia, the Creek Nation and Alabama, 1806–1836* (Tuscaloosa: University of Alabama Press, 1989), 26; Hawkins, *Letters*, Vol. II, 326.

81. Benjamin Hawkins to Henry Dearborn, 22nd January 1807, *Letters*, Vol. II, 511; Benjamin W. Griffith, *McIntosh and Weatherford, Creek Indian Leaders* (Tuscaloosa: University of Alabama Press, 1988), 60; Southerland and Brown, *The Federal Road*, 25.

82. Benjamin Hawkins to Henry Dearborn, 16th September 1807, *Letters*, Vol. II, 521.

83. *Ibid.*, 521, 524.

84. Benjamin Hawkins to Henry Dearborn, 8th October 1807, *Letters*, Vol. II, 527; Benjamin Hawkins to James Forbes, 29th May 1806, Henry Wilson Papers, reel 1500D, PKY.

85. James Durouzeaux to Vicente Folch, 25th May 1809, PC, leg. 221B, 10, reel 310, PKY; Benjamin Hawkins to Henry Dearborn, 16th October 1808, *Letters*, Vol. II, 540.

86. Stephen Folch, "Journal of a Voyage to the Creek Nation from Pensacola in the year 1803," 5th May 1803, PC, leg. 2372, 1, reel 436, PKY.

87. John Halstead to General John Mason, 31st July 1810, 331, Records of the Creek Trading House, Letter Book, 1795–1816, reel 94-O, PKY; Stipend to be paid by the U.S. to the Creeks in 1811, "Creek Letters, 1800–1819," Vol. I, GDAH; John Halstead to Benjamin Hawkins, 2nd May 1811, 337, Records of the Creek Trading House, Letter Book, 1795–1816, reel 94-O, PKY.

88. Benjamin Hawkins to William Eustis, 24th February 1811, *Letters*, Vol. II, 583.

89. Benjamin Hawkins to the Big Warrior, Little Prince and Others, 16th June 1814, in *Indian Affairs: Treaties*, ed. Charles J. Kappler (Washington, DC: U.S. Govt. Print. Off., 1904), 845.

90. Tallassee Fixico to Benjamin Hawkins, 5th July 1813, *Letters of Benjamin Hawkins, 1797–1815* (LBH), ed. Louise F. Hays (typescript in GDAH), 209.

91. Joel W. Martin, *Sacred Revolt: The Muskogees' Struggle for a New World* (Boston: Beacon Press, 1993), 120–121.

92. For more on Tecumseh and the nativist movement, see Luella Bruce Creighton, *Tecumseh: The Story of the Shawnee Chief* (London: Macmillan & Co., 1965); Amy H. Sturgis, *Tecumseh: A Biography* (Westport, CT: Greenwood Press, 2008); R. David Edmunds and Russell David, *Tecumseh and the Quest for Indian Leadership* (Boston: Little Brown, and Company, 1984); Sandy Antal, *A Wampum Denied: Procter's War of 1812* (Ottawa: Carleton University Press, 1997); Guy St-Denis, *Tecumseh's Bones* (Montréal: McGill-Queen's University Press, 2005); and John Sugden, *Tecumseh: A Life* (London: Pimlico, 1999).

93. Benjamin Hawkins to William Eustis, 21st September 1811, *Letters*, Vol. II, 591.

94. *Ibid.*

95. For more on the Shawnees, see Sami Lakomäki, *Gathering Together: The Shawnee People Through Diaspora and Nationhood, 1600–1870* (New Haven: Yale University Press, 2014); Stephen Warren, *The Worlds the Shawnees Made: Migration and Violence in Early America* (Chapel Hill: University of North Carolina Press, 2014); Benjamin Hawkins to William Eustis, 3rd October 1811, *Letters*, Vol. II, 592.

96. Benjamin Hawkins to Governor Mitchell, 29th April 1811, *Letters*, 143, GDAH; Hoboithle to the President of the United States, 15th May 1811, "Creek Letters, 1800–1819," Vol. I, GDAH; Benjamin Hawkins to William Eustis, 3rd October 1811, *Letters*, Vol. II, 592.

97. Mauelshagen and Davis, *Partners in the Lord's Work*, 70.

98. Benjamin Hawkins to William Eustis, 6th April 1812, *Letters*, Vol. II, 605; Benjamin Hawkins to William Eustis, 25th May 1812, *Letters*, Vol. II, 609; Benjamin Hawkins to the chiefs of the Creek nation, June 1812, LBH, 156, GDAH; Chiefs of the Creek nation to Benjamin Hawkins, 17th June 1812, LBH, 159, GDAH; Benjamin Hawkins to William Eustis, 22nd June 1812, *Letters*, Vol. II, 610; C. Limbaugh to Benjamin Hawkins, 27th July 1812, LBH, 164, GDAH; Benjamin Hawkins to the Governor Mitchell, 7th September 1812, Lockey Collection (LC), PKY.

99. Benjamin Hawkins to William Eustis, 25th May 1812, *Letters*, Vol. II, 609; Benjamin Hawkins to William Eustis, 22nd June 1812, *Letters*, Vol. II, 610; Chiefs of the Creek nation to Benjamin Hawkins, 17th June 1812, LBH, 159, GDAH; Extract of a letter from William Henry to John J. Henry, 26th June 1812, *American State Papers, Class II: Indian Affairs* (Washington, DC: Gales and Seaton, 1832), Vol. I, 814; Benjamin Hawkins to William Eustis, 13th July 1812, *Letters*, Vol. II, 612.

100. John Sugden, 'Early Pan-Indianism: Tecumseh's Tour of the Indian Country, 1811–1812,' *American Indian Quarterly*, 10, 4 (Autumn, 1986), 279.

101. Benjamin Hawkins to William Eustis, 9th June 1812, *Letters*, Vol. II, 609.

102. Chiefs of the Creek nation to Benjamin Hawkins, 17th June 1812, LBH, 159, GDAH.

103. Benjamin Hawkins to William Eustis, 3rd August 1812, *Letters*, Vol. II, 613.

104. William Bartram, *Travels of William Bartram*, ed. Mark van Doren (New York: Dover Publications, 1955), 313.

105. Benjamin Hawkins to Governor Mitchell, 13th July 1812, LBH, 163, GDAH; Benjamin Hawkins to William Eustis, 13th July 1812, *Letters*, Vol. II, 612.

106. H. S. Halbert and T. H. Ball, *The Creek War of 1813 and 1814* (Chicago: Donohue & Henneberry, 1895), 99–100.

107. Halbert and Ball, *The Creek War*; George Stiggins, *Creek Indian History: A Historical Narrative of the Genealogy, Traditions, and Downfall of the Ispocoga or Creek Indian Tribe of Indians* (Birmingham: Birmingham Public Library Press, 1989), 83–186; Martin, *Sacred Revolt*, 142; Claudio Saunt, *A New Order of Things: Property, Power and the Transformation of the Creek Indians, 1733–1816* (Cambridge: Cambridge University Press, 1999), 249–259.

108. Halbert and Ball, *The Creek War*, 143–76; Stiggins, *Creek Indian History*, 107–114; Hawkins, *Letters*, Vol. II, 664–665; Frank L. Owsley, 'Fort Mims Massacre,' *The Alabama Review* XXIV (January, 1971), 192–204; Martin, *Sacred Revolt*, 157.

109. Halbert and Ball, *The Creek War*, 105–286; Stiggins, *Creek Indian History*, 97–136; Hawkins, *Letters*, Vol. II, 681, 748, 757; Frank L. Owsley, *Struggle for the Gulf Borderlands: The Creek War and the Battle of New Orleans, 1812–1815* (Gainesville: University Press of Florida, 1981), 30–86.

110. Hawkins, *Letters*, Vol. II, 687.

111. *Ibid.*, 744.

112. Treaty at Fort Jackson, ASPIA, Vol. I, 826–827; Benjamin Hawkins to George Graham, 1st August 1815, *Letters*, Vol. II, 743.

113. Robbie Franklyn Ethridge, *Creek Country: The Creek Indians and Their World* (Chapel Hill: University of North Carolina Press, 2003), 197.

114. Hawkins, *Letters*, Vol. II, 744.

115. *Ibid.*, 717.

116. Andrew Jackson O'Shaughnessy, *An Empire Divided: The American Revolution and the British Caribbean* (Philadelphia: University of Pennsylvania Press, 2000). For more on the British Empire after the American Revolution, see Alfred Leroy Burt,

The Evolution of the British Empire and Commonwealth from the American Revolution (Boston: D.C. Heath & Col., 1956); Eliga H. Gould, The Persistence of Empire: British Political Culture in the Age of the American Revolution (Chapel Hill: University of North Carolina Press, 2000); Jerry Bannister and Liam Riordan, eds., The Loyal Atlantic: Remaking the British Atlantic in the Revolutionary Era (Toronto: University of Toronto Press, 2012).

117. Tyson Reeder, 'Liberty with the Sword: Jamaican Maroons, Haitian Revolutionaries, and American Liberty,' Journal of the Early Republic, 37, 1 (Spring, 2017), 84–94.
118. Extract of a Letter from John Merody to Lord Balcarres, 19th July 1795, CO 137/95, NA.
119. Balcarres to Portland, 19th July 1795, CO 137/95, NA.
120. For more on the Louisiana Purchase, see Mary Kay Phelan, Story of the Louisiana Purchase (New York: Crowell, 1979); John Keats, Eminent Domain: The Louisiana Purchase and the Making of America (New York: Charterhouse, 1973); Ann Gaines, Louisiana Purchase in American History (Berkeley Heights: Enslow Publishers, 2000); Christopher Collier, Jeffersonian Republicans, 1800–1823: The Louisiana Purchase and the War of 1812 (New York: Benchmark Books, 1999).
121. R. S. Cotterill, 'Federal Indian Management in the South, 1789–1825,' The Mississippi Valley Historical Review, 20, 3 (Dec., 1933), 339.

Bibliography

Primary Sources

British Library, London, United Kingdom

Acts of Assembly Passed in the Island of Jamaica from 1681 to 1733 Inclusive.
Edward Long Manuscripts.

Galileo Online Digital Library of Georgia (website)

South-eastern Native American Documents, 1730–1842.

Georgia Department of Archives and History, Morrow, Georgia, United States

Colonial Records of the State of Georgia.
"Creek Indian Letters, Talks, and Treaties, 1705–1839."
"Creek Letters, 1800–1819."
"Indian Treaties: Cessions of Land in Georgia, 1705–1837."
"Letters of Benjamin Hawkins, 1797–1815."
Miscellaneous Creek Indian Documents.
South-eastern Native American Documents Database.
Treaty at Fort Wilkinson with the Creek Indians, 1802.
Unpublished Letters of Timothy Barnard, 1784–1820.

Library of Congress, Washington, D.C., United States

Archivo Nacional de Cuba Collection (microfilm).

National Archives, Kew, United Kingdom

CO 137/94	CO 137/95	CO 137/96
WO 1/92	WO 1/96	

National Archives of Jamaica, Spanish Town, Jamaica

Journals of the House of Assembly, Vols. I–X.

National Archives and Records Office, Washington, D.C., United States

Foreign Letters of the Continental Congress and the Department of State.
Records of the Bureau of Indian Affairs.

P. K. Yonge Library, University of Florida, Gainesville, United States

Archivo General de Indias (microfilm).
East Florida Papers (microfilm).
Papeles Procedentes de Cuba (microfilm).
Records of the Creek Trading House, Letter Book, 1795–1816.

Special Collections, University of Georgia, Athens, United States

Southeastern Native American Documents, 1730–1842.

Published Sources

Antal, Sandy, *A Wampum Denied: Procter's War of 1812* (Ottawa: Carleton University Press, 1997).

Bannister, Jerry, and Liam Riordan, eds., *The Loyal Atlantic: Remaking the British Atlantic in the Revolutionary Era* (Toronto: University of Toronto Press, 2012).

Botkin, Frances R., *Thieving Three-Fingered Jack: Transatlantic Tales of a Jamaican Outlaw, 1780–2015* (New Brunswick: Rutgers University Press, 2017).

Bridges, G. W., *The Annals of Jamaica* (London: John Murray, 1827).

Burt, Alfred Leroy, *The Evolution of the British Empire and Commonwealth from the American Revolution* (Boston: D.C. Heath & Col., 1956).

Campbell, Mavis, *The Maroons of Jamaica, 1655–1796: A History of Resistance, Collaboration & Betrayal* (Trentin: Africa World Press, 1990).

Carey, Bev, *Maroon Story: The Authentic and Original History of the Maroons in the History of Jamaica, 1490–1880* (St. Andrew, Jamaica: Agouti Press, 1997).

Chappell, Absalom Harris, *Miscellanies of Georgia; Historical, Biographical, Descriptive, etc.* (Columbus, GA: Gilbert Printing Company, 1928).

Cochran, Thomas C., ed., *The New American State Papers, 1789–1860* (Wilmington: Scholarly Resources, 1972–81).

Coker, William S., and Thomas D. Watson, 'Indian Traders of the Southeastern Spanish Borderlands: Panton, Leslie & Company and John Forbes & Company, 1783–1847,' *Louisiana Historical Association*, 28, 1 (Winter, 1987), 243–272.

Collier, Christopher, *Jeffersonian Republicans, 1800–1823: The Louisiana Purchase and the War of 1812* (New York: Benchmark Books, 1999).

Cotterill, R. S., 'Federal Indian Management in the South, 1789–1825,' *The Mississippi Valley Historical Review*, 20, 3 (Dec., 1933), 333–352.

Creighton, Luella Bruce, *Tecumseh: The Story of the Shawnee Chief* (London: Macmillan & Co., 1965).

Dallas, Robert C., *The History of the Maroons: From Their Origin to the Establishment of Their Chief Tribe at Sierra Leone: Including the Expedition to Cuba, for the Purpose of Procuring Spanish Chasseurs; and the State of the Island of Jamaica for the Last Ten Years: With a Succinct History of the Island Previous to That Period* (London: Printed by A. Strahan . . . for T. N. Longman and O. Rees. . ., 1803).

Edmunds, R. David, *Tecumseh and the Quest for Indian Leadership* (Boston: Little, Brown, and Company, 1984).

Ethridge, Robbie Franklyn, *Creek Country: The Creek Indians and Their World* (Chapel Hill: University of North Carolina Press, 2003).

Finkelman, Paul, ed., *Free Blacks in a Slave Society* (New York: Garland, 1989).

Gaines, Ann, *Louisiana Purchase in American History* (Berkeley Heights: Enslow Publishers, 2000).

Glasrud, Bruce A., and Milton S. Jordan, eds., *Free Blacks in Antebellum Texas* (Denton, TX: University of North Texas Press, 2015).

Gould, Eliga H., *The Persistence of Empire: British Political Culture in the Age of the American Revolution* (Chapel Hill: University of North Carolina Press, 2000).

Griffith, Benjamin W., *McIntosh and Weatherford, Creek Indian Leaders* (Tuscaloosa: University of Alabama Press, 1988).

Halbert, H. S., and T. H. Ball, *The Creek War of 1813 and 1814* (Chicago: Donohue & Henneberry, 1895).

Hart, Richard, *Slaves Who Abolished Slavery* (Kingston: University of the West Indies, Institute of Social and Economic Research, 1985).

Hawkins, Benjamin, *Letters of Benjamin Hawkins, 1796–1806* (Savannah, 1916).

Hoefte, R., 'Free Blacks and Coloureds in Plantation Suriname: The Struggle to Rise,' *Slavery & Abolition*, 17, 1 (1996), 102–129.

Hudson, Angela Pulley, *Creek Paths and Federal Roads: Indians, Settlers, and Slaves and the Making of the American South* (Chapel Hill: University of North Carolina Press, 2010).

Jamaica, *The Laws of Jamaica: 1760–1792* (London: A. Aikman Printer's to the King's Most Excellent Majesty, 1811).

Kappler, Charles J., ed., *Indian Affairs: Treaties* (Washington: U.S. Government Printing Office, 1904).

Keats, John, *Eminent Domain: The Louisiana Purchase and the Making of America* (New York: Charterhouse, 1973).

Lakomäki, Sami, *Gathering Together: The Shawnee People Through Diaspora and Nationhood, 1600–1870* (New Haven: Yale University Press, 2014).

Landers, Jane G., ed., *Against the Odds: Free Blacks in the Slave Societies of the Americas* (London: F. Cass, 1996).

Laurence, K. O., *The Settlement of Free Negroes in Trinidad Before Emancipation* (Diego Martin, Trinidad: John Hilton Hackshaw, 1999).

Lindsay, Alexander Crawford, *Lives of the Lindsays: Or a Memoir of the Houses of Crawford and Balcarres . . .* (Wigan: Privately Printed, 1840).

Martin, Joel W., *Sacred Revolt: The Muskogees' Struggle for a New World* (Boston: Beacon Press, 1993).

Mauelshagen, Carl, and Gerald H. Davis, eds., *Partners in the Lord's Work: The Diary of Two Moravian Missionaries in the Creek Indian Country, 1807–1813* (Atlanta: School of Arts and Sciences Research Papers, Georgia State College, 1969).

McDowell, William L., ed., *Documents Relating to Indian Affairs, Colonial Records of South Carolina*, Vol. II (Columbia: South Carolina Archives Department, 1958).

Nicholls, Michael L., 'Creating Identity: Free Blacks and the Law,' *Slavery & Abolition*, 35, 2 (2014), 214–233.

O'Shaughnessy, Andrew Jackson, *An Empire Divided: The American Revolution and the British Caribbean* (Philadelphia: University of Pennsylvania Press, 2000).

Owsley, Frank L., 'Fort Mims Massacre,' *The Alabama Review*, 24 (Jan., 1971), 192–204.

Owsley, Frank L., *Struggle for the Gulf Borderlands: The Creek War and the Battle of New Orleans, 1812–1815* (Gainesville: University Press of Florida, 1981).

Phelan, Mary Kay, *Story of the Louisiana Purchase* (New York: Crowell, 1979).

Reeder, Tyson, 'Liberty with the Sword: Jamaican Maroons, Haitian Revolutionaries, and American Liberty,' *Journal of the Early Republic*, 37, 1 (Spring, 2017), 84–94.

Robinson, Carey, *The Iron Thorn: The Defeat of the British by the Jamaican Maroons* (Kingston: Kingston Publishers Limited, 1993).

Rowe, Jill E., *Invisible in Plain Sight: Self-Determination Strategies of Free Blacks in the Old Northwest* (New York: Peter Lang, 2017).

Saunt, Claudio, *A New Order of Things: Property, Power, and the Transformation of the Creek Indians, 1733–1816* (Cambridge: Cambridge University Press, 1999).

Southerland, Henry deLeon Jr., and Jerry Elijah Brown, *The Federal Road Through Georgia, the Creek Nation and Alabama, 1806–1836* (Tuscaloosa: University of Alabama Press, 1989).

St-Denis, Guy, *Tecumseh's Bones* (Montréal: McGill-Queen's University Press, 2005).

Stiggins, George, *Creek Indian History: A Historical Narrative of the Genealogy, Traditions, and Downfall of the Ispocoga or Creek Indian Tribe of Indians* (Birmingham: Birmingham Public Library Press, 1989).

Sturgis, Amy H., *Tecumseh: A Biography* (Westport, CT: Greenwood Press, 2008).

Sugden, John, 'Early Pan-Indianism: Tecumseh's Tour of the Indian Country, 1811–1812,' *American Indian Quarterly*, 10, 4 (Autumn, 1986), 273–304.

Sugden, John, *Tecumseh: A Life* (London: Pimlico, 1999).

Thompson, Alvin O., *Flight to Freedom: African Runaways and Maroons in the Americas* (Kingston: University of West Indies Press, 2006).

Warren, Stephen, *The Worlds the Shawnees Made: Migration and Violence in Early America* (Chapel Hill: University of North Carolina Press, 2014).

3   Runaways and Rebellions
Maroons and Creeks as Hunters and Harbourers

In March 1739, after decades of bloody battles, the First Maroon War drew to a close with the signing of peace treaties between the colonial government and Maroons in the west and east of Jamaica. As discussed earlier, rather than just confirming peace between Maroons and colonists, the peace treaties also included several clauses intended to determine future interactions between Maroons and enslaved people. These clauses have haunted the Maroons ever since. The main clauses which dealt with these interactions were outlined at the beginning of Chapter 1, namely Cudjoe's Clause Six which required the Leewards to "take, kill, suppress, or destroy" all of the "rebels wheresoever they be throughout the island,"[1] and Quao's Clause Four which stated that the Windwards should "destroy all other . . . rebellious negroes" and "bring in such other negroes as shall from time to time runaway from their respective owners."[2] Quao's treaty, therefore, not only states that the "rebels" are runaway slaves, but also requires the Windwards to treat them as "rebels" as soon as they run away from their masters. However, Quao's treaty further included Clause Eight which instructed the Windwards to "take up any runaway Negroes that shall abscond from their respective Owners, he or they shall carry them to their respective Masters or Owners, and shall be paid for doing so, as the Legislature shall appoint."[3] Whilst the wording differed slightly in each treaty, the intent was the same; Maroons were to assist the colonial government in locating any slaves who would in the future run away from their masters, whether with the intention of rebelling or otherwise.

In the 1790 Treaty of New York, similar concerns also led federal officials to insert clauses which dealt with the return of runaways and of rebellions. There were, however, several key differences. Article Three read,

> the Creek Nation shall deliver as soon as practicable to the commanding officer of the troops of the United States, stationed at the Rock-Landing on the Oconee River, all citizens of the United States, white inhabitants or negroes, who are now prisoners in any part of the said nation.[4]

The issue here seems to have been the return of people, regardless of race, who had been taken against their will to Creek lands, although it is not impossible that the federal government also expected those who had willingly fled to the

Creeks to be returned. This article was so important to the federal government that it continued,

> and if any such prisoners or negroes should not be so delivered, on or before the first day of June ensuing, the governor of Georgia may empower three persons to repair to the said nation, in order to claim and receive such prisoners and negroes.[5]

As in Jamaica, absent slaves, whether those who fled or were abducted, were lost property and lost financial investment and had to be reclaimed. Whilst these "prisoners" were not strictly runaways, the United States was clearly determined to recover its people and its property. Indeed, subsequent demands, which will be discussed later in this chapter, explicitly called for the return of runaways for payment. With these clauses, slaveholders in Jamaica and the United States intended both to deter future abductions or runaways and to remove a haven for those intending to flee captivity.

One major difference between the demands in Jamaica and those in the United States was that members of the Creek Nation had already been acting as slave-catchers for decades, whereas, by the very notion of their history, Maroons had not. Returning slaves had been enshrined in the articles of friendship between the Creeks and South Carolina.[6] According to this 1732 agreement, Creeks who returned escapees to a British garrison would be rewarded.[7] Later, in spring 1767, in Augusta, the British Indian agent John Stuart won a promise from the Creeks to return fugitive slaves.[8] In fact, in almost every treaty prior to removal, Creeks were requested to return runaway slaves. By including similar demands in the Maroon treaties, we can see how these former communities of "wild negroes" were being re-imagined as allies in the fight against slave flight—much in the same way that Native American communities had been recruited for decades. The inclusion of these clauses alone, however, does not necessarily mean that they were adhered to. Therefore, it is imperative to explore how these clauses were received and the extent to which they were acted on by both Maroon and Creek communities.

News of the signing of the treaties spread quickly throughout Jamaica, but it is not clear how these particular clauses were viewed by Maroon communities. There are unfortunately no Maroon-produced records which reference these stipulations or the treaties at all. The colonial sources, as ever, have to be read with caution. For example, Colonel John Guthrie, the man tasked with negotiating the peace terms, stated that the Leeward Maroons had "offered . . . to take up for the future all Runaway Negroes" rather than this clause being forced upon them. Whilst this is wildly unlikely, numerous examples show both Leeward and Windward Maroons carrying out their treaty obligations, albeit to varying degrees. On the estates, it appears the treaties were, unsurprisingly, poorly received. Colonel Guthrie, the British representative who signed the treaties, died in mysterious circumstances shortly after the announcement of the treaties and was rumoured to have been poisoned by disgruntled slaves who, under the treaty, were to be returned to their owners. A few months later, groups of slaves were said to have "met in great Bodies to consider of Mutinying."[9] It was said that they met "openly" and "insolently" in Spanish Town to form "rebellious" companies and to name commanders amongst themselves. The plot, however, was soon uncovered. Its leaders were rounded up and executed whilst others were transported to French or Spanish territories to be sold as slaves. During these years, the number of slaves in Jamaica had risen by 35,000, whilst the white population increased by only 1500.[10] According to Mavis Campbell, many of these large numbers of slaves saw the treaties as nothing more than a reward for disobedience.[11] Discontent was sure to have spread across the estates.

As alluded to earlier in the chapter, the Treaty of New York, signed between the Creek Nation and the federal government of the United States, had a different impact upon Creek-black relations because earlier treaties had also tried to regulate those relations. African American people had been present throughout British colonisation, and Creeks had been continually been requested to return any runaways. However, the number of African American people bordering Creek country was fairly low until mid-way through the eighteenth century. Then, in 1751, Georgia permitted slavery, leading to dramatic growth in the number of slaves in the region. In 1763, when Britain assumed control of Florida from Spain, the enslaved population in the region expanded significantly.[12] According to Peter H. Wood, the black population of Georgia and Florida had more than quadrupled, from 4100 to roughly 18,000 between 1760 and 1775.[13] This outweighed the 14,000 Creeks who lived in the region at the time. As the black population grew, so did the frequency of contact between Native Americans and black people. One of the most frequent forms of contact was that between Creeks and runaway slaves who fled nearby European settlements. In the colonial era, the vast majority of Creeks adopted these runaways into their clans. Such adoption gave the person full rights and, according to the naturalist William Bartram, all captives could be liberated upon marrying a Creek.[14] Of course, the reaction of the slave colonies was to try to prevent "Indian country" from becoming a haven for runaways.[15] As such, the first formal agreement was reached in 1767, where Creeks agreed to return fugitive slaves.[16] Whilst, in a shadowing of what was to come, many Creeks refused to adhere to the agreement and, in fact, actively hid runaway slaves, colonial officials saw fit to declare that the agreement "cannot fail of having a very good effect by breaking that intercourse between the negroes and savages which might have been attended with very troublesome consequences had it continued."[17]

In fact, into the Revolutionary era, the image of Creek country as a haven for runaways persisted. In 1777, the Spanish Governor of Louisiana, Luis de Unzaga, reported to his British counterpart, Peter Chester, in Pensacola that slaves were frequently fleeing from the vicinity of New Orleans, crossing Lake Pontchartrain, and finding refuge with Native Americans. He implored Chester to do something as the problem was said to be getting worse with every passing day, but little was done.[18] As the end of the Revolution neared, American officials continued to press Creek leaders for the return of stolen property, especially slaves.[19] Whether these slaves had truly been stolen or had fled of their own accord is difficult to determine given the previous flight of many slaves to the Nation. For example, when Britain evacuated East Florida in 1783 and 1784, 4745 blacks were said to be missing, many of whom had fled to Creek territory.[20] One Georgian volunteered to enter Creek country in an effort to locate these slaves. He explained,

> I have in my employ a very good blacksmith which I would take on with me and place in the most central part of the nation where he could take care of negroes as we would collect them, and place irons on them to prevent their escape.[21]

Despite the best efforts of these people now called Americans, many of the runaways remained in Creek country.

This led to the image of Creek country as a safe haven for runaways continuing into the post-revolutionary period. In November 1785, eight slaves ran away from a Spanish official in New Orleans, led by a man called Pitter, who had once belonged to the Spanish commissioner. The group set out to seek asylum in Creek country and included the slave King, who was also familiar with the land. He headed for his former owner, an Englishman, and in May 1786 was reportedly "with him in the Talapusa Nation."[22] In this early period of Creek-American relations, the Creeks were doing little to discourage runaways from fleeing to their lands. That said, however, not all runaways in Creek country found life to their suit. In 1781, when three slaves absconded from Spanish-controlled Pensacola and headed for the Creek Nation, one of them, a sailor, escaped and returned to the Spanish port a few days later. His skills had been of little use in the Creek Nation, and he was said to prefer to seek work elsewhere.[23]

Nevertheless, many runaways still aimed for Creek country when setting out on the search for freedom, and the archival record is full of such examples. In 1787, the Executive Deputy of Georgia wrote to the Cheehaw King requesting his assistance in locating some runaway slaves. One Andrew Wouldhove of Liberty County, near the Altamaha, had lost a family of slaves who had fled to Creek country.[24] On another occasion, the "free fellow Bill" absconded to the Creeks in 1792 when his employer, John Forrester of East Florida, refused to pay his wages.[25] When a company slave in Pensacola, "the rascally Negroe Tom," fled his owners, he also struck out for Creek country.[26] These African Americans may have been encouraged by the contradictory stance different Creeks took to returning or harbouring runaways. Even Alexander McGillivray was known to authorise the return of some slave runaways and not others. For example, in 1789, he wrote of an African American runaway named Luis who apparently escaped from Mobile and "was long in this Country & no one Claiming him he passed as free & used to go where he pleased."[27] Despite this,

McGillivray went on to reiterate that any African Americans that ran away and went into the Nation "shall always be deliverd to their owners wherever demanded."[28] It is quite possible that such declarations were made only to placate Spanish and American officials who were in search of their runaways. Despite McGillivray's public proclamations, instances of Creeks shielding runaways continued to occur. A man named Benjamin Sims wrote that a young slave absconded from him and took with him one of Sims's horses. Sims had been told that the slave had "made his way good to the Creek nation."[29] Likewise, A. B. Harris claimed that the Creek town called Masacusa was an "assailom [asylum] for negroes."[30] This practice of harbouring runaways continued into the nineteenth century. In 1808, Benjamin Hawkins was infuriated by the lack of Creek effort in hunting runaways. He wrote to the Nation that if they did not "alter their conduct," then he would "shut my door against all of you." He reiterated that the Creeks must "collect and restore such negroes" as "you are bound to do so by treaty."[31]

However, Creek country had not always been the preferred destination for runaways. Before 1790, slaves living in Georgia tended to head for St. Augustine, rather than the Creek lands, when running away. There they could secure their freedom, offered to American slaves who wished to convert to Catholicism. In 1788, for example, a group of twenty-one slaves from Georgia fled to the Spanish city. They joined thirty-six others in St. Augustine who had fled under "the pretext of religion."[32] This was all to change in July 1790. As part of a larger policy to halt the spread of revolutionary ideas in the New World, the Spanish government ordered the Governor of St. Augustine to desist from freeing fugitive slaves that made it to Florida.[33] This ultimately had the unintended consequence of encouraging more runaways to flee to Creek country. The slaves' new preferred destination of the Creek Nation was set not only because of the decree, but as a result of the continuing willingness of some Creeks to harbour the runaways. In 1799, Georgia's Governor noted that those slaves who had fled his state "will very probably be concealed by some negro fellows who was in the [Creek] nation and run away some years ago."[34]

These slaves were inspired by the welcome many received once in Creek country. In 1795, for example, ten Creeks entered Spanish settlements along the St. Johns River and had "in their company two negroes stolen in past years." It was alleged that they

> already speak Indian, and through them the savages have indicated that the adjacent country belongs to them, and that they will hunt in it as long as they like. Here one should add that the aforementioned negroes are praising to the residents' slaves the good life that people of their colour enjoy in the nation where they eat the same as their masters and work only when they wish without fear of punishment.[35]

Potential runaways were also actively encouraged to run away by Creeks and their black companions. One, Peter, a black translator for the "witch" Cohiti, travelled around the south-east spreading news of the "good life" and apparently bribing slaves to flee to the Nation. They were said to be "daily inconveniencing the settlers by conspiring with their negroes and . . . persuading them to flee."[36]

Conversely, there is little evidence that Maroon country continued to be seen as a haven for runaways after the signing of the peace treaties. However, this dirge of evidence could be a result of relying on colonial sources when studying the Jamaican Maroons. It is possible that certain slaves were harboured in Maroon towns after the peace treaties, but their very presence would be hidden from authorities and, therefore, would be non-existent in the archival record. Indeed, Bev Carey has suggested that the Maroons looked carefully at how slaves had escaped: if it was achieved quietly; if the slave established his cottage in the remote clearing in the woods; if such a clearing housed one family, or several. In other words, if the slaves had attempted to do as the Maroons had done and establish themselves without fanfare, then those villages could remain undisturbed in their remote places. However, any that did not act in such a manner would be viewed as renegades disturbing the peace.[37] It does seem that Carey is correct in that some runaways were left to establish small communities in the more remote areas of Jamaica. R.C. Dallas wrote that it was "very well known" that a small body of runaways established themselves in the mountains, where they raised huts, and made provision grounds, on which some had lived for "upwards of twenty years."[38] The Maroons may have been unaware of their existence but, as Maroons frequently travelled in the woods to hunt runaways, visit market towns, or hunt wild boar, it is extremely unlikely that this particular community would have escaped their attention for upwards of two decades. Therefore, the Maroons, it seems, had allowed the settlement to develop. By early 1795, however, a party of Maroons attacked the settlement. Some of these so-called Congo settlers returned to their owners whilst some were said to have joined the Trelawnys in their later war. Indeed, during the Second Maroon War, a party of British soldiers were said to have met a party of these runaway "Congo negroes," about thirty-five in number, settled "deep in the woods" towards Black River and, from the "appearance of the provisions," were alleged to have been there "some time."[39]

These allegations of Maroons harbouring runaway slaves led to rumours swirling that they were on the brink of joining with slaves to overthrow white rule. In 1765, when a slave rebellion took place, a "good deal of alarm was occasioned by the statements of some of the prisoners that the Maroons were to have joined them and divided the country with them."[40] In 1765 and 1766, Coromantin disturbances broke out again. In one uprising, thirty-three Akan slaves suddenly rose up and, in the space of an hour, killed nineteen colonists on an estate in Westmoreland. The rebellion, however, was soon crushed, but the Maroons were notable for their lack of engagement.[41] Again, in 1776, Thistlewood wrote that it was "strongly reported the Maroon Negroes are at the bottom of the Negro conspiracy."[42] Given the rumours of Maroon involvement in slave uprisings, and the presence of the Congo settlement, it would not be entirely surprising to learn that some runaways continued to be welcomed in Maroon towns even after the treaties.

However, it also cannot be denied that Maroons could be, and were, called upon to hunt runaways. As early as 1741, the colonial government requested the assistance of Maroons in locating runaways, stating that the Maroons were so skilled in hunting runaways that "they have been known to trace parties of runaway Negroes to a great distance by the smell of their firewood."[43] Their real usefulness was to be tested in an incident in 1742 during a rebellion, the very existence of which suggests how poorly the treaties were received by parts of the enslaved population. In that year, Leeward Maroons and slaves from a nearby plantation belonging to a Colonel Foster joined forces. The Maroons were said to be "Head men who were dissatisfied with the Treaty" and were "of the same kind" as the slaves.[44] The authorities apparently discovered that "the rebellion . . . was concerted between the Coromantee [Coromantin] negroes of those plantations, and some of the same country in the woods." The conspirators first intended "to cut off all those there that were born in the woods or came from other countries," and the rest of the slaves at Foster's were to destroy the white people.[45] Apparently, Cudjoe discovered that "some of His Chief men, who were dissatisfied with the treaty . . . had Entered into private Caballs with the Negroes in the Neighbouring Plantations, and incited them to revolt."[46] In response, he and Captain Accompong immediately armed "a sufficient number of the most faithful of their people," attacked the rebels, killed some, took others prisoner and chased the rest home to their plantations.[47] Cudjoe then turned to dealing with his own men who had been involved in the plot. In keeping with another of the treaty clauses, Cudjoe delivered them to the English, suggesting he deemed their actions as worthy of the death penalty. The men were tried under colonial justice. Two were sentenced to death, and the other two were sentenced to transportation from the island. However, as a gesture of goodwill, Governor Edward Trelawny pardoned the two men sentenced to death as it was their first offence. Cudjoe disagreed and insisted the men be returned to him so he could deal with them "upon his own authority." Upon their arrival in the Leeward territory, he promptly hanged them. Several of the plantation slaves were also tried and were executed or transported.[48] It is safe to assume that the planters would have been thrilled to spread the news of Cudjoe's punishment far and wide.

The repercussions of Cudjoe's form of justice were immediate and, in the eyes of the colonists, effective. Cudjoe's actions were said to have "struck a Terror" among the enslaved population, who "became more tractable" than they had been for years, largely because they had "met with No Encouragement from the Negroes in the Mountains."[49] Jamaican colonists were said to be, unsurprisingly, delighted with how the Leeward Maroons had taken to their new roles. The Assembly applauded "the use such an example must be of in preventing other negroes, for the future, from running away in bodies in hopes of being protected by them."[50] William Beckford, a planter, wrote that if a slave tried to escape, the Maroons were sure to capture him or to return his head.[51] R. C. Dallas reiterated this and alleged that the Maroons were "careless" whether they brought in a runaway alive, or only his head.[52] The latter practice became so prevalent that a law was passed allowing mile-money for every runaway produced alive in addition to the usual rewards.[53] It was very clear from this law of 1741 that colonists had made a capital investment in their slaves and preferred to have the slave returned to them to be punished and sent back to work. The law stated,

> And as it is justly to be apprehended, that from the different Encouragements given by the said Laws, Cudjo and Quaw and the several Negroes under their Command in Trelawny and Crawford Towns . . . may be induced to kill all straggling and runaway Negroes that may fall in their Way, with Intention to receive the greater Reward of Ten Pounds . . . rather than to bring them in alive, and receive the lesser Reward of Ten Shilling for them as Stragglers or Runaways.

It was decided that £3 plus mile-money, a not inconsequential amount of money, be paid to any Maroon who returned a runaway alive.[54] The introduction of this law suggests that Maroons were adhering to their treaty obligations to an extent that took even the colonists by surprise.

It was not just individual, or small groups of, runaways that concerned the colonists. Arguably, more of a concern was the threat of large-scale slave rebellion.[55] In this case, too, the Maroons were thought to be a boon to the colony. Edward Long reported that

> no insurrection of moment occurred for many years. Some trifling disturbances happened, and some plots were detected, but they came to nothing; and indeed the seeds of rebellion were in a great measure rendered abortive, by the activity of the Maroons, who scoured the woods, and apprehended all straggling and vagabond slaves that from time to time deserted from their owners.[56]

Indeed, when a small rebellion broke out in Kingston in 1746, forty mercenaries from Crawford Town helped to suppress it.[57] Again, in 1752, the Maroons were called out, and George Currie of Accompong earned a reward of £100 for killing a rebellious slave named Quaco Venter. The Committee of the House considered the action a "very extraordinary service" because Venter was a "dangerous rebel" who had killed many and was a "great terror in the area."[58] He was accused of committing "much mischief" and was apparently involved in "several murders." The colonists were delighted when the Maroons brought this "terror" to justice.[59]

The fidelity of the Maroons was truly tested when the large-scale Tacky's Rebellion exploded in 1760. The violence broke out in St. Mary and soon spread to St. James, Kingston, St. Johns, Clarendon, Westmoreland and St. Dorothy. On 10th April, the Lieutenant Governor wrote that he "had sent

Expresses to the Commanding Officers of Crawford Town, Nanny Town, and Scots Hall with Orders to March Immediately a company from each place."[60] It is worth noting here that both Leeward and Windward Maroons were called upon and also responded. Indeed, it was Windward Maroons from Scotts Hall who first arrived at the meeting point with colonial forces. However, in a hint towards the financial motivations of the Maroons, they at first refused to act further without a payment of the head-money owed to them.[61] The colonists present immediately contributed some money, and they all proceeded to march on the rebellious slaves. They engaged in the first hostilities in St. Mary and "killed a few" of those located.[62] After further skirmishes, the forces encountered Tacky and his band apparently wandering in the woods, and the Maroons "immediately pursued" the slaves in "full cry." The chase was of "no long duration" and Tacky was shot through the head.[63] During the rebellion, "about" sixty colonists were killed, while the number of blacks lost through execution, transportation, suicide or battle "was not less than one thousand"—the whole loss sustained by the country in "ruined buildings, cane-pieces, cattle, slaves and disbursements was at least 100,000 pounds."[64] Tacky's Rebellion represented one of the largest threats to Jamaican society, and it was a Maroon who nullified that threat.[65]

Despite this, the Maroons' participation was deeply criticised in some quarters of colonial society. The planter-historian Bryan Edwards claimed that when one body of Maroons was confronted by the rebels, all of them threw themselves flat on the ground and continued in that position "until the rebels retreated."[66] Edwards then wrote a note in his private copy of Edward Long's account stating, that during one attack at Down's Cove, the Maroons "behaved most shamefully" during the fight by "lying the whole time on their faces."[67] These claims led to a debate between planter-historians over the extent to which Maroons were involved in other skirmishes during the rebellion. Edward Long believed that the Maroons were the "principal instruments" in suppressing the insurrection.[68] On the other hand, Edwards claimed that the Maroon role in parts of the 1760 rebellion has been overstated.[69] He does not dispute the fact that Tacky was killed by a Maroon but contends that, on other occasions, parties of Maroons arrived "two or three days" after an outbreak, leaving it to colonial troops to defeat the rebels in skirmishes such as one at Heywood Hall. Edwards even went as far as to claim that, after one skirmish, the Maroons were sent into the woods to pursue the surviving rebels. The Maroons "rambled around" for a day or two and returned with a collection of human ears which they claimed to have cut off from the heads of rebels they had killed. Their claim was believed, and they received reward money; yet, afterwards, it was found they had not killed anyone but had cut the ears off already-dead bodies.[70] No colonial source, however, challenges the claim that it was a Maroon who ultimately killed Tacky. Indeed, both the Leeward and the Windward Maroons subsequently received financial reward for their actions in Tacky's Rebellion. The Leewards received £450 whilst the Windwards were granted £230.[71] The Lieutenant-Governor assured the Council that the "parties from the Negro Towns" were in pursuit of the remaining rebel parties and were "employed in Scouring the Woods where they had Secreted themselves."[72] So confident of the Maroons' success, the Council lifted the imposition of martial law even before the rest of the rebellious slaves had been rounded up. The Governor, however, may have acted too hastily as, by June, another uprising broke out at Manchioneal in the parish of St. Thomas-in-the-east. Companies of colonists soon convened to face the rebels and again called upon the Maroon towns. Two detachments from the "Negro Towns" joined with the colonial troops to place the rebels "between their two fires" and eventually quelled the rebellion.[73]

Such actions led to Maroons continually being called upon to hunt runaways. The infamous colonist Thomas Thistlewood made numerous observations in his diaries of Maroons being "out on the hunt." In 1763, he noted that "the Wild Negroes" had captured eleven runaways in a hut in the mountains. The Maroons were said to have killed three and taken the rest to be tried at Savanna-la-Mar. Some were eventually hanged and others burnt alive for the murder of a Mr. Wright.[74] In other examples, in 1764, Cudjoe's men caught a "negro wench" who had cut out a sailor's tongue and another who had "a vast deal of Obeah of different kinds."[75] In the 1780s, Maroons were called upon when Three Fingered Jack, the biggest threat to colonial society since Tacky, terrorised the island.[76] Jack terrified British colonists for almost two years during the late 1770s and early 1780s. With no progress being made in his capture, the Assembly offered a reward of £200 for "the apprehending, or bringing in the head of that daring rebel, called Three Finger Jack, who hath hitherto eluded every attempt against him."[77] He was eventually killed by a party of Scotts Hall and Moore Town Maroons. These examples demonstrate that certain Maroons were fulfilling their treaty obligations of hunting runaways and putting down slave rebellions.

Creeks, too, increasingly turned towards slave-catching. As mentioned earlier, Native Americans in the south-east had half-heartedly served as slave-catchers for decades, but this was to change following the influence of Alexander McGillivray, particularly after 1790. The Treaty of New York's secret articles had made McGillivray a brigadier-general for the United States and paid him a handsome salary, making him more inclined to American interests. But even before the treaty was signed, his literacy had enabled Spanish and American officials to send letters directly into Creek country describing the appearance of fugitive slaves. His literacy meant that he could also keep lists of runaways indefinitely, and use them to describe the fugitives to fellow Creeks.[78] In November 1785, for example, Arturo O'Neill, Governor of Spanish West Florida, informed McGillivray about Louis McCarty's slave Ciro, who had run away from New Orleans. O'Neill described Ciro as a creole from Illinois, twenty-two years old and five feet, three fists high. A few months later, McGillivray captured the fugitive, who had been "roving about the country."[79] In another example, in 1786, McGillivray reviewed a list of runaways and noted that some belonged to a man called Martin Paloa. He wrote to O'Neill to assure Paloa that he would "preserve the negro list, and if chance should direct any to these parts you may be assured of them."[80] Almost eight months later, McGillivray secured their return.[81] This does not mean, however, that McGillivray diligently and unquestionably returned all runaways that he located. On one occasion, a Gerardo Bine entered Creek territory with a Spanish passport to catch two runaway slaves. He travelled to McGillivray's house with the intention of explaining his reasons for entering Creek country. McGillivray met him at his door, examined Bine's papers and replied that he did not understand his passport, declaring it as good only for toilet paper. He then told Bine to leave Creek country and refused to allow him to search for the runaways.[82]

Despite this rejection of Bine, other slaves were located and returned to their owners. For example, the Lower Creeks, Philatouche and Ninnywageechee, who were themselves of African descent, led attacks against settlements and captured African Americans to return to their owners.[83] McGillivray's records are full of instances in which other Creeks also participated in hunting for runaways.[84] In one example from 1787, a settler called Benjamin James wrote that he owned three African Americans in the territory of Cumberland but that a man called Amey had stolen those slaves. James "immediately sent of twelve indians for my negroes who fetch'd them to me."[85] Clearly, some Creeks were willing to undertake the wishes of Spanish and American officials to return runaway slaves.

It is clear that many Maroons and Creeks needed financial motivation to go slave-catching. In Jamaica, the 1741 law had stipulated that Maroon officers should be paid "2/6 per day and volunteers should receive 7 1/2d with a lump sum of 6/3 for those who had not previously volunteered."[86] These amounts were revised in 1780 to

> the Officer among the Negroes in each Party in the Rank of Captain, Two shillings and six Pence per Day, to a lieutenant, One Shilling and Three Pence per Day, and to every common Man, One Ryal per Day, when on actual duty, and no longer.[87]

However, despite these strict guidelines, Maroons frequently went unpaid. The displeasure of certain Maroons with this issue has already been highlighted in the discussion of Maroon action during Tacky's Rebellion, but other examples arose, too. In December 1791, in a petition from the superintendent of Scotts Hall, it was stated that a Colonel Gray of Scotts Hall was frequently sent out with slave-catching parties and was entitled to £70 which he had never received. Thirty-one years after his initial claim, Gray was finally paid the money he was owed.[88] Although there were difficulties in obtaining their rewards, limits were later placed on the amount of money each community could earn through this activity. It was decided that each town should be prevented from earning more than £500 per annum through slave-catching. The colonial government soon realised the folly of setting such a limit—it only served to discourage Maroons from aiding the government when the town's earnings neared the maximum. Despite this, the limit does not seem to have impacted negatively on the financial income of the Maroon communities—the committee had investigated and found that nearby inhabitants were in the practice of privately hiring Maroons to hunt their runaways.[89] As a consequence, it was decided that no superintendent should order out parties at the request of any one individual unless there was an affidavit stating that there were runaway slaves establishing quarters nearby.[90] This clearly did not reduce the payments enough as, five years later, the Governor gave instructions to all the superintendents of the Maroon towns "not to send out in future parties on the requisition of any private individual, unless the person desiring such party engage to make good all the expence of pay and subsistence of said party."[91] The government itself, however, also surpassed the limit itself on several occasions, sometimes even exceeding £1000. In 1787, a committee of the House examined party accounts and ruled that they were "considerable"—resolving to further reduce payments for slave-hunting.

Limits on payments for hunting runaways had, unsurprisingly, always led to ambivalence when it came to slave-catching, and colonists had early on realised that financial incentive would help motivate slave-catchers. In 1761, the colonial government requested that Trelawny Town send a party of Maroons to find some slaves that were "skulking" in the woods. The Maroons did not respond positively enough so, to encourage them, two planters, Mr. Cope and Mr. Goodin, promised that they would give the Maroons twenty shillings per head for all the slaves that killed, over and above what they already received.[92] Eventually, £115 was paid for this service, so it appears that, whatever grievances the Maroons felt, the colonists soon found some Maroons willing to do as the colonists requested. The economic motivations of Maroons can also be seen in another example from 1761. On this occasion, Maroons were sent out against rebellious slaves and, initially, were said to have done a "good service" and to have killed "twelve or fifteen negroes" in one skirmish. Their "good service" was soon forgotten as they became somewhat "discontented and mutinous."[93] This discontent was said by Bryan Edwards to have arisen from the inability of the authorities to pay the Maroons what they were due. These examples highlight the primary motivation of the Maroons when it came to hunting runaways—money. As will be discussed later, Maroons had little other option for financial gain and became reliant on this controversial practice for income.

Similarly, in Creek country, many were motivated by financial reward. When discontent rumbled through the Nation, and Americans found it difficult to locate Creeks willing to hunt runaways, increased rewards were constantly offered. This was initially set at $12.50—a not inconsequential amount of money in Creek country.[94] In terms easier to understand, every captured runaway was officially worth a gun and three blankets—the equivalent of approximately forty pounds of dressed deerskins in weight.[95] Returning an African American runaway, therefore, was far more profitable than spending months on the hunt for ever-decreasing deerskins. This price does not seem to have been desirable enough, however, and Benjamin Hawkins was forced to increase the offer to $25 in 1808.[96] Indeed, on some occasions Creeks were even offered $50 to capture slave runaways. This had been the case in 1787 when the family of slaves belonging to Andrew Wouldhove absconded from his estate. Wouldhove argued that their capture would be a good deed and would "tend to make both people whites and reds better friends."[97] Creeks, however, held out for additional money rather than simply good favour.

The act of hunting runaways for profit seems to have led some Creeks into viewing African Americans in terms of financial value. Abner Hammond, a traveller through Creek country, noted the presence of African Americans in the Nation. He claimed that "six or eight negroes" might be recovered by paying to the holders of them nearly their value.[98] This implies, then, that some Creeks were beginning to see African American captives in economic terms rather than as people to potentially adopt into their clan. By 1801, certain Creeks were explicitly referring to African Americans as "property." In a letter to John Forbes, the Creek chief Mad Dog wrote that the traders in Creek country had "property enough in negroes, cattle, horses." He reiterated that he did not mean Euro American traders alone, that he included the Native American factors who had accumulated property.[99]

These ambivalent stances from both Maroons and Creeks led to some hatching plans with enslaved people. One example of this, which has yet to be explored elsewhere in the scholarship, is a claim made in the Journals of the Assembly of Jamaica. This alleged that a deception was conjured up between some slaves and Maroons. Apparently the "wild negroes" would catch runaways within the limits of plantations, or towns, "frequently by consent, and at the instance of such runaways, who are in connivance with the said wild negroes, and obtain them a part of the said reward."[100] If true, this clearly shows that the treaties did not herald the end of Maroon-slave collaboration. There is the possibility that this charge against the slaves and Maroons was false; however, there must have been a certain amount of close interaction between the groups for it to have at least seemed plausible. At first, it seems unlikely that a slave would risk punishment for this plan. However, if a slave had a lenient master who accepted short-term runaways, or *petit marronage*, as part of the system, then perhaps the reward may have outweighed the punishment.[101] Nevertheless, if true, the participation of Maroons in this act shows their recognition of slaves as property to be returned for money, even if those slaves were in collusion with the Maroons. This may have been a case of both sides feeling unable to change the system and so trying to play it to their mutual advantage. In an interesting comparison, Joshua Piker has claimed that Creek slave-catchers were willing to create business by helping such slaves to escape.[102] If true, this hints at the alliances that some enslaved peoples formed with Creeks in the late eighteenth and early nineteenth centuries. Similar to the Maroon case, some pragmatic Creeks and slaves may have been attempting to work the system to their advantage.

As illustrated by heterogeneous attitudes towards slave-catching, the complicated relations between Maroons, Creeks and enslaved people continued into the Second Maroon War and the Creek War of 1813. In Jamaica, almost as soon as hostilities broke out, rumours abounded that slaves were joining the Trelawny Town Maroons. Of even greater concern for Jamaican whites was the claim that some of the slaves who had been serving with the British soldiers had deserted and joined the Maroons.[103] Other archival evidence certainly supports the assertion that slaves could, and did, flee their estates to link up with the Trelawnys. It is difficult, however, to quantify exactly how many did so. Henry Shirley, a Jamaican planter, reported that from "the best accounts," upwards of two hundred slaves joined the Trelawnys.[104] Shirley's account is given credibility by the fact that the figure was based on General Walpole's observances. Although fighting against the Maroons, Walpole railed against the way in which the colonial government treated the Maroons, as discussed earlier. At the conclusion of the war, Walpole was offered five hundred guineas and a ceremonial sword to mark his contribution to the defeat of the Maroons, but he was so disgusted by the colonial government's treatment of the Trelawnys that he refused both and sailed to England. If Walpole's observations were correct, then approximately the same number of able adult slaves fought as able adult Trelawnys. However, the presence of two hundred slaves represents an incredibly low percentage of the entire enslaved population. Shirley's account then actually suggests that the tensions between the slaves and the Maroons, dating back to before the First Maroon War, continued into the Second Maroon War and beyond.

It is certain, though, that at least some slaves did join with the Maroons to fight the British during the Second Maroon War. At the beginning of October 1795, Balcarres reported to the Secretary of War that "forty negroes are missing from one estate; it is possible they may have joined the Trelawny Maroons." Rather hopefully, Balcarres added "If it is true, I think it would weaken instead of strengthening the Maroons."[105] Indeed there were some claims that the initiation rituals that runaways were subject to were so severe that some regretted the choice they had made. According to R. C. Dallas, however, once a runaway had joined, they "could not retract." Many were no doubt sustained by the hope that, if peace was agreed, they would be included under the terms as Maroons. One Maroon leader, Johnson, apparently treated many runaway allies harshly, but he also did not hesitate to raise them to leadership levels if they had proved themselves worthy. One slave eyewitness, called Jumbo, alleged that Johnson had made a Coromantin "negro" named Cudjoe a captain and raised another belonging to the estate of Whittaker, named Casacrui, to the same rank.[106] It was perhaps the treatment of these runaways which incited a further fifty-four slaves to "join the Maroons in rebellion" from St. Elizabeth.[107]

According to the archival sources, the prospect of fighting the colonists alone was not enough to convince slaves to join the Trelawnys, and other methods had to be found. In an examination following the war, Thomas Sadler testified that, in the raids on the plantations, what the Maroons could not carry away, they "distributed amongst the negroes belonging to the plantation."[108] In other words, the Trelawnys encouraged slaves to join them by offering incentives—a situation which mirrored how colonial society had induced Maroons to ally with the government earlier in the century. Sadler further reported that Parkinson, a Maroon leader, told the slaves that they only wanted to kill "backras," and the enslaved population had nothing to fear from them. This actually hints at the continued distance between some Maroons and certain slaves—if the Maroons were particularly close to the slaves, they would not have had to reassure them that they only wanted to kill whites. This is further supported by the fact that Parkinson told the slaves that "he did not mean to force them, that he was fighting to make all the negroes free."[109]

A similar situation was also seen in the United States when Redstick warriors attempted to reassure enslaved people that they had no quarrel with them. As the Redsticks stormed Fort Mims in the war of 1813, one warrior encountered a black man cowering in the corner of a house. The Redstick approached the man and told him not to worry because the Master of Breath "has ordered us not to kill any but white people and half breeds."[110] It seems that in both cases, the enslaved population was wary after some Maroons and Creeks had spent decades hunting runaways. Perhaps the slaves were uncertain whether the wars would be successful and wanted to avoid the repercussions that would follow defeat. Either way, the majority of the slaves continued to reside on the plantations and "wait and see."

When assessing the likelihood of slaves joining with the Trelawnys, Dallas claimed that in the north and west, the slaves or "the majority of them were actually the determined enemies of the Maroons," presumably because of Maroon actions over the previous half-century. On the other hand, in Clarendon "whence the Maroons originally came," a degree of family connections was still acknowledged among them, and emissaries had been employed to ascertain their inclination.[111] Of those few hundred who did join the Maroons, many were apparently welcomed into the ranks. The colonial government despaired that the Maroons were receiving runaways with "great triumph."[112] Balcarres constantly worried that "the Maroons of Trelawny Town could command the aid of the plantation negroes at pleasure."[113] The prospect of hordes of slaves joining the Maroons sent shockwaves throughout the island, particularly in light of the recent uprising in Haiti. The worst fears of the whites were becoming a reality.

The British wasted no time in fighting fire with fire and compelled slaves to join their forces. They did this through two main methods—financial reward and the promise of freedom. On 19th November, the Westmoreland vestry presented thirty dollars to three armed slaves whose good behaviour entitled them "the praise and remembrance of the community."[114] The colonial government did not stop with offering financial rewards to the slaves who fought the Maroons. Balcarres issued a statement that assured slaves that he thought it "highly probable" that the House of Assembly would purchase the freedom of "any slave, who takes, or kills, a Trelawny Maroon in arms."[115] This at once shows the continued tensions between slaves and Maroons, and highlights the failure of the colonial government to attract enough slaves to fight the Maroons. The British were unlikely to free any slaves unless necessary and would not have deemed it so if slaves were volunteering in significant numbers. This continued offer of financial reward and promised freedom, therefore, shows that the colonial government had failed in its attempt to create utter disharmony between the Maroons and the enslaved population of Jamaica. If anything, the Second Maroon War demonstrates the apathy of the slaves when deciding whether to join a side—presumably because of the fear that they may choose the "wrong" side.

As alluded to earlier, African American slaves also joined the Redsticks when war broke out in the United States in 1813. It is almost impossible to ascertain how many did so, perhaps even harder than in the Maroon case. We are limited to fleeting mentions of African American allies of the Redsticks mentioned in the archives. For example, before the battle of Fort Mims, a group of African Americans informed the Redsticks of American attack plans, and when the attack began, a black man named Siras was said to have "cut down the Pickets" so the Redsticks could enter the fort.[116] In one account of the battle, Hillis Hadjo, a leading prophet, recalled that during the Fort Mims attack, "the blacks were the first in" and that one African American had single-handedly "killed seven Americans in that affair."[117] According to the later reminisces of an eyewitness, Alexander McGillivray's former slaves had actually helped set fire to the fort.[118] On another occasion, when Redstick morale was on the wane, their African American allies were said to have urged them on in battle, fighting together to defeat the enemy.[119]

In a reflection of the contradictory attitudes demonstrated by Maroons towards Afro-descended peoples, Redsticks scalped some blacks at Fort Mims, but they also abducted 243 from the fort and its surrounding area.[120] It is unclear whether these slaves were abducted in the true sense or if they had "got with the Indians" of their own accord. However, once they arrived where the Redsticks were taking them, a town called Eccanachaca near present-day Montgomery, Alabama, they assisted in the defence of that town when it came under attack by the Americans.[121] Again, it is not apparent whether they were forced into this role, although it seems they took to it rather well when the attack began. One American officer contended that the "negroes were the last to quit the ground" during the battle. These African Americans paid a price for their part in the fighting, as ten or twelve were eventually killed by American soldiers.[122] After the hostilities, an American officer claimed that, "It was customary with the hostile Indians to make the negro men with them fight against the white people."[123] The Americans, at least, seemed to place the blame for African American actions at the feet of the Redsticks. The alliance between Redsticks and African Americans, however, continued after the defeat of the Redsticks when both groups retreated to Seminole country to regroup and launch later attacks.[124]

Therefore, as we have seen, there are examples of both Maroons and Creeks, to varying degrees, participating in the act of slave-catching—as dictated by the amalgamation of laws, treaties and individual instigation which demanded it. Further, the motivations of both groups bear similarities. That said, we can never read too much into the actions of communities who have left behind few records. We can only rely on fragments of European-authored sources which quote Maroon and Creek voices to decipher their actions. Some may have held grudges against particular African Americans for past grievances; others may have been driven by hunger and the need for money to purchase food. Indeed, motivations to hunt runaways could be contradictory with earlier actions, even within the same person as exemplified by McGillivray's willingness to hunt or harbour runaways waxing and waning dependent on his contact with the Spanish, British and Americans. On those occasions when Maroons or Creeks did hunt slaves, it could be argued that both groups contributed to the consolidation of slavery in Jamaica and the United States. However, the reality of the situation does not allow for a clear demarcation of defending or resisting slavery by either group. Instead, the willingness to return slave runaways was often connected to the state of the relationships with the British or Americans when a particular incident occurred. There is no evidence which proclaims a stated support for either side of the argument. Instead, the act of returning runaways could be used as a pawn in the larger power games both within and without Maroon and Creek society. Both groups could withhold their assistance in locating runaways in order to better their negotiating stance—whether their desired goals were greater financial reward, an improved peace treaty, or more land. In the south-east of the United States, and even more so in Jamaica, Europeans were terrified of slave revolt so, given the decreasing economic might of the Creeks and the already limited trade opportunities of Maroons, hunting runaways became a weapon which both communities could wield at the negotiating table given the relative lack of alternative options.

Whatever the motivation, it is likely that both Maroons and Creeks also used the act of hunting runaways to hone their traditional skills. John N. Grant sees slave-catching as one of the few ways that Maroons could use their unparalleled ability as woodsmen and exercise their love of combat, as well as offering both excitement and payment.[125] Young Maroons may have relished the opportunity to prove themselves as men by hunting and catching runaways. This is why, in some ways, it is surprising that the colonial government advocated hunting runaways so strongly. Hunting runaways meant that the Maroons kept physically fit, enhanced their knowledge of the interior of the island, and were able to exercise their martial skills—all of which could pose a threat to the colonial order of the island. In other words, such an act presented opportunities to continue many Maroon traditions and, thus, solidify their identity as a separate community. Similarly, young Creeks were disproportionately impacted by the decreasing deerskin trade. Unable to prove their masculinity by hunting deer, slave-catching provided warriors an opportunity to maintain their skills of tracking and, if necessary, attacking. In this way, it is difficult to understand why the colonial and federal governments would encourage Maroons and Creeks to partake in acts which provided such training.

In other ways, it is not hard to see why colonial and federal officials wrote clauses into peace treaties with Maroon and Creek communities obliging them to hunt runaways. Firstly, a slave rebellion was always feared across the slave-holding societies of the Caribbean and the United States.[126] Rumours of plots and uprisings played on the minds of many slave-owners and led to severe punishments for dissent and disobedience.[127] Even more of a threat was the thought of rebellious slaves joining with armed groups of Maroons or Creeks who had honed their fighting skills across the mountains of Jamaica, or the hills and plains of the south-east. White British and Americans, therefore, tried to sow dissension between such potential allies at every opportunity—incentives for slave-catching being a particularly effective one. Secondly, because of their movement across and around difficult territories during their hunts, whether for wild boar or deer, Maroons and Creeks had knowledge of the likely haunts of slave runaways that Europeans could never hope to achieve. Finally, the image and practice of a Maroon or Creek being ordered by a white man to hunt slave runaways was a strategic coup for both governments. The actual motivations of Maroons and Creeks when hunting runaways may have mattered little to white Jamaicans and Americans. The act painted Maroons and Creeks as subservient and contributed to the long battle to undermine the independence of these semi-autonomous communities. In other words, it was a propaganda victory for the British and the Americans.

It does seem from this study that there was a higher frequency of slave-catching by Maroons than for Creeks. There are several possible reasons for this. A significant one is that those Maroons who were inclined to hunt runaways had more opportunity to do so than their Creek counterparts. The proportion of the population that was enslaved was far larger in Jamaica than in the United States, meaning that colonists feared more runaways.[128] In addition to this, there was only a small free black population, often within urban areas, in which potential runaways could hope to hide themselves in Jamaica.[129] If slaves did not run to the urban free black population, the next likely destination was the mountainous interior of the island—the domain of the Maroons. Further, the relative lack of other free communities in Jamaica capable of hunting slaves meant that colonists had to rely on Maroons, so, as a result, they were called upon more often.[130] Conversely, runaway slaves in the south-eastern United States could, and did, flee to the Spanish territories, other indigenous communities, or the North.[131] Creeks were able only to effectively hunt runaways in their own lands, which simply reduced the opportunities for Creeks to partake in the act, even if they had desired to do so.

It must not be overlooked that many, if not the majority of, Maroons and Creeks who did hunt runaways were motivated by financial reward. Indeed, there are records of both groups withholding their services until additional rewards were offered or arrears paid. These demands were often made when the request to hunt the runaway was received, demonstrating how slave-catching had become a negotiation tool of both groups. The financial side of the arrangement is important as an explanation for the motivation of Maroon and Creek slave-catchers, but also as a reason why Creeks seemed to hunt fewer slaves than Maroons. Quite simply, Creeks were less dependent on the income generated by slave-catching than Maroons. As will be explored in Chapter 6, Creeks could sell their wares to U.S.-owned trade stores, individual traders, or the Spanish. Whilst Maroons could also take their goods to the colonial markets of Jamaica, they grew little that colonists could not procure elsewhere. Few Maroon communities cultivated a surplus of produce and, aside from the selling of jerked pork and tobacco, had limited income.[132] Therefore, out of necessity, many Maroons had to turn to slave-catching.

A major difference between the Maroons and Creeks with regard to enslaved people was in the suppression of rebellions. As shown, Maroons frequently participated in this act, but there is no evidence that any Creeks aided in the suppression of any slave uprisings. One of the primary reasons for this was again location. Maroons were simply better placed to assist the colonial government during a slave uprising. Their location in the heart of the island and their extensive knowledge of tracks, roads and paths, along with their frequent activity of hunting wild boar, meant that they were ideally situated to aid the colonists. Conversely, Creeks, living in their still vast territories, far removed from the larger concentrations of slaves in the coastal regions, would take days, if not weeks, to assemble and provide any kind of military support. Therefore, even if there had been any desire to aid the Americans, the feasibility of doing so was affected by such a location.

Also worth considering is the fact that Maroons seemed to have a more amicable relationship with the local whites in Jamaica than Creeks did with the local whites in Georgia. This will be explored in more detail in Chapter 6, but suffice to say here that this situation meant that Maroons may have been more willing to come to the aid of local whites in times of rebellion than many Creeks were. Or, viewed from a different angle, local whites in Georgia would have been unlikely to turn to the Creeks for help in times of rebellion because of their fractious relationship. There was constant fighting along the frontier and if slaves rebelled near Creek territory, it is unlikely that Georgian settlers would think that many Creeks would come to their aid.

Why did the British trust Maroons to suppress slave rebellions? After all, these were communities made up of former slaves, descendants of slaves and indigenous Africans who had fought alongside parts of the enslaved population during the First Maroon War. There are several possibilities. One is that the Maroons were a formidable fighting force that had never tasted defeat—a worthy ally for any government. It could also have been that the government had little other option—unlike the United States, with its borders shared with numerous indigenous communities, Jamaica had no alternative. Without the Maroons on their side, actively suppressing the rebellions, colonists would have been at the mercy of a large slave rebellion. Also important were the actions of the Maroons themselves. As outlined in Chapter 1, the Maroons immediately took to their new duties with vigour. Without this, and Cudjoe's strong centralised power, it is unlikely that the colonial government would have trusted the Maroons with suppressing rebellions. It was, of course, not unusual for British colonists to enlist the support of indigenous communities when fighting resistance to their rule.[133] Therefore it is unsurprising that a similar tactic was utilised in Jamaica.

Why, then, did the federal government not utilise any willing Creeks in the same manner? The Creeks were also undoubtedly a fighting force to be reckoned with, yet the Creeks were not involved with suppressing slave rebellions in the way that Maroon groups were. As with the low levels of slave-catching, one of the primary reasons again seems to have been the location of many Creeks. Far removed from the sites of slave rebellions, it would have made little sense to attempt to muster Creek warriors to march across the south-east in an attempt to quell any uprising that may have broken out. The Euro Americans who lived near the border with the Creek territory generally owned only a handful of slaves, a situation which was not amenable to slaves launching a large-scale rebellion. The slave rebellions which did break out in the United States during the period under study were far away from Creek territory, for example, Gabriel's Rebellion in 1800 which broke out in Virginia, meaning suppression of them was less associated with the Creeks.[134] In addition, given the reluctance of the majority of Creeks to assist the United States in any way, federal officials would have found it difficult to find any volunteers willing to aid in the suppression of a rebellion. Conversely, slaves in Jamaica lived in relative proximity to each other; the plantations were large and grouped closely together, meaning rebellion could spread quickly across the island. As a consequence, slave rebellions simply broke out more often in Jamaica than in the United States, meaning colonists had to find an effective ally.

Therefore, we can see that in both cases, contradictory actions took place within communities, towns, and even within individuals when it came to the return of runaways and suppressing rebellions. There is no clear way to determine which Maroons and Creeks took part and which refused to do so. To generalise, we can see that both communities, in the pre-treaty years, were often havens for slave runaways but that, with the signing of the treaties, there was a turn towards slave-catching usually for economic reasons. But, whilst some Maroons and Creeks took part in such acts, others continued to provide shelter for runaway slaves, whether because of familial ties, hatred of European society, in defiance of slavery, or for any other of a myriad of reasons. The outbreak of war forced some into taking sides but largely continued the complex situation, with some slaves being welcomed into the ranks while others joined the Americans or British. The British and Americans strove to force divides between these semi-autonomous communities and the enslaved populations that resided in the regions. Neither was wholly successful in this endeavour and the complexities which had been present before the peace treaties continued once they were signed.

Notes

1. *Journals of the House of Assembly of Jamaica (JHA)*, 1st March 1739, Vol. III, National Archives of Jamaica, Spanish Town, Jamaica (NAJ).
2. JHA, 23rd June 1739, Vol. III, NAJ.
3. *Ibid.*
4. Treaty of New York, August 1790, Entry No. 108, RG11, National Archives, Washington DC, USA (NA).
5. *Ibid.*
6. For more on Creeks, colonists, and slaves see Gary Zellar, *African Creeks: Estelvste and the Creek Nation* (Norman: University of Oklahoma Press, 2007); John T. Juricek, *Endgame for Empire: British-Creek Relations in Georgia and Vicinity* (Gainesville: University Press of Florida, 2015).
7. Joshua Piker, 'Colonists and Creeks: Re-thinking the Pre-Revolutionary Southern Backcountry,' *The Journal of Southern History*, 70, 3 (Aug., 2004), 514.
8. Claudio Saunt, *A New Order of Things: Property, Power and the Transformation of the Creek Indians, 1733–1816* (Cambridge: Cambridge University Press, 1999), 52.
9. Edward Long Papers, Add. Ms. 12431, British Library, London, United Kingdom (BL).
10. Frank Wesley Pitman, *The Development of the British West Indies, 1700–1763* (New Haven: Yale University Press, 1917), 121.
11. Mavis Campbell, *The Maroons of Jamaica, 1655–1796: A History of Resistance, Collaboration & Betrayal* (Trentin: Africa World Press, 1990), 147.
12. See Wilbur H. Siebert, 'Slavery and White Servitude in East Florida, 1726–1776,' *Florida Historical Quarterly*, 10 (1931), 3–23; and Siebert, 'Slavery and White Servitude in East Florida, 1776–1785,' *Florida Historical Quarterly*, 10 (1932), 139–161.
13. Peter H. Wood, 'The Changing Population of the Colonial South: An Overview of Race and Region, 1785–1790,' in *Powhatan's Mantle: Indians in the Colonial Southeast*, eds. Peter H. Wood, Gregory A. Waselkov and M. Thomas Hatley (Lincoln: University of Nebraska Press, 1989), 38.
14. William Bartram, *Travels of William Bartram*, ed. Mark van Doren (New York: Dover Publications, 1955), 183. For more on Native American adoption, see Max Carocci and Stephanie Pratt, eds., *Native American Adoption, Captivity, and Slavery in Changing Contexts* (New York: Palgrave Macmillan, 2012).
15. John Stuart to Thomas Gage, 26th September 1767, Thomas Gage Papers (TGB), American series, reel 140H, P. K. Yonge Library of Florida History, University of Florida, Gainesville (PKY).
16. John Alden, *John Stuart and the Southern Colonial Frontier: A Study of Indian Relations, War, Trade, and Land Problems in the Southern Wilderness, 1754–1775* (London: Oxford University Press, 1944), 233.
17. John Stuart to Thomas Gage, 2nd July 1768, Thomas Gage Papers, American series, reel 140H, PKY.
18. Luis de Unzaga y Amezaga to Peter Chester, 7th March 1777, PC, leg. 190, 478, reel 261, PKY.
19. Governor Martin to Tallassee King, 19th July 1782, ST, bnd. 6677, PC leg. 121/40, PKY.
20. Patrick Riordan, 'Seminole Genesis; Native Americans, African Americans, and Colonists on the Southern Frontier from Prehistory through the Colonial Era' (Ph.D. diss., Florida State University Press, 1996), 250–252.
21. Murdoch McLeod to James Jackson, 6th May 1799, Creek Indian Letters, Talks and Treaties, 1705–1839, ed. Louise F. Hays (typescript in Georgia Department of Archives and History), Vol. II, 558–559.
22. Estevan Miró to Arturo O'Neill, 29th November 1785, PC, leg. 3B, 1079, reel 155, PKY; Nota de los Negros, 29th November 1785, PC, leg. 3A, 721, reel 154, PKY;

Arturo O'Neill to Estevan Miró, 16th December 1785, PC, leg. 37, bnd. 1, doc. 50, reel 169, PKY; Estevan Miró to Arturo O'Neill, 26th May 1786, PC, leg. 40, 63, reel 193, PKY.

23. Arturo O'Neill to Bernardo de Gálvez, 15th October 1781, PC, leg. 36, 249, reel 183, PKY.

24. Executive Deputy of Georgia to the Chehaw King, 5th March 1799, Reel 12, ANC, LOC.

25. Carlos Howard to Juan Nepomuceno de Quesada, 21st April 1792, EF, bnd. 128K1, 1795–218, reel 51, PKY.

26. *Ibid.*

27. Alexander McGillivray to Captain Folch, 2nd March 1790, PC, leg. 52, Elizabeth Howard West Papers, PKY.

28. Alexander McGillivray to Vicente Folch, 2nd March 1789, Reel 5, Archivo Nacional de Cuba (ANC), Library of Congress, Washington, D.C., United States (LOC).

29. Benjamin Sims to Jerrard Irwin, 11th July 1807, Reel 17, ANC, LOC.

30. B. Harris to D. Mitchell, 8th November 1810, Reel 18, ANC, LOC.

31. Benjamin Hawkins to Chiefs of the Twelve Towns of the Lower Creeks, 24th April 1808, in *The Collected Works of Benjamin Hawkins*, ed. H. Thomas Foster (Tuscaloosa: University of Alabama Press, 2003), 535.

32. Memorial of Alexander Bisset, 1st October 1788, LOC, PKY; Vicente Manuel de Zéspedes to José de Ezpeleta, 3rd November 1788, Lockey Collection (LC), Archivo General de Indias, Seville (AGI), (microfilm in leg. 1395, PKY; Josef de Espeleta to Vicente Manuel De Zéspedes, 19th December 1788, EF, bnd. 1B, 318, reel I, PKY).

33. Luis de las Casas to Juan Nepomuceno de Quesada, 21st July 1790, EF, bnd. 1C, 527, reel I, PKY.

34. Article Three, Treaty of New York, August 1790, Entry No. 108, RG11, NA.

35. Carlos Howard to Juan Nepomuceno de Quesada, 16th April 1795, EF, bnd. 128K10, 1795–218, reel 51, PKY.

36. Andrew Atkinson to Carols Howard, 15th May 1795, EF, bnd. 128K10, doc. 1795–287, reel 51, PKY.

37. *Ibid*, 438.

38. Robert C. Dallas, *The History of the Maroons: From Their Origin to the Establishment of Their Chief Tribe at Sierra Leone: Including the Expedition to Cuba, for the Purpose of Procuring Spanish Chasseurs: And the State of the Island of Jamaica for the Last Ten Years: With a Succinct History of the Island Previous to That Period* (London: Printed by A. Strahan. . ., for T.N. Longman and O. Rees. . ., 1803), Vol. I, 101.

39. Examination of a Negro Man Slave Named Sambo, the Property of Richard Hampton Reid Esq. one of the Baggage Negroes Sent with the Detachment Under the Command of Captain Charles Brown on the 16th October 1795, CO 137/96, National Archives, Kew, United Kingdom (NA).

40. W. J. Gardner, *The History of Jamaica from Its Discovery . . . to the Year 1872* (1st edition 1873), new edition (London: T. Fisher Unwin, 1909), 14.

41. Edward Long, *The History of Jamaica: Or, General Survey of the Ancient and Modern State of That Island: With Reflections on its Situations, Settlements, Inhabitants, Climate, Products, Commerce, Laws, and Government* (London: F. Cass, 1970), Vol. II, 465.

42. Thomas Thistlewood in *In Miserable Slavery: Thomas Thistlewood in Jamaica, 1750–86*, ed. Douglas Hall (Macmillan: London and Basingstoke, 1989), 244.

43. Dallas, *History of the Maroons*, Vol. I, 90.

44. James Knight, "History," Add. Ms. 12415, BL.

45. JHA, 1st May 1742, Vol. III, NAJ.

46. Edward Long Manuscripts, BM: Ad. MS. 12431, BL.

47. JHA, 1st May 1742, Vol. III, NAJ.

48. James Knight, "History," Add. Ms. 12415, BL; JHA, 1st May 1742, Vol. III, NAJ.

49. Edward Long Manuscript, BM: Ad. MS. 12431, BL.

50. *JHA*, 2nd December 1742, Vol. III, NAJ.
51. William Beckford, to James Knight, 11th October 1740, Add. Ms 12431, 1740; 19th August 1741, Add. Ms. 12431, BL.
52. Dallas, *History of the Maroons*, Vol. I, 97.
53. *Ibid.*
54. *Acts of Assembly Passed in the Island of Jamaica from 1681 to 1733 Inclusive* (BL), CSF., 154/4, 251.
55. For more on Caribbean slave rebellions, see Johannes Postma, *Slave Revolts* (Westport, CT: Greenwood Press, 2008); Junius P. Rodriguez, ed., *Encyclopedia of Slave Resistance and Rebellion* (Westport, CT: Greenwood Press, 2007); Michael Craton ed., *Testing the Chains: Resistance to Slavery in the British West Indies* (Ithaca: Cornell University Press, 1982); Gelien Matthews, *Caribbean Slave Revolts and the British Abolitionist Movement* (Baton Rouge: Louisiana State University Press, 2006); Eugene D. Genovese, *From Rebellion to Revolution: Afro-American Slave Revolts in the Making of the Modern World* (Baton Rouge: Louisiana State University Press, 1979).
56. Long, *History*, Vol. II, 447.
57. *JHA*, 27th January 1746, Vol. IV, NAJ.
58. *JHA*, 12th April 1752, Vol. IV, NAJ.
59. *JHA*, 2nd and 4th November 1752, Vol. IX, NAJ.
60. Minutes of the Meeting Held at Spanish Town, 10th April 1760, CO 137/32, NA.
61. Long, *History*, Vol. II, 451.
62. *Ibid.*
63. Bryan Edwards, *The Proceedings of the Governor and Assembly of Jamaica, in Regard to the Maroon Negroes: Published by Order of the Assembly. To Which Is Prefixed, an Introductory Account, Containing, Observations on the Disposition, Character, Manners, and Habits of Life, of the Maroons, and, a Detail of the Origin, Progress, and Termination of the Late War Between Those People and the White Inhabitants* (London: John Stockdale, 1796), 268.
64. Long, *History*, Vol. II, 462, 471.
65. Although there is historical debate about whether Tacky's revolt constituted a singular, coherent event, Bollettino casts the battles in the larger context of the Seven Years' War. Maria Alessandra Bollettino, 'Slavery, War and Britain's Atlantic Empire: Black Soldiers, Sailors, and Rebels in the Seven Years' War' (Ph.D. diss., University of Texas at Austin, 2009), 21.
66. Edwards, *The History, Civil and Commercial. . .*, 545.
67. Richard Hart, *Slaves Who Abolished Slavery: Blacks in Rebellion* (Kingston: University of the West Indies Press, 2002), 137.
68. Long, *The History of Jamaica*, 445.
69. Edwards, *The History, Civil and Commercial. . .*, 61.
70. *Ibid.*, 543.
71. *JHA*, 28th July 1760, Vol. V, NAJ.
72. Council Minutes, 17th April 1760, CO 137/42, NA.
73. Long, *The History of Jamaica*, 447.
74. Thistlewood in *In Miserable Slavery*, 128–129.
75. *Ibid.*, 133.
76. For more on Three Fingered Jack, see Frances R. Botkin, *Thieving Three-Fingered Jack: Transatlantic Tales of a Jamaican Outlaw, 1780–2015* (New Brunswick: Rutgers University Press, 2017).
77. *JHA*, 18th and 22nd December 1781, Vol. VII, NAJ.
78. Jack Goody, *The Domestication of the Strange Mind* (Cambridge: Cambridge University Press, 1977), Chapter Five; Goody, *The Interface Between the Written and the Oral* (Cambridge: Cambridge University Press, 1987), Chapter Eight.
79. Estevan Miró to Arturo O'Neill, 15th October 1785, PC, leg. 40, 48, reel 193, PKY; Arturo O'Neill to Estevan Miró, 7th November 1785, PC, leg. 37, bnd. 1, doc. 43, reel 169, PKY; Alexander McGillivray to Arturo O'Neill, 21st

February 1786, PC, leg. 199, 770, reel 383, PKY; Arturo O'Neill to Estevan Miró, 12th March 1786, PC, leg. 37, bnd. 2, doc. 67, reel 169, PKY; Estevan Miró to Arturo O'Neill, 25th April 1786, PC, leg. 37, bnd. 8, doc. 304, reel 169, PKY.

80. Alexander McGillivray to Arturo O'Neill, 10th February 1786, PC, leg. 199, 767, reel 383, PKY.

81. Alexander McGillivray to Arturo O'Neill, 5th October 1786, PC, leg. 199, 791, reel 383, PKY.

82. Arturo O'Neill to Esteban Miró, 10th September 1788, Reel 4, ANC, LOC.

83. John Forrester to Governor Juan Nepomuceno de Quesada, 23rd April 1793, EFL; Jack Kinnard to the Cuseta King, Hallowing King, Young Prince, and Chiefs of the Lower Creeks, 25th May 1793, EFL.

84. Claudio Saunt, '"The English Has Now a Mind to Make Slaves of Them All": Creeks, Seminoles and the Problem of Slavery,' *American Indian Quarterly*, 22, 1/2 (Winter–Spring, 1998), 166.

85. Benjamin James to Mather and Strother, 23rd July 1787, Reel 3, ANC, LOC.

86. Long, *History of Jamaica*, Vol. I, 223.

87. *Acts of Assembly Passed in the Island of Jamaica from 1681 to 1733 Inclusive* (BL), CSF., 154/7, 204.

88. *JHA*, 7th December 1791, Vol. IX, NAJ.

89. *JHA*, 18th December 1781, Vol. VII, NAJ.

90. *JHA*, 11th December 1787, Vol. XIII, NAJ.

91. *JHA*, 12th December 1792, Vol. IX, NAJ.

92. *JHA*, 12th November 1761, Vol. V, NAJ.

93. *Ibid.*

94. Benjamin Hawkins to Daniel Stewart, 13th October 1799, in *The Collected Works of Benjamin Hawkins*, ed. H. Thomas Foster (Tuscaloosa: University of Alabama Press, 2003), 213.

95. Kathryn E. Holland Braund, *Deerskins and Duffels: The Creek Indian Trade with Anglo-America, 1685–1815* (Lincoln: University of Nebraska Press, 1996), 74.

96. Benjamin Hawkins to Chiefs of the Twelve Towns of the Lower Creeks, 24th April 1808, *Collected Works*, 535.

97. Executive Deputy of Georgia to the Chehaw King, 5th March 1799, Reel 12, ANC, LOC.

98. Abner Hammond to James Jackson, 8th November 1798, Reel 11, ANC, LOC.

99. Mad Dog to John Forbes, 31st May 1801, Reel 13, ANC, LOC.

100. *JHA*, 1st December 1769, Vol. VI, NAJ.

101. For more on this so-called *petit marronage*, see F. Gomes, 'Africans and Petit Marronage in Rio de Janeiro, 1800–1840,' *Luso-Brazilian Review*, 47, 2 (2010), 74–99; Marcus Peyton Nevius, 'Lurking About the Neighbourhood: Slave Economy and Petit Marronage in Virginia and North Carolina, 1730 to 1860' (Ph.D. diss., Ohio State University, 2016.

102. Piker, 'Colonists and Creeks,' 526.

103. Dallas, *History of the Maroons*, Vol. I, 176.

104. Henry Shirley to Major General Taylor, 20th October 1795, CO 137/96, NA.

105. Alexander Crawford Lindsay, *Lives of the Lindsays: Or a Memoir of the Houses of Crawford and Balcarres. . .* (Wigan: Privately Printed, 1840), 77–78.

106. *Ibid.*, 23, 88.

107. *Ibid.*, 23, 92–93.

108. *Ibid.*

109. *Ibid.*

110. Report of Benjamin Hawkins, 17th September 1813, enclosed in Hawkins to Armstrong, 21st September 1813, in *Letters of Benjamin Hawkins, 1796–1806* (Savannah: Published by the Georgia Historical Society, 1916), Vol. II, 665.

111. Dallas, *History of the Maroons*, Vol. II, 143.

112. Henry Shirley to Major General Taylor, 20th October 1795, CO 137/96, NA.

113. Copy of a Letter from the Magistrates of St. James, 18th July 1795, 3rd August 1795, WO 1/92, NA.

114. Carey Robinson, *The Iron Thorn: The Defeat of the British by the Jamaican Maroons* (Kingston: Kingston Publishers Limited, 1993), 198.

115. Balcarres to the Duke of Portland, 3rd August 1795, WO 1/92, NA.

116. "A Historical Narration of the Genealogy, Traditions, and Downfall of the Ispocoga or Creek Tribe of Indians," PKY; Extract of a communication from the chiefs at Coweta to Benjamin Hawkins, 16th September 1813, *Letters of Benjamin Hawkins*, 1797–1915, ed. Louise F. Hays (typescript in GDAH), 248.

117. Colonel Nicolls to Alexander Cochrane, August through November 1814, Cochrane Papers, MS 2328, 59, reel 65M, No. 1, PKY.

118. Thomas Simpson Woodward, *Woodward's Reminiscences of the Creek, or Miscogee Indians, Contained in Letters to Friends in Georgia and Alabama* (Tuscaloosa: Alabama Book Stores, 1939), 99.

119. "A historical narration of the genealogy, traditions, and downfall of the Ispocoga or Creek tribe of Indians, Written by One of the Tribe," original in the Draper Manuscripts, State Historical Society of Wisconsin, (microfilm reel, 1461, PKY).

120. Mateo González Manrique to Juan Ruiz de Apodaca, 2nd October 1813, PC, leg. 1794, 1821, reel 113, PKY; Extract of a communication from the chiefs at Coweta to Benjamin Hawkins, 16th September 1813, LBH, 248, GDAH; Benjamin Hawkins to John B. Floyd, 26th September 1813, *LBH*, Vol. II, 667.

121. Article from *Mobile Register*, September 1884, Draper ss. 10U10, reel 146E, PKY.

122. *United States Serial Set (USSS)*.H.doc 200 (20-I), 173: 12, Florida State University (FSU).

123. *USSS*.H.doc 200 (20-I), 173: 12 (FSU).

124. *USSS*.H.doc 200 (20-I), 173: 11 (FSU). For more on the Seminole War, see John Missall and Mary Lou Missall, *The Seminole Wars: America's Longest Indian Conflict* (Gainesville: University Press of Florida, 2004); Joe Knetsch, *Florida's Seminole Wars, 1817–1858 (The Making of America)* (Mount Pleasant: Arcadia Publishing, 2003); Henrietta Buckmaster, *The Seminole Wars* (New York: Macmillan, 1966); Deborah A. Rosen, *Border Law: The First Seminole War and American Nationhood* (Cambridge, MA: Harvard University Press, 2015).

125. John N. Grant, *The Maroons in Nova Scotia* (Halifax: Formac, 2002), 21.

126. J. T. Sharples, 'Discovering Slave Conspiracies: New Fears of Rebellion and Old Paradigms of Plotting in Seventeenth-Century Barbados,' *The American Historical Review*, 120, 8 (2015), 811–843; Carl Lawrence Paulus, *The Slaveholding Crisis: Fear of Insurrection and the Coming of the Civil War* (Baton Rouge: Louisiana State University Press, 2017).

127. For more on slave punishments, see J. Savage, 'Unwanted Slaves: The Punishment of Transportation and the Making of Legal Subjects in Early Nineteenth-Century Martinique,' *Citizenship Studies*, 10, 1 (2006), 35–53; Diana Paton, 'Punishment, Crime, and the Bodies of Slaves in Eighteenth Century Jamaica,' *Journal of Social History*, 34, 4 (2001), 923–954; Ramesh Mallipeddi, *Spectacular Suffering, Witnessing Slavery in the Eighteenth-Century British Atlantic* (Charlottesville: University of Virginia Press, 2016); Glenn McNair, *Criminal Injustice: Slaves and Free Blacks in Georgia's Criminal Justice System* (Charlottesville: University of Virginia Press, 2009); James M. Campbell, *Slavery on Trial: Race, Class, and Criminal Justice in Antebellum Richmond, Virginia* (Gainesville: University Press of Florida, 2007); Peter M. Beattie, *Punishment in Paradise: Race, Slavery, Human Rights, and a Nineteenth-Century Brazilian Penal Colony* (Durham: Duke University Press, 2015); Gwenda Morgan and Peter Rushton, *Banishment in the Early Atlantic World: Convicts, Rebels and Slaves* (London: Bloomsbury Academic, 2013); A. K. Brown, '"A Black Mark on Our Legislation": Slavery, Punishment, and the Politics of Death in Nineteenth-Century Brazil,' *Luso-Brazilian Review*, 37, 2 (2000), 95–122; A. De V. Phillips, '"Doubly Condemned": Adjustments

to the Crime and Punishment Regime in the Late Slavery Period in the British Caribbean Colonies,' *Cardozo Law Review*, 18, 2 (1996), 699–716; James M. Campbell, *Crime and Punishment in African American History* (Basingstoke: Palgrave Macmillan, 2012); Diana Paton, *No Bond but the Law: Punishment, Race, and Gender in Jamaican State Formation, 1780–1870* (Durham: Duke University Press, 2004).

128. Barry Higman, *Slave Population and Economy in Jamaica, 1807–1834* (Barbados: University of the West Indies Press, 1995); Paul Finkelman, ed., *Slave Trade and Migration: Domestic and Foreign* (New York: Garland, 1989).

129. Gad Heuman, *Between Black and White: Race, Politics and the Free Coloureds in Jamaica, 1792–1865* (Oxford: Clio Press, 1981); Alexander X. Byrd, *Captives and Voyagers: Black Migrants Across the Eighteenth-Century British Atlantic World* (Baton Rouge: Louisiana State University Press, 2008).

130. Kenneth Morgan, *Slavery and the British Empire: From Africa to America* (Oxford: Oxford University Press, 2007), 133.

131. Jane Landers, *Black Society in Spanish Florida* (Urbana: University of Illinois Press, 1999); Nathaniel Millett, 'Slave Resistance During the Age of Revolution: The Maroon Community at Prospect Bluff, Spanish Florida' (Ph.D. diss., University of Cambridge, 2002); Don H. Hagist, *Wives, Slaves, and Servant Girls: Advertisements for Female Runaways in American Newspapers, 1770–1783* (Yardley: Westholme Publishing, 2016); Paul Finkelman, ed., *Rebellions, Resistance, and Runaways Within the Slave South* (New York: Gardland, 1989); Lathan A. Windley, *A Profile of Runaway Slaves in Virginia and South Carolina from 1730 Through 1787* (New York: Routledge, 2014); John Hope Franklin and Loren Schweninger, *Runaway Slaves: Rebels on the Plantation* (Oxford: Oxford University Press, 2000); Cassandra Pybus, *Epic Journey of Freedom: Runaway Slaves of the American Revolution and Their Global Quest for Liberty* (Boston: Beacon Press, 2006).

132. Dallas, *History of the Maroons*, Vol. I, 110.

133. Jarvis Brownlie, '"Our Fathers Fought for the British": Racial Discourses and Indigenous Allies in Upper Canada,' *Histoire Sociale/Social History*, 50, 102 (2017), 259–284; Tanja Bührer, Flavio Eichmann, Stig Förster and Benedikt Stuchtey, eds., *Cooperation and Empire: Local Realities of Global Processes* (New York: Berghahn Books, 2017); John C. Mitcham, *Race and Imperial Defence in the British World, 1870–1914* (Cambridge: Cambridge University Press, 2016).

134. Douglas R. Egerton, *Gabriel's Rebellion: The Virginia Slave Conspiracies of 1800 and 1802* (Chapel Hill: University of North Carolina Press, 1993).

Bibliography

Primary Sources

Beinecke Rare Book and Manuscript Library, Yale University, New Haven, United States

Thomas Thistlewood Papers.

British Library, London, United Kingdom

Acts of Assembly Passed in the Island of Jamaica from 1681 to 1733 Inclusive.
Edward Long Manuscripts.

Galileo Online Digital Library of Georgia (website)

South-eastern Native American Documents, 1730–1842.

Georgia Department of Archives and History, Morrow, Georgia, United States

Colonial Records of the State of Georgia.
"Creek Indian Letters, Talks, and Treaties, 1705–1839."
"Creek Letters, 1800–1819."
"Indian Treaties: Cessions of Land in Georgia, 1705–1837."
"Letters of Benjamin Hawkins, 1797–1815."
Miscellaneous Creek Indian Documents.
South-eastern Native American Documents Database.
Treaty at Fort Wilkinson with the Creek Indians, 1802.
Unpublished Letters of Timothy Barnard, 1784–1820.

Florida State University, Tallahassee, United States

United States Serial Set (USSS).

Library of Congress, Washington, D.C., United States

Archivo Nacional de Cuba Collection (microfilm).

National Archives, Kew, United Kingdom

CO 137/96	CO 137/97	CO 137/98
WO 1/95	WO 1/96	

National Archives of Jamaica, Spanish Town, Jamaica

Journals of the House of Assembly, Vols. I–X.

National Archives and Records Office, Washington, D.C., United States

Foreign Letters of the Continental Congress and the Department of State.
Records of the Bureau of Indian Affairs.

P. K. Yonge Library, University of Florida, Gainesville, United States

Archivo General de Indias (microfilm).
East Florida Papers (microfilm).
Papeles Procedentes de Cuba (microfilm).
Records of the Creek Trading House, Letter Book, 1795–1816.
Thomas Gage Papers.

Special Collections, University of Georgia, Athens, United States

Southeastern Native American Documents, 1730–1842.

Ph.D. Sources

Bollettino, Maria Alessandra, 'Slavery, War and Britain's Atlantic Empire: Black Soldiers, Sailors, and Rebels in the Seven Years' War' (Ph.D. diss., University of Texas at Austin, 2009).

Millett, Nathaniel, 'Slave Resistance During the Age of Revolution: The Maroon Community at Prospect Bluff, Spanish Florida' (Ph.D. diss., University of Cambridge, 2002).

Nevius, Marcus Peyton, 'Lurking About the Neighbourhood: Slave Economy and Petit Marronage in Virginia and North Carolina, 1730 to 1860' (Ph.D. diss., Ohio State University, 2016).

Riordan, Patrick, 'Seminole Genesis; Native Americans, African Americans, and Colonists on the Southern Frontier from Prehistory through the Colonial Era' (Ph.D. diss., Florida State University Press, 1996).

Published Sources

Alden, John, *John Stuart and the Southern Colonial Frontier: A Study of Indian Relations, War, Trade, and Land Problems in the Southern Wilderness, 1754–1775* (London: Oxford University Press, 1944).

Bartram, William, *Observations on the Creek and Cherokee Indians* (New York: American Ethnological Society, 1853).

Beattie, Peter M., *Punishment in Paradise: Race, Slavery, Human Rights, and a Nineteenth-Century Brazilian Penal Colony* (Durham: Duke University Press, 2015).

Botkin, Frances R., *Thieving Three-Fingered Jack: Transatlantic Tales of a Jamaican Outlaw, 1780–2015* (New Brunswick: Rutgers University Press, 2017).

Braund, Kathryn E. Holland, *Deerskins and Duffels: The Creek Indian Trade with Anglo-America, 1685–1815* (Lincoln: University of Nebraska Press, 1996).

Brown, A. K., '"A Black Mark on Our Legislation": Slavery, Punishment, and the Politics of Death in Nineteenth-Century Brazil,' *Luso-Brazilian Review*, 37, 2 (2000), 95–122.

Brownlie, Jarvis, '"Our Fathers Fought for the British": Racial Discourses and Indigenous Allies in Upper Canada,' *Histoire Sociale/Social History*, 50, 102 (2017), 259–284.

Buckmaster, Henrietta, *The Seminole Wars* (New York: Palgrave Macmillan, 1966).

Bührer, Tanja, Flavio Eichmann, Stig Förster and Benedikt Stuchtey, eds., *Cooperation and Empire: Local Realities of Global Processes* (New York: Berghahn Books, 2017).

Byrd, Alexander X., *Captives and Voyagers: Black Migrants Across the Eighteenth-Century British Atlantic World* (Baton Rouge: Louisiana State University Press, 2008).

Campbell, James M., *Slavery on Trial: Race, Class, and Criminal Justice in Antebellum Richmond, Virginia* (Gainesville: University Press of Florida, 2007).

Campbell, James M., *Crime and Punishment in African American History* (Basingstoke: Palgrave Macmillan, 2012).

Campbell, Mavis, *The Maroons of Jamaica, 1655–1796: A History of Resistance, Collaboration & Betrayal* (Trentin: Africa World Press, 1990).

Carocci, Max, and Stephanie Pratt, eds., *Native American Adoption, Captivity, and Slavery in Changing Contexts* (New York: Palgrave Macmillan, 2012).

Craton, Michael, ed., *Testing the Chains: Resistance to Slavery in the British West Indies* (Ithaca: Cornell University Press, 1982).

Dallas, Robert C., *The History of the Maroons: From Their Origin to the Establishment of Their Chief Tribe at Sierra Leone: Including the Expedition to Cuba, for the Purpose of Procuring Spanish Chasseurs: And the State of the Island of Jamaica for the Last Ten Years: With a Succinct History of the Island Previous to That Period* (London: Printed by A. Strahan . . . for T. N. Longman and O. Rees. . ., 1803).

Edwards, Bryan, *The Proceedings of the Governor and Assembly of Jamaica, in Regard to the Maroon Negroes: Published by Order of the Assembly. To Which Is Prefixed, an Introductory Account, Containing, Observations on the Disposition, Character, Manners, and Habits of Life, of the Maroons, and, a Detail of the Origin, Progress, and Termination of the Late War Between Those People and the White Inhabitants* (London: John Stockdale, 1796).

Egerton, Douglas R., *Gabriel's Rebellion: The Virginia Slave Conspiracies of 1800 and 1802* (Chapel Hill: University of North Carolina Press, 1993).

Finkelman, Paul, ed., *Free Blacks in a Slave Society* (New York: Garland, 1989).

Finkelman, Paul, ed., *Rebellions, Resistance, and Runaways within the Slave South* (New York: Gardland, 1989).

Foster, H. Thomas, ed., *The Collected Works of Benjamin Hawkins* (Tuscaloosa: University of Alabama Press, 2003).

Franklin, John Hope, and Loren Schweninger, *Runaway Slaves: Rebels on the Plantation* (Oxford: Oxford University Press, 2000).

Gardner, W. J., *The History of Jamaica from Its Discovery . . . to the Year 1872* (1st edition 1873), new edition (London: T. Fisher Unwin, 1909).

Genovese, Eugene D., *From Rebellion to Revolution: Afro-American Slave Revolts in the Making of the Modern World* (Baton Rouge: Louisiana State University Press, 1979).

Gomes, F., 'Africans and Petit Marronage in Rio de Janeiro, 1800–1840,' *Luso-Brazilian Review*, 47, 2 (2010), 74–99.

Goody, Jack, *The Domestication of the Strange Mind* (Cambridge: Cambridge University Press, 1977).

Goody, Jack, *The Interface Between the Written and the Oral* (Cambridge: Cambridge University Press, 1987).

Grant, John N., *The Maroons in Nova Scotia* (Halifax: Formac, 2002).

Hagist, Don H., *Wives, Slaves, and Servant Girls: Advertisements for Female Runaways in American Newspapers, 1770–1783* (Yardley: Westholme Publishing, 2016).

Hall, Douglas, ed., *In Miserable Slavery: Thomas Thistlewood in Jamaica, 1750–86* (London and Basingstoke: Palgrave Macmillan, 1989).

Hart, Richard, *Slaves Who Abolished Slavery* (Kingston: University of the West Indies, Institute of Social and Economic Research, 1985).

Heuman, Gad, *Between Black and White: Race, Politics and the Free Coloureds in Jamaica, 1792–1865* (Oxford: Clio Press, 1981).

Higman, Barry, *Slave Population and Economy in Jamaica, 1807–1834* (Barbados: University of the West Indies Press, 1995).

Juricek, John T., *Endgame for Empire: British-Creek Relations in Georgia and Vicinity* (Gainesville: University Press of Florida, 2015).

Knetsch, Joe, *Florida's Seminole Wars, 1817–1858 (The Making of America)* (Mount Pleasant: Arcadia Publishing, 2003).

Landers, Jane G., ed., *Against the Odds: Free Blacks in the Slave Societies of the Americas* (London: F. Cass, 1996).

Landers, Jane, *Black Society in Spanish Florida* (Urbana: University of Illinois Press, 1999).

Lindsay, Alexander Crawford, *Lives of the Lindsays: Or a Memoir of the Houses of Crawford and Balcarres . . .* (Wigan: Privately Printed, 1840).

Long, Edward, *The History of Jamaica; or, General Survey of the Ancient and Modern State of That Island: With Reflections on its Situations, Settlements, Inhabitants, Climate, Products, Commerce, Laws, and Government*, Vol. II (London: F. Cass, 1970).

Mallipeddi, Ramesh, *Spectacular Suffering, Witnessing Slavery in the Eighteenth-Century British Atlantic* (Charlottesville: University of Virginia Press, 2016).

Matthews, Gelien, *Caribbean Slave Revolts and the British Abolitionist Movement* (Baton Rouge: Louisiana State University Press, 2006).

McNair, Glenn, *Criminal Injustice: Slaves and Free Blacks in Georgia's Criminal Justice System* (Charlottesville: University of Virginia Press, 2009).

Missall, John, and Mary Lou Missall, *The Seminole Wars: America's Longest Indian Conflict* (Gainesville: University Press of Florida, 2004).

Mitcham, John C., *Race and Imperial Defence in the British World, 1870–1914* (Cambridge: Cambridge University Press, 2016).

Morgan, Gwenda, and Peter Rushton, *Banishment in the Early Atlantic World: Convicts, Rebels and Slaves* (London: Bloomsbury Academic, 2013).

Morgan, Kenneth, *Slavery and the British Empire: From Africa to America* (Oxford: Oxford University Press, 2007).

Paton, Diana, 'Punishment, Crime, and the Bodies of Slaves in Eighteenth Century Jamaica,' *Journal of Social History*, 34, 4 (2001), 923–954.

Paton, Diana, *No Bond but the Law: Punishment, Race, and Gender in Jamaican State Formation, 1780–1870* (Durham: Duke University Press, 2004).

Paulus, Carl Lawrence, *The Slaveholding Crisis: Fear of Insurrection and the Coming of the Civil War* (Baton Rouge: Louisiana State University Press, 2017).

Phillips, A. De V., '"Doubly Condemned": Adjustments to the Crime and Punishment Regime in the Late Slavery Period in the British Caribbean Colonies,' *Cardozo Law Review*, 18, 2 (1996), 699–716.

Piker, Joshua, 'Colonists and Creeks: Re-thinking the Pre-Revolutionary Southern Backcountry,' *The Journal of Southern History*, 70, 3 (Aug., 2004), 503–540.

Pitman, Frank Wesley, *The Development of the British West Indies, 1700–1763* (New Haven: Yale University Press, 1917).

Postma, Johannes, *Slave Revolts* (Westport, CT: Greenwood Press, 2008).

Pybus, Cassandra, *Epic Journey of Freedom: Runaway Slaves of the American Revolution and Their Global Quest for Liberty* (Boston: Beacon Press, 2006).

Robinson, Carey, *The Iron Thorn: The Defeat of the British by the Jamaican Maroons* (Kingston: Kingston Publishers Limited, 1993).

Rodriguez, Junius P., ed., *Encyclopedia of Slave Resistance and Rebellion* (Westport, CT: Greenwood Press, 2007).

Rosen, Deborah A., *Border Law: The First Seminole War and American Nationhood* (Cambridge, MA: Harvard University Press, 2015).

Saunt, Claudio, "The English Has Now a Mind to Make Slaves of Them All": Creeks, Seminoles and the Problem of Slavery,' *American Indian Quarterly*, 22, 1/2 (Winter–Spring, 1998), 157–180.

Saunt, Claudio, *A New Order of Things: Property, Power, and the Transformation of the Creek Indians, 1733–1816* (Cambridge: Cambridge University Press, 1999).

Savage, J., 'Unwanted Slaves: The Punishment of Transportation and the Making of Legal Subjects in Early Nineteenth-Century Martinique,' *Citizenship Studies*, 10, 1 (2006), 35–53.

Sharples, J. T., 'Discovering Slave Conspiracies: New Fears of Rebellion and Old Paradigms of Plotting in Seventeenth-Century Barbados,' *The American Historical Review*, 120, 8 (2015), 811–843.

Siebert, Wilbur H., 'Slavery and White Servitude in East Florida, 1726–1776,' *Florida Historical Quarterly*, 10 (1931), 3–23.

Siebert, Wilbur H., 'Slavery and White Servitude in East Florida, 1776–1785,' *Florida Historical Quarterly*, 10 (1932), 139–161.

Windley, Lathan A., *A Profile of Runaway Slaves in Virginia and South Carolina from 1730 Through 1787* (New York: Routledge, 2014).

Wood, Peter H., 'The Changing Population of the Colonial South: An Overview of Race and Region, 1785–1790,' in *Powhatan's Mantle: Indians in the Colonial Southeast*, eds. Peter H. Wood, Gregory A. Waselkov and M. Thomas Hatley (Lincoln: University of Nebraska Press, 1989).

Woodward, Thomas Simpson, *Woodward's Reminiscences of the Creek, or Miscogee Indians, Contained in Letters to Friends in Georgia and Alabama* (Tuscaloosa: Alabama Book Stores, 1939).

Zellar, Gary, *African Creeks: Estelvste and the Creek Nation* (Norman: University of Oklahoma Press, 2007).

4 African Americans in Maroon and Creek Country

Inserting clauses to encourage Maroons and Creeks to hunt runaways was just one method colonial and federal officials deployed in the attempt to prevent a grand alliance with the enslaved population. Another addressed the occurrence of slave ownership. In Jamaica, paramount to British thinking was preventing the presence of any slaves in Maroon towns, whether as property or otherwise. Colonial officials, not wanting to give Maroons the opportunity to accumulate vast wealth, as was the reason a limit on the amount paid for slave-catching was given, repeatedly tried to block the buying or selling of slaves. Not only that, however, the colonists were terrified of collusion between the two groups and wanted to limit any reason for Maroons and slaves to be in close quarters.

The first official reference to Maroon slave-holding was just five years after the peace treaties. A motion put to the Assembly stated that several merchants were found to be selling slaves to Maroons. The House was against this and demanded a clause to prevent the Maroons from keeping slaves be inserted into a proposed bill. Not long after, the bill was passed and entitled "An Act for the better order and government of the Negroes belonging to the several Negro towns, and for preventing them from purchasing of slaves."[1] The colonial government wanted to prevent Maroons and slaves from being unobserved in close quarters, but this act also represented the first step in trying to reduce Maroons to the same status as other free blacks in Jamaica. Slave-holding was to be a preserve of the colonists.

Regardless of the efforts of the colonial government, the laws introduced in Jamaica did not prevent what the authorities deemed slave-owning. It is incredibly difficult to determine how many Maroon-owned slaves there were, however. The only references we have are fleeting ones such as a 1773 document from Robert Brereton, the superintendent-general of all the Maroon towns. When asked by the colonial government to submit his report on Maroon population numbers, he stated that he found "about twenty slaves in all the towns, belonging to the Maroon officers." To further demonstrate the difficulty in identifying Maroon-owned slaves, he went on to say that the Maroon officers "do not care to acknowledge or give me an account of" the slaves present.[2] Therefore, we can deduce that these slaves were identified as slaves purely through Brereton's own observations.

Indeed, these "slaves" may not have been slaves at all. Bev Carey contends that "many" free blacks went to live among the Maroons, whilst others merely lived there until they could fend for themselves. But they were always welcome as long as they would adhere to the traditions of the Maroons.[3] Indeed, early nineteenth-century formal returns to the government showed that "free persons and their personal slaves," living among the Maroons, amounted to up to 30 per cent of the total persons listed.[4] Therefore, it is possible that those counted as Maroon slaves were actually free persons living in the towns, or slaves belonging to those free people. This opaque system on who was a Maroon, free black or slave served the Maroon communities well, allowing them to escape, to a certain extent, the scrutiny of the colonial government.

In contrast to Jamaica, where legal methods were used to prevent Maroon slave ownership, federal officials in the United States never legislated on Creek ownership of African Americans. However, the federal government did actively encourage Creeks to own slaves as part of its aim to turn Creeks into farmers and ranchers. There were no specific schemes for this promotion of slavery but, if it meant giving up the hunt, then federal representatives were delighted when Creeks took to slavery. Indeed, in 1797, Benjamin Hawkins visited one Creek town and observed that only one of the inhabitants had "good government" over his nine black slaves. Hawkins implored other slave-owners to improve their control over their slaves, noting that those with better control had the superior plantations.[5]

It is quite clear from records that, contrary to the Maroon case, significant numbers of enslaved people were found within Creek country. According to Claudio Saunt, the largest concentration of African American slaves, estimated to be around three hundred, was on the "mixed-blood and Indian countryman plantations" on the Coosa and Tallapoosa rivers.[6] For instance, Sophia and Elizabeth Durant, sisters of the notable Creek leader Alexander McGillivray, who lived in Ocheubofau, owned eighty and thirty slaves, respectively. Richard Bailey of Autossee owned eight, as did the Upper Creek headman Efau Haujo, and Alexander Cornell owned nine.[7] The Indian countryman Richard Grierson, who lived among the upper Tallapoosa, owned forty.[8]

Slave ownership, however, was not a new concept introduced to the Creeks by Euro Americans. According to Saunt, small numbers of Creeks began keeping slaves in the 1760s.[9] Indeed, when William Bartram travelled around the Creek Nation in the 1770s, he described Creek-owned slaves who were indigenous themselves. When he visited a Lower Creek chief who "owned" many Yamasee captives, Bartram highlighted the difficulty of trying to understand the capacity in which these indigenous slaves were held. He noted that they were "dressed better than he [the chief]" yet still waited upon the chief with "signs of the most abject fear."[10] The complexity of what constituted a slave was clear even before the years of colonisation, when some captives were tortured and killed for ceremonial and religious purposes, whilst others were adopted into native clans and hence, into their communities.[11] As William Bartram observed of this second group, slaves, "both male and female, are permitted to marry amongst them: their children are free, and considered in every respect equal to themselves."[12] The treatment of slaves in Creek society before the American Revolution was, therefore, ambiguous and could be ruthless with slaves owned by "fear" or in a manner which represented the first step in tribal adoption.

It is clear that African-descended people, perhaps even slaves, lived in both Maroon and Creek society, but how did this come to pass? In Jamaica, clues can be ascertained from a 1751 re-enactment of the 1744 Act. In this, it was stated that "some of the Negroes lately in Rebellion" have "purchased Slaves." It was further believed that the Maroons intended to buy more which the colonial government believed would be "of ill Consequence to the Island, if not prevented." It was decreed that any Maroon who purchased a slave would forfeit the said slave to the King. Further, "if any Merchant, Factor, or other Person" sold a slave to any of the Maroons, then that person would forfeit the sum of £100. Intriguingly, there was also an explicit penalty for any person who held the slave "in Trust for or to the Use of the aforesaid Negroes." This phrase suggests that local colonists were aiding some Maroons in circumnavigating the ban on Maroon slave ownership. The seriousness of this charge is reflected in the penalty—a forfeit also of £100, the same as for those actively selling slaves to Maroon communities.[13] These sums were a not insignificant amount in mid-eighteenth-century Jamaica.

Further clues are obtained from the 1780 re-enactment of the 1744 law. The colonial government felt it necessary to re-emphasise the ban on slave ownership following complaints that the Maroons were still purchasing slaves, apparently on the open market. However, upon investigation by a committee, the complaints were found to be "groundless."[14] This did not prevent yet another re-enactment of the law in 1791, in the act entitled "for the better order and governing" of the "negro towns" which again explicitly prevented them from purchasing slaves.[15] There seems little reason for the colonial government to have continually re-issued the 1744 act, if there had been no evidence of what colonists identified as slave-owning in Maroon towns. Despite the efforts of the colonial government, Maroons continued to use local colonists to buy slaves on their behalf. Records on this are particularly rare but, in one post-war account, we can see the difficulties the superintendents faced when trying to ascertain the frequency of slave-holding, and evidence of how third-party ownership by local colonists enabled some Maroons to own slaves. In 1797, James Anderson the superintendent of Charles Town, reported,

> There are a few slaves in the town, but cannot ascertain the number; I understand that they have no title to them, being made out in other people's names; others staying with them for a certain time, for past favours.[16]

Anderson's account is also one of the few records which allude to how these slaves were kept—"for a certain time, for past favours." It is unclear whether these past favours were due from colonists or from the slaves themselves. It is possible local planters lent Maroons their slaves in payment on a quid pro quo basis.

In contrast, a large body of evidence reveals how "slaves" came to be present in Creek country after the American Revolution. In 1779, Governor James Wright of Georgia enquired into the presence of "thousands" of refugee slaves in Creek country with a view to re-claiming them. His hopes were quickly dashed when he was told that the Creeks claimed them as their property. These Creeks explained that they "were told by the General before they went into Carolina, that whatever plunder they got should be their own property" and that they saw "the Kings Army Seize upon all the Negroes they could get— upon which they did the same, and intend to carry them to the Nation."[17] By 1783, there was a thriving slave trade to Pensacola. It was reported that "the Indians and White Pepel [sic] is Constantly Carrying Droves of Negroes" to Pensacola. The Spanish Governor buys "the chief of them" and encourages them to "fetch" more slaves, telling them they would "receive the cash for all they fetch there."[18]

The slave trade did not only involve Creeks taking slaves to European settlements to sell them; it also took place within Creek country itself. John Cannard, the infamous mestizo rancher, carried on a trade in African American captives with other Lower Creeks which made him one of the wealthiest men in the territory. Euro American traveller Caleb Swan explained that Cannard's newfound wealth "raised him to the dignity of a chief, and enabled him to go largely into trade, by which he supplies all the Indians around him."[19] Other Creeks began to follow Cannard's example. In 1791, a group of Chehaw warriors "took" a party of slaves from John Whitehead's plantation in Liberty County, Georgia, and sold them to others living among the Chehaws. A Creek headman named Humlathluchee, or Big Eater, bought two people named Hector and Daphney and later sold or gave Daphney's two children to other Creeks. Finally, "a negro wench named Rose" was resold more than once in the Creek Nation before eventually being traded to Panton, Leslie, and Company in Pensacola.[20] Creeks apparently went further afield as well. Alexander McGillivray, for example, arranged to purchase slaves from Jamaica, and John Cannard travelled to the slave market in Savannah.[21]

However, it is important to note that Creeks had been trading enslaved people for centuries. Gary Zellar argues that the Creek involvement in the Indian slave trade imprinted the practice of treating people as commodities on the Creek people.[22] By as early as 1703, the Creeks had become South Carolina's premier slave-trading partners. Over the next two years, Creek warriors targeted the Apalachees of Spanish Florida for capture with a view to sale. According to Alan Gallay, during that time Creeks sold some two thousand to four thousand Apalachees as slaves and secured a reputation as the American South's most powerful native nation.[23] What changed, as the eighteenth century progressed, was the shift in focus to trading African Americans. During a two-year period in the Creek-Georgia border war, Creek warriors captured at least 140 Georgians, nearly 80 per cent of whom were enslaved African

Americans.[24] There could be many reasons for this—one possibility is that the Creeks wanted the captives to work for them, and African Americans would have been most useful with their knowledge and expertise of agriculture. Furthermore, if they wished to trade the captives on for a profit, the Creeks would have been aware that no American market would purchase Euro American captives and only African American slaves would be worthwhile for sale. Whatever the reason, however, this was a marked increase in the capture of African Americans during raids.

Sometimes, these "abducted" slaves also joined the Creeks of their own accord. On one occasion, for example, a "horrid banditti of negroes" fled from South Carolina and headed for Creek country.[25] Another African American was said to have "got with the Indians" and then "made his escape with them to the nation."[26] Slaves such as these were, on occasion, re-captured by American forces, and it is little surprise that they would have then downplayed their freedom in Creek country. Making themselves appear to be passive objects in the raids, and then as slaves forced to toil for Creek masters, may have been an attempt to avoid harsher punishments upon their re-capture.

Once these African Americans were present in Maroon and Creek towns, under what conditions were they held? It is clear from the numerous laws and reports from superintendents that some form of slave-holding took place in Maroon towns throughout the post-treaty period. However, it is possible that it was a type of Maroon slavery that was unique to Jamaica, with African roots but influenced by the European slavery on the island. Unfortunately, it is almost impossible to explore such acts. We can only aim to deduce, from fleeting mentions in the archives, how African Jamaicans in Maroon communities were treated. For example, Zell, an Ibo belonging to a colonist called Isaac Lascelles, said he was forced away with three other slaves by a group of Maroons and made to carry salted provisions and yams. Another example is Jamaica, a slave belonging to a man named John Reid, who was employed for two weeks by Maroons catching thatch and looking for wild yams.[27] These cases suggest that African Jamaicans could be utilised for a short period to complete small agricultural tasks. If local planters hired their slaves out to Maroons, as seems to be the case with the slave Jamaica, it seems likely that local colonists did not object to how harshly or leniently Maroons treated their slaves. There is, of course, the possibility that these accounts had several falsehoods. Zell's claim that he was "forced" to join the Maroons could have been to avoid punishment for running away and joining the colonists' enemies. Jamaica may also have underplayed the role he was allowed in Maroon society to avoid retribution if he was granted more freedom than his British master would usually allow. The cases of Zell and Jamaica show the difficulties of trying to determine what characteristics Maroon slavery had. Neither person was fully incorporated into society, but neither do they seemed to have been treated particularly harshly. Whether or not the claims of Zell and Jamaica are true, their cases are evidence that there was a degree of interaction between Maroons and slaves, perhaps representing a form of slavery, which went entirely against the colonial government's demands. In this way, the act of slave ownership (in the colonial government's view) was retaliation against colonial society.

The type of agriculture practiced in Maroon communities was suited to the small-scale tasks completed by people such as Zell and Jamaica. Maroon agriculture, both pre- and post-treaty, was based on planting provision grounds, rearing livestock, hunting and fishing. Maroon women also grew crops such as plantains, coffee, cocoa, cassava, corn, yam, papaw, pineapples, citrus, avocado and pears. Their treaty lands were held in common, and Maroons were forbidden from giving or selling any portion of the land to an outsider. As the treaties outlined the produce which Maroons could cultivate, there was no need to trade inclandestinely as they had in the pre-treaty days. As such, Maroons travelled to market days and openly traded. There is no evidence that they adhered to the treaty clauses which obliged them to secure a licence or "ticket" in order to carrying their produce to market. This, however, never seemed to be an issue which the colonial government raised with any of the Maroon towns.

Maroon skills were not limited to agricultural work. There is some evidence, provided by colonists such as J. Lewis who wrote to James Knight, that some Maroons acquired technical skills as well. He wrote that the Maroons

> forged their own Iron works, making Knives, Cutlasses, Heads of Lances, Bracelets, Rings and a variety of other kinds of necessaries; they have Bellows, made of wood, about 6 feet high and 16 inches wide through which they make hollow and a hole at the Bottom through which the air passes.[28]

This is in contrast to R. C. Dallas's claim that "They were none of them mechanics, all their knowledge of that kind was confined to the art of erecting a house, and repairing a gun."[29] It is also clear that they manufactured the abeng from a combination of the horn of a cow and leather. Such small-scale agricultural or industrial works would have lent itself to the short-term hiring of slaves from nearby colonists.

Agricultural work also formed a large part of the slaves' day in Creek country. In many ways, Creek-owned slaves were more akin to tenant farmers than their American-owned counterparts. They lived with their owners and tended agricultural fields, but the crops were theirs except for a small payment to their owners.[30] Slaves also took care of ranching and other tasks; but all of the work was divided between them and the matrilineage, so they were never the main labourers. An example of this is George, a slave in Creek country, who said "I made fences, dug the ground, planted corn, and worked hard, but the people were kind to me."[31] George may have been treated well, but these tasks imply he was still considered an outsider by Creek society—the tasks that he was instructed to do were usually given to Creek women rather than to men.[32] Christina Snyder suggests that Creek masters assigned their African American captives tasks inconsistent with their own gendered division of labour in order to reinforce the notion of African Americans as the other.[33] Treating a black person as "the other," in this case by gendering their tasks, suggests an incorporation of Euro American practices. However, any non-Creek male, regardless of race, could be made to do these tasks. It was not the colour of the skin but the length of time in Creek society that determined the type of labour. Once incorporated into Creek society, or having been born to a Creek parent, a person could take part in the same activities as Creek men to prove themselves to the community in order to be accepted. For example, a white trader who brought his Euro American wife with him was often tolerated but not incorporated into society as a Creek, whereas a white trader who married a Creek woman could become part of society because his marriage connected him to a clan and a matriline.[34] If a slave did not marry a Creek person, then their opportunity to connect to a clan was by completing menial tasks for a family and eventually being adopted into their clan.

Despite the best efforts of Hawkins and his civilisation plan, slaveholders in Creek country struggled to replicate the conditions in Euro American settlements that were conducive for plantation slavery. Quite simply, the terrain was not suited to it, and vast, unpatrolled forests offered slaves a quick escape. It was not just the landscape, however. Many Creeks simply had little inclination to produce a substantial agricultural surplus. One notable Creek slaveowner was Alexander McGillivray's sister, Sophia Durant, and she, like many other Creeks, had little desire to work her slaves to produce additional crops. U.S. Indian agent Benjamin Hawkins noted that Sophia's slaves were a "burthen" to her because "they are all idle."[35] He went on to say that "The black people here are an expense to their owners," that they "do nothing the whole winter but get a little wood, and in the summer they cultivate a scanty crop of corn barely sufficient for bread."[36] Sophia in fact allowed her slaves a good deal of autonomy. In 1795, for example, one of them visited William Panton to secure money that the Spanish Indian agent Marcos de Villiers owed him, before journeying to Pensacola to trade further with him.[37] In other words, this slave was not only permitted to travel alone to Pensacola but had also acquired enough property and capital to lend money and trade with a notable Spanish official. On another occasion, in December 1796, Hawkins reported meeting slaves travelling down the Tallapoosa to a gathering at Durant's. Every Christmas, the slaves stated, they had a "proper frolic of rum drinking and dancing." They explained, "The white people and Indians met generally at the same place with them and had the same amusement."[38]

This lenient attitude towards slave ownership continued into the 1790s. In 1795, Spanish officials complained that ten Indian men, women, and children had been in the area for some time "burning forests and pastures and even introducing themselves into the houses of the residents." A Spanish officer called Carlos Howard reported that "they have in their company two negroes stolen in past years" who praise "the good life that people of their colour enjoy in the nation where they eat the same as their masters and work only when they wish with-out fear of punishment."[39] Indeed, this supports Angela Pulley Hudson's argument that Creek-owned slaves were frequently afforded considerable latitude in their daily tasks and were often known to travel great distances within the Nation.[40] This was in stark contrast to how the majority of Euro Americans treated their slaves. In fact, on some occasions, observers seemed to detect little difference between Creeks and their African slaves. Kathryn Braund has described the Creek slaves as "like their employers," stating that they "joined in games and dancing, courted Creek women, drank rum, swapped tall tales with warriors."[41] According to Claudio Saunt, this treatment led to whites never knowingly purchasing slaves who had belonged to Indians for fear of their nearly certain flight back to Creek country.[42]

The casual labour frequently practiced within Creek country clearly differed greatly from that found on the coastal plantations, but this should not undermine the experiences of some Creek-owned slaves who found themselves owned by a particularly cruel master. Often, but not always, it was on the plantations of mestizos that Creek-owned slaves were mistreated. One example, John Cannard, "a noted trader, farmer, and herdsmen" who lived between the Flint and Chattahoochee rivers, owned forty bondsmen and bondswomen and was regarded as one of the largest slaveholders in the area.[43] One visitor to his property wrote, "He is a despot, shoots his negroes when he pleases, and has cut off the ears of one of his favourite wives, with his own hands, in a drunken fit of suspicion."[44] Another mestizo, the rather aptly named Bully, lived on the Apalachicola and reportedly owned, and mistreated, sixty-one slaves.[45] The link between mestizos and cruel treatment of slaves is too tentative to push any further, but the correlation between mestizos and larger concentrations of slaves can be made. Many of those in Creek country who owned considerable numbers of slaves were either white people living in Creek country or their mestizo children. For example, those named earlier in this chapter, Sophia Durant and Elizabeth, Richard Bailey, Alexander Cornell Richard Grierson and John Cannard, all fall into this category.[46]

Owning large numbers of slaves was an American ideal which slowly permeated Creek society; another was the progression of hereditary slavery. An example is that of the slave, Lucy. One summer morning in 1787 a Creek war party crossed the Oconee River and attacked the farmstead of John Lang, seizing his twelve-year-old African American slave, Lucy. The Creeks took her back to the Nation where she stayed—bearing children and even living to see her grandchildren born, and remain enslaved, under Native American masters.[47] The statement that her children and grandchildren would be enslaved is a hallmark of Euro American slavery rather than the adoption-type slavery practiced in Creek society. However, what is not clear is under what conditions Lucy was made to work. Was she held in the same conditions as traditional Creek slaves, or was her enslavement more akin to that of American slavery? Perhaps we will never know, but it seems that the hereditary method of enslavement was being utilised in some Creek families by the late eighteenth century. Another example is from 1793 when a slave named Mary was stolen from Liberty County, Georgia. She was taken to Creek country where she gave birth to four children whom "the Indians kept because they were born upon their hands."[48] In previous Creek traditions, the status of slave was not passed down through the generations. However, the interpretation of this case rests on whether the children were actually free. The document says that the Creeks "kept" the children which could mean they were kept as slaves, but it could also mean they were being kept through adoption into Creek society. Either way, the children were removed from their mother, which went against the traditional matrilineal structure of Creek society.

Whilst it is clear that African-descended people were present in both Maroon and Creek society, one question that we must ask is: were these people, identified as slaves in European sources, really slaves? In Jamaica, it is not clear whether Maroons viewed these so-called slaves as their property, or if they were held under some other kind of condition. Historians are divided over the issue. Alvin O. Thompson believes that Maroon slaves had few rights in this period, similar to European-owned slaves, whereas Eugene Genovese argues that the Maroons practised a "mild, familial slavery" reminiscent of the kind practised in Africa.[49] Mavis Campbell expands upon Genovese's suggestion by stating that Maroon slaves may have been treated in a similar manner to slaves living in the Asante kingdom of Africa, who scholarly consensus understands as the ancestors of Maroons.[50] Slavery amongst the Asante people arose as a social mechanism for the assimilation of "outsiders" into early Akan society. As the Asante were matrilineal, children born of male slaves and Asante women were absorbed into the Asante people through the matriclans.[51] Bev Carey, herself of Maroon descent, concurs with this view, stating that the Maroon tradition regarding owning slaves had its roots among the Asante people.[52] She writes that slavery among Asante was commonplace, but that the type of slavery was, in the first place, a method to integrate strangers into the community.[53] Further, the Asante might offer a family member to put in service to discharge a family obligation and thereby avoid war and bloodshed. In other words, in the Maroons' ancestral land, a type of slavery existed, but one which was markedly different to that in the European plantations in Jamaica.[54] It is, therefore, not impossible that Maroon slavery could have replicated, at least partially, Asante slavery.

The notion of ownership in Creek society is also complex. Andrew Frank has outlined that, throughout their pre-removal history, Creeks welcomed countless African, native and European outsiders into their villages as spouses and occasionally adopted others into their families, frequently as repayment for some kind of debt.[55] The initial step to adoption was often ownership by clan rather than individual.[56] This was the case in the 1780s with Sambo, who in 1788 was owned by the Tiger or Panther Clan in Chiaja and was referred to as "one of his family property" by the Chehaw Tiger King.[57] Formal adoption into a Creek clan gave the newcomer full rights, but it often took time to receive a warm welcome, at least until their commitment to the community had been shown. To do so, these adopted slaves were sometimes asked to work the land, but not in the same way that slaves were expected to in Euro American areas. Kevin Kokomoor has argued that Creek owners simply asked the African Americans among them to participate in the same communal style agriculture as was practiced by all families in their villages.[58] This difference in treatment seemed to foster a milder form of slavery than that typically practised on the vast, cotton plantations of the Deep South.

People identified as slaves in Creek country by Americans also often had a different status in Creek country. One such example is that of the Scots Creek named Boatswain who owned "Private Plantations" near Hitichi on the Chattahoochee River. He was visited there in the 1770s by William Bartram, who received a grand welcome and served with "excellent Coffee . . . in China Dishes by Young Negro Slaves."[59] These so-called slaves, however, were part of Boatswain's "family" and were only in servitude until they married a Creek, at which point they became "Indians, or Free Citizens."[60] This supports Andrew Frank's claim that Creeks had a "non-racial worldview" well into the nineteenth century,[61] and Daniel Littlefield's assertion that Creek slavery was not even a "loose equivalent" of the plantation slavery of Georgia and the Carolinas.[62]

On an individual level, and away from slave-owning, both Maroons and Creeks interacted with enslaved peoples in other forms—further complicating Maroon and Creek notions of slavery. Evidence in the archival sources shows that slaves entertained Maroons on their plantations, a continuation of pre-treaty practices. Shortly before the Second Maroon War, a man called Robertson said that fourteen or fifteen Maroons were welcomed at a place called Oliphant's by the gardener of Mr. Mure.[63] These slaves took part in Maroon dances and games, socialising until sunrise the next morning. These social interactions with slaves were so pivotal to the Maroons that Bev Carey has claimed, from a Maroon point of view, that the clause which banned such engagements was the most restrictive covenant in the 1791 laws.[64] Indeed, Carey further claims that when a slave, who had been freed because of "an essential service to the public, such as revealing a conspiracy, or valiantly fighting against rebels and invaders," wished to escape the draconian laws dictating the lives of free blacks, then they often headed for Maroon country, resulting in Maroons, slaves and free persons visiting each other, entertaining each other and cohabiting together.[65]

Personal contact between Maroons and slaves also took the form of sexual interaction. Balcarres, then Governor of Jamaica, wrote in July 1795 that the Trelawny Town Maroons had "increased to 660, exclusive of their numerous children by slaves residing on the low plantations."[66] Carey Robinson claims that planters turned a blind eye to this because they believed that children born from a Maroon father would be stronger and, therefore, more valuable.[67] By interacting with enslaved women, but not attempting to aid their escape, Maroons may have, at first, seemed to condone slavery. However, if we place too much blame for this at the feet of the Maroon men, it risks the outdated practice of stripping slaves of any agency or control over their lives. Perhaps slave women chose to stay on their plantations rather than take the uncertain risk of flight to a community caught between two worlds. Once these women stayed on the plantations, their children, too, were bound to reside with them. This practice, however, would have followed the Asante matrilineal tradition, which said that the child stayed with the mother. Another possibility is that the Maroon men actually cohabited with slave women, as Edward Long has claimed.[68] In these cases, it may not have been the case that Maroon men abandoned their children on the plantations. Instead, they may have cohabited with their wives and children on the plantations while keeping a foothold in Maroon society as well. There were certainly reports that, immediately following the outbreak of the Second Maroon War, the Trelawny Town Maroons sent messengers to tell their brethren who lived on the plantations what had happened.[69]

Sexual relations and shared offspring were also present in Creek country. For example, Ninnywageechee, also known as the Little Negro Factor and the Black Factor, was an "Indian and negro mestizo, [a] trader among the Lower Creeks."[70] Another, Philatouche, was of African descent and a notable leader in Chiaja.[71] Likewise, Sean Michael O'Brien states that the prominent Creek chief Cusseta Hadjo (also called Cusseta Tustunnuggee or Jim Boy) was said to be part African American.[72] All of these examples show that African American people not only intermarried with Creeks, but that their offspring could gain a prominent status within Creek society. In fact, Creeks were said to have intermarried with slaves more than other indigenous nations, such as the Cherokee. In a nineteenth-century joke, a Creek says to a Cherokee, "you Cherokees are so mixed with whites we cannot tell you from whites." The Cherokee replied, "You Creeks are so mixed with negroes we cannot tell you from negroes."[73] The offspring of these intermarriages went on to play an important role in Creek society, with some becoming village factors or prominent chiefs—highlighting the inclusiveness of Creek society.

Slaves did not necessarily have to marry into Creek society to be accepted as part of the community, however. Three enslaved men, Isaac, Pearo and Orange, freed themselves in 1788 and headed for Creek country. The three of them were granted refuge and subsequently became warriors. This shows that, while certain African American men were given the female-gendered tasks of agricultural work, others could pursue the more masculine role of warrior once they had proved their commitment to the community. Seven weeks after their initial escape, they returned to their old plantation with a Creek war party and killed three enslaved African Americans and captured six more.[74] Even slaves who had been owned by Creek masters had the opportunity to be freed and to join Creek society. In 1798, David Randon visited Benjamin Hawkins to free his wife Suckey and his five mulatto children. Slaves could also free themselves, as was the case early in the nineteenth century when "Negro Jim," belonging to Chief Walker, purchased his freedom for $330.[75]

However, even whilst some slaves were incorporated into Maroon and Creek society, Euro American attitudes towards the black population slowly began to permeate both communities. Christina Snyder and Claudio Saunt have placed this turning point in Creek history as the nineteenth century, but there were also examples prior to that.[76] In 1783, five Alabama Indians murdered two black slaves, and blood satisfaction for the murders was sought. The Creeks agreed to everything except taking the lives of two Indians in the place of the dead slaves because they believed these were not "equivalent" to the Indians.[77] This hints at the changing attitude towards African Americans. Creeks had always given satisfaction for murders committed by their people. In the border violence with white settlers, Creeks often agreed to kill one of their own people in retribution for a Creek murdering a white person; therefore, this refusal to give satisfaction because the slaves were not "equivalent" cannot simply be related to the slaves being outsiders. Further evidence of this attitude is seen in 1795, when a Yuchi man camped near Tensaw shot and killed a slave of that town. A Tensaw boy asked the Yuchi "why he had killed the Negro" to which the Yuchi responded "that he had killed him because he is the same as a dog."[78] Similarly, in 1792, two Pensacola convicts, Josef Antonio Beltrán, of Spanish descent, and Leonardo de la Trinidad Poveda, of African descent, murdered a Creek Indian named Esnite. According to Arturo O'Neill, Beltrán was sentenced to death "as much for being the most guilty as for it being understood that the Indians would not be satisfied with the death of Leonardo de la Trinidad because, being a Negro, they look on him with the greatest contempt."[79]

Similarly, Maroons began to single out slaves for their animosity. During the event which triggered the Second Maroon War, that of the flogging of two Maroons, it was the sentence being carried out by a slave which particularly angered the Trelawnys. However, rather than this simply being a result of the race of the slaves, this may have been a result of the decades of discord promoted by the colonial government. Indeed, one Maroon representative warned the British not to "subject us to insult and humiliation from the very people to whom we are set in opposition."[80] It was the slave status of the flogger in particular that increased the humiliation of these Maroons. Every action the colonial government had taken from the end of the First Maroon War was implemented with the intention of deepening the division between Maroons and enslaved people. The choice of a slave to carry out the sentence cannot, therefore, have been accidental.

Such animosity, however, did not prevent enslaved peoples from being incorporated into Trelawny ranks during the Second Maroon War. As stated in the previous chapter, the Trelawny leader, Johnson, promoted a Coroman-tin "negro" named Cudjoe to the rank of captain and raised another belonging to the estate of Whittaker, named Casacrui, to the same rank.[81] It was perhaps the treatment of these runaways which incited a further fifty-four slaves to "join the Maroons in rebellion" from St. Elizabeth.[82] The years of attempted division by the colonial government had not wholly succeeded.

As we have seen, both Maroons and Creeks did own African slaves, in some capacity, during the time period under question. This is unsurprising given the history of both communities. Creeks had a long history of enslavement which included slaves of indigenous, African and European descent.[83] Similarly, those Maroons born in Africa would have been familiar with the different types of slavery practiced across the region, whilst those born in Jamaica would have observed the European-style slavery under which African slaves toiled on the plantations of the English. Therefore, it should come as no surprise that some form of slave ownership took place in these free communities.

What is harder to discern is under what status these slaves were owned. It is difficult to say definitively, given the scant archival records to do with Maroon slave ownership, but the type of slavery practiced by both Maroons and Creeks also appears to have been similar, particularly in the early years of the study. Creek-style slavery was often the first step towards adoption into a particular clan, and was focused on small, agricultural-based tasks with considerable freedom to work for themselves. Maroon-style slavery was based around similar tasks and, most likely, followed that of slavery in Asante societies; in other words, being held for a fixed period of time in payment for a family debt or as part of the adoption process. Those slaves held under such conditions in Maroon and Creek country largely appear to have been treated rather leniently, and the actual number of slaves in those communities seems to have been relatively low.

Whilst it is not clear what types of jobs were given to the slaves of Maroons, it seems they echoed the work of Creek slaves. A male slave in Creek country was often required to complete agricultural tasks. Likewise, Maroons seem to have, at first, instructed male slaves to perform agricultural tasks in order to "prove" themselves to Maroon leaders. Female slaves would presumably be required to perform agricultural tasks alongside the Maroon women. It may also have been that agricultural tasks were given to these new male slave recruits because slaves in both the United States and Jamaica would not have been trained to hunt wild boar (in the Maroon case) or deer (in the Creek case) and so would have been no use to the warriors whose responsibility it was for such undertakings. In other words, tasks were seemingly handed out on account of the needs of the community rather than on status or race. However, in both cases, as suggested in the archival evidence, former slaves could be raised to the status of warrior or even leader. This is some of the strongest evidence of the Maroon and Creek inclusiveness towards African Americans which continued into the inter-war period and beyond.[84]

The influence of European society on slavery practices was not completely absent, however. White society did have more of an impact on both Maroon and Creek slave ownership when it came to buying and selling individuals. Maroons appear to have acquired slaves through third-party sellers, presumably local colonists, and so were involved in the slave economy, albeit only on a small scale. On the other hand, Creeks had participated in a slave trade with Europeans for centuries and continued to do so. What did change, however, is that more of an emphasis was placed on buying and selling black people rather than on any other race. In earlier years, Creeks had shown no preference when it came to the race of those they were trading; this changed with the creeping influence of European society. As stated earlier, the change to trading African Americans was most likely because of economic, rather than racist, reasons. African Americans simply represented a higher profit margin because of their desirability on the American markets.

These differing trends in the acquisition of what Europeans termed slaves highlights the most pertinent difference when comparing Maroon and Creek slave ownership—namely that the colonial government outlawed the practice for Maroons, whereas Creeks were actively encouraged by the federal government to adopt American-style slavery. It is not difficult to understand why the colonial government forbade the act—a "slave" present in a Maroon town was also a possible ally and link to other slaves who may ally with the Maroons against the colonists. Further, if slavery had been permitted, it would have been easier for Maroons to claim runaways as their slaves and, thus, harbour them from the brutal conditions of the coastal plantations. Finally, racist property laws in Jamaica prevented Maroons from acquiring large amounts of wealth, and this extended to wealth in slaves. Therefore, the disallowance of slave ownership was intended to eradicate links to slaves, prevent Maroon territory from being a haven for runaways, and to stop Maroons from gaining influence through wealth. On the other hand, Creeks were encouraged to own slaves. As part of the civilisation plan, the federal government believed that if Creeks could be encouraged to give up the deer hunt, and to become farmers and ranchers with slaves, they would need less land whilst becoming worthy trading partners. As such, Benjamin Hawkins made it a particular effort of his to encourage the use of African slaves in Creek communities, and he decried the lack of effort on the Creek part.

The types of economies in Jamaica and the United States also played a role here. Jamaica was a wholly slave-based society; the entire economy of the island revolved around slavery and the colonial government needed to control that system. More importantly, there was a strict racial hierarchy, and the colonial government could not allow an African-descended people to raise themselves to be an equal of a European.[85] On the contrary, the United States, whilst allowing slavery, did not have an economy as reliant on slavery in the manner that Jamaica's was. The south-eastern United States was also based on a strict racial hierarchy but allowing Creeks to trade in black people did not impact significantly upon this.[86] In fact, it merely consolidated the existing hierarchy of whites on top, blacks on bottom and Native Americans in between. That the majority of Creeks refused to participate in such American-style slavery was not for want of trying on the part of the federal government.

In this way, we can see that the encouragement, or discouragement, of African slavery became another pawn in the battle to control the Maroons and Creeks. But the attempts or not at adopting European-style slavery also became a battleground in resisting that control. Creeks were pushed to adopt American-style slavery and, largely, refused in defiance of the federal government. Conversely, Maroons were outlawed from owning African slaves but continued to do so, also in an act of defiance towards the colonial government. Maroons may not have classed those in their communities as slaves, but the British certainly did and explicitly outlawed their presence in repeated rounds of legislation. Therefore, ownership can be construed as an act of defiance by the Maroons.

The few cases of slave ownership did not prevent personal relationships forming between enslaved people and Maroons and Creeks. In particular, cases of intermarriage are relatively common. Such acts went completely against the wishes of the colonial and federal governments. That the Maroons and Creeks ignored their respective governments on this matter is another example of their resistance to white society. Maroons and Creeks cared so little for these European-imposed policies that there are numerous records of the offspring of such unions. The main difference seems to be that Maroon children were raised on the plantations whilst Creek children were brought up in Creek country. Maroons may have felt that the child had a greater chance of survival on a plantation than in Maroon country, especially if the master was benign. The proximity of Maroon settlements, as a result of the geography of Jamaica, meant that Maroons could, and did, visit their families on the plantations. In the Creek case, intermarriage was more likely to take place with African Americans already living in Creek country and, therefore, the children would be brought up in Creek villages. Given the growing classification of African Americans as inferior, American territory would have been no place to introduce a child of a Creek-African marriage.

Interestingly, the intermarriage of slaves with either Maroons or Creeks does not seem to have occasioned much horror from the white population. Indeed, the colonists of Jamaica noted the benefits of slave children having Maroon fathers. Importantly, this desire for Maroons and slave women to have children was a view held by local whites, rather than the colonial government of Jamaica. This hints at the split in opinion between official and unofficial policy within Jamaica, a scenario assessed in greater detail in Chapter 6. Suffice to say here that local whites were perhaps more interested in increasing the value and productivity of their slaves than in adhering to an island-wide policy of divide-and-rule, particularly as the Maroons enjoyed a relatively good relationship with the local whites.

The seeming lack of interest from any whites in the United States regarding Creek-black unions is more difficult to understand. The American government, much like the colonial government in Jamaica, wanted to implement a divide-and-rule policy which would suggest they would discourage any unions with black people. Furthermore, once Benjamin Hawkins began to instigate the civilisation plan, which encouraged Creeks to turn to a version of slavery more associated with the whites of Georgia, it seems odd that little would be done to prevent marriages with slaves. The answer lies in the possibility that the white Americans did not have a significant influence on the day-to-day lives of Creeks. There was little the government could do if a Creek wanted to marry a black person if they lived deep within Creek country. The United States could not enforce its laws on a sovereign nation and could do little but hope its racist policies would permeate Creek society through the mestizo children of Americans and the Creek children educated in the United States as part of the Treaty of New York.

Such interpersonal relationships were an act of resistance against the white governments which tried to implement policies of divide and rule, but they also highlight a whole web of interactions distinct from the European world that was occurring in these regions. Peace with the Jamaican and American governments did not change this, and there was nothing either could do to prevent it from happening. These intermarriages and shared children are one of the most definitive examples of how free communities continued to negotiate their worlds on their terms.

Notes

1. *Journals of the House of Assembly (JHA)*, 12th and 17th May 1744, Vol. III, National Archives of Jamaica (NAJ).
2. *JHA*, 26th November 1773, Vol. VI, NAJ.
3. Bev Carey, *Maroon Story: The Authentic and Original History of the Maroons in the History of Jamaica, 1490–1880* (St. Andrew, Jamaica: Agouti Press, 1997), 440.
4. *Ibid.*
5. Benjamin Hawkins, *Letters of Benjamin Hawkins, 1796–1806* (Savannah: Published by the Georgia Historical Society, 1916), Vol. I, 287.
6. Claudio Saunt, *A New Order of Things: Property, Power and the Transformation of the Creek Indians, 1733–1816* (Cambridge: Cambridge University Press, 1999), 116–117. Indian countrymen were Europeans who had settled in Creek country, often with a Creek wife.
7. Benjamin Hawkins, *The Collected Works of Benjamin Hawkins* (Tuscaloosa: University of Alabama Press, 2003), 15, 22, 24, 292.
8. *Ibid.*, 301–306.
9. Saunt, *A New Order of Things*, 51.
10. William Bartram, *Travels of William Bartram*, ed. Mark van Doren (New York: Dover Publications, 1955), 164.
11. Christina Snyder, *Slavery in Indian Country: The Changing Face of Captivity in Early America* (Cambridge, MA: Harvard University Press, 2010), 35.
12. Bartram, *Travels of William Bartram*, 167.
13. *Acts of Assembly Passed in the Island of Jamaica from 1681 to 1733 Inclusive* (BL), CSF., 154/4, 332–333.
14. *JHA*, 18th December 1781, Vol. VI, NAJ.
15. Jamaica, *The Laws of Jamaica: 1760–1792* (London: A. Aikman Printer's to the King's Most Excellent Majesty, 1811), 476.
16. *Votes of the House of Assembly of Jamaica*, Appendix (not numbered), 1st November 1797, (BL).
17. At a council held in the Council Chamber at Savannah, 26th July 1779, *Colonial Records of the States of Georgia*, ed. Allen D. Chandler (Atlanta: Franklin Printing, 1904–1916), Vol. XXXVIII, 186–187, GDAH.
18. Patrick Carr to John Martin, 13th December 1782, Creek Indian Letters, Talks and Treaties, 1705–1839, ed. Louise F. Hays (typescript in GDAH), I-40–41.
19. Caleb Swan, 'Position and State of Manners and Arts in the Creek, or Muscogee Nation in 1791,' in *Historical and Statistical Information Respecting the History, Condition and Prospects of the Indian Tribes of the United States*, ed. Henry Rowe Schoolcraft (Philadelphia: Lippincott, Grambo and Company, 1851), 261.

20. Affidavit of John Whitehead, 5th September 1791, in *Indian Depredation Claims, 1796–1920* ed. Larry C. Skogen (Norman: University of Oklahoma Press, 1996), 211; Affidavit of David Garvin, 4th February 1803, *Indian Depredations*, 89.
21. Alexander McGillivray to the Intendant-General Martin Navarro, 7th November 1785, in D. C. Corbitt, 'Papers Relating to the Georgia-Florida Frontier, 1784–1800. Part II,' *Georgia Historical Quarterly*, 21 (1937), 75; William Laurence to William Panton, 15th August 1798, Heloise H. Cruzat Papers, MS 19, George A. Smathers Libraries, University of Florida, United States (GAS).
22. Gary Zellar, *African Creeks: Estelvste and the Creek Nation* (Norman: University of Oklahoma Press, 2007), 7.
23. Alan Gallay, *The Indian Slave Trade in Colonial America: The Rise of the English Empire in the American South, 1670–1717* (New Haven: Yale University Press, 2003), 148–149.
24. Return of Depredations Committed by the Creek Indians since the Commencement of Hostilities in the State of Georgia, *American State Papers*, 77; "Return of Persons Killed, Wounded, and taken Prisoners. . . ," Miscellaneous Creek Indian Documents, RG 4-2-46, (GDAH).
25. James Jackson to the Governor of Georgia, 21st July 1793, CIL, Vol. I, 334–337. GDAH.
26. Affidavit of Nathan Atkinson, 31st October 1802, "Indian Depredations, 1787–1825," 2, pt. 1: 85.
27. Carey Robinson, *The Iron Thorn: The Defeat of the British by the Jamaican Maroons* (Kingston: Kingston Publishers Limited, 1993), 192.
28. Edward Long Papers, Add. Ms. 12431, BL.
29. Robert C. Dallas, *The History of the Maroons: From Their Origin to the Establishment of Their Chief Tribe in Sierra Leone: Including the Expedition to Cuba, for the Purpose of Procuring Spanish Chasseurs; and the State of the Island of Jamaica for the Last Ten Years: With a Succinct History of the Island Previous to That Period* (London: Printed by A. Strahan . . . for T. N. Longman and O. Rees. . ., 1803), Vol. I, 109.
30. Kathryn E. Holland Braund, 'The Creek Indians, Blacks and Slavery,' *The Journal of Southern History*, 57, 4 (Nov., 1991), 623–631.
31. John Rippon, ed., 'An Account of the Life of Mr. David George from Sierra Leone in Africa Given by Himself in a Conversation with Brother Rippon of London, and Brother Pearce of Birmingham,' in *The Baptist Annual Register for 1790, 1791, 1792 & Part of 1793, Including Sketches of the State of Religion Among Different Denominations of Good Men at Home and Abroad* (London: Dilly, Button and Thomas, 1793–1802), 474.
32. Barbara Krauthamer, 'A Particular Kind of Freedom in the American Southeast,' in *Women and Slavery*, eds. Gwyn Campbell, Suzanne Miers and Joseph C. Miller (Athens: Ohio University Press, 2008), 115.
33. Christina Snyder, 'Conquered Enemies, Adopted Kin, and Owned People: The Creek Indians and Their Captives,' *The Journal of Southern History*, 73, 2 (May, 2007), 282.
34. Robbie Franklyn Ethridge, *Creek Country: The Creek Indians and Their World* (Chapel Hill: University of North Carolina Press, 2003), 112.
35. Journal of Benjamin Hawkins, 24th December 1796, *Letters of Benjamin Hawkins* (Savannah: Published by the Georgia Historical Society, 1916), Vol. I, 24.
36. Journal of Benjamin Hawkins, 25th December 1796, *LBH*, Vol. I, 29.
37. Enrique White to Barón de Carondelet, 22nd November 1795, Papeles Procedentes de Cuba, Archivo de Indias, Seville (microfilm, leg. 32, 1149, reel 387, PKY).
38. Journal of Benjamin Hawkins, 25th December 1796, *LBH*, Vol. I, 29.
39. Carlos Howard to Juan Nepomuceno de Quesada, 16th April 1795, EFL, PKY.
40. Angela Pulley Hudson, *Creek Paths and Federal Roads: Indians, Settlers, and Slaves and the Making of the American South* (Chapel Hill: University of North Carolina Press, 2010), 73.
41. Braund, 'The Creek Indians, Blacks, and Slavery,' 609.
42. Saunt, *A New Order of Things*, 123.

43. Claudio Saunt, 'The English Now Has Mind to Make Slaves of Them All": Creeks, Seminoles and the Problem of Slavery,' *American Indian Quarterly*, 22, 1/2 (Winter–Spring, 1998), 168–169.

44. Swan, 'Position and State of Manners and Arts,' 263.

45. *Ibid.*, 206–261; John Pope, *A Tour Through the Southern and Western Territories of the United States of North-America; the Spanish Dominions on the River Mississippi, and the Floridas; the Countries of the Creek Nations; and Many Uninhabited Parts* (Richmond: Printed by John Dixon, 1792), 64–65.

46. Hawkins, *Collected Works*, 15, 22, 24, 292.

47. Affidavit of John Lang, 27th October 1802, in *Indian Depredation Claims*; Affidavit of John McMichael Jr., 2nd July 1787, *ibid.*; Affidavit of David McMichael, 2nd July 1787, *ibid.*, 104–105.

48. Affidavit of William Smith, 4th June 1821, *ibid.*

49. Eugene D. Genovese, *From Rebellion to Revolution: Afro-American Slave Revolts in the Making of the Modern World* (Baton Rouge: Louisiana State University Press, 1992), 57; Alvin O. Thompson, *Flight to Freedom: African Runaways and Maroons in the Americas* (Kingston: University of West Indies Press, 2006), 216.

50. Mavis Campbell, *The Maroons of Jamaica, 1655–1796: A History of Resistance, Collaboration & Betrayal* (Trentin: Africa World Press, 1990), 21.

51. Paul E. Lovejoy, *Transformations in Slavery: A History of Slavery in Africa* (Cambridge: Cambridge University Press, 2000), 165.

52. Carey, *Maroon Story*, 433.

53. *Ibid.*, 435.

54. *Ibid.*, 436.

55. Andrew Frank, *Creeks & Southerners: Biculturalism on the Early American Frontier* (Lincoln: University of Nebraska Press, 2005), 11.

56. Saunt, 'The English Has Now a Mind to Make Slaves of Them All,' 169.

57. John Millar to Arturo O'Neill, 28th September 1788, East Florida Papers (EFL), film 55-A. P. K. Yonge Library, University of Florida, United States (PKY).

58. Kevin Kokomoor, 'A Reassessment of Seminoles, Africans, and Slavery on the Florida Frontier,' *Florida Historical Society*, 88, 2 (Fall, 2009), 219.

59. William Bartram, *Observations on the Creek and Cherokee Indians* (1853), 156–157.

60. *Ibid.*, 156.

61. Frank, *Creeks & Southerners*, 129.

62. Daniel F. Littlefield Jr., *Africans and Creeks from the Colonial Period to the Civil War* (Westport, CT: Greenwood Press, 1979), 51.

63. Bryan Edwards, *The Proceedings of the Governor and Assembly of Jamaica, in Regard to the Maroon Negroes: Published by Order of the Assembly. To Which Is Prefixed, an Introductory Account, Containing, Observations on the Disposition, Character, Manners, and Habits of Life, of the Maroons, and, a Detail of the Origin, Progress, and Termination of the Late War Between Those People and the White Inhabitants* (London: John Stockdale, 1796), 62.

64. Carey, *Maroon Story*, 458. The 1791 laws brought many restrictions against the Maroons, particularly focused on reducing their freedom of movement. Further details of these will be discussed in subsequent chapters.

65. *Ibid.*, 440.

66. Balcarres to the Duke of Portland, 25th August 1795, WO 1/92, National Archives, Kew, England (NA).

67. Robinson, *The Iron Thorn*, 130.

68. Carey, *Maroon Story*, 440.

69. Robinson, *The Iron Thorn*, 151.

70. John Cannard to Juan Nepomuceno de Quesada, 25th May 1793, Reel 43, EFL, PKY; John Cannard to the kings, principals, and chiefs of the Lower Creeks, 25th May 1793, Reel 43, EFL, PKY; James Burges to Robert Leslie, 1st July 1793, Reel 43, EFL, PKY.

71. Alexander McGillivray identified Philatouche as the leader of Chiaja in his letter to Manuel Vicente de Zéspedes, 3rd August 1786, Reel 43, EFL, PKY.
72. Sean Michael O'Brien, *In Bitterness and Tears: Andrew Jackson's Destruction of the Creeks and Seminoles* (Guilford: Lyon's Press, 2005), 5.
73. *Ibid.*, 4.
74. Affidavit of John Elliott, 3rd August 1789, *Indian Depredations*, 234.
75. 23rd March 1798, 17th October 1802, Benjamin Hawkins' Letterbook, Independence National Historical Park, Philadelphia (INHP).
76. Snyder, *Slavery in Indian Country*, 124; Claudio Saunt, *Black, White, and Indian: Race and the Unmaking of an American Family* (Oxford: Oxford University Press, 2006), 11.
77. Arturo O'Neill to Henrique Grimarest, 19th March 1783, Reel 184, EFL, PKY.
78. Manuel de Lanzos to Enrique White, 19th February 1795, Reel 418, EFL, PKY.
79. Arturo O'Neill to Barón de Carondelet, 5th July 1792, PC, leg. 39, 766, reel 162, PKY.
80. Balcarres to Portland, 25th August 1795, CO 137/95, NA.
81. Lindsay, *Lives of the Lindsays*, 23, 88.
82. *Ibid.*, 23, 92–93.
83. Zellar, *African Creeks*; Saunt, '"The English Has Now a Mind to Make Slaves of Them All"'; John Reed Swanton, *Early History of the Creek Indians and Their Neighbours* (Gainesville: University Press of Florida, 1998); Saunt, *Black, White, and Indian*; Steven C. Hahn, *The Invention of the Creek Nation, 1670–1763* (Lincoln: University of Nebraska Press, 2004).
84. Michael Mullin, *Africa in America: Slave Acculturation and Resistance in the American South and the British Caribbean, 1736–1831* (Urbana: University of Illinois Press, 1994), 293; H. S. Halbert and T. H. Ball, *The Creek War of 1813 and 1814* (Chicago: Donohue & Henneberry, 1895), 211–218.
85. S. D. Smith, *Slavery, Family, and Gentry Capitalism in the British Atlantic: The World of the Lascelles, 1648–1834* (Cambridge: Cambridge University Press, 2010), 329.
86. Trevor Burnard, 'Freedom, Migration and the American Revolution,' in *Empire and Nation: The American Revolution and the Atlantic World*, eds. Eliga H. Gould and Peter S. Onuf (Baltimore: Johns Hopkins University Press, 2005), 295.

Bibliography

Primary Sources

Beinecke Rare Book and Manuscript Library, Yale University, New Haven, United States

Thomas Thistlewood Papers.

British Library, London, United Kingdom

Acts of Assembly Passed in the Island of Jamaica from 1681 to 1733 Inclusive.
Edward Long Manuscripts.

Galileo Online Digital Library of Georgia (website)

South-eastern Native American Documents, 1730–1842.

George A. Smathers Libraries, University of Florida, Gainesville, United States

Heloise H. Cruzat Papers.

Georgia Department of Archives and History, Morrow, Georgia, United States

Colonial Records of the State of Georgia.
"Creek Indian Letters, Talks, and Treaties, 1705–1839."
"Creek Letters, 1800–1819."
"Indian Treaties: Cessions of Land in Georgia, 1705–1837."
"Letters of Benjamin Hawkins, 1797–1815."
Miscellaneous Creek Indian Documents.
South-eastern Native American Documents Database.
Treaty at Fort Wilkinson with the Creek Indians, 1802.
Unpublished Letters of Timothy Barnard, 1784–1820.

Library of Congress, Washington, D.C., United States

Archivo Nacional de Cuba Collection (microfilm).

National Archives of Jamaica, Spanish Town, Jamaica

Journals of the House of Assembly, Vols. I–X.

National Archives and Records Office, Washington, D.C., United States

Foreign Letters of the Continental Congress and the Department of State.
Records of the Bureau of Indian Affairs.

P. K. Yonge Library, University of Florida, Gainesville, United States

Archivo General de Indias (microfilm).
East Florida Papers (microfilm).
Henry Wilson Papers.
Papeles Procedentes de Cuba (microfilm).
Records of the Creek Trading House, Letter Book, 1795–1816.

Special Collections, University of Georgia, Athens, United States

Southeastern Native American Documents, 1730–1842.

Published Sources

Bartram, William, *Observations on the Creek and Cherokee Indians* (New York: American Ethnological Society,1853).

Braund, Kathryn E. Holland, 'The Creek Indians, Blacks and Slavery,' *The Journal of Southern History*, 57, 4 (Nov., 1991), 601–636.

Burnard, Trevor, 'Freedom, Migration and the American Revolution,' in *Empire and Nation: The American Revolution and the Atlantic World*, eds. Eliga H. Gould and Peter S. Onuf (Baltimore: Johns Hopkins University Press, 2005), 283–305.

Campbell, Mavis, *The Maroons of Jamaica, 1655–1796: A History of Resistance, Collaboration & Betrayal* (Trentin: Africa World Press, 1990).

Carey, Bev, *Maroon Story: The Authentic and Original History of the Maroons in the History of Jamaica, 1490–1880* (St. Andrew, Jamaica: Agouti Press, 1997).

Chandler, Allen D., ed., *Colonial Records of the States of Georgia* (Atlanta: Franklin Printing, 1904–1916),

Corbitt, D. C., 'Papers Relating to the Georgia-Florida Frontier, 1784–1800. Part II,' *Georgia Historical Quarterly*, 21 (1937), 73–82.

Dallas, Robert C., *The History of the Maroons: From Their Origin to the Establishment of Their Chief Tribe at Sierra Leone: Including the Expedition to Cuba, for the Purpose of Procuring Spanish Chasseurs: And the State of the Island of Jamaica for the Last Ten Years: With a Succinct History of the Island Previous to That Period* (London: Printed by A. Strahan . . . for T. N. Longman and O. Rees. . ., 1803).

Edwards, Bryan, *The Proceedings of the Governor and Assembly of Jamaica, in Regard to the Maroon Negroes: Published by Order of the Assembly. To Which Is Prefixed, an Introductory Account, Containing, Observations on the Disposition, Character, Manners, and Habits of Life, of the Maroons, and, a Detail of the Origin, Progress, and Termination of the Late War Between Those People and the White Inhabitants* (London: John Stockdale, 1796).

Ethridge, Robbie Franklyn, *Creek Country: The Creek Indians and Their World* (Chapel Hill: University of North Carolina Press, 2003).

Foster, H. Thomas, ed., *The Collected Works of Benjamin Hawkins* (Tuscaloosa: University of Alabama Press, 2003).

Frank, Andrew, *Creeks & Southerners: Biculturalism on the Early American Frontier* (Lincoln: University of Nebraska Press, 2005).

Gallay, Alan, *The Indian Slave Trade in Colonial America: The Rise of the English Empire in the American South, 1670–1717* (New Haven: Yale University Press, 2003).

Genovese, Eugene D., *From Rebellion to Revolution: Afro-American Slave Revolts in the Making of the Modern World* (Baton Rouge: Louisiana State University Press, 1979).

Hahn, Steven C., *The Invention of the Creek Nation, 1670–1763* (Lincoln, NE: University of Nebraska Press, 2004).

Halbert, H. S., and T. H. Ball, *The Creek War of 1813 and 1814* (Chicago: Donohue & Henneberry, 1895).

Hawkins, Benjamin, *Letters of Benjamin Hawkins, 1796–1806* (Savannah: Published by the Georgia Historical Society, 1916).

Hudson, Angela Pulley, *Creek Paths and Federal Roads: Indians, Settlers, and Slaves and the Making of the American South* (Chapel Hill: University of North Carolina Press, 2010).

Jamaica, *The Laws of Jamaica: 1760–1792* (London: A. Aikman Printer's to the King's Most Excellent Majesty, 1811).

Kokomoor, Kevin, 'A Reassessment of Seminoles, Africans, and Slavery on the Florida Frontier,' *Florida Historical Society*, 88, 2 (Fall, 2009), 209–236.

Krauthamer, Barbara, 'A Particular Kind of Freedom in the American Southeast,' in *Women and Slavery*, eds. Gwyn Campbell, Suzanne Miers and Joseph C. Miller (Athens: Ohio University Press, 2008).

Lindsay, Alexander Crawford, *Lives of the Lindsays: Or a Memoir of the Houses of Crawford and Balcarres . . .* (Wigan: Privately Printed, 1840).

Littlefield, Daniel F., Jr., *Africans and Creeks from the Colonial Period to the Civil War* (Westport, CT: Greenwood Press, 1979).

Long, Edward, *The History of Jamaica: Or, General Survey of the Ancient and Modern State of That Island: With Reflections on Its Situations, Settlements, Inhabitants, Climate, Products, Commerce, Laws, and Government*, Vol. II (London: F. Cass, 1970).

Lovejoy, Paul E., *Transformations in Slavery: A History of Slavery in Africa* (Cambridge: Cambridge University Press, 2000).

Mullin, Michael, *Africa in America: Slave Acculturation and Resistance in the American South and the British Caribbean, 1736–1831* (Urbana: University of Illinois Press, 1994).

O'Brien, Sean Michael, *In Bitterness and Tears: Andrew Jackson's Destruction of the Creeks and Seminoles* (Guilford: Lyon's Press, 2005).

Pope, John, *A Tour Through the Southern and Western Territories of the United States of North-America; the Spanish Dominions on the River Mississippi, and the Floridas; the Countries of the Creek Nations; and Many Uninhabited Parts* (Richmond: Printed by John Dixon, 1792).

Rippon, John, ed., *The Baptist Annual Register for 1790, 1791, 1792 & Part of 1793, Including Sketches of the State of Religion Among Different Denominations of Good Men at Home and Abroad* (London: Dilly, Button and Thomas, 1793–1802).

Robinson, Carey, *The Iron Thorn: The Defeat of the British by the Jamaican Maroons* (Kingston: Kingston Publishers Limited, 1993).

Saunt, Claudio, '"The English Has Now a Mind to Make Slaves of Them All": Creeks, Seminoles and the Problem of Slavery,' *American Indian Quarterly*, 22, 1/2 (Winter–Spring, 1998), 157–180.

Saunt, Claudio, *A New Order of Things: Property, Power, and the Transformation of the Creek Indians, 1733–1816* (Cambridge: Cambridge University Press, 1999).

Saunt, Claudio, *Black, White, and Indian: Race and the Unmaking of an American Family* (Oxford: Oxford University Press, 2006).

Skogen, Larry C., ed., *Indian Depredation Claims, 1796–1920* (Norman: University of Oklahoma Press, 1996).

Smith, S. D., *Slavery, Family, and Gentry Capitalism in the British Atlantic: The World of the Lascelles, 1648–1834* (Cambridge: Cambridge University Press, 2010).

Snyder, Christina, 'Conquered Enemies, Adopted Kin, and Owned People: The Creek Indians and Their Captives,' *The Journal of Southern History*, 73, 2 (May, 2007), 255–288.

Snyder, Christina, *Slavery in Indian Country: The Changing Face of Captivity in Early America* (Cambridge, MA: Harvard University Press, 2010).

Swan, Caleb, 'Position and State of Manners and Arts in the Creek, or Muscogee Nation in 1791,' in *Historical and Statistical Information Respecting the History, Condition and Prospects of the Indian Tribes of the United States*, ed. Henry Rowe Schoolcraft. (Philadelphia: Lippincott, Grambo and Company, 1851).

Swanton, John Reed, *Early History of the Creek Indians and their Neighbours* (Washington, DC: U.S. Govt. Print. Off., 1922).

Thompson, Alvin O., *Flight to Freedom: African Runaways and Maroons in the Americas* (Kingston: University of West Indies Press, 2006).

van Doren, Mark, ed., *Travels of William Bartram* (New York: Dover Publications, 1955).

Zellar, Gary, *African Creeks: Estelvste and the Creek Nation* (Norman: University of Oklahoma Press, 2007).

5 Desirable Lands?

Land Disputes on the Maroon and Creek Borders

A critical issue, characteristic of free, non-European communities across the colonial experience, which affected both Maroons and Creeks is that of the land hunger of Europeans which was present, to varying extents, in both cases under consideration here. However, how this manifested itself differed in each case. I will now examine the forms these land disputes took in both the Maroon and Creek examples, highlighting the commonalities and differences along the way.

Both Maroon and Creek treaties included clauses which addressed land and land disputes. In Cudjoe's treaty, Clause Three stated that the Trelawnys "shall enjoy and possess" all the lands lying between Trelawny Town and the Cockpits, to the amount of fifteen hundred acres, bearing north-west from the said town.[1] Quao's Maroons were granted "a certain quantity of land" to raise "provisions, hogs, fowls, goats, or whatever stock they may think proper." However, the treaty explicitly restricted the Windwards from growing sugarcane.[2] Similarly, Cudjoe's treaty stated in Clause Four that the Trelawnys could plant the lands with "coffee, cocoa, ginger, tobacco, and cotton, and to breed cattle, hogs, goats, or any other stock." They were allowed to bring any produce to market after applying for a licence to the Custos, or any other magistrate in the parish they wished to sell their goods.[3] In other words, Maroons were officially granted their own treaty lands by the colonial government. What was ignored, however, was that the Maroons had previously had the run of almost the entire interior of the island, and the peace treaties, therefore, actually represented a significant loss of territory rather than a gain.

It was not only the land itself which was referenced in the treaties—how land was to be used was also a significant point. In particular, hunting was predicted to be a source of contention between Maroons and nearby colonists, and clauses were included to try to prevent future disputes. Cudjoe's treaty stated in Clause Five that the Leeward Maroons had liberty to hunt "where they shall think fit," except within three miles of any "Settlement, Crawl or Pen." In the event that Cudjoe, or his followers, should meet with nearby settlers whilst on the hunt, then the "Hogs" were to be equally divided between both parties. In the Windward treaty, Clause Thirteen said that neither "Captain Quao, nor any of his People, shall hunt within Three Miles of any Settlement." When it came to disputes over hunting, Clause Seven instructed that "in case of any of the Hunters belonging to the Inhabitants of this Island, and the Hunters belonging to Captain Quao, should meet, in order to hinder all Disputes, Captain Quao will order his People to let the Inhabitant Hunters have the Hog." In other words, solutions to any potential disputes were outlined in the treaties, and those solutions always favoured the colonists. The clause in Cudjoe's treaty gave colonists an advantage because, as Maroons were skilled hunters, sharing the spoils meant a better return on hunting. The Windward treaty, which required disputes over hogs to be resolved by the Maroons handing over their haul, benefited colonists even more.

Land was also a critical issue in relations between Creeks and Americans. Looking back, it seems almost inevitable that land would be a major source of conflict between Creeks and white settlers, given the restless determination to expand which contributed to the outbreak of the American Revolution. This emphasis on land acquisition was clear during the peace negotiations at the end of that war. In the Treaty of Paris, the new United States won from Britain the Mississippi River as the western boundary and the 31st parallel as the boundary on the south. What Britain failed to do, however, was gain the agreement of the indigenous inhabitants who lived in this area. Such a decision is striking given that the British had previously recognised Native Americans as owners of their lands.[4] With one sweeping decision, decades of violence would ensue as Americans and nations such as the Creeks battled for the land handed over in the Treaty of Paris. Creeks initially paid little heed to this agreement signed by European powers but, once Georgians poured into the region to claim their war spoils, Creeks were forced to address the consequences of the treaty.

The initial stance of the federal government, when it came to Native American land policy, was formulated in the Articles of Confederation, ratified in 1781. Following British policy set in the Proclamation of 1763, the Articles of Confederation demarcated a clear boundary line between Native Americans and Euro Americans, which, in effect, sealed international recognition of Native American national land claims.[5] According to the Articles of Confederation, Native American lands could be acquired only through negotiations conducted by the federal government with representatives of Native American communities with the authority to make land cessions.[6] This became known as the Treaty System. In the south-east, state governments almost immediately challenged the federal government's authority to negotiate land boundaries. This attempted assertion of states' rights led to Article Nine of the Articles of Confederation that reads, "The United States in Congress assembled have the sole and exclusive right and power of regulating the trade, and managing all affairs with the Indians, not members of any of the states, provided the legislative right of any State, within its own limits, be not infringed or violated."[7] The southern states, all of which made outrageous territorial claims as their "own limits," used this clause to their advantage. What followed was an immense land grab that rendered Native American policy under the Articles of Confederation useless and set in motion the land wars which followed in the subsequent decades.

The first negotiations over land were conducted with representatives of the state of Georgia, who moved more quickly than federal officials did with forming treaties with the Creek Nation. In 1783, Hoboithle Micco and Neha Micco led a small number of Creeks to Augusta, in Georgia, where they and twelve others ceded land bordering the Oconee and Apalachee rivers on one side, and the Ogeechee River on the other, in what was called the Treaty of Augusta. In 1785, seventeen Creeks, again including Hoboithle Micco and Neha Micco, confirmed this cession to Georgia in the Treaty of Galphinton, and in addition ceded land east of a line drawn from the fork of the Ocmulgee and Oconee rivers to the source of the St. Marys River. A year later, at the Treaty of Shoulderbone Creek, Georgia used strong-arm tactics to intimidate and coerce several Creek leaders, once again led by Hoboithle Micco and Neha Micco, into confirming the prior cessions and promising satisfaction for thefts and murders committed since those treaties.[8] As it turned out, many of these men did not have the necessary authority to conclude these agreements. Alexander McGillivray immediately derided the terms of the treaties, damned the Fat King and the Tame King and told Georgians that if they wanted the land, they must "come and take it."[9] Treaties such as these laid further groundwork for the future clashes over land. Georgians used these treaties to legitimise their land claims, whilst Creeks argued these agreements were worth nothing.

A few years later, McGillivray led his delegation to New York to sign the Treaty of 1790. The delegation settled terms that confirmed the cession along the Oconee originally made in 1783 at Augusta but retained for the Creeks the additional lands ceded in 1785 at Galphinton.[10] The treaty also transferred the remaining Creek territory claimed by Georgia from state to federal jurisdiction. McGillivray and others believed that the federal government would be less aggressive than Georgia in its efforts to take possession of Creek lands.[11] This miscalculation led to decades of confrontations over land.

What followed these agreements with colonial and federal officials was years of land disputes; how these disputes manifested themselves, however, differed. Let us first look at Maroon land disputes. Following the land grants in the Leeward and Windward treaties, the first clash over land came in the mid-1750s. An internal dispute in Trelawny Town led a Captain Furry to remove himself, along with some followers, to lands outside of the old town in order to form a new community. The land which Furry and his followers settled on, though, was alleged to have been owned by a Dr. Mark Hardyman. He had obtained, in 1755, 300 acres of land in the vicinity with the intention of erecting a sugar plantation with mills. In a petition to the colonial government, Hardyman stated that Furry had "separated himself from [the] said town, and built houses, and planted provisions, on the petitioner's said land, in the place where the works must have been erected." According to the petition, the land was three miles beyond the limits of Trelawny Town and Hardyman, therefore, requested the government to order Furry and his followers to return to within their boundaries. The House deliberated over the matter for two weeks, eventually concluding in Hardyman's favour. It recommended that Furry return to within the Trelawny borders.[12] However, the House did suggest some provisions be made for Furry and his followers. In particular, it advised that the superintendent of Trelawny Town should:

> fall, settle and plant, thirty acres of provisions, in as effectual a manner as a certain quantity of land, now possessed by Furry, belonging to Dr. Mark Hardyman is, and also to assist the Negroes living with the said Negro Furry, on the land of Dr. Hardyman, to build houses, and make a town, as good as what he shall be dispossessed of . . . and the expence [sic] to be incurred by this service, shall be supported by the public.[13]

For his part, Hardyman offered £50 in compensation for the improvements Furry had made on the land and "to prevent any inconvenience" to him and his people.[14] This inflammatory matter was dealt with without resorting to violence, and a solution was found, albeit one that involved Maroon submission. It is clear that the compensation offered by both the colonial government and Hardyman was intended to avoid bloodshed.

The endeavours of the colonial government to solve the dispute between Hardyman and Furry's Maroons without violence are indicative of its accommodating stance towards the Maroons in the early post-treaty years. Yet, as with frequent non-payment for hunting runaways and to surveyors of land, the colonial government fell back to its usual habits. By 1770, the Trelawny Town superintendent, petitioning on behalf of Furry, stated that the said Maroons had returned within the Trelawny boundaries and had "fallen, cleared, and planted at their own expence [sic] thirty acres of land, and have erected and built fourteen houses, within the 1500 aces granted them" but had never received any pay as promised.[15] The superintendent-general, William Ross, wrote in his report that Furry and his followers "think it hard" that the money voted to them had not been paid. With this pressure, the House finally acquiesced and agreed to pay £150 to Furry's Maroons.[16] The colonial government was clearly employing its typical delaying tactics when it came to payments promised.

Later in that decade, the Accompong Maroons were also accused of infringing on colonists' lands. In 1758, a survey was taken and Accompong Town was said to be encroaching on the lands of Francis Smith, James Smith and Edward Smith to the extent of 430 acres. Later in the month, James Smith Jr. petitioned the Assembly stating that Accompong's land covered fifty-nine acres of his property, "some of the best and most easy part of the said land" making the value of the rest of his land "much diminished."[17] Quite why it took him so long to realise that his best lands were occupied by Accompong Town is unclear. Perhaps a financial motive can be deduced as he subsequently decided to sell the fifty-nine acres to Accompong Town and was willing to make title "to his Majesty, his heirs, and successors for the use of the said Negroes."[18] It seems that by claiming it as his "best" lands, Smith may have been able to acquire a better price. There is no further mention of the rest of the 430 acres belonging to the earlier Smiths on which the Accompongs were said to be encroaching.

The non-violent dispute resolution found in Furry's case was once again utilised in 1770 when Charles Town and Trelawny Town both complained of encroachments by white settlers. The colonial government demanded an inquiry and instructed both towns to be re-surveyed. Once the surveys had been carried out, the Maroons of Charles Town were said to be satisfied with the outcome. Trelawny Town, however, did not agree with the results of their survey, contending that most of their provision grounds had been left outside the boundary and that "great part of that [their land] which was run out for them, is rocks and cockpits."[19] Apparently, the dispute was settled by the intervention of the custos of St. James, John Palmer, and some other gentlemen, even though in the eyes of the English, "there is no doubt that Maroons were encroaching."[20] In a further incident, when another survey of Charles Town was taken, it was discovered that the town was occupying ninety-four acres of land belonging to the Kildair property. The Maroons, having possessed it, were "unwilling to give [it] up, having their provisions chiefly upon that land; therefore," the superintendent wrote, "in order to pacify the Maroons, I was under the necessity of stoping [stopping] Mr. Graham, the surveyor, from proceeding upon the lines, till a fair statement of their claims, should be laid before Your Honour."[21] The archival evidence does not reveal how this event ended, but Mavis Campbell has claimed that it was again likely that a local man helped to settle the dispute without resort to violence.[22] These examples of planter intervention reiterate the argument, outlined in Chapters 1 and 2, that the relationship between the colonial government and Maroons was growing increasingly strained. Disputes were more likely to be solved without violence when a trusted local was involved rather than a colonial official.

Non-violent dispute resolution also occurred at the behest of Maroons themselves. In a petition written by a George Gray and "other Maroon Negroes of Charles Town," it was stated that they had initially settled on lands where there were no white settlers adjoining them; hence "they were able to raise large quantities of goats, hogs and other stock, so as to live very comfortably." However, this tranquil setting was soon disturbed. Gray elaborated that within "these few years past," several sugar works and other plantations had been settled near their town, and upon the lands where their stock used to range. Consequently, they could not raise stock of any kind without encroaching on the neighbouring plantations, as the land allotted to them was "steep and hilly." According to Gray, this resulted in disputes between them and white settlers. Maroon stock trespassed on the cane pieces, while the cattle of the white settlers ruined Maroon provision grounds.[23] The Charles Town Maroons claimed to strive for a peaceful end to this particular dispute, saying they did not wish to put the country to further expense. A "run of land" on either side of the Spanish River, about six miles from their present town, was offered to them in exchange. Situated as it was, the Maroons felt this land would enable them to raise stock without inconvenience to themselves, and there would be no trespassing on their neighbours' land. They pointed out that this would remove every cause of "murmurings and disputes" about stock trespassing which is "now too frequent between them and the white settlers in their neighbourhood," which had not yet turned violent but could have had the "murmurings" continued.[24] The authorities seemed convinced by the arguments of the Charles Town Maroons and agreed to the land exchange.

The petition of George Gray highlights how white settlement had moved inland as the mid-eighteenth century progressed and placed increasing pressure on the borders of Maroon territory. Wandering stock was a difficult problem as both sides seemingly used lands outside of their official territory for grazing. However, rather than this descending into a situation which provoked violent retaliation, as was so often the case in other contexts including the Creek example, a solution was found which seemed acceptable to both the Charles Town Maroons and the affected colonists.[25] This case suggests that, in the decades after the conclusion of formal hostilities, both local whites and Maroons were determined to preserve the tranquillity of their relations. The petitioning Maroons do not seem to have taken the trespassing as the first step in the acquisition of their lands by local whites, as was the case in many other colonial contexts.[26] At this point, both government representatives and local settlers seemed to work together to solve disputes peacefully with Maroon communities.

The claim of "disputes and murmurings" may have been a veiled threat of what might occur if suitable alternative land was not provided for the Maroons, but Maroons asserted their rights in other ways, too. In 1781, a group of Maroons settled on lands belonging to Charles Douglas. The landowner objected to this, and talks were opened to resolve the issue. Douglas said that he would give the lands up if, in return, the Maroons would give him an equal quantity to the northeast where he had another plot—to which the Maroons agreed. Two surveyors were appointed, one by the colonial government and, importantly, one by the Maroons.[27] The Douglas case is yet another example of negotiation between Maroons and settlers to find a solution beneficial to both sides. In this example, Maroons were even allowed to appoint their own surveyors to assess disputed land boundaries, and surveyors were not simply imposed upon them by government officials. It is important to note, however, that such planter negotiation was not likely to be for altruistic reasons. If planters could see more of a benefit from removing Maroons from the land, then they would more often than not have attempted to do so.

The year 1781 also marked the time when certain Maroons became less willing to negotiate disputes with planters. In December 1781, John Cosens lodged a petition explaining that he wanted to clarify the boundaries of his land. He employed surveyors to ascertain the limits, but a group of Moore Town Maroons prevented them from proceeding. It seems that this could have been more a result of necessity than of belligerence. A committee employed to review the case said it appeared that Moore Town was entitled to 1000 acres in the peace treaties, but only 500 had been granted and laid out.[28] Clearly, Moore Town believed this land belonged to them, and they were willing to prevent it from being taken. The committee ruled that the Maroons were encroaching but recommended no action be taken because they had been living on those lands for forty years.[29] Yet again, this situation was investigated, and, whilst not accepting of the Maroon rights to the land, there was no attempt to remove them from the disputed territory. A similar case occurred in 1787, when a survey of Trelawny Town was taken and it was concluded that their provision grounds, as well as their grazing areas, were encroaching on neighbouring lands.[30] Yet, again, nothing was done to remove the alleged squatters.

Just four years later, the Trelawny Maroons sent another petition to the House to claim that they were in need of more lands. Colonel Montague James, Captain Zachary Bayly and Captain James Lawrence complained that a great part of their allotted 1500 acres consisted of

> very high rocky mountains totally unfit for cultivation, that the rest had been under cultivation since 1739, and, the soil, being of a light texture, had become exhausted as to be totally insufficient and inadequate to the support of the present number of the Maroons, who, in the meantime, are greatly increased.[31]

The Maroons openly stated that "trespasses are made on the lands of adjoining proprietors, and a scene of great distress and confusion must ensue, unless measures are taken to prevent it."[32] Again, necessity rather than belligerence seems to have been the cause of the alleged encroachments. Still, however, the colonial government refused to grant more lands.

As the 1790s progressed, and with the spectre of Haiti hanging over the island, some Maroons began to act more belligerently when it came to land disputes. In 1793, a local planter, David Schaw, complained that the Maroons' stock was continually trespassing on his and his slaves' provision grounds. Schaw claimed that, thus far, he had not been able to procure the assistance of the Maroons in making a dividing fence, and he was obliged to "throw up the whole of those grounds to the material injury of himself and slaves."[33] Whilst no violence occurred, the Maroons' apathy in finding a solution is clear. That neither the colonial government nor Schaw himself was able to procure their assistance shows that it was becoming difficult for some planters to negotiate disputes with the Maroons. As will be shown in the following chapter, it was increasingly only a select group of planters who were able to negotiate with the Maroons.

Therefore, as we can see from the above examples, land disputes between Maroons and local colonists were frequent but never violent. As the eighteenth century passed, certain Maroons became less willing to negotiate over land disputes and acted increasingly belligerent, but still violence never broke out.

In contrast, Creek land disputes were often violent and involved far more actors than in the Maroon case. Let us first examine the small groups of settlers who encroached upon Creek territory. As outlined at the beginning of the chapter, the federal government had reacted to reports of frontier settlement by making intrusions of any sort illegal in the proclamations of the Continental Congress. Enforcing this, however, was always difficult. By treaty, Hawkins had the authority to forcibly eject any intruders, but the budget for doing so was always low. The federal government never allocated sufficient money to maintain a military or police force which would be able to expel the squatters. Creeks soon realised, despite frequent promises and treaty stipulations, that the federal government had no real interest in preventing encroachments by illegal settlers. As a result, individuals and families often moved into disputed areas against federal law.[34] Two of the most famous of these settlements were Wofford's settlement in Georgia and Muscle Shoals in Tennessee.[35] The settlers defended their actions by claiming the lands had been ceded to them but, legally speaking, this was impossible. If any attempts were made to remove the intruders, they simply went to the state governments which were full of land speculators, such as William Blount, happy to question Creek rights to land.[36] State laws did exist which ruled against squatting, theft, murder, and other crimes, but in Georgia and Tennessee, Native American testimony was not allowed in a court of law. Thus any land disputes were incredibly difficult to resolve through the courts.[37] It was not until 1809 that Governor Jared Irwin of Georgia finally issued a proclamation that forbid hunting, cutting cedar, building fish traps, or driving stock on Creek lands subject to a fine of $100 or six months' imprisonment.[38] The proclamation, however, was largely ignored, and intrusion continued. Once the settlements were established, pressure could be put on the Native Americans to cede the land rather than face the difficult task of trying to remove the squatters.

An example of such individual intrusion is that of Captain Roderick Easley. He and a few other men entered a disputed area at High Shoals, Georgia, cleared some land, and built a "dairy establishment." The Creeks sent numerous warnings to Easley, and Hawkins ordered him off the land several times.[39] For three years Easley simply ignored the Creeks and Hawkins. He claimed he had legal title to the land, although he had no evidence to back this up.[40] Rather than resort to violence, Hawkins urged Creek headmen to resolve the dispute through American channels. Thus they visited Governor Irwin, who re-issued his proclamation, but Easley continued to ignore the demands. Pressed to act, Hawkins issued a warrant for Easley's arrest.[41] Once arrested, he was to appear before court but skipped bail and fled the area.[42] This was one of the first times that a land dispute made it to court—despite the unsatisfactory outcome.[43] More often than not, however, other methods were used to resolve the disputes.

For example, following a raid in 1787 which went wrong, a William Anderson Jones went missing from his farm in the Oconee valley. Neighbours reported sounds of gunshots and went in search of the source but found only Jones's horse.[44] After three days, Jones's body was discovered. He had been "Barbarously Killed and scalped and stripped naked and a Large Bayonet stuck through his Body which pin'd him to the ground."[45] Jones's killing was allegedly to stake the Creeks' claim for the right to use the Oconee River's east bank. Later that year, Creek warriors again retaliated against American use of the east bank by attacking the settlement of Greenesborough, burning the courthouse and several other buildings.[46] Violence was also utilised by American forces. In 1788, Georgians reported killing ninety-one Creeks. It was noted that these attacks were undertaken "with an exterminating spirit," often targeting Creek civilians. Creek women were said to be "flayed when partly alive" and "pregnant women were ripped open the men's privates cut off and put in the women's mouths with other monstrosities of the like nature." Children were also caught up in the violence, being mutilated and "so mangled that they couldn't be known by Relations."[47]

Such violence was often said to be a result of a pre-meditated Georgian policy of killing Creeks to provoke a violent response which, in turn, would allow the Georgians to further attack Creek settlements and ultimately force land cession. In 1798, for example, on the banks of the Oconee, Georgians killed a Creek chief and severely wounded two others. William Panton laid the blame for the actions on many of the "principal people" of Georgia, saying they were doing everything they could to trigger a war with the Creeks in order to seize land as far south as Ocmulgee. The headmen of the involved villages demanded satisfaction from the Georgians but, in Panton's opinion, it was unlikely they would receive it. Crucially, he then stated, "it [satisfaction] will be taken and this is exactly what the Georgians want."[48] This supports Reginald Horsman's argument that as the Creeks desperately fought to preserve their lands from white encroachment, their "savage" actions were used to condemn them.[49]

These small groups of settlers also brought cattle and livestock with them which exacerbated the problem. Creeks frequently complained of trespass on their lands by American-owned stock, and the Americans did likewise. Frustrated, both sides often took to killing the livestock that crossed into their territory.[50] It was not just the wanderings of cattle which caused problems, however. Straying livestock created problems because both Creeks and Americans crossed into each other's territory searching for strays. In both cases, the search parties went armed and were frequently accused of theft while looking for their own wandering livestock. Armed groups of men roving along the frontier caused concern on both sides. Federal officials and Creek headmen sought a peaceable solution to rounding up strays and to curbing the rampant thefts,[51] with Benjamin Hawkins even trying to issue hunting passes so that everyone in the woods could be accounted for.[52] Like many of his other efforts, he struggled to enforce such actions.

The most likely reason for Creeks to react with such horror to the intrusion of cattle on their lands was because it represented the more permanent presence of Euro Americans. As will be shown, Creeks could be very hospitable towards travellers; but, as the years passed, and the presence of people near the border usually pre-empted a loss of land, Creeks increasingly turned to violence. Robbie Ethridge has claimed that the most common form of Creek resistance to encroachment was raiding and harassing American settlers, especially those who illegally settled on Creek lands.[53] George Stiggins certainly supported this view. He claimed that the Creeks were inclined to believe that murdering recent settlers would teach the white people not to move into their country.[54] Alexander McGillivray agreed and said that if "peaceable remonstrances" failed to remove the squatters, then his people would not be "quiet spectators."[55] Every sight of an American settler on the move caused concern throughout Creek country, and the more who came, the more likely they would be met with violence. This was particularly so in the years after the Louisiana Purchase when settlers streamed across the south-east towards New Orleans.

Following this, Americans seized upon the excuse of wandering stock to push their boundaries even further into Creek territory. In 1805, Tustunnuggee Hutkiss, or William McIntosh, travelled to Washington to negotiate the Treaty of Washington with the Americans. President Thomas Jefferson wanted to push the boundary between Georgia and the Creeks to the Fork of the Oconee and Ocmulgee rivers. He claimed this was because "neither your cattle nor ours regard a marked line—they trespass on both sides & thos produces trespasses by men."[56] Notably, there is no suggestion to draw the boundary back towards the American territory to some suitable river there. It is entirely possible that federal officials turned a blind eye to cattle roaming over the boundary in order to build a better case to push the boundaries back. Americans at least were in the practice of erecting fences, so there was no reason they could not prevent stock intrusion through the use of fences.[57] That they did not suggests an ulterior motive.

Creeks did not just face threats to their lands from these small groups and their livestock. Of even greater concern were the powerful land companies which formed to take advantage of the loopholes left in the ambiguous American Indian policy.[58] The claims of these speculators were truly audacious. For instance, the Yazoo land companies, the nucleus of which formed as early as 1785, claimed holdings from present-day Vicksburg, Mississippi, to Muscle Shoals on the Tennessee River in Tennessee, all of which were Indian lands.[59] These claims were made not by opportunistic settlers but by some of the most influential men in the region. In 1788, James Robertson, John Sevier, James Wilkinson and Andrew Jackson, the later President, intended to grab a large portion of the territory around the Mississippi River.[60] The Tennessee Land Company, formed in 1789, boasted William Blount, the Governor of the Southwest Territory, as a prominent shareholder and laid claim to four million acres of Native American land along the Tennessee River.[61] The tactics of speculators appalled not only Creeks but also the wider political community. It led to Louis LeClerc Milfort, the French military officer, to deduce that, "Americans are very dishonest."[62] Creeks had a name for these land speculators: *ecunnaunuxulgee*, or "those greedily grasping after our lands."[63] Still, speculators operated freely throughout south-eastern Indian territory.

When the land grabs of these companies began to cause political outcry in 1790, the federal government responded with the Trade and Intercourse Act.

The Act intended to stop land speculation and thus smooth the path to more peaceful negotiations over land between federal officials and Creek chiefs. Section Four of the Act stated clearly that only the federal government could acquire Native American lands.[64] This section outraged the supporters of states' rights, and it did not stop the land speculators. As many of these speculators were members of state governments, they simply formulated subsequent state legislation to undermine Section Four.[65] Despite outward appearances, however, such confusion over land speculation actually benefited the federal government. Since the federal government's real agenda was expansion, there was little attempt to regulate Native American land purchases. Indeed, the ambiguities and contradictions served U.S. aims.

In the early years after the American Revolution, the federal government could not be overt in its aims of land acquisition; but, as the Western Confederacy was slowly defeated, that changed in the last years of the eighteenth century. The Treaty of New York, as has already been discussed, involved a significant cession of a significant portion of Creek territory. Then, in 1796, the United States again approached the Creek Nation with a view to concluding a treaty. In St. Marys, Georgia, Benjamin Hawkins, George Clymer, and Andrew Pickens met with representatives of the Creeks and signed the Treaty of Colerain on 29th June 1796. The treaty confirmed the agreements made prior in the Treaty of New York whilst also binding the Creek Nation to acknowledgement of the boundaries established between the United States, the Choctaws, Chickasaws, and Cherokee, as outlined in the Treaties of Hopewell and Holston signed in 1791. These had been controversial treaties because they concerned land which had been promised to the Creeks in the Treaty of New York. Therefore, the Treaty of Colerain included the cession of lands which overlapped with other Native American groups, as well as a new agreement which ceded the lands roughly between the Ogeechee and Oconee rivers in Georgia.

Some Creeks could not understand this incessant desire for Creek land by the Americans because they believed there was more than enough for everyone. Prominent Creeks, such as Uhollimicco, Cutchatustonico and Oposehajoe, wrote to the federal government and asked why the white men wanted to draw lines through the "red people's" land, asking "can't we all live as we allways [sic] lived and by [sic] and sell in peace." They go on to "beg that our great friends will set still and throw away this drawing."[66] Letters such as this one highlight the growing discontent within Creek communities of the land cessions granted to the United States.

The discontent of many Creeks was exacerbated when surveyors arrived to run the line between the United States and Spain, as determined in the 1795 Treaty of San Lorenzo. In 1799, a joint team began surveying and marking the 31st parallel—the official boundary between Spanish West Florida and the United States. The Quaker Andrew Ellicott, who had previously laid out the capital at Washington, D.C., was enlisted to lead the team, and the National Council was instructed to send warriors to protect the surveyors. The delegation started at the Mississippi River and headed eastwards, blazing trees and erecting stone markers to show the boundary. Unsurprisingly, the closer they got to Creek lands, the greater the opposition. After increasing harassment, Ellicott and his men were forced to abandon their supplies and equipment upon reaching the Chattahoochee River and fled to Spanish Saint Marks. Hawkins, as official representative of the federal government, was enraged and demanded the National Council take action. Alexander Cornell, also known as Oche Haujo, marched seventy-two Upper Creek warriors to Tallassee on the Tallapoosa. Upon arrival, he burned the house of a Creek called Isstechah, then beat the man, cut his ears and part of one cheek off, and shoved a sharp stick up his "fundament."[67] The divide between those Creeks who accepted the land cessions and those who did not was growing. According to William Panton, some of the Creeks who did not protest were considering removing themselves out of the country rather than remain to be "cooped up."[68] It is possible the federal government hoped that the Creeks would grow tired of being closed in from all sides and voluntarily move to lands west of the Mississippi. This is reminiscent of the policy used by the colonial government in Jamaica towards the Maroons. From the 1760s onwards, the colonial government restricted the freedom of the Maroons to such an extent that they hoped the Maroons would relinquish their "right" to be a Maroon and become just like any other free black person in Jamaica. Both of these strategies represent indirect ways the governments attempted to influence the Maroons and Creeks into giving up their identity and, therefore, their lands.

Finally, in the early nineteenth century, a new way of gaining Creek land became popular—debt extinguishment. The most significant cession using this new method was acquired by Forbes and Company, the successor to Panton, Leslie and Company and the main trading house operating in the Deep South. In return for extinguishing all debts owed by the Creek Nation to the trading company, Creeks agreed to land cessions in 1804 and 1811.[69] Let us first look at the 1804 agreement which ceded to Forbes a tract of land between the Apalachicola and St. Marks rivers, amounting to nearly 1.4 million acres.[70] The cession wrote off a debt of approximately $66,500.[71] Part of the agreement also provided for the establishment of a trading post on the Apalachicola River at Prospect Bluff. By 1810, however, Creeks owed another $19,388 at this store, and again Creek leaders agreed to cede land to cover the debts. This agreement included St. Vincent Island and the adjacent coast at the mouth of the Apalachicola, as well as land between the Wakulla and St. Marks rivers and a tract at the north-western corner of the original cession.[72] Those Creeks who agreed to the cession benefited significantly from the extinguishment of their debts, making it an attractive deal. For example, Ninnywageechee owed $239, John Cannard $1338, his brother William $783, Kinache $1673, Thomas Perryman $250 and John Galphin $404.[73] These men were all prominent in Creek society. It is no surprise that those who had the influence to push through agreements gained the most from the land cessions.

Therefore, by the outbreak of the Redstick War, Creeks had faced land pressure from individual squatters, illegal settlements, state governments, land speculators, the federal government and, finally, the U.S. trading houses. The civilisation plan, brought in as a tool to reduce Creek dependence on their hunting grounds, also contributed to their loss of land by encouraging credit and, consequently, debt—to be extinguished through land cession.

As we have seen, therefore, both Maroons and Creeks were embroiled in land disputes with various actors. But what caused these disputes? In Jamaica, aside from certain individuals not recognising the boundary lines of other groups, one of the primary causes was the confusion over the size of the land granted in the peace treaties. Cudjoe's treaty explicitly stated that he and his followers were to be given 1500 acres, but Quao's said only that they were to be given a "certain quantity" of land to raise the same cash crops as stipulated in Cudjoe's.[74] This ambiguity lent itself to flexible interpretations by both Maroons and the authorities.[75]

Additionally, the colonial government itself found the varying land grants confusing and hard to administer. This can be seen in the earlier survey of Accompong Town where it was found that the Accompong lands were "binding to the eastward and southward on the lands belonging to George Roxstead, Samuel Smith, George Currie, and Alexander Stanhope, and such other lands as are now taken up."[76] By 1791, however, the boundaries had become: to the east, on lands patented by James Smith and George Roxstead; south, on land patented by Alexander Stanhope and partly on land laid out for George Currie; west and south-west, by rocky mountains and cockpits; and south-easterly, on land patented by Edward and Francis Smith. It was clear that surveys were needed to ascertain boundaries, but these could be delayed for decades, meaning neither side knew who the land truly belonged to. For example, in 1751 a motion was passed by the Assembly recommending that the lands adjoining Scotts Hall be used for the settling of white families. By the following month, an agreement had been made to purchase "nearby land called Scotts Hall," some five hundred acres, for £600. This was executed in November 1751, but the land was not officially surveyed until 1775.[77] For almost twenty-five years, no one knew whom the land was allotted to, and thus disputes easily occurred. This implies that land encroachment was not necessarily a pre-meditated policy of colonial settlers or Maroons to gain more land, but was perhaps more a policy of the colonial government to indirectly put pressure on Maroon communities by refusing to properly survey lands granted to the Maroons in the treaties. It may have suited the colonial government to have confusion over land boundaries, as small-scale, non-violent disagreements kept the Maroons occupied and, therefore, less of a threat. However, such disagreements may have also suited the Maroons, as they could use the lack of clarity to negotiate and swap lands for areas more useful to them—as was the case with the Charles Town Maroons.

A further cause of clashes over land in Jamaica was the poor quality of the lands that Maroons held. After several surveys and additional land grants, the Leewards "legally" held 2500 acres; yet by 1758 yet, even at this early stage of Maroon-colonist relations, there would have been incredible pressure on the lands to support the population. We do not have accurate figures, but the Leeward population in 1738 was said to be 470 persons, although it is not clear whether this included Accompong Town. The land pressure was compounded by the low quality of much of the land. R. C. Dallas wrote that a third of the original grant was "merely rocks . . . overrun with a species of fern and Foxtail grass, which are certain indications of a poor soil."[78] Mavis Campbell has argued that this would allow for "about 100" arable acres of land.[79] If true, Maroons may have been leaving their treaty lands more out of necessity than out of belligerence. This situation was only to get worse as the time passed. Contradictorily, some colonists believed Maroon lands to be fertile and well suited for coffee, pens or provisions and so deemed them desirable for agriculture.[80] These differing views contributed to land disputes breaking out between colonists and Maroons.

In the United States, different reasons abounded. What exacerbated the situation were the differing Euro American and Creek views of land. In 1787, William Panton wrote that Creeks looked on their lands as "their blood and their life, which they must fight for rather than part with."[81] Similarly, the Hallowing King of the Cowetas said, in the spring of 1789, "Our lands are our life and breath; if we part with them, we part with our blood. We must fight for them."[82] The problem developed because white settlers never saw Creek fields and streams as Creeks did—animated with a thousand nonhuman spirits. Instead, as Joel D. Martin has pointed out, the Americans saw the land as aching for development.[83] This fundamental difference was the cause of many violent encounters in the Creek borderlands. Creeks viewed their land as sacred and tied to their society, so, even if they did not use it to hunt on or live on, the land was still in use in some manner. However, the majority of Americans did not understand this, or chose to ignore it, and saw no reason that they could not claim the land for their own as, they argued, Creeks were not utilising it to its potential.

With this in mind, Angela Pulley Hudson has argued that, ever since the Congress of Pensacola in 1784, Creeks observed with much discontent the encroachments made upon their lands by Americans "in every quarter that we possess." But they were particularly concerned with the actions of the inhabitants of Georgia, who "had encroached greatly to our prejudice on our best hunting grounds on the Oconee River and all its waters." These were a result of the generous, if unrealistic, land grants in the West promised to Georgian Patriots.[84] This in itself would not have been a huge complication if the Creeks had agreed to the land cession. However, the Creeks never consented to these rewards given to Georgian Patriots and, more catastrophically, as Hudson says, these men were not content to wait for the necessary legislative acts and appropriations, and began to pour west within a few months of the Treaty of Paris.[85] In 1786, Yntipaya Masla, a principal warrior of the Lower Creeks, said to St. Augustine's Spanish Governor Vizente Manuel de Zéspedes, "The Georgians, when they were English, had their frontier separated fifteen days' journey from our towns." However, since the American Revolution that had "so encroached upon and usurped our land that at present they are distant from us only two days' march, thus not leaving us land enough for our hunting."[86]

A further complication was the contradicting federal and state treaties signed with Creek representatives. As treaty-making was the sole preserve of the central government, in both the Articles of Confederation and these state treaties 1789 Constitution, federal officials could not and would not accept these treaties as valid. Creeks, being an independent Native American nation, had to be dealt with by the national government only. Despite this, Georgians continued to use the treaties as evidence of their right to settle. They moved onto Creek lands, declaring themselves the rightful owners, while the Creeks refused to recognise such claims.

In a similar manner to the Maroon case, a problem that exacerbated the situation was that the borders were seemingly never explained to the Creeks. In 1786, Creeks insisted all settlers be removed from their lands and to "ascertain and draw a boundary line or rather to explain the old one between us and the English." The Governor of Georgia took advantage of this request by insisting upon a boundary line that plainly proved his intention to wrest more than one half of the Creeks' most valuable lands from the Nation. The Creeks were increasingly frustrated and threatened that "the only alternative that was left us, war with arms in our hands." However, at this point, many Creek leaders urged caution to go along with action. They told their warriors to "conduct themselves with moderation and to shed no blood on no pretense but where self defence made it absolutely necessary."[87] At this early point, Creeks seemed determined not to resort to violence to solve the land issue, although Alexander McGillivray did later warn against the "extirpation of the first inhabitants of this Country" by depriving "us of Lands which have been ours from the beginning of time—the possession of which is absolutely necessary to our Subsistence."[88]

Despite this, some Creeks were, in fact, willing to give up some of their land—land which they did not see as spiritual. Creek negotiations with Europeans had included discussions over land for centuries, and Creeks had often used parts of their land as a bargaining tool to gain something that they did not hold in abundance. Remember, for many years before this period, Creeks had more land than they could use for hunting, and not all of it imbued with spirits, so it was more useful for them to give up some of it in return for goods that they did need. Creeks could be open to negotiations; however, they took exception when Americans took more lands than the Creeks were prepared to give up. McGillivray wrote in 1788, "I will most cheerfully consent to conclude a peace upon this basis [land cession but no further encroachments]." But he opposed such actions when Americans seized not just the agreed few miles of country, but an area which extended to several hundred miles.[89] Creeks were willing to trade their land but, understandably, only those lands that would not affect their traditional lifestyles. As Stuart Banner recognised of other communities, Native American political leaders were far from gullible individuals, and whilst not all sales went in the manner in which were intended, there was political manoeuvring.[90]

Kathryn Holland Braund agrees that Creeks were willing to negotiate over some of their lands. She claimed that if Creeks believed some lands had lost value due to lack of game or conflict with colonists, then they made the best use of the land and traded it off.[91] If this analysis is accurate, then the Creeks may have been using a pre-planned strategy when selling off lands following the Revolution. The lands they initially sold may have become useless in their eyes, and they may have preferred to trade it for cancellation of debts. In order to get the best deal possible, Creeks would have had to emphasise how important the lands were to them while actually preferring the cancellation of debt to keeping useless lands. Unfortunately for the Creeks, Euro Americans were not content with taking lands on Creek terms but continued to acquire Creek lands after the point when the Creeks no longer had enough to survive on.

Now that we have looked at some of the most significant causes of land disputes, the most pertinent question to examine is, why did Maroon land disputes never turn violent? One reason that violent clashes did not break out over land was because, despite Alvin O. Thompson's claim to the contrary, it appears that colonial settlers after the peace treaties generally did not place much emphasis on gaining the land that Maroons held.[92] Clearly, Jamaican whites wished to colonise and settle the vast majority of the island. Indeed, General Walpole stated in the 1790s that sugar plantations nearly encircled the Trelawny Town lands and "every where encroach upon the base of these mountains."[93] However, the lands that Maroons held were often of poor quality for growing many crops, and colonists most likely felt that the protection Maroons provided to the island was far more valuable than acquiring some rocky outcrops.

In addition to this, colonists still had plenty of available land in Jamaica to expand into rather than strip their Maroon allies of what little land they held. Bryan Edwards claimed that Jamaica had four million acres of land, of which 3¾ million was cultivable, yet only one-quarter was actually under cultivation.[94] Edward Long further stated that 80,000 acres in St. Elizabeth and 100,000 acres in St. James, both parishes bordering Maroon territory, were still not being cultivated in the mid-eighteenth century.[95] This shows that Jamaica had an abundance of land available if the planters desired it. The land that was desirable to the planters was the low-lying, flat land good for sugar cultivation, not the mountainous rocky interior the Maroons inhabited. Maroon lands were not even particularly useful for other purposes, such as plantation provision grounds, being in such an over-worked and exhausted condition.

The evidence of Edwards and Long contradicts Michael Craton's theory that the Maroons were hemmed in, or at least leads us to question the extent to which that was the case.[96] Parts of the island which were supposed to have been settled extensively following the peace treaties with the Maroons still had not seen significant expansion by the 1770s. The colonial government deemed the situation to be unsatisfactory enough that Acts had to be passed encouraging settlement of the vacant lands. For example, in Portland in 1776, the colonial government agreed to grant each person a quantity of land "not exceeding 500 acres," in proportion to the number of slaves and white men they were willing to bring with them.[97] An Act such as this would have been redundant if the area had been settled to the extent that the colonial government had envisioned. The same was true in the west of the island. Following the American Revolution, Loyalist planters fled the thirteen former colonies, with many arriving in Jamaica. The colonial government debated how to provide for them, and it was suggested that they be given lands in St. Elizabeth. There were rumours of unclaimed crown lands stretching across 20,000 acres or more—land which would be perfect for growing sugarcane.[98] Undoubtedly, there had been expansion of sugar plantations across Jamaica; prior to the peace treaties, St. George had only four small sugar plantations, but sixty had been established by the 1750s.[99] However, the evidence suggests that the image of Maroons being confined to their land like "reservations" seems inaccurate.[100] Local whites had acres of land to expand into if they so wished without taking Maroon land.

Despite this abundance of land, white Jamaicans would most likely have still advocated stripping Maroons of their small landholdings if they had not been turned into an effective security force. As it was, Maroons often provided such protection to white Jamaicans that the colonists wanted to avoid any event which would remove this protection. The importance of this is demonstrated by Edward Long, who remarked that when Moore Town moved to new territory in 1768, it was "much better situated" for giving "speedy protection" to the estates on each side of the Rio Grande.[101] In fact, Long went on to claim that some planters went as far as making secret deals with the Maroons, paying them a sort of retainer to protect their properties.[102] Balcarres, Governor of Jamaica during the Second Maroon War, echoed Long in identifying planters as paying "protection money" to the Maroons to safeguard their properties.[103] This reliance on Maroons was unsurprising given the precarious position of the sugar islands and the planters as well. The sugar islands' free populations were too small to provide an adequate militia, thus leaving them vulnerable to attack.[104] The planters looked for alternative solutions and realised that the Maroons could offer them something which was hard to find elsewhere— defence against the large enslaved population. Once the peace treaties had been signed, enough land was opened up to satisfy the colonists. More important in the inter-war period was ensuring those lands were safe to grow sugar and to live on.

In contrast, the Creek Nation still held huge tracts of fertile land in the south-east—lands which were desirable to the swarms of settlers pushing westwards. One of the causes of the American Revolution had been discontent with the 1763 Proclamation banning any westward expansion.[105] New American citizens were not content with keeping to existing lands when they had fought a war for the right to expand. This began with the Treaty of Paris in which Britain ceded significant portions of Creek territory to the United States without consultation with the Creeks themselves. Georgia Patriots had also been promised lands as a reward for loyalty and were intent on claiming what they saw as their right. Both sides believed the land to be theirs and were willing to take up arms to defend it. Perhaps violence would not have been so frequent if Creeks represented a reliable security force, as the Maroons did in Jamaica. But, as Chapter 3 outlined, Creeks were often reluctant to act as slave-catchers and were never called upon to assist in times of slave rebellion. Indeed, settlers on the frontier would have been far more concerned about a Native American attack than a slave rebellion. One of the biggest threats of the late eighteenth century was the Western Confederacy and, far from being a possible ally against the Confederacy, Creeks were actually a possible ally *for* the Confederacy. Therefore, rather than attempting to peacefully settle land disputes, settlers saw Creeks as an existential threat and often violently pressed their claims.

It is unsurprising to note that on a rudimentary level, one major point of comparison is that both Maroons and Creeks were plagued by land disputes. Land was, and still is, a contentious issue across the globe. From the Americas to Australia, European-descended settlers clashed with autonomous communities over the right to own, and use, land. The Maroons and Creeks were no different. For the Maroons, land represented their identity as a semi-autonomous community in Jamaica. Their landholdings were increasingly the only thing that distinguished them from other free blacks, increasing their determination to protect their possession. Their land also provided sustenance and economic opportunities, although never enough to fully avoid reliance on interaction with the British. Similarly, land was integral to Creek life. As Joel Martin pointed out, it was imbued with thousands of different spirits and was what their identity as a community was based upon.[106] It, too, provided provisions for Creeks to live on and enabled them to become a largely self-sufficient society, at least until prolonged contact with Europeans began to change the Creeks' lifestyle.

The most striking difference between the two communities, when it comes to land, is that Creeks were gradually stripped of their landholdings, whilst Maroons were actually granted land in the early years after the treaties. The common image of an encounter between a non-white community and a European one is of land cession rather than gain. This marks the Maroon experience as different from that of the Creeks, and of the majority of free communities in the Americas. Admittedly, the treaties themselves had resulted in significant land loss for the Maroons, but the subsequent land grants of the 1750s are unusual in the context of European encounters with non-white communities.

However, the actual practice of granting land by the colonial government belies the reality of the situation. Granting land implies control over the land and the authority to transfer control to another party. Whilst British settlers in Jamaica may have deferred to the authority of the colonial government, there is little evidence to suggest that Maroons did the same. In fact, many of the cases in which Maroons were granted additional lands grew out of a petition from a colonist after Maroons had already settled on the lands. The colonial government granting the lands to the Maroons, therefore, was a reaction to action taken by Maroons. The opposite was true with the Creeks. Federal representatives negotiated with Creek leaders to gain lands which had been under Creek control but had been lost to American settlers, often through illegal settlement. Land cession was, therefore, most often a reaction to the expansionist acts of the Americans.

Another marked difference between Maroons and Creeks in land disputes is how those disputes were dealt with. Maroons and Jamaican whites alike petitioned the colonial government and, on occasion, some local whites even intervened to settle land disputes; whereas American settlers tended to simply settle on lands, provoke violence, and retaliate with their own violence. One reason for this lack of violence in Jamaica was that there is no record of any encroachment on Maroon treaty lands by colonists. The only encroachment which occurred was on disputed lands, not granted in the treaties, which both sides saw as rightfully theirs. Conversely, in the United States, white encroachment of Creek lands was endemic, even on lands which had been specifically cited as Creek lands by the federal government.

The lack of violence in solving disputes in the Maroon case was often a result of the intervention of local white settlers, who were in contact with both sides and worked to settle the disagreement. Such intermediaries were almost totally lacking in the Creek case. Many of the reasons for this absence had to do with the geography of the regions. The Maroon settlements, whilst difficult to access, were much closer to colonial settlements than the majority of Creek towns were to American settlements. Furthermore, being employed to hunt runaways led many male Maroons to scour the island, often seeking hospitality and refreshments at British-owned estates. Likewise, Maroon women often made the journey into colonial towns to sell their wares at the markets. In other words, Maroons came into frequent contact with colonists. In the United States, however, Creek settlements were further away from their American counterparts. Hunting runaways was limited to within Creek country and the slave hunters had little contact with American slave-owners, instead receiving instructions from prominent men within the Creek Nation such as Alexander McGillivray or Benjamin Hawkins. In addition, Creeks sold their goods to the United States from within their own lands at the U.S. trading stores and to the U.S. traders scattered across the territory. The white men who lived closest to Creek country were expansion-minded settlers used to the hard-living that came with life on the farthest fringes of the new American nation. Very few of them would have wanted to act as mediators if the opportunity ever even presented itself.

Other explanations abound, too. Maroons had little motivation for violent responses to land disputes. As outlined above, Maroons were often granted new lands, albeit in small amounts, when they petitioned the colonial government. There was little incentive to launch a war for additional lands when they could gain more from peaceful methods. Colonists also had little motivation for violence over land. At this point, Jamaica still had an abundance of available land, should any colonist wish to expand, and the small landholdings of the Maroons did not outweigh their attractiveness as a security force and slave patrol. On the other hand, Creeks were consistently being stripped of their lands by the federal government, state governments, trading companies and individual settlers. Negotiation was not working and many Creeks, particularly of the younger generation, saw no option but to attack. Likewise, the frontier settlers of the United States saw their opportunity to expansion being blocked by Creek settlements and their lands seemingly "not being used." These men wanted to push westwards and were not willing to wait for politicians in the capital to negotiate new cessions. Far from being a security force and slave patrol, as Maroons were, Creeks represented a haven for slaves to run to, and a potential ally for European empires and indigenous confederations to unite with. These men gained nothing from an alliance with the Creeks.

Furthermore, violence was actually a specific tactic deployed by Americans to gain land from the Creeks. American citizens would attack Creek settlements with the view that it would lead to retaliation by the Creeks. The Americans, most often Georgian settlers, could then justify unleashing their full force on the Nation with the aim of pushing Creeks further back into their territory.[107] Such a tactic was not viable in Jamaica. Constantly plagued by the possibility of a Maroon-slave uprising, colonists were not willing to risk sparking such an alliance by attacking Maroon settlements to gain a few more acres of land when colonists already had access to the vast majority of the land in Jamaica. The position of the American regions with greater concentrations of enslaved people was further removed, so the possibility of a Creek-slave alliance was much lower than in Jamaica.

A further reason for the lack of violence was that Maroons were not as troubled by internal division in the way that Creeks were. That is not to say that the Maroons were a homogenous group acting as one, but simply that the small size of the Maroon population, in comparison to that of the Creeks, was significant. Creek communities were split along ethnic lines, often spoke different languages and, as they entered the nineteenth century, were troubled by the rise of the mestizos. This internal confusion led to quarrels, competing land cessions and diverging tactics on how to deal with the American threat. Conversely, as the years passed, Maroon communities found a common language, and Maroons born in Jamaica began to outnumber those born in Africa. Mulatto children born to Maroon mothers and British fathers tended to live outside of the communities, reducing their influence; whereas mestizo children, born to Creek mothers and American fathers, often stayed in Creek country but frequently showed a tendency towards the American culture of their fathers.[108] While there was internal dissension on how to deal with disputes within Maroon communities, there was a more homogenous approach when actually negotiating with the British.

In both cases, land grants of the various treaties were both confusing and inaccurately explained. Furthermore, surveys to ascertain the boundaries of Maroon and Creek lands were delayed and the location of the borders was hardly clarified. Such inaction in Jamaica can be explained by, for example, the colonial government's typical tardiness in paying for services. But there were other reasons, too. Confusion over the borders could actually benefit both Maroons and colonists. Informal use of land on both sides of the Maroon/ British border meant pieces of land could be, and were, exchanged for more desirable tracts elsewhere. Furthermore, confusion over the land grants meant that the colonial government could "gift" lands to the Maroons, which they were already using, whilst seeming to be conciliatory and open to negotiation, thus placating the Maroons and promoting their non-violent co-existence. Conversely, unmarked borders meant that American settlers could pour into Creek territory and settle on the lands, and once in possession, the federal government could negotiate with Creek leaders for lands which had already been lost to the Creeks, meaning the Creeks were more likely to give them up and, thus, the territory would be formally attributed to the United States. Further, land cessions negotiated with the state government of Georgia were often later formalised in treaties between the Creek Nation and the federal government. This issue of federal versus state treaties was not present in Jamaica, meaning land disputes in Jamaica had one fewer layer of confusion than Creek disputes.

Another significant factor which was lacking in the Maroon case was the presence of traders and trading factories which, as a specific tactic outlined by the likes of Thomas Jefferson, led Creeks to agree to land cessions in return for the cancellation of debts. This was a result of the more subsistence style of agriculture practised by Maroons in comparison to the Creeks. In particular, Maroons were explicitly banned from trading in the cash crop of the island, sugar, meaning Maroons were unlikely, as a community, to get into debts similar to what was seen with the Creeks. If anything, the colonial government was frequently in debt to the Maroons for services related to hunting runaways. The reverse, however, of cancelling these debts in return for additional lands did not occur in the Jamaican case.

Not to be overlooked is the differing aspirations of the settlers in Jamaica and the United States. As Barry Higman has shown, Jamaican whites created a plantation society whereas American whites established a settler society.[109] The majority of whites in Jamaica arrived to earn their fortune, making enough money to move back to England and place the running of their estates in the hands of plantation managers and overseers. Few whites intended to stay in Jamaica and raise their families; there were few schools and no universities.[110] Whites in Jamaica were, therefore, less interested in developing the colony than they were in developing the plantation system.[111] This contrasted to the white Americans in places such as Georgia. Whites in Georgia also arrived to make their fortune, but they intended to stay in the United States and consolidate their society through establishing schools, transport links, infrastructure and, most importantly, land acquisition to aid population growth.[112] This explains the different ways in which interactions over land manifested themselves. Maroons inadvertently aided Jamaican whites in achieving their goals, whereas, in the view of Georgians, Creeks prevented white American society from expanding to its fullest potential. The period under examination in Jamaica covers the so-called "golden years" of the planters. Planters were making more money than ever, and this was directly related to peace with the Maroons. To continue generating money at such high levels, the planters required stability over everything else. Jamaica was experiencing a large slave rebellion approximately every five years, and the planters relied on the Maroons to bring security and stability to the island.[113] As outlined in Chapter 3, the British had Maroons to thank for killing notorious slave leaders such as Tacky and Three Fingered Jack. Relinquishing some land in return for stability of the island and the opportunity to increase their wealth was a small price to pay. Furthermore, peace with the Maroons had opened up vast, fertile lands for colonists to develop sugar plantations and increase their wealth. Even more land was subsequently becoming available for sugar cultivation in places like Tobago and Dominica, so there was little need for Jamaican whites to strip the Maroons of their land to cultivate their cash crops.[114] Peace with the Creeks did not have the same effect. Those whites remaining in the southeast after the American Revolution were largely enemies of the British. They had fought for self-determination and to pursue the dream of owning their own property. These men and women wanted land, and lots of it. The problem was that large indigenous communities such as the Creeks hemmed the white population in towards the coastal regions. This was exacerbated as the years passed and the population grew. Once the Louisiana Purchase was finalised, white settlers flooded through Creek territory towards the new land in the west. The refusal of Creeks to give up their lands after the Louisiana Purchase was, in itself, enough to raise the Americans' ire.

Overall, land was a constant issue in both Maroon and Creek history. There are some similarities between the two experiences, but the comparison in this chapter is notable because of the differences. This is largely accounted for by the fact that the colonial government, in its view at least, controlled the vast majority of land in Jamaica whilst the reality was that Maroons still roamed the internal mountains of the island in much the same way as they had for generations. When their lands were pushed to breaking point, Maroons settled elsewhere, often being granted additional lands by the colonial government. Those colonists who lost out on the lands, after they were transferred to the Maroons, were placated by compensation and the availability of lands elsewhere. Other colonists recognised that the usefulness of the Maroons as security against internal and external threats outweighed the possibility of a few extra acres being gained in the high mountains of Jamaica. Conversely, the Creek Nation had possessed their land for centuries and saw no expansion after the American Revolution, whilst suffering continually from settler incursions and land cessions. Their hunting grounds were decimated, leading them to rely on American traders and trading stores for their goods, traders who were all too happy to encourage getting into debt, knowing they could then request lands as a payment for that debt. Creeks were increasingly pushed to react violently to these incursions, and those very reactions were used to strip even more land from them.

Acknowledgements

Parts of this chapter have previously been published in Helen McKee, 'From Violence to Alliance: Maroons and White Settlers in Jamaica, 1739–1795,' *Slavery & Abolition*, 39, 1 (2018), 27–52.

Notes

1. *Journals of the House of Assembly of Jamaica (JHA)*, 1st March 1739, Vol. III, National Archives of Jamaica, Spanish Town, Jamaica (NAJ).
2. *JHA*, 23rd June 1739, Vol. III, NAJ.
3. *JHA*, 1st March 1739, Vol. III, NAJ.
4. Stuart Banner, *How the Indians Lost Their Land: Law and Power on the Frontier* (Cambridge, MA: Harvard University Press, 2005), 12, 18.
5. Luis De Vorsey, *The Indian Boundary in the Southern Colonies, 1763–1775* (Chapel Hill: University of North Carolina Press, 1966), 3, 35.
6. Proclamation of the Continental Congress, 22nd September 1783, in Francis Paul Prucha, *Documents of United States Policy* (Norman: University of Oklahoma Press, 2000), 3.
7. *Ibid.*
8. Randolph C. Downes, 'Creek-American Relations, 1790–1795,' *The Journal of Southern History*, 8 (Aug., 1942), 354.
9. Alexander McGillivray to Estevan Miró, 26th November 1786, PC, leg. 206, 734, PKY.
10. Treaty of New York, August 1790, Entry No. 108, RG11, NA.
11. Alexander McGillivray to Estevan Miró, 26th February 1791, Papeles Procedentes de Cuba, Archivo de Indias, Seville (microfilm, leg. 2004, 733, P. K. Yonge Library of Florida History, University of Florida, Gainesville (PKY).
12. *JHA*, 13th October 1758, Vol. V, NAJ.
13. *Ibid.*
14. *JHA*, 29th September 1758, Vol. V, NAJ.
15. *JHA*, 13th October 1758 Vol. V, NAJ; *JHA*, Petition of John James superintendent of Trelawny Town, on behalf of Furry and others, 24th November 1770, Vol. V, NAJ.
16. *JHA*, 20th October 1770 and 20th December 1770, Vol. V, NAJ.
17. *JHA*, 21st October 1758, Vol. VI, NAJ.
18. *JHA*, 24th and 31st October 1758, Vol. VI, NAJ.
19. *JHA*, 19th December 1791, Vol. V, NAJ.
20. *Ibid.*
21. Notes on Survey Diagram of Charles Town by William Frazer, ST. JAMES 60, National Library of Jamaica, Kingston, Jamaica (NLJ).
22. Mavis Campbell, *The Maroons of Jamaica, 1655–1796: A History of Resistance, Collaboration & Betrayal* (Trentin: Africa World Press, 1990), 171.
23. *JHA*, Petition of George Gray and others to Assembly, 28th November 1776, Vol. IV, NAJ.
24. *Ibid.*
25. Stuart Banner, *Possessing the Pacific: Land, Settlers, and Indigenous People from Australia, to Alaska* (Cambridge, MA: Harvard University Press, 2007); Banner, *How the Indians Lost Their Land*; Lindsay Gordon Robertson, *Conquest by Law: How the Discovery of America Dispossessed Indigenous Peoples of Their Lands* (Oxford: Oxford University Press, 2005); Brett Troyan, *Cauca's Indigenous Movement in Southwestern Colombia: Land, Violence, and Ethnic Identity* (Lanham: Lexington Books, 2015);

Edward Cavanagh, *Settler Colonialism and Land Rights in South Africa: Possession and Dispossession on the Orange River* (New York: Palgrave Macmillan, 2013).

26. For example, in Banner, *Possessing the Pacific*; Banner, *How the Indians Lost Their Land*.
27. JHA, Petition of John Cosens and others, 30th November 1781, Vol. VII, NAJ.
28. JHA, Petition of John Cosens and others, 18th December 1781, Vol. VII, NAJ.
29. *Ibid.*
30. JHA, 17th September 1787, Vol. VII, NAJ.
31. JHA, Petition of Montague James . . . to Assembly, 7th March 1792, Vol. IX, NAJ.
32. *Ibid.*
33. A Petition of David Schaw to the Assembly, Sir Adam Williamson to the Duke of Portland, 14th January 1795, Minutes of the House of Assembly, CO 137/91, NA.
34. Benjamin Hawkins, *Letters of Benjamin Hawkins, 1796–1806* (Savannah: Published by the Georgia Historical Society, 1916), Vol. I, 107, and Vol. II, 409.
35. Francis Paul Prucha, *American Indian Policy in the Formative Years: The Indian Trade and Intercourse Acts, 1790–1834* (Cambridge, MA: Harvard University Press, 1962), 158–162.
36. Prucha, *American Indian Policy in the Formative Years*, 137–47; Florette Henri, *The Southern Indians and Benjamin Hawkins, 1796–1816* (Norman: University of Oklahoma Press, 1986), 43, 194–195; James Wilkinson to Governor Josiah Tatnell, 10th June 1802, Entry No. 1, RG 75, National Archives and Records Office, Washington, D.C., United States (NARO); 9th June 1802, "Benjamin Hawkins' Journal of Occurrences," American Philosophical Society Library, Philadelphia (APSL).
37. Proclamation, 19th July 1790, Letters of Timothy Barnard, GDAH, 109–110; Hawkins, *Letters*, Vol. II, 504.
38. Hawkins, *Letters*, Vol. II, 555.
39. *Ibid.*, 574.
40. *Ibid.*, 560.
41. *Ibid.*, 574.
42. *Ibid.*, 578.
43. *Ibid.*
44. Deposition of David McMichael, 2nd July 1787, 'Indian Depredations' GDAH, Vol. I, pt. 1:105.
45. *Ibid.*
46. George Matthews to James White, 15th November 1787, ASPIA, Vol. I, 23.
47. Kathryn E. Holland Braund, 'Reflections on "Shee Coocys" and the Motherless Child: Creek Women in a Time of War,' *Alabama Review*, 64, 4 (Oct., 2011), 272.
48. William Panton to Manuel Gayoso de Lemos, 6th February 1798, ANC, LOC.
49. Reginald Horsman, *Race and Manifest Destiny: The Origins of American Racial Anglo-Saxonism* (Cambridge, MA: Harvard University Press, 1981), 114.
50. Prucha, *American Indian Policy in the Formative Years*, 158; Early County to the Governor of Georgia and Benjamin Hawkins, 1808, Entry No. 1065, RG 75, NA.
51. Hawkins, *Letters*, Vol. I, 184, Vol. II, 496; Richard Thomas, "His Book," 491.
52. Hawkins, *Letters*, Vol. I, 169, 275.
53. Robbie Franklyn Ethridge, *Creek Country: The Creek Indians and Their World* (Chapel Hill: University of North Carolina Press, 2003), 215.
54. George Stiggins, *Creek Indian History: A Historical Narrative of the Genealogy, Traditions, and Downfall of the Ispocoga or Creek Indian Tribe of Indians* (Birmingham: Birmingham Public Library Press, 1989), 71.
55. Alexander McGillivray to Arturo O'Neill, 28th March 1786, in *McGillivray of the Creeks*, ed. John Walton Caughey (Norman: University of Oklahoma Press, 1938), 104.
56. Jefferson, "President's Talk to the Creeks," 2nd November 1805, Records of the Bureau of Indian Affairs, RG75, NARO.

57. Colin G. Calloway, *White People, Indians and Highlanders: Tribal Peoples and Colonial Encounters in Scotland and America* (Oxford: Oxford University Press, 2008), 201; William E. Burns, *Science and Technology in Colonial America* (Westport, CT: Greenwood Press, 2005), 105.

58. De Vorsey, *Indian Boundary*; Prucha, *American Indian Policy in the Formative Years*; Henri, *The Southern Indians*; Wilma Dunaway, *The First American Frontier: Transition to Capitalism in Southern Appalachia, 1700–1860* (Chapel Hill: University of North Carolina Press, 1996).

59. Henri, *The Southern Indians*, 64; Thomas D. Clark and John D. W. Guice, eds., *The Old Southwest, 1795–1830: Frontiers in Conflict* (Norman: University of Oklahoma Press, 1996), 67–82.

60. Henri, *The Southern Indians*, 62–63.

61. McGillivray, *McGillivray*, 259; Henri, *The Southern Indians*, 67.

62. Louis LeClerc Milfort, *Memoirs or a Quick Glance at My Various Travels and My Sojourn in the Creek Nation* (New York: Beehive Press, 1972), 90.

63. Hawkins, *Letters*, Vol. I, 146.

64. Trade and Intercourse Act, 22nd July 1790, in Prucha, *Documents of United States Policy*, 15; Prucha, *American Indian Policy in the Formative Years*, 45–46.

65. Prucha, *American Indian Policy in the Formative Years*.

66. John Forrester to William Panton, 14th November 1796, Reel 13, Archivo Nacional de Cuba (ANC), Library of Congress, Washington, D.C., United States (LOC).

67. Report of Tustunnue Haujo and Robert Walton to Benjamin Hawkins, 4th November 1799, *Letters of Benjamin Hawkins, 1797–1815*, ed. Louise F. Hays (typescript in GDAH), 44.

68. William Panton to Manuel Lemos, 19th July 1798, Reel 13, ANC, LOC.

69. Daniel H. Usner, 'American Indians on the Cotton Frontier: Changing Economic Relations with Citizens and Slaves in the Mississippi Territory,' *The Journal of American History*, 72, 2 (Sept., 1985), 301–304.

70. William S. Coker and Thomas D. Watson, *Indian Traders of the Southeastern Spanish Borderlands: Panton, Leslie and Company and John Forbes and Company, 1783–1847* (Pensacola: University of West Florida Press, 1986), 251–255.

71. *American State Papers: Public Lands* (Washington, DC: Gales and Seaton, 1859), Vol. IV, 161–163.

72. Coker and Watson, *Indian Traders*, 268–270.

73. "List of Debts Due by Indian Traders and Factors to Panton, Leslie and Co. at Their Store at Appalachy. . . ," Forbes-Innerarity Papers, 85/15, reel 147P, PKY.

74. *Journals of the House of Assembly of Jamaica (JHA)*, 1st March 1739, Vol. III, National Archives of Jamaica, Spanish Town, Jamaica (NAJ).

75. Campbell, *The Maroons of Jamaica*, 138.

76. JHA, 26th October 1756, Vol. IV, NAJ.

77. JHA, 16th October 1751, Vol. IV; 14th November 1751, Vol. IV; 8th December 1775, Vol. VI, NAJ.

78. Robert C. Dallas, *The History of the Maroons: From Their Origin to the Establishment of Their Chief Tribe at Sierra Leone: Including the Expedition to Cuba, for the Purpose of Procuring Spanish Chasseurs; and the State of the Island of Jamaica for the Last Ten Years: With a Succinct History of the Island Previous to That Period* (London: Printed by A. Strahan . . . for T. N. Longman and O. Rees. . ., 1803), Vol. I, 84.

79. Campbell, *The Maroons of Jamaica*, 183.

80. JHA, 7th December 1775, Vol. VI, NAJ.

81. James White to Henry Knox, 24th May 1787, in *American State Papers*, 24.

82. Walter Lowrie and Matthew St. Claire Clarke, eds., *American State Papers, Class II: Indian Affairs*, 2 vols. (Washington, DC: Gales and Seaton, 1832), 23. For more on the Creek relationship to the land, see David W. Miller, *The Taking of American Indian Lands in the Southeast: A History of Territorial Cessions and Forced Relocations, 1607–1840* (Jefferson: McFarland, 2011).

83. Joel W. Martin, *Sacred Revolt: The Muskogees' Struggle for a New World* (Boston: Beacon Press, 1993), 92.

84. Angela Pulley Hudson, *Creek Paths and Federal Roads: Indians, Settlers, and Slaves and the Making of the American South* (Chapel Hill: University of North Carolina Press, 2010), 27.

85. *Ibid.*

86. Vizcente Manuel de Zéspedes and Yntipaya Masla, "Talk That Zéspedes the Governor of Florida had with Yntipaya Masla, principal warrior of the Lower Creek Indians, called Toclatoche, on the ten articles that were proposed and the answers that he gave to each of them in order," 29th May 1786, quoted in Caughey, *McGillivray of the Creeks*, 115.

87. Alexander McGillivray to Esteban Miró, 1st May 1786, ANC, LOC.

88. Alexander McGillivray to Generals Pickins and Mathews, 4th June 1788, PC, leg. 201, 1045, reel 279, PKY.

89. Alexander McGillivray to Arturo O'Neill, 15th April 1788, (ANC), MSS17376, LOC.

90. Banner, *How the Indians Lost Their Land*, 4.

91. Kathryn Holland Braund, *Deerskins and Duffels: The Creek Indian Trade with Anglo-America, 1685–1815* (Lincoln: University of Nebraska Press, 1996), 153.

92. Alvin O. Thompson, *Flight to Freedom: African Runaways and Maroons in the Americas* (Kingston: University of West Indies Press, 2006), 298.

93. Balcarres to the Duke of Portland, Some Opinions Respecting the Present State of the Maroon War, 31st December 1795, CO 137/96, NA.

94. Bryan Edwards, *The Proceedings of the Governor and Assembly of Jamaica, in Regard to the Maroon Negroes: Published by Order of the Assembly. To Which Is Prefixed, an Introductory Account, Containing, Observations on the Disposition, Character, Manners, and Habits of Life, of the Maroons, and, a Detail of the Origin, Progress, and Termination of the Late War Between Those People and the White Inhabitants* (London: John Stockdale, 1796), 247–248.

95. Edward Long, *The History of Jamaica: Or, General Survey of the Ancient and Modern State of that Island: With Reflections on its Situations, Settlements, Inhabitants, Climate, Products, Commerce, Laws, and Government*, Vol. I (London: F. Cass, 1970), 191, 213.

96. Michael Craton, *Testing the Chains: Resistance to Slavery in the British West Indies* (Ithaca: Cornell University Press, 1982), 213–214.

97. Jamaica, *The Laws of Jamaica: 1760–1792* (London: A. Aikman Printer's to the King's Most Excellent Majesty, 1811), 221–222.

98. Maya Jasanoff, *Liberty's Exiles: The Loss of America and the Remaking of the British Empire* (London: Harper Press, 2011), 258–259.

99. Campbell, *The Maroons of Jamaica*, 146–147.

100. Kamau Brathwaite, *Nanny, Sam Sharpe, and the Struggle for People's Liberation* (Kingston: Published by the API for the National Heritage Week Committee, 1977), 248.

101. Long, *History of Jamaica*, 176.

102. Edward Long Manuscripts, Add. Ms. 12431, British Library (BL), UK.

103. Carey Robinson, 'Maroons and Rebels (A Dilemma),' in *Maroon Heritage: Archaeological, Ethnographic, and Historical Perspectives*, ed. E. Kofi Agorsah (Barbados: Canoe Press, 1994), 91.

104. J. H. Parry and P. M. Sherlock, *A Short History of the West Indies* (London: Macmillan, 1971), 136. For more on the militia, see Trevor Burnard, *Planters, Merchants, and Slaves: Plantation Societies in British America, 1650–1820* (Chicago: University of Chicago Press, 2015), 79; Roger Norman Buckley, *The British Army in the West Indies: Society and the Military in the Revolutionary Age* (Gainesville: University Press of Florida, 1998).

105. For more on this, see Colin Calloway, *The Scratch of a Pen: 1763 and the Transformation of North America* (Oxford: Oxford University Press, 2006).

106. Martin, *Sacred Revolt*, 92.
107. William Panton to Manuel Gayoso de Lemos, 6th February 1798, ANC, LOC.
108. Claudio Saunt, *A New Order of Things: Property, Power, and the Transformation of the Creek Indians, 1733–1816* (Cambridge: Cambridge University Press, 1999), 46, 49, 159.
109. Barry Higman, *Plantation Jamaica, 1750–1850* (Kingston: University of West Indies Press, 2008), 4.
110. Amy Marie Johnson, 'Expectations of Slavery: African Captives, White Planters, and Slave Rebelliousness in Early Colonial Jamaica' (Ph.D. diss., Duke University Press, 2007), 148; Christer Petley, *Slaveholders in Jamaica: Colonial Society and Culture During the Era of Abolition* (London: Pickering & Chatto, 2009).
111. Although others, such as Trevor Burnard, have challenged the idea of a large absentee population in Jamaica, there is no doubt that Jamaica had a more transitory population than the United States. Trevor Burnard, 'Passengers Only: The Extent and Significance of Absenteeism in Eighteenth-Century Jamaica,' *Atlantic Studies*, 1, 2 (2004), 183–185, 190–191.
112. Richard Middleton and Anne Lombard, *Colonial America: A History to 1763* (Oxford: Wiley-Blackwell, 2011), 261.
113. Richard B. Sheridan, 'The Jamaican Slave Insurrection Scare of 1776 and the American Revolution,' in *Origins of the Black Atlantic*, eds. Laurent DuBois and Julius S. Scott (New York: Routledge, 2010), 27.
114. Richard B. Sheridan, *Sugar and Slavery: An Economic History of the British West Indies* (Baltimore: Johns Hopkins University Press, 1973), 457, 461.

Bibliography

Primary Sources

British Library, London, United Kingdom

Acts of Assembly Passed in the Island of Jamaica from 1681 to 1733 Inclusive.
Edward Long Manuscripts.

Galileo Online Digital Library of Georgia (website)

South-eastern Native American Documents, 1730–1842.

Georgia Department of Archives and History, Morrow, Georgia, United States

Colonial Records of the State of Georgia.
"Creek Indian Letters, Talks, and Treaties, 1705–1839."
"Creek Letters, 1800–1819."
"Indian Treaties: Cessions of Land in Georgia, 1705–1837."
"Letters of Benjamin Hawkins, 1797–1815."
Miscellaneous Creek Indian Documents.
South-eastern Native American Documents Database.
Treaty at Fort Wilkinson with the Creek Indians, 1802.

Library of Congress, Washington, D.C., United States

Archivo Nacional de Cuba Collection (microfilm).

National Archives, Kew, United Kingdom

Adm. 1/240	CO 137/18	CO 137/21
CO 137/32	CO 137/40	CO 137/42
CO 137/56	CO 137/69	CO 137/73
CO 137/90	CO 137/91	CO 137/92
CO 137/94	CO 137/95	CO 137/96
CO 137/97	CO 137/98	WO 1/92
WO 1/96		

National Archives of Jamaica, Spanish Town, Jamaica

Journals of the House of Assembly, Vols. I–X.

National Archives and Records Office, Washington, D.C., United States

Foreign Letters of the Continental Congress and the Department of State.
Records of the Bureau of Indian Affairs.

National Library of Jamaica, Kingston, Jamaica

Notes on Survey Diagram of Charles Town by William Frazier.
Roger Hope Elletson Letter Book, 1766–1770.

P. K. Yonge Library, University of Florida, Gainesville, United States

Archivo General de Indias (microfilm).
East Florida Papers (microfilm).
Papeles Procedentes de Cuba (microfilm).
Records of the Creek Trading House, Letter Book, 1795–1816.

Special Collections, University of Georgia, Athens, United States

Southeastern Native American Documents, 1730–1842.

Ph.D. Sources

Johnson, Amy Marie, 'Expectations of Slavery: African Captives, White Planters, and Slave Rebelliousness in Early Colonial Jamaica' (Ph.D. diss., Duke University Press, 2007).

Published Sources

Agorsah, E. Kofi, ed., *Maroon Heritage: Archaeological, Ethnographic, and Historical Perspectives* (Barbados: Canoe Press, 1994),
Banner, Stuart, *How the Indians Lost Their Land: Law and Power on the Frontier* (Cambridge, MA: Harvard University Press, 2005).

Banner, Stuart, *Possessing the Pacific: Land, Settlers, and Indigenous People from Australia, to Alaska* (Cambridge, MA: Harvard University Press, 2007).

Brathwaite, Kamau, *Nanny, Sam Sharpe, and the Struggle for People's Liberation* (Kingston: Published by the API for the National Heritage Week Committee, 1977).

Braund, Kathryn E. Holland, *Deerskins and Duffels: The Creek Indian Trade with Anglo-America, 1685–1815* (Lincoln: University of Nebraska Press, 1996).

Braund, Kathryn E. Holland, 'Reflections on "Shee Coocys" and the Motherless Child: Creek Women in a Time of War,' *Alabama Review*, 64, 4 (Oct., 2011), 255–284.

Buckley, Roger Norman, *The British Army in the West Indies: Society and the Military in the Revolutionary Age* (Gainesville: University Press of Florida, 1998).

Burnard, Trevor, 'Passengers Only: The Extent and Significance of Absenteeism in Eighteenth-Century Jamaica,' *Atlantic Studies*, 1, 2 (2004), 178–195.

Burnard, Trevor, *Planters, Merchants, and Slaves: Plantation Societies in British America, 1650–1820* (Chicago: University of Chicago Press, 2015).

Burns, William E., *Science and Technology in Colonial America* (Westport, CT: Greenwood Press, 2005).

Calloway, Colin, *The Scratch of a Pen: 1763 and the Transformation of North America* (Oxford: Oxford University Press, 2006).

Calloway, Colin G., *White People, Indians and Highlanders: Tribal Peoples and Colonial Encounters in Scotland and America* (Oxford: Oxford University Press, 2008).

Campbell, Mavis, *The Maroons of Jamaica, 1655–1796: A History of Resistance, Collaboration & Betrayal* (Trentin: Africa World Press, 1990).

Caughey, John Walton, *McGillivray of the Creeks* (Norman: University of Oklahoma Press, 1938).

Cavanagh, Edwards, *Settler Colonialism and Land Rights in South Africa: Possession and Dispossession on the Orange River* (New York: Palgrave Macmillan, 2013).

Clark, Thomas D., and John D. W. Guice, eds., *The Old Southwest, 1795–1830: Frontiers in Conflict* (Norman: University of Oklahoma Press, 1996).

Coker, William S., and Thomas D. Watson, *Indian Traders of the Southeastern Spanish Borderlands: Panton, Leslie and Company and John Forbes and Company, 1783–1847* (Pensacola: University of West Florida Press, 1986), 251–255.

Craton, Michael, ed., *Testing the Chains: Resistance to Slavery in the British West Indies* (Ithaca: Cornell University Press, 1982).

Dallas, Robert C., *The History of the Maroons: From Their Origin to the Establishment of Their Chief Tribe at Sierra Leone: Including the Expedition to Cuba, for the Purpose of Procuring Spanish Chasseurs; and the State of the Island of Jamaica for the Last Ten Years: With a Succinct History of the Island Previous to That Period* (London: Printed by A. Strahan . . . for T. N. Longman and O. Rees. . ., 1803).

De Vorsey, Luis, *The Indian Boundary in the Southern Colonies, 1763–1775* (Chapel Hill: University of North Carolina Press, 1966).

Downes, Randolph C., 'Creek-American Relations, 1790–1795,' *The Journal of Southern History*, 8 (Aug., 1942), 350–373.

Dunaway, Wilma, *The First American Frontier: Transition to Capitalism in Southern Appalachia, 1700–1860* (Chapel Hill: University of North Carolina Press, 1996).

Edwards, Bryan, *The Proceedings of the Governor and Assembly of Jamaica, in Regard to the Maroon Negroes: Published by Order of the Assembly. To Which Is Prefixed, an Introductory Account, Containing, Observations on the Disposition, Character, Manners, and Habits of Life, of the Maroons, and, a Detail of the Origin, Progress, and Termination of the Late War Between Those People and the White Inhabitants* (London: John Stockdale, 1796).

Ethridge, Robbie Franklyn, *Creek Country: The Creek Indians and Their World* (Chapel Hill: University of North Carolina Press, 2003).

Hawkins, Benjamin, *Letters of Benjamin Hawkins, 1796–1806* (Savannah, 1916).

Henri, Florette, *The Southern Indians and Benjamin Hawkins, 1796–1816* (Norman: University of Oklahoma Press, 1986).

Higman, Barry, *Plantation Jamaica, 1750–1850* (Kingston: University of West Indies Press, 2008).

Horsman, Reginald, *Race and Manifest Destiny: The Origins of American Racial Anglo-Saxonism* (Cambridge, MA: Harvard University Press, 1981).

Hudson, Angela Pulley, *Creek Paths and Federal Roads: Indians, Settlers, and Slaves and the Making of the American South* (Chapel Hill: University of North Carolina Press, 2010).

Jamaica, *The Laws of Jamaica: 1760–1792* (London: A. Aikman Printer's to the King's Most Excellent Majesty, 1811).

Jasanoff, Maya, *Liberty's Exiles: The Loss of America and the Remaking of the British Empire* (London: Harper Press, 2011).

Littlefield, Daniel F., Jr., *Africans and Creeks from the Colonial Period to the Civil War* (Westport, CT: Greenwood Press, 1979).

Long, Edward, *The History of Jamaica; or, General Survey of the Ancient and Modern State of That Island: With Reflections on its Situations, Settlements, Inhabitants, Climate, Products, Commerce, Laws, and Government*, Vol. II (London: F. Cass, 1970).

Lowrie, Walter, and Matthew St. Claire Clarke, eds., *American State Papers, Class II: Indian Affairs*, 2 vols. (Washington, DC: Gales and Seaton, 1832).

Martin, Joel W., *Sacred Revolt: The Muskogees' Struggle for a New World* (Boston: Beacon Press, 1993).

Middleton, Richard and Anne Lombard, *Colonial America: A History to 1763* (Oxford: Wiley-Blackwell, 2011).

Milfort, Louis LeClerc, *Memoirs or a Quick Glance at My Various Travels and My Sojourn in the Creek Nation* (New York: Beehive Press, 1972).

Miller, David W., *The Taking of American Indian Lands in the Southeast: A History of Territorial Cessions and Forced Relocation, 1607–1840* (Jefferson: McFarland, 2011).

Parry, J. H., and P. M. Sherlock, *A Short History of the West Indies* (London: Palgrave Macmillan, 1971).

Petley, Christer, *Slaveholders in Jamaica: Colonial Society and Culture During the Era of Abolition* (London: Pickering & Chatto, 2009).

Prucha, Francis Paul, *American Indian Policy in the Formative Years: The Indian Trade and Intercourse Acts, 1790–1834* (Cambridge, MA: Harvard University Press, 1962).

Robertson, Lindsay Gordon, *Conquest by Law: How the Discovery of America Dispossessed Indigenous Peoples of Their Lands* (Oxford: Oxford University Press, 2005).

Saunt, Claudio, *A New Order of Things: Property, Power, and the Transformation of the Creek Indians, 1733–1816* (Cambridge: Cambridge University Press, 1999).

Sheridan, Richard B., *Sugar and Slavery: An Economic History of the British West Indies* (Baltimore: Johns Hopkins University Press, 1973).

Sheridan, Richard B., 'The Jamaican Slave Insurrection Scare of 1776 and the American Revolution,' in *Origins of the Black Atlantic*, eds. Laurent DuBois and Julius S. Scott (New York: Routledge, 2010).

Stiggins, George, *Creek Indian History: A Historical Narrative of the Genealogy, Traditions, and Downfall of the Ispocoga or Creek Indian Tribe of Indians* (Birmingham: Birmingham Public Library Press, 1989).

Thompson, Alvin O., *Flight to Freedom: African Runaways and Maroons in the Americas* (Kingston: University of West Indies Press, 2006).

Troyan, Brett, *Cauca's Indigenous Movement in Southwestern Colombia: Land, Violence, and Ethnic Identity* (Lanham: Lexington Books, 2015).

Usner, Daniel H., 'American Indians on the Cotton Frontier: Changing Economic Relations with Citizens and Slaves in the Mississippi Territory,' *The Journal of American History*, 72, 2 (Sept., 1985), 297–317.

6 Contact Across the Borders

Maroon and Creek Interaction With White Settlers

Clashes over land were not the only point of contact between Maroons and Creeks on the one hand, and white Jamaicans and Americans on the other. Each side was familiar to the other as they traversed the regions in which they lived and negotiated interactions with those outside of their communities. In Jamaica, Maroons frequently met colonists as they roamed the island hunting runaways, travelling to markets, or visiting their families. Some of the most striking evidence of this is found in the diaries of Thomas Thistlewood. He often recorded instances of coming across the "wild Negroes" in search of prize money on the roads of Westmoreland parish. One such encounter was with Cudjoe in May 1750 on the road to St. James. Thistlewood wrote he "met Colonel Cudjoe, one of his wives, one of his sons, a Lieutenant and other attendants." Cudjoe shook Thistlewood by the hand "and begged a dram of us, which we gave him. He brought to my memory the picture of Robinson Crusoe."[1] Again in early 1751, Thistlewood met another Maroon leader, Accompong. The Maroon leader wore "a ruffled shirt, blue broad cloth coat, scarlet cuff to his sleeves, gold buttons, & he had with [that] white cap, and black hat, white linen breeches puffed at the rims"[2] Maroon captains in such military dress were familiar sights around the island, even into the 1790s and 1800s. R. C. Dallas noted that chiefs "wore a kind of regimentals," and "some old military coat finely laced . . . with this . . . a ruffled shirt, linen waistcoat and trousers, and a laced hat."[3] Thus dressed, Kathleen Wilson states, Maroon captains and their men became distinctive figures, roaming across plantations with their rifles in hand, selling their game in the markets of Kingston and Spanish Town or sailing to offshore islands to search for runaways.[4]

On another occasion in 1753, Thistlewood met with Cudjoe "just by the Styx Bridge and shook him by the hand."[5] Later, Thistlewood wrote of a time at his plantation, Egypt, when two of Cudjoe's men who, on a furlough for nine days, stopped in and drank some punch.[6] These instances show the extent to which Maroons were integrated into colonial society. Interactions were not just limited to hunting slave runaways but took place on a social and personal level as well. Maroons were even said to spend the night at plantations near their lands. Two Maroons stayed the evening at Thomas Thistlewood's plantation, being allowed to "sleep in the cookroom for the night."[7] Not only that,

Thistlewood also wrote of dining with some Maroons on his estate. In 1760, at the height of the terror caused by Tacky's Rebellion, he entertained Colonel Witter, Mr. Cope and four other white men alongside Cudjoe and Quao.[8] Thistlewood's interactions with Maroons are fascinating in light of his brutal treatment of slaves. At first, it is hard to understand how Jamaican planters reconciled their deep-seated racism with their behaviour towards Maroons. Thistlewood liked to consider himself as an enlightened thinker and possibly thought of his interactions with Maroons such as Cudjoe as part of his scientific curiosity. He may also have entertained the famous Maroon leader to express his interest in the exotic. Short of any statement from such planters, we will never know. These examples, however, do show that Maroons, in the eyes of some colonists, were distinct from the enslaved population and warranted different treatment. That treatment, however, was not to be equal to how fellow colonists were entertained.

Michael Mullin has written of other social encounters between Maroons and colonists. According to him, white Jamaicans witnessed Maroon dances and other ceremonies, enjoyed their hospitality and slept with and married some of their women.[9] Mullin further claims that white visitors were aware that they would be welcome in Trelawny Town whilst Cudjoe was alive because "A rule with Cudjoe was, 'always, never to provoke whites.'"[10] It seems unlikely that this was because Cudjoe was fearful of the whites, but rather that he could see the benefits of non-violent co-existence with them. Some colonists were even said to have responded to this amicable stance by learning the Maroons' Kromanti language.[11]

In addition to these social interactions, some Maroons named their children after prominent planters in the area. For example, the leader of the Trelawny Maroons at the outbreak of the Second Maroon War was Montague James—James was a prominent surname in the area at the time, and it is likely that he was named for the Jameses who were the beloved superintendents of the Trelawny Town Maroons. Other examples of Maroon names are found in a letter signed in 1796, following the conclusion of the war. Names of prominent colonists from Trelawny and St. James, including Shaw, Bayley and James, feature throughout.[12] Carey Robinson argues that this act could have been a client's acknowledgement of the patron, or it could have been a mere ploy: an attempt to flatter prominent colonists into supporting the Maroons and becoming their advocates.[13] Mavis Campbell posits that this practice can be traced back to Africa where a common tradition was to choose the name of an authority figure or that of a respected individual as a sign of respect.[14] Conversely, Trevor Burnard has argued that freed slaves frequently chose to abandon African names in favour of English ones upon their manumission.[15] Names of African origin had generally lost their connection with Africa and become more associated with slavery in both black and white minds. African names, notably Quashie and Sambo, became reminders more of their humiliations than their proud African past.[16] If Maroons felt the same, it is likely they too would abandon African names, particularly as the ethnogenesis of the communities led them to distance themselves from an enslaved status. It is notable, however, that the English names chosen were from prominent local families. Whether Maroons were doing this to curry favour with local whites or as a genuine sign of respect, the act demonstrates a certain degree of familiarity between the two following the First Maroon War and a desire to promote mutually beneficial relations.

In many ways, it is unsurprising that powerful white men in Jamaica negotiated with powerful Maroon leaders; after all, this process was replicated in many encounters with African kings, tribal leaders and wealthy merchants in African trading zones. In a time when slavery was not yet thought of as scientific, and therefore Africans were not considered congenitally inferior to Europeans, many colonists across the empire were willing to work with influential Africans in order to make economic and political gains. What is surprising, however, is that this negotiated alliance did not break out into violence in over half a century. When compared to similar interactions in African contexts, the Jamaican Maroons' uneasy alliance with colonists is all the more remarkable. For example, absent completely are the violent skirmishes that broke out between the Ndebele and Rhodesian colonists after a period of alliance.[17]

The amicable relations between Maroons and certain colonists was often a result of joint efforts to locate runaways. There is evidence that white men joined Maroon parties when out hunting for runaways. Again, we rely on the diaries of Thomas Thistlewood. He wrote in February 1754 that a white man with "wild negroes armed" called to beg refreshment because they were hunting "Woodcock's Negroes."[18] The tale of Sam Grant, told in Chapter 1, is another example. Grant was engaged in a runaway hunt in the Hellshire Hills in St. Catherine accompanied by white rangers under Colonel Bennett when the violence broke out that led to his trial.[19] Colonists and Maroons spending days on the hunt increased their contact but also led to colonists utilising Maroons as a quasi-police force. In 1763, Cudjoe's men chased eleven runaways, killed three and took the rest who were tried at Savanna-la-Mar. Some of the runaways were hanged and others burnt alive "by a slow fire behind the Court House" because they allegedly confessed to the murders of a Mr. Wright and Mr. Grizzle at Round Hill in Hanover.[20] Further examples of Maroons hunting runaways in the eighteenth century can be found throughout the archives.[21] However, white settlers were not just reliant on the Maroons' martial assistance; on occasion, Maroons were even said to provide them with information on slave runaways or uprisings. Thistlewood claimed that, long before one small rebellion, Colonel Cudjoe "wrote to Col. Barclay & the Gentlemen of this parish . . . to warn them of this that has happened."[22] The relationship between some planters and Maroons, therefore, seems to have gone beyond employment to one of providing intelligence on the enslaved population. In the process of uniting under a Maroon identity, it seems clear that Maroons were aligning themselves closest to local whites. Indeed, when rebel actions threatened the colony, such as in the time of Three Fingered Jack, Maroons quelled the threats.[23]

Maroons were also employed by colonists in other ways: for example, some Maroons hired themselves out to planters to clear and plant large tracts of land.[24] This began to happen so often that a law was enacted to ensure Maroons received their due payment.[25] This 1791 law made it not:

> lawful for any white person or persons whomsoever to hire, work, or employ in his, her, or their service, . . . any maroon . . . without first entering into a written agreement with such maroon or maroons, two parts of which shall be signed by both parties . . . and such agreement to be signed and subscribed by one credible white person as witness, one of which shall be delivered to the Maroons . . . and the other kept by the person or persons so hiring or employing him, her, or them.[26]

Many details of this type of employment have been lost, given the informal nature of many of the arrangements. Fleeting mentions, however, can be detected. Bryan Edwards, for example, remarked that a Mr. Gowdie hired one of the Trelawny Town Maroons to work for him, showing no difference in wages to those that he would have paid to a white overseer.[27] Gowdie was even said to be an "affectionate and indulgent master."[28] The Maroon historian, Bev Carey, points out a similar circumstance when she says that Maroons offered themselves for hire to planters, settling on their back lands as an act of convenience to be near their employment but being selective as to what kind of work they undertook.[29] Indeed, the Maroon economy benefited when external events impacted the colony. During the American Revolution, plantation supplies from the American colonies were disrupted and the Charles Town Maroons, with their access to the woodlands surrounding their territories, took the opportunity to manufacture lumber and supply it to Jamaican estates. These examples show a degree of interaction with colonial society but, perhaps more importantly, they suggest a labour relationship which was not based upon compulsion.

The cutting of roads in Jamaica soon became important to the economic life of the Maroons. The act had been written into the Leeward treaty but, according to Mavis Campbell, the payment of such work was not ratified by law.[30] Therefore, it became necessary in 1771 and 1780 to pass laws which authorised the receiver general to pay the Maroons who worked on the roads. It was written that, once every year, the Maroons were to repair the roads leading to their settlements. Each man was to be paid "one Ryal per day, Oath being first made by the Superintendent . . . residing in the Towns, of the Number of Negroes actually employed, and the Time they worked on the said Roads: Provided always, that such Pay do not exceed the Sum of Ten Pounds to each Negro Town in each year."[31] The financial limit, however, proved to be too low. When Superintendent-General Robert Brereton instructed the two Leeward towns to "go upon the roads" in 1773, they refused and asked, "what was £10 per year to go on such roads?"[32] Consequently, in 1781, a committee of the House agreed that the financial reward was too small and, by 1791, the limit had been raised to £50.[33] These examples show that, far from being removed from colonial society, Maroons interacted on many levels with colonists and were an integral part of island life.

Similarly, some Creeks also formed good relations with certain Americans who lived in, or near, their territories. In one example, a group of Americans making the long trek across the south-east was intercepted by some Creeks near Tuckabatchee. Rather than this being the beginning of a violent clash, the group escorted the Americans to Big Warrior's territory where he received them "very kindly" and told them he had provided a house for them in town.[34] This hospitable reception was most likely given because the group was only passing through Creek territory rather than attempting to settle on the Nation's lands. Indeed, the kindness of Creeks to strangers in their land was well known at the time saying, "as moral men, they certainly stand in no need of European civilization. They are just, honest, liberal, and hospitable to strangers."[35] Those simply passing through Creek country were often welcomed as a temporary source of income; the same reception, however, could not be expected by those who intended to settle.

Another way to avoid an encounter descending into violence was to be educated in Creek culture. For example, in 1792, about twelve miles from the Oconee River, an American met two Creeks who presented their guns cocked. However, finding the American able to answer them in their own language, they stopped and talked to him.[36] Creeks, unsurprisingly, usually responded well to this behaviour, and white traders were encouraged to learn the language from their Creek wives if they married into the Nation. The benefit of speaking a Creek language has been outlined by Theda Perdue. Fluency in a native language not only made a trader's life more enjoyable, but it also enabled him to interact directly with his customer, follow local politics, which often had a considerable impact on his livelihood and sometimes his life, and act as translator for other foreigners, a role that enhanced his status in the community.[37]

Learning one of the many languages of the Creek Nation was certainly beneficial to smoothing relations, but a lack of language could be forgiven if an outsider had something to offer. One man spoke of a time in his youth when he visited a Creek town. He said that they had no iron hatchets, pots or guns, but that they made use of their own stone utensils. The man said that he was the first who brought the white peoples' goods into the town, and the Creeks welcomed him because of it.[38] Many Creeks differentiated between those outsiders who wanted only their land, usually with little in return, and those who came among their community with skills, or goods, to offer. Perdue has highlighted how such a stance was typical of south-eastern Native Americans, saying that they accepted foreigners "on their own terms and for their own purposes." Indeed, those welcomed into Creek country were expected to live by Creek rules.[39]

Even into the nineteenth century, outsiders could be indispensable members of the community and Creeks were willing to risk violence to protect them. In 1808, a man called Kendall Lewis was playing a game of cards with another called Edward Denton. A disagreement ensued, and Lewis murdered Denton. Fleeing to a Creek village to escape justice, Lewis soon learnt the language and became interpreter and advisor to his village's chief, Big Warrior. The U.S. authorities had not given up, though, and offered a $100 reward for Lewis's capture. However, by this time, he was an indispensable member of Creek society and elders resolved to shield him. When agents came looking, Hawkins instructed local Christian missionaries to keep him hidden.[40] Creeks, therefore, not only incorporated white Americans into their communities but also risked sparking a war to protect them.

Interactions in both Maroon and Creek society also took the form of sexual contact. In Jamaica, the mentions of this are fleeting, but there is evidence in the archival record. After the outbreak of the Second Maroon War, when the colonial government offered Maroons the opportunity to relinquish their Maroon identity and live as free people in Jamaica, a relatively small group accepted the offer. Interestingly, many of the group were Maroon women who had mulatto or quadroon children.[41] According to Mavis Campbell, when a second group of twenty-two relinquished their identity, all except seven women were of mixed blood. Of those seven, three had liaised with white men and had produced mulatto children.[42] Such examples demonstrate the sexual contact between colonists and Maroon women. These women may not have been coerced into these sexual relations in the same way that slave women were, but it is still most likely that they were pressured into these acts, whether by Maroon and/or colonial society, by their economic situation or by members of their own family. It is clear that simply being a free woman, whether black or white, did not curtail the opportunities for men to exploit and coerce women into sexual relations. Scholars must not only look to other examples of rape and sexual exploitation in colonial settings to understand that a woman "voluntarily" leaving her community to live with a white man may actually have been coercion.[43] There is no evidence of any sexual relations between Maroon men and European women, although this does not mean it did not occur. Taboo though it was, some European women were said to have formed sexual relationships with their male slaves, and it would not be impossible for this to have been replicated with Maroon men.[44]

Sexual interaction, often in the form of intermarriage, also occurred in Creek country—most frequently between traders and Creek women. As shown by Theda Perdue, the best way for a trader to integrate himself into Creek society was to marry a native woman and thereby socially bind himself to the community. Examples of these marriages abound in the records. For example, Richard Bailey married a Creek woman in the 1790s and remained in Creek country for forty years.[45] By marrying a Creek woman, Bailey demonstrated his commitment to Creek society. Kathryn Braund has argued that virtually every trader took an Indian wife and raised a mixed-blood family. The majority of Creeks accepted these unions as visible testimony of a trade alliance, and there were advantages for those traders who took a Creek wife. At the most basic level, marriage to a Creek woman linked an outsider to a specific clan, which supported him, protected him and also guaranteed a certain number of customers from the clan network.[46] Having a Creek wife could also protect these traders from certain treatment. Andrew Frank has shown that on several occasions, Creeks evicted unmarried traders, but married ones avoided this fate.[47]

Marriage with a Creek woman did not always automatically result in full incorporation into Creek society, however. In 1796, Mr. Marshall, a trader of twelve years with two Creek wives, explained his ignorance of Creek households by saying "that during the whole of his residence he had not entered 3 of the Indian houses, that whatever business he had with the men he went to their doors, mentioned it to them."[48] There were also instances when a married trader encountered problems regardless of his Creek wife. In 1798, several Creek chiefs agreed to banish six traders and packhorsemen who "meddle in public affairs, are constantly circulating reports injurious to our peace." Creek leaders of the town gave Richard Bailey, John Shirley, William Lyons, Samuel Lyons, Francis Lessly and Robert Killgore twenty-four days to leave the Nation. Charles Weatherford, who was married to one of McGillivray's sisters, a woman of the Wind clan, was also sentenced to banishment. However, at the intervention of Opoie Hutke of Ocheubofau and "in consideration of his family on the Indian side," he was given a reprieve. Hutke assured the Creek leaders that he would "attend to Weatherford's conduct and endeavour to make him reform his behaviour." The leaders were satisfied with this promise but swore that if Weatherford "do misbehave again, he is then to be removed without any favour or affection."[49] In other words, having a link to a clan was more important than simply marrying a Creek woman.

Intermarriage between Creeks and white settlers was not limited to the instances where a Creek woman married a Euro American man. Although there were comparatively few intermarried white women, Andrew Frank argues that at least two dozen European women had Creek husbands. Frank believes that the small number of European women in Creek country was due to Creek social structure. Women would have had trouble finding a place within female-controlled villages, especially as they would not have relatives in the town, access to property, independent status or social obligations unless they married into a Creek clan. They would be nonentities. Therefore, most women who married Native Americans were adopted captives rather than voluntary migrants.[50] Some of these captives stayed in Creek country until their relatives bargained with their captors.[51] Others went on to marry into Creek society, whether willingly or not. In one case, Jenny Stephenson was given to Passcote Emautlau "in payment for a brother of his who was killed accidentally." Stephenson had four children whilst in Creek country but subsequently petitioned Hawkins to return her to the United States.[52] Other women chose to stay—one example is Hannah Hale. Hale became a rancher and slave owner, and now living in a matrilineal society, she did not have to worry about her husband's relatives leaving her destitute if he died. After spending almost twenty years with her Creek husband, a headman of Thlotlogulgau, and raising five children, Hale decided to visit her mother in Georgia. Once there, her relatives refused to let her return to Creek country and her husband had to ask Hawkins to intercede. After lengthy discussions, Hawkins eventually convinced her family to release her to his care, and they returned to Creek country.[53] Hale had not only made a life for herself in Creek country but, according to Hawkins, would have possessed all the rights of a Creek woman, including the right to "throw away her husband whenever she chooses."[54]

When it comes to examining interactions between Maroons and Creeks on the one hand, and settlers and colonists on the other, it is imperative also to study the role of superintendents and federal officials who lived amongst these communities. In the interest of time and space, these men will be represented by Major John James, superintendent-general for the Maroon towns in Jamaica, and Benjamin Hawkins, U.S. representative to the Creek Nation. John James was the most famous of the superintendents employed by the colonial government to reside in Maroon territory. He initially became superintendent of Trelawny Town in 1767, and then major-commandant of all Maroons in 1779.[55] His post mainly consisted of travelling the island settling disputes with white residents and going out with Maroon parties in search of runaways. James, in many ways, was suited for the job as he was full of qualities which were attractive to the Maroons he lived amongst. It is worth here quoting R. C. Dallas at length:

> Nature never produced a form more calculated for vigour and activity. Barefoot, he equalled the speed of the hardiest Maroon over rocks and precipices, darting on with an agility peculiar to himself. He was indefatigable in every pursuit to which the Maroons were accustomed, and nothing that he pursued escaped him. Hunting the wild boar had been his earliest amusement and employment. . . . When dreadful disputes took place among the Maroons, their cutlasses brandished against one another and serious mischief likely to ensue, he would run among the thickest of them, knock down the most refractory, put them into irons, and afterwards punish them. . . . They loved, venerated and feared him. He arranged and settled their accounts for their labour, adjusted differences, and neither suffered them to be imposed upon, nor to impose upon others. Had he been born a Maroon, he could not have been better acquainted with their character, disposition, and prejudices.[56]

Because of some dispute over housing, however, John James withdrew from Trelawny Town and went to reside on his own estate. The Trelawnys apparently deeply missed having James living with them and, with a view to having him returned, they complained to the Assembly that he had not been living in their town. Their aim, apparently, was simply to have him reinstated within Maroon territory itself. It came as a surprise, then, when the House dismissed James for negligence in 1792. In a move which was to have tragic consequences, he was replaced by Thomas Craskell. Craskell was the son of the island's engineer, and his character certainly did not suit the Maroons. It was claimed that when the "young men" quarrelled, Craskell "instead of interfering with his authority to adjust their differences" would appear frightened and ran to his house "for safety."[57]

After the flogging of the two Maroons in the lead-up to the Second Maroon War, James once again became instrumental. On learning of the trouble, Major James and his son rushed to the Trelawny territory where, because of their popularity, they acted as a calming influence. One view is that the Jameses helped the Trelawnys to list their grievances in writing. Another view, stated by James Merody, was that the Jameses used the tense situation to attempt to secure their own reinstatement. Merody claimed to the colonial government that Major James had held private talks with the Trelawnys where he not only "took down in writing" all their complaints, but also "reminded them of many old grievances which they had complained of whilst he was their Superintendent and which they had forgotten."[58] Merody also alleged that he had heard Major James tell the Trelawnys that if they wished to have him back as their superintendent then "they must insist positively upon it with the Governor."[59] The speed at which James had reached the Trelawnys meant he had installed himself in the town before the magistrates sent to negotiate with the Maroons arrived. When John Tharp, James Stewart and the rest of the delegation appeared in the town, they found Major James and his group had already mitigated much of the Trelawny's anger, although the gathering of the armed men that they met still displayed in their "countenances and manners . . . a spirit of violence."[60]

This spirit of violence was said to have been encouraged by Major James and his son. Captain James, the son of Major James, was alleged to have told the Trelawnys that he wished their complaints "accommodated" but, if the events led to rebellion, then he would "flog the Negroes from his Estate to oblige them to join the Maroons." Merody's deposition concluded with a statement which, if true, shows the extent to which the relationship between the colonial government and the Trelawny Maroons had deteriorated. He stated that they declared that "Major James was the only Person wearing a red Coat who should be permitted to enter their town."[61] Major James later joined colonial troops to fight the Trelawnys, but they never lost their support of him. On one occasion, he had led a party through unfamiliar territory to the mouth of a defile, where their presence was detected by a Maroon look-out. A voice echoed around the slopes enquiring whether Major James was with them and "if he is let him go back, we do not wish to hurt him; but as for the rest of you, come on and try battle if you choose."[62] Perhaps wisely, the party chose to retreat.

Benjamin Hawkins was held in a similar regard by many Creeks—although this had not always been the case. In their first transaction, Creeks were very distrustful of Hawkins and his office. George Stiggins claimed that the Creeks held frequent debates among themselves "in contemplation of killing him."[63] They considered killing him because some Creeks believed that he was imposed on them by the government as a spy and to shackle their liberties. But as the years passed, attitudes towards Hawkins began to change. Stiggins elaborates: "They loved him for his virtuous and disinterested greatness of mind, for he expressed to them his hopes and wish for their welfare. He took pains to learn their language."[64] This underlines the point made earlier in this chapter that local whites were welcomed into Creek society if they married a Creek woman or learnt the indigenous language. The fact that Hawkins took the time to learn their language implied his commitment to Creek society and, therefore, eased his acceptance into the community. In fact, he was subsequently given the honorary high-ranking title of *istiatcagagi*, or "beloved man," denoting wisdom, accomplishment and trust.[65]

Many of Hawkins's successful dealings with Creeks were a result of his knowledge of the language and his willingness to converse with Creeks about numerous topics. Indeed, Hawkins was not the distant figure that previous Indian agents had been. His ability to converse in the local languages meant that he could help calm tempers when disputes arose. In many ways, Hawkins was an advocate of the Creeks and did not adhere to the later policies of reduction or removal. This stance won him significant support within Creek country. George Stiggins claimed that Creeks "could not but admire his [Hawkins's] firm candid and honest deportment" when participating in public meetings.[66] Indeed, Hawkins eventually became close friends with many Creek men, especially the Tuckabatchee headman Oche Haujo, known as Alexander Cornell, at whose death Hawkins wrote, "We have not his equal among us."[67] As the years passed, Creeks continued to praise Hawkins and his efforts within the Creek Nation. Hopoie Micco, a Creek chief, wrote to him saying Hawkins had long been in their land doing good for them. Hopoie Micco even called him "an old chief among us" and stated that they appointed him "our agent, to see justice done in our affairs, as well as the white people."[68] This shows the esteem in which Hawkins seems to have been held by many Creeks, or at least the esteem in which those Creeks were willing Hawkins to believe they held him. There is no doubt that several, if not the majority, of the Creeks had an affection for Hawkins as a person, if not for his policies. However, despite his commitment to the Creeks, his interaction with them unquestionably aided the federal government in its aim of convincing Creeks to ally with it against any other foreign power. His civilisation plan was clearly an attack on the Creek way of life and, therefore, he remains a controversial figure in Creek society. Indeed, his introduction of the National Council and the "lawmenders" contributed to the frequent violence in the region.

The presence of men such as John James and Benjamin Hawkins within these communities had a severe impact. In the Maroon case, it is because they aided in non-violent dispute resolution which kept the island largely free of Maroon trouble until the Second Maroon War. In the Creek Nation, it contributed to the cycle of violence already present on the frontier. Violence was a product of many things—from land disputes, to kidnapping, or to pure criminality. However, what compounded these problems was how they were resolved. As outlined in Chapters One and Two, in his civilisation plan, Hawkins attempted to, and largely succeeded in, altering Creek justice. First, however, we will look at how disputes were resolved in Jamaica.

When a dispute broke out between Maroons and colonists, most often over land, one of the most important factors in it staying peaceful was the role of these mediators who intervened to discuss matters with both sides and attempted to find a non-violent solution. Take for example, the case surrounding Sam Grant from Chapter 1. When Grant fled the scene, he at first retreated to his town, Scotts Hall, and from there to Charles Town and subsequently Moore Town. Thus, all the Windward communities were joined in the dispute—no doubt striking fear in the hearts of colonists and encouraging many to handle the situation carefully. When colonial officials approached the Maroons in an attempt to calm tempers, it was said they were received with "great haughtiness" and their leader, Cudjoe, addressed them with "insolence." He stated, "You see, it is true Gentlemen, but a handful of Men here, but dont' [sic] expect to treat us ill on that account. Tho' we take up rebels and runaways, we know how to make use of them, and if you persist, we can bring twenty blacks to one white."[69]

At this point, we see the intervention of "some gentlemen" to quell the dispute. It was agreed that Grant should be brought to justice and a trial was arranged with two justices and three freeholders. After hearing the evidence, Grant was acquitted on account of his actions being committed in self-defence. Perhaps the "gentlemen" who had intervened suggested a trial to calm the colonists, with an agreed acquittal to quieten the Maroons. Grant's trouble did not end there, however. He then faced a Maroon trial and was reminded that he, as a soldier, was expected to take his own life if guilty. The Captain of Scotts Hall said he was honour bound to do so and, if guilty, should "go this instant into the wood and shoot yourself." But Grant argued that he was innocent because the first killing was accidental and occurred while trying to protect his superior, while the second genuinely was in self-defence.[70] He was subsequently also acquitted by in the Maroon trial.

Following the incident with Sam Grant and Captain Davy, fears ramped up among the colonists. One colonist speculated on the prospect of war with the Maroons, writing "It would be a very unequal warfare . . . with a parcel of savages who have nothing to lose; and what might still be worse it is to be feared, that if we had the fortune to extirpate them, our great wilderness which occupies the middle range of the Island, would soon be filled again by another set of Banditti more Savage than these." The colonist concluded that the best solution would be "a uniform adherence to justice in all our dealings with them."[71]

Such examples of intervention by trusted locals also occurred in many of the land disputes outlined in Chapter 5; for example, the occasion in 1770 when Maroons of Trelawny Town complained of encroachments by white settlers. That particular dispute was said to have been settled by the intervention of the custos of St. James, John Palmer and some other gentlemen, even though in the eyes of the English, "there is no doubt that Maroons were encroaching."[72] In the incident in which Charles Town Maroons were accused of encroaching upon the Kildair property, it was again alleged that a local man helped to settle it without resort to violence.[73]

These interventions were not just over small matters. Indeed, the richest body of sources that deal with this issue are from the Second Maroon War. It is worth examining these in detail. When the Second Maroon War broke out, many of the local planters of St. James advised Balcarres that they thought it best to appease the Maroons by promising that their causes of complaint would be enquired into by the Legislature.[74] These men did not stop with writing letters. Discussions were held, and it was proposed to send "four . . . justices to meet four chosen Maroons" to settle all disputes.[75] However, the Trelawnys did not welcome the magistrates in the cordial manner that was expected. James Merody, who was assistant to Thomas Craskell, by then superintendent of the Trelawny Town Maroons, deposed that the local men pleaded with the Maroons to surrender themselves early on, but the younger Maroons refused and said the militia were fools to think of coming into their woods to fight with them.[76] The Maroons did not appear to be overly aggressive towards the magistrates, but their refusal to back down and negotiate shows the extent to which the Maroons had been aggrieved. However, their willingness to meet peacefully with these local magistrates, despite their feelings of discontent, suggests their quarrel could have been more related to their treatment by the colonial government rather than by individual local planters.

The four men who travelled to Trelawny Town were James Stewart, who was specifically asked to attend by the Trelawnys, Jarvis Gallimore, Edward Knowles and James Galloway. Stewart reported that:

> The Maroons, collected in a body of about three hundred men, received us, armed with their usual weapons, and displayed at our entrance into the town evolutions peculiar to their mode of fighting. The gentlemen, first with them, had mitigated much of their rage; but yet their countenances and manners indicated a spirit of violence, which was strongly expressed by the language and gestures employed in the detail of grievances which I have enclosed to you.[77]

Stewart's account suggests that by mere negotiation and communication, much of the discontent had been appeased. He went on:

> under such circumstances, little time could be afforded for deliberation. We therefore thought it, at the instant, not bad policy to appease them by a promise, that their causes of complaint should be enquired into by the legislature, in order that they might be redressed, with which dependence they appeared satisfied: but would not by any means consent to Mr. Craskell's return to his office, and insisted that major James should remain with them all night, which he agreed to do.[78]

As far as Stewart was concerned, this seemed enough to placate the Maroons until their complaints were heard. He informed them of the intended meeting of the House of Assembly early the following month where he suggested their complaints could be heard. This led to an "appearance of satisfaction" amongst them so Stewart and the others left the town in the evening, apparently believing the matter to be settled.[79]

The apparent mutually beneficial alliance between white settlers in nearby parishes and the Maroons was called into question by the events that followed. On 20th July, the Trelawnys allegedly threatened to burn Vaughan's estates and the estate of Fairfield where their beloved former superintendent Major James lived, stating that they desired nothing more than to fight the St. James' Regiment. However, this letter is suspect because one of the initial reasons for the hostility was the desire to reinstate Major James as their superintendent; yet, apparently, a few days later they were willing to burn the estate where he lived. Whether the letter was authentic or not, the colonial government took it as a reason to order five regiments of the Cornwall county militia to hold themselves in readiness.[80] Balcarres, then Governor of Jamaica, further claimed in a subsequent letter that "They have threatened the destruction of the two plantations nearest them."[81] We cannot be sure whether this was a ploy by Balcarres to justify hostilities against the Maroons. Perhaps his statements were true, but it is also possible that he claimed that local plantations were under threat in order to gain the alliance of these local planters in the fight against the Trelawny Maroons. Indeed, Balcarres intentionally misconstrued other events in the lead-up to the Second Maroon War, so he could surely have been capable of doing so again. For example, there is the occasion when he received a note from Montague James, the colonel of Trelawny Town, stating:

> Gentlemen,
> The Maroons wishes [sic] nothing else from the country but battle; and they desires not to see Mr Craskell up here at all. So are waiting every moment for the above on Monday.
> Colonel Montague, and all the rest.[82]

This rather assertive note, however, also had a postscript. It said, "Mr David Schaw will see you on Sunday morning for an answer. They will wait till Monday, nine o'clock, and if they don't come up, they will come down themselves."[83] Balcarres duly sent a copy of the letter to the Duke of Portland the following day. However, he omitted the postscript, thus making the Trelawnys sound more provocative and less willing to parlay.

Even after this apparent threat to burn local plantations, some of these colonial mediators continued to try to advise the Trelawny Town Maroons. They strongly recommended that the Maroons comply with the Governor to prevent "those terrible evils."[84] This support shown by a group of local white settlers is repeated throughout the archival evidence. For example, James Palmer, the custos of St. James, regarded the decision to send three troops of light horse to reinforce the militia as "provocative."[85] He went on to urge the Governor to reappoint "with as little delay as possible" Major John James in order to convince the Trelawnys that the colonists were not "delaying the business in order to collect force."[86] Further, on 25th July, a senior magistrate about to sail with the fleet from Negril wrote urging that the Maroons' demands, which he termed "not unreasonable," be satisfied.[87] Finally, the gentlemen of the area around the Maroon territory assembled, formed themselves into a council of war and heard the story of the Maroons. They described them as a "quiet innocent people" and said the colonial troops ought to retire.[88] This backing of the Maroons by local whites was sustained throughout the Second Maroon War apparently out of a genuine desire to avoid hostilities.

Balcarres took a dim view of the actions of the local magistrates. He wrote to inform General Williamson, who was away leading British troops in Saint Domingue, that the insurrection amongst the Maroons had subsided "for the moment" but was critical of the magistrates having "conceded everything." He lamented that "by such want of exertion, and such timidity among magistrates, are countries lost."[89] It is no surprise, however, that these local colonists desired a more amicable end to the tensions. One of them, Vaughan, explicitly outlined their fears in one letter. He stated that "as a further motive" for settling the affair without open hostility, it was best to inform the Governor that the "negroes of several estates" had been making complaints against their management. Vaughan had witnessed one such complaint coming from "all the negroes" at Content Estate and was told by a Mr. Barrett of another from Anchovy Bottom. As the days passed, reports of more complaints reached Vaughan, and he wondered, "Whence does this arise, but from the times; and what check have we so effectual as the maroons?"[90]

The magistrates who had met with the Trelawnys and heard their complaints continued to argue their case. At a meeting of their fellow planters and property owners, the magistrates outlined the Maroons' grievances. First, they complained of the whipping of the two Maroons at Montego Bay by a slave, declaring it to have been an infringement of the treaty. Second, they pointed out their original land grant was worn out, and they therefore were asking for an additional quantity, citing the adjoining properties of Vaughan and David Schaw as well as the lands commonly called and known as Crews or Robert Kenyon as desirable. Third, they complained against the conduct of Thomas Craskell arguing that he was not qualified for the office of superintendent of their town; that he lacked authority, "and as they have experienced the disposition and abilities of captain John James (their late superintendent), they are desirous of his reappointment to the office, and are adverse to the appointment of any other person."[91] The colonists from St. James and Trelawny who attended this meeting were "of the opinion" that such requests should be complied with.[92] As history has shown us, however, Balcarres ignored this advice and launched a military attack against the Trelawny Maroons.

It was becoming increasingly clear that there was a split in colonial society over how to deal with the Trelawnys. In private, Balcarres acknowledged this lack of consensus. In fact, he was concerned that men such as John James aimed to lead the Maroons in rebellion to reap rewards for himself. Balcarres lamented, "I think the soul and heart of the country is with me, excepting the two parishes of Trelawny and St. James who are under the absolute sway and dominion of a Major James." He claimed that James was a man of considerable property connected by relationship with all of the men in those two parishes. Balcarres accused him of being rebellious but "clear sighted enough to perceive that the Maroons with himself at their head, and supported by the negroes, were to give law to this country."[93] Balcarres, however, forged ahead with the Second Maroon War.

Even after the Second Maroon War finally came to a close, the criticism of the colonial government continued by these St. James and Trelawny planters. According to Richard Hart, the decision to transport the Trelawny Maroons out of the island "in breach of the treaty" occasioned "surprise and disgust among many white residents."[94] This attitude came from some of the most powerful men in Jamaica. John Tharp, for example, one of the largest slave-owners in Jamaica, expressed his disagreement with the deportation. At his death in 1805, his personal estate was worth over £362,000 including 2990 slaves, meaning support for the plight of the Trelawny Maroons came from the very elite of Jamaican society.[95] General Walpole, leader of the colonial forces, also mentioned the "violent opposition party" in Jamaica which asserted that the colonial government had "broken faith with the Maroons," a view Walpole agreed with. As stated earlier, Walpole was so disgusted by the treatment of the Trelawny Town Maroons that he refused a ceremonial sword and five hundred guineas granted to him for his achievements, and promptly resigned his commission.[96]

What makes this situation remarkable is that those planters who seemed to recognise the mutual benefits of an alliance were mostly planters from a certain sector of Jamaican society. This challenges Scott V. Parris's assertion that the partners of the Maroon societies were underdogs in the economic and political struggles against greater labour and capital-intensive European interests, or what has been called "exploitative" forms of colonial enterprise.[97] Flávio dos Santos Gomes also argued that Brazilian Maroons, as well as Maroon communities in general, preferred to make alliances with impoverished white overseers rather than wealthy estate owners.[98] Similarly, N. A. T. Hall contends that poor whites in the Danish West Indies provided shelter for so-called maritime Maroons as opposed to wealthier Danes.[99] The evidence presented here contradicts these arguments. Consistently throughout the examples in this book, it is a group of extremely wealthy and influential Jamaican planters, such as John Tharp, who had the closest relations with Maroon communities. It is not hard to understand why Maroons may have been more eager to form alliances or relationships with these planters rather than overseers, or indeed with slaves themselves. Amicable interactions with white society, and with wealthy planters in particular, would have helped to achieve the goal of creating a unified Maroon identity. By allying with local white planters, Maroons distanced themselves from their former identities as the enemies of the colony and re-characterised themselves as associates of the elite of Jamaican society.

Likewise, established planters in Jamaica with several estates had far more to lose from unrest on the island than overseers and managers. Another colonist who mediated in Maroon-colonist disputes was John Palmer, who had connections to Rose Hall estate in St. James and also owned other properties on the island, including Palmyra estate. Palmer was not just a landowner; he was also custos of St. James. It was such men who voiced the greatest concern for the plight of the Trelawny Maroons during and after the Second Maroon War.

However, the divide between support and objection was not clearly defined along class lines. Some of the colonists discussed here were far removed from the striking wealth of John Tharp. Take, for example, Thomas Thistlewood, who was in frequent contact with Maroons. Thistlewood arrived in Jamaica in 1750 and, for the first seventeen years, worked primarily as an overseer on a sugar plantation. In 1767, he made the move to plantation owner with his property, Brednut Island Pen. Therefore, Thistlewood was not from the lowest echelons of society, but he was certainly not on a level with men such as John Tharp and John Palmer when it came to wealth and influence. A further example of tolerance of the Maroons from men lower in colonial society comes from the 1730s. The minutes of a meeting of the Assembly held on 7th July 1737 reported that Job Williams, a "poor man" of St. Ann's, had refused refreshments to a party from the barracks at Cave River, in Clarendon, who were on the hunt for Maroons, declaring that "the rebels never hurted him, and that he would not relieve any party sent in pursuit of them."[100] Clearly, not all white settlers favoured waging war against the Maroons, even in the context of the First Maroon War. Williams and the Maroons had apparently worked out a means of peaceful co-existence. A similar situation occurred in the early 1790s when one man wrote that his "brother's residence bordered on Trelawny Town and his intercourse with the Maroons was always of a friendly nature."[101] The author implies in the letter that his brother was not a man of powerful influence and wealth.

Other scholars who have mentioned this local support of the Maroons, albeit briefly, speak of the geographic divisions of the colonists. Carey Robinson claims that, at first, some of the white Jamaicans on the northern coast of Jamaica thought that the Trelawny Maroons had been unfairly treated, but in the general hysteria which soon gripped the island, all voices eventually became united in the belief that they must be brought low.[102] Bev Carey disputes Robinson's claim that it was the northern colonists who showed initial support to the Maroons. Carey suggests that those on the south coast found the Maroons harmless and opposed the declaration of martial law, but those on the north coast felt threatened.[103] Her claim, however, contrasts with most of the archival evidence which suggests that it was the planters of St. James and Trelawny, both northern parishes, who supported the Maroons and opposed action against them. The view that whites in the northern parishes, rather than the southern parishes, were more sympathetic to the Maroons is supported by a letter written by Balcarres in 1795. He wrote that there is "an imperium in imperio, and that is the parishes of St. James and Trelawny, who at first opposed and thwarted every thing that was done." Balcarres raged that at all times those planters had opinions of their own, not regulated by those of the Legislature and the other parishes.[104]

As stated earlier, the motivations for these men's actions may have been the security Maroons provided to them, the lack of interest in Maroon lands, or scientific curiosity, but this would have been true for many other colonists of the time. Why, then, in the 1790s when the Maroons had lost the support of the colonial government and other white Jamaicans, did this group of men from St. James and Trelawny actively argue on behalf of the Maroons? Unfortunately, none of these men have left records explaining their actions. Most likely it was because of their proximity to the Maroons, which meant that the security Maroons provided, in terms of hunting runaways and quelling rebellions, was most important to them. The mere presence of Maroons in the region would have had an impact not felt in more urban areas like Kingston and St. Andrew. According to Richard B. Sheridan, violent protest by slaves was nearly endemic in seventeenth- and eighteenth-century Jamaica, where outbreaks occurred on an average of every five years.[105] Orlando Patterson termed it a little more conservatively when he wrote that "hardly a decade went by without a serious, large-scale revolt threatening the entire system"[106] As I outlined previously, the planters certainly had the Maroons to thank for killing notorious slave leaders such as Tacky and Three Fingered Jack.[107] The presence of the Maroons meant that colonists had a fairly reliable defence force which only incurred costs when it was actually called out, rather than the running costs of a standing army. Further, as can be seen with the formation of the West India Regiment, difficult decisions had to be made about whether former slaves were soldiers and under which conditions and laws they would serve.[108] The benefit of using the Maroons as a defence force was that these discussions were not as critical. There was no debate as to whether Maroons were beholden to military law or slave court jurisdiction, as there was with slave regiments.[109] In other words, Maroons as soldiers did not present the same social problems as West India regiments and provided the most effective protection to plantations closest to their territories.

When it comes to the wealthier, local landowners who had relatively peaceful interactions with Maroons, it is likely that such men, who were profiting massively from a stable Jamaica, would have recognised that Maroons contributed significantly to the position they found themselves in. As Barry Higman has shown, many whites arrived in Jamaica to earn their fortune, making enough money to move back to England and place the running of their estates in the hands of managers and overseers.[110] In contrast, the men who supported the Trelawny Maroons were often men from families who had settled in Jamaica for generations and may have felt they owed more to the Maroon presence than their absentee counterparts. Transiency continued to be a fundamental feature throughout the seventeenth and eighteenth centuries. Jamaica was a place for sojourners, a land in which to make a quick fortune before heading home to Britain.[111] Perhaps these planter-settlers held a grudging affinity for Maroons who also called the island home.

This split in white society, whether along class or geographic lines, is not out of character for other areas of Jamaican colonial society. Edward Long spoke of Jamaican colonists "wilfully seeking occasions" to quarrel with their Governors.[112] Indeed, since there were no real political parties in Jamaica, politically the island was a free-for-all: factions of various groups vying against each other continuously.[113] Splits in white society were frequent, whether planters fighting for power with merchants, or Spanish Town residents competing with Kingston residents for influence. A split in opinion in how to deal with the Maroons is therefore not surprising, but it does highlight another division within colonial society—that of St. James and Trelawny colonists against representatives of other parishes.

The deep-seated racism of many planters, including those wealthy settlers in St. James and Trelawny, at first seems at odds with their behaviour towards Maroons. However, as has been seen in other contexts, certain groups of Europeans were ready or compelled to overlook their partners' former slave status in forming alliances against common enemies. For example, Robert Nelson Anderson showed how Brazilian Maroons traded with their Portuguese neighbours, exchanging foodstuffs and crafts for arms, munitions and salt.[114] White men frequently overcame their differences with black men in other colonial contexts, and this was also the case in Jamaica. Aba Karama argued that there were two possible routes that colonial policy could follow: pacification and containment, or suppression and extermination.[115] It seems that Jamaican society was increasingly split between the two policies, with the St. James and Trelawny planters leaning towards pacification and containment. As the population ratio rose to sixteen blacks for every white person by the end of the eighteenth century, white fears of black Jamaicans increased and led many to fear the Maroons as well. The St. James and Trelawny planters, however, chose to put their faith in the Maroons who had quelled slave rebellions and contained the communities within their lands.

Such a situation was also likely to have been satisfactory to the majority of Maroons. The Maroons had endured constant warfare from at least 1655, and arguably even longer because of their origins as runaways from Spanish settlements. Theirs was a society that had never had the opportunity to flourish. They had always been free, but it was an uncertain freedom: their settlements constantly had to move, and population decline was a recurring problem.[116] Peace with local whites brought an opportunity to end the persistent strain of being a society incessantly at war. It brought opportunities to solidify their freedom, to have safer access to resources and the chance to form a more stable environment to encourage natural reproduction. Indeed, even after the conclusion of the Second Maroon War, Maroons petitioned the colonial government to request that they be allowed to settle in "other parts of his Majesty's dominions" if they were to be transported from the island so that they "might again obtain an opportunity of proving the sincerity of their repentance."[117]

It is worth noting here that even if Maroons harboured a desire to free all the slaves, evidence has shown that they were pragmatic if nothing else. Allying with the enslaved population and fighting the colonists would only bring more war as Britain would pour its army into Jamaica to try to keep hold of the colony and, if the British were successful, the Maroons would lose the acknowledged freedom they had fought so hard for. That is not to say that the Maroons were not willing to defend their interests if threatened, but that, from both the Maroon and white side, there seems to have been little motivation for violence.

A factor also not to be overlooked is the apparent blood oath which was concluded between the Maroon representatives and colonists in 1739. Kenneth Bilby has presented convincing evidence that this occurred, using both archival evidence and oral traditions.[118] It is alleged that during the ceremonies in which the treaty papers were signed, Colonel Guthrie and Cudjoe mixed their blood with some rum and drank it as a sign of the new alliance. If true, this would provide another reason why Maroons were willing to negotiate difficult situations with local white planters rather than resort to violence. Indeed, Barbara Kopytoff has posited that contemporary Maroons view their treaties as "sacred charters" which underpin and assure their very existence as separate people.[119] These sacred charters acted as a springboard for Maroons to redefine themselves and their role in Jamaica. Maroons began to shed their former identity as former slaves, and all the connotations which that identity entailed, to create a new one as Maroon societies. Trevor Burnard has argued that freed people's escape from the stigma of slavery was more complete if they had both forenames and surnames, particularly ones not common in slavery.[120] If Burnard is correct in his assertion, then it is possible that Maroons believed that their freedom was "complete" by associating with powerful slave-owners and forming a new identity.

Overall, this section has demonstrated the non-violent relations between Maroons and Jamaican planters in the inter-war period. The most important point from this analysis for scholars of different regions or colonies is that none of these interactions were characterised by violence. This is somewhat surprising because violence as a standard between white settlers and free, non-white communities can be found in numerous settings. From the American West to colonies across Africa, Australia and Latin America, examples of violent interactions are highlighted time and again in the archival record.[121] There are, of course, examples throughout the colonial sphere which also point to the diplomatic negotiations, cultural exchange and tentative alliances found throughout borderland contexts.[122] Therefore, it is perhaps not surprising that this chapter has uncovered examples of closeness between Maroons and planters in Jamaica, but what is significant is the lack of any violence between the two sides until the Second Maroon War. The situation is even more surprising considering the violence of colonial Jamaican society. Michael Craton has claimed that the island experienced almost as many slave rebellions as all the other British colonies put together.[123] However, violence was not just inherent throughout enslaved groups resisting slavery; it was also synonymous with how those enslaved people were subsequently punished, by both individual plant-ers and the state.[124] Yet violence was not a feature of the relationships formed between Maroons and local planters.

This lack of violence requires us to re-think the Maroon position in Jamaica, and the position of wealthy colonists within the British Empire. The findings here highlight that the ending of formal hostilities with a colonial empire did not necessarily mean the ending of Maroon, or indeed other free, non-white communities' power. The peaceful handling of what the colonists deemed Maroon land encroachments brings to light the reliance local Jamaican plant-ers had on Maroon communities when it came to expanding and consolidat-ing the society they were creating. It further encourages us to recognise that peoples of different cultures could avoid violence when they shared common goals or at least were not obstacles to the goals of the other party. In other words, violence in a region, in this case Jamaica, did not automatically equate to violence in every context in that region. The mutual recognition of the benefits of an alliance between Maroons and local planters reminds us that interactions and relationships on frontiers and borderlands were shaped as much by free, non-white communities as by colonial forces.

Now let us turn to the effects of Benjamin Hawkins's changes to Creek justice and how they impacted upon the cycle of violence. The contemporary white view of Creeks was that they committed indiscriminate violent acts towards white settlers. However, equally prevalent was the violence commit-ted by Georgians against Creeks. Once again, animosity was exacerbated by different interpretations of a similar act. Christina Snyder claims that Creek warriors targeted what they deemed unlawful settlements, but settlers retali-ated by killing Indians indiscriminately.[125] The problem was that both sides viewed their attacks as justified. Creeks blamed whites for land encroachment, and whites blamed Creeks for not using their land "properly." Therefore, the cycle of violence was set.

The majority of instances of violence in the borderlands were launched with a specific goal in mind. For example, in 1786, Georgians intended to hold a congress at Skalop Creek with about four hundred Talapuche men, women and children. The Georgians subsequently ambushed the Talapuche with three thousand armed men and took them all prisoner. They released one to tell the Talapuche nation that they must submit to the following demands: first, to give the Americans the land which they had demanded; second, to surrender all the property which the Talapuche had allegedly taken during the war with England; third, satisfaction for "all the murders that they [the Tala-puche] committed on their citizens last summer."[126] These demands represent three of the most common causes of violence between the Creek Nation and the citizens of Georgia; land, property and retribution.

Violence was certainly a characteristic of the frontier. For example, in mid-March 1793, thirty Lower Creeks led by the mestizo John Galphin attacked a trading store on the St. Marys River, killing two men including the storekeeper.[127] Two days later, another party murdered four more whites just a few miles from the first site.[128] Then, a couple of weeks later, Creeks, once again led by John Galphin, raided plantations in East Florida, stealing slaves, cattle, horses and household belongings, then burning down buildings.[129] Acts such as these, launched by either side, often had specific motives, which I will discuss in more detail. However, on a few occasions, the violence was not linked to resistance or other political motivations. Take, for example, Benjamin Harrison, the leader of the gang that attacked Padjeeligau in 1795. He was known across the Deep South as a notorious "Indian hater." A man who engaged in brutal acts had also apparently been on the losing side, wearing a patch over one eye and having "a piece out of one side of his nose."[130] Creeks detested him and wanted him punished, but he eluded them and the white authorities for years. He surfaced from time to time to kill "Indians," as he had sworn vengeance against "every Indian he saw."[131]

Creeks, too, could commit brutal acts. In 1813, Hawkins wrote to Tustanagee Thlucco, Oche Hanjo and every chief of the Upper Creeks, of an incident that had been reported to him by General Robertson, the Agent of the Chickasaws. Hawkins explained that seven Americans were murdered near the mouth of the Ohio River "showing all the savage barbarity that could be invented." One pregnant woman had been cut open, a child taken out and stuck on a stake, and the Chickasaws had been charged with the murder. Subsequently, a party of Creeks acknowledged that they had actually committed the murder. Two of the principal men of the Creek Nation were found to be in the party; one named Tustunnuggeeooche of Wewocau and the other Oostanaulah Kecoh Tustkey living in Tuskegee. This particular act caused such outrage because it was not done by "thoughtless, wild young people, but deliberately, by a party under the command of two chiefs." The outrage was exacerbated even further because it was found that the chiefs were those "sent by the Creek nation on a public mission of peace and friendship to the Chickasaws."[132]

However, more often, acts were committed by young warriors avenging acts such as those committed by the "Indian-hater" Benjamin Harrison. One of the reasons was the usual attribute given to the young of protesting that which their elders try to impose upon them. There were, however, more practical reasons as well. As the loss and destruction of their traditional hunting grounds continued, young warriors had less opportunity to hone their skills and to prove themselves as warriors. Conducting raids on the Georgia frontier presented them with such opportunities, whilst also discouraging further settlement and, thus, further impact on their traditional hunts. In 1795, Creek headmen noted that white settlements south of the Oconee caused "much distress and displeasure among our young warriors" because of the destruction of their hunting grounds.[133]

Young warriors were also motivated by pan-Indian messages to resist American encroachments. For example, in 1793, a delegation of ten Shawnees travelled through the Deep South urging Creeks to take up arms against the

United States.[134] The Shawnees claimed the Creeks were "ruining" themselves by ceding land to the Americans.[135] This inspired young warriors to strike frontier settlements with vengeance. Despite the pleas of the Indian agent James Seagrove, and of prominent Creek leaders like Efau Hadjo, warriors from several Upper and Lower Creek towns sent warriors.[136] In one attack, thirty Lower Creeks attacked a trading store on the St. Marys, killing two men.[137] Raids continued on several settlements, killing whites and stealing livestock.[138] Raiding and harassing American settlers soon became the most common form of Creek resistance to land sales. Alexander McGillivray often encouraged such violence as a form of resistance. For instance, he instructed Creek hunters to attack if they saw any American settlements appearing in the area, although on one occasion he ended up lamenting that his "orders have been a little exceeded" because the hunters destroyed some boats which held passports from Governors.[139] Nevertheless, there was no regret about the order to attack.

Violence in, and of, itself was not the only problem. How that violence was punished also led to further violence. In September 1793, when Creek warriors raided the Georgia frontier, a party of Georgia light horsemen responded by taking revenge on the settlement of Hothlitaiga. They razed it to the ground, killed and scalped six men, and took three women and five girls prisoner. Such revenge confused Creeks because Hothlitaiga had not sent warriors as part of the raiding party which had previously attacked American settlements. Creeks were seeing that the American form of justice was often indiscriminate, and innocent people were increasingly likely to get caught up in the violence.

Traditional Creek justice revolved around the clan and worked on the principle of exchange, a life for a life, to "placate the soul of the departed" which remained in turmoil until satisfaction was given.[140] William Bartram, who visited the Creeks in the 1770s, explained that they believed it was "the Supreme Being, as the high arbiter of human transactions, who alone claims the right of taking away the life of man."[141] When a person was killed, therefore, the victim's clan had to exact revenge; ideally, by killing the person who committed the murder.[142] However, if the perpetrator had escaped, then one of his family was to be killed in his place.[143] There could be no compromise when it came to satisfaction—it lay at the very foundation of the Creek belief system. One visitor to the Nation explained that "It lies with the family injured to revenge their own quarrel. If a man is killed, his family will revenge it upon him who committed the murder, but if he escaped they will kill one of his family, and none of the rest of the tribes will offer to interfere."[144] Creek justice also differed markedly from its European counterparts in its disregard of intent or motive. In other words, it exacted the same punishment on those who caused accidental death as they did on those who intentionally took a life.[145] After white settlers killed eleven people from Kasihta in 1787, residents of that town "for some time appeared enraged and threatened to take a severe revenge of the Georgians, yet they did not act with a proper spirit on the occasion). Finally, "the family of the murdered Indians who resided in other towns" took satisfaction.[146] Justice was therefore, a clan issue rather than a national one—although the clans were spread across the entirety of the region.[147]

Among the Creek Nation, every killing of a Creek resulted in a spiritual imbalance, and the only way to correct it was through the death of one responsible for that disparity. This principle was so important to the Creek Nation that any person who did not avenge "crying blood" would be known throughout the Nation and considered "utterly sunk in cowardice."[148] Retaliation, which was similar to this notion of blood revenge, was the basic principle of international law among the south-eastern Indians. Retaliation was enacted whenever a Creek was killed by an outsider, and it followed the same principles of restoring spiritual balance to the world.[149] The difference between blood revenge and retaliation was that, with retaliation, a whole nation was liable and could be held responsible for the actions of one person.[150] Therefore, any individual could plunge their nation into war by maliciously or even accidentally killing a member of another nation. This system of retaliation was used as a way of provoking Creeks into war. Indeed, as one Anna Vansant reported in her deposition regarding the death of her husband, Isaac, "The doctrine in her neighborhood was, let us kill the Indians, bring on a war, and we shall get land."[151]

White frontier people operated with a similar principle of blood for blood, although their method often had little to do with spirituality. When one member of an American frontier community was killed by a Creek, they, too, sought vengeance through the death of someone from the Nation, and not necessarily the person responsible for the slaying or their family. According to Philip Henry Gosse, in the southern backcountry, "every man is his own law-maker and law-breaker, judge, jury, and executioner."[152] For example, in 1804, Mr. Patrick of Clarke County, Georgia, killed a Creek man and wounded another because he thought he recognised one of their horses as having been stolen from a friend of his.[153] The Governor of Georgia, John Milledge, soon became aware of the incident and ordered Lieutenant William Walton to arrest Patrick. Upon arriving in the settlement, Patrick was nowhere to be found, with other residents apparently shielding him from the law. When questioned, they responded that the death of a Creek was owed to them because a Mr. Moreland had been earlier killed by a group of Creeks. They refused to release Patrick to the authorities unless the Creeks handed over Moreland's killers. Sensing a diplomatic crisis, Milledge decided not to act.[154] American settlers were using the Creek form of justice as a means to justify their indiscriminate killing of Creeks.

Confusingly, Creeks and Americans often blamed each other when they reacted to violence in a similar way. When some Upper Creeks killed a couple of Georgia frontier settlers in 1787, the Georgians quickly exacted vengeance, killing some nearby Creek hunters. As it turned out, the Georgians had killed Lower Creeks. The Lower Creek chiefs responded by saying to the Americans, "you always promised that the innocent should not suffer for the guilty." Pre-empting any reply of ignorance from the Americans, the Creeks wrote that the Americans must have known they were friendly "or we would not have been among you and hunting." However, they concluded with a point which detracts from their argument. The Lower Creeks stated that they looked upon all white people as one and supposed the Americans must do the same to Indians which is the reason "you have killed your friends."[155] The Creeks were complaining that Americans did not differentiate between different Indians, yet they admitted that they did exactly the same with Americans.

Creeks did not always resort immediately to violence to solve disputes, however. On occasion, some Creeks appealed to Benjamin Hawkins to deal with the problem. Similarly, white people who had apparently been the victim of a crime committed by a Creek person were known to petition the Creek leader, Alexander McGillivray, to punish the attackers. In 1792, General Robertson was wounded by Creeks "so bad that his life is dispard [sic] of" and some women were kidnapped. A planter named Hoggarth pleaded with McGillivray to help him in his efforts to locate the women and return them home.[156] This is particularly interesting as it highlights how McGillivray's influence stretched beyond the limits of Creek country. It also implies that, into the 1790s, some Americans felt that petitioning a Creek leader would be more successful than contacting an American leader to resolve the situation.

Retribution within Creek country was also not always violent. McGillivray punished the trader, Timothy Lane, for "his many crimes" by having his trade suspended "as an example to others it being the mildest punishment I could inflict." Lane was left with "his necessarys" and departed with all of his horses and other effects.[157] One possible reason for this was that Lane was a trader, rather than a white settler who lived illegally on Creek lands. As Kathryn Holland Braund has argued, traders were regularly welcomed in the village square and were present at all ceremonial occasions in Creek life.[158] Therefore, instances such as this highlight the extent to which whites could be incorporated into Creek society. Their alleged crimes were addressed with restraint, and some Creeks genuinely tried to ascertain the causes of violence and administer punishments accordingly.

The lack of violence in certain circumstances is attributed to the fact that Creeks and Americans, on occasion, communicated with each other about administering justice. In 1792, a young American was killed by some Indians near Kars Bluff on the Oconee River. Creeks assured the Americans that they intended to "make an example" of whomever it was that committed the murder. The Creeks pleaded for patience and for the whites to give them time to locate the perpetrator, as they had done when they waited twelve months to take satisfaction for a man who was killed the previous May.[159] This letter reveals the determination of these Creeks to punish crimes on their terms, but it also hints at the dialogue between the two sides. Even in potentially inflammatory circumstances, such as violent retribution for murder, both sides could communicate and try to negotiate a solution in the years shortly after the Revolution. As time passed, this was to change.

Open communication did not always result in a satisfactory conclusion for either side, however, precisely because of the different interpretations of what constituted punishment. In 1798, some Creek men killed a white man on the Oconee River. When the friends of the man went to inspect the scene, they found a note which read:

> Friends and Brother . . . we are sorry that we are obliged to take our due satisfaction ourselves; you have often promised to give satisfaction in the Likke [sic] cases, but never have done itt [sic] once. Now we have gottitt [sic], our harts are strait [sic], and itt [sic] is all over. We are now good friends as ever we was [sic] and can take you by the hand in friendship again.[160]

The cultural differences here appear to have been the cause of the problem. The Creeks were willing to forgive the violent act as long as retribution was sought. The Americans refused to do this because it would involve punishing a family member of the accused. The result was that nothing was done, and the Creeks resorted to "violence," in the Americans' eyes and "satisfaction," in the Creeks' eyes. A similar outcome was seen in 1798, when Tussekiah Mico and Yeauholau Mico stated they had fired across the Oconee and killed a white man, Nicholas Vines, on his own plantation in Hancock County. They left a letter to explain their actions, stating that the act was for the satisfaction for a previous murder. They presumably hoped that an explanation would avoid any retribution from the family of Vines.[161]

This system of satisfaction had continued more or less as usual throughout the period under study. Increasingly found alongside it, however, was an alternate form of justice encouraged by Americans. When the United States emerged from the ashes of the American Revolution, Creeks came under pressure to create a centralised, executive force which would keep its people in check through an ordered system of punishments, or face the wrath of the new republic. This began with Alexander McGillivray. He tried, and failed, to introduce a law which required rustlers to return stolen animals and pay a fine of thirty chalks (the method of payment used in the deerskin trade) or fifteen dollars. Those who did not, or could not, pay were to be sentenced to thirty lashes of the whip by the injured party.[162] It is clear McGillivray was trying to enforce some kind of regulated punishment, but with a nod to Creek justice by including the victim as part of the punishment. The law, however, was frequently ignored. According to Caleb Swan, the Scots Indian also called on his kin to act as "constables" to "pursue, take up, and punish, such characters as he may direct," and on some occasions, to act as "executioners."[163] As with his whipping law, this, too, was frequently ignored.

Under the guidance of Benjamin Hawkins, however, Creeks were again pressured into changing their justice system to one more akin to the American one. It was increasingly encouraged to place the power for punishment in the hands of a small number of "national leaders" who were to represent the "nation."[164] Many Creeks refused to follow this increased emphasis on individual responsibility. In 1784, the Governor of Georgia remarked to Hoboithle Micco that he should not defend the murder of an "innocent" white woman, killed for satisfaction. The Governor explained that the Americans would try to find the murderer and execute him and insisted "the Indians should do the same in regard to those who had killed the white woman, for . . . (as the laws of the white people (stated)) . . . if Blood was spilt in the land that blood ought to wash out by the blood of the murderer and that he thought both murders ought to die." Hoboithle Micco simply responded that "that was not their rule and that they being perfectly satisfied on their side, thought the white people ought to be so too."[165]

Many Creeks continued to use their traditional justice system, alongside other Creeks who tried to impose the new one. Unsurprisingly, however, both Creeks and settlers often abandoned their preferred justice system when it suited them. For example, in early summer 1787, Georgians killed twelve Kasihtas, Lower Creeks, in retaliation for murders committed by Creeks from Okchoy, an Upper Creek town. Lower Creek leaders asked for satisfaction, reminding the Georgia Governor, "It was your rule that the innocent should not suffer for the guilty."[166] The Governor responded that they should take satisfaction from the Upper Creeks because they had indirectly caused the murders by killing white settlers.[167] At this, Creeks fell back on their "life for a life" justice system.[168]

Faced with Hawkins's insistence and the threat of spiralling vengeance raids, it fell to the National Council to attempt to reframe Creek crime and punishment based on American principles. The National Council was, as shown in Chapter 2, led by Creeks with pro-American sentiments, many of whom were mestizos and, therefore, knowledgeable about the fundamentals of Euro American judicial concepts.[169] They revoked clan blood revenge, agreed to punish individuals responsible for assaults against Americans, and established a warrior police, "the lawmenders," to this end. They also attempted to define horse stealing and other thefts as criminal actions subject to state punishment. The effect of such decrees was limited by the fact that vast numbers of Creeks refused to recognise their authority—leading to yet more violence.

Therefore, what developed on the Creek frontier was a cycle of violence exacerbated by the dispute resolution of either violent blood revenge or, after the introduction of Hawkins's policies, violent punishments meted out by a non-elected, centralised National Council. These two systems overlapped and were used alongside each other, causing mass confusion and contributing to further violence.

As we can see, life on the frontier of Maroon and Creek country differed greatly. First, however, we can also identify some commonalities. On an individual level, there were occasions to interact in a more social sphere—from overnight stays at Jamaican plantations to learning the Creek language, these meetings usually were in small groups and, crucially, did not involve interactions with those wanting to settle on Creek or Maroon lands. Both cases also had examples of intermarriage and/or sexual relations between Maroons and Creeks on the one hand, and local white settlers on the other.

These individual, more amicable interactions did not preclude violence from being rife on the Creek frontier. Conversely, there was a total lack of violence between Maroons and white settlers, apart from during times of warfare. Indeed, any disputes which did occur were resolved non-violently, often with the intervention of a mediator. This is in stark contrast to the cycle of violent retribution that was present in the Creek case. But why did these differences occur? Many of the reasons are similar to the presence, or lack of, violence in land disputes. Local white settlers in Jamaica were willing to act as mediators in disputes because the presence of friendly Maroons served them well. Their slaves were caught if they ran away, or they were discouraged from even attempting to run away by the Maroon threat. Maroons were willing to ally with the colonists when other European empires threatened the island and the peace treaties had already granted the vast majority of Jamaican land to the Crown which would, thus, be available for settlement by colonists. In other words, continued peace was more conducive for better profits than violent retribution over a few acres of land or any other dispute.

In contrast, in the case of Creeks and Americans, violence which erupted over land or other kinds of disputes was rarely dealt with satisfactorily for either side. Differing views of punishment meant that, even if either side had wanted to, violence was difficult to avoid. The seeming random acts of retribution committed by Americans made no sense to Creeks. Likewise, Creeks avenging a murder by attacking the alleged murderer's family enraged Americans as it seemed to be a separate act of violence. Matters were exacerbated when Benjamin Hawkins utilised blood revenge in his formation of a National Council-led proto-police force. These U.S.-backed warriors attacked their own people as punishment for Creek depredations, leading to an increased hostility towards both the National Council and its federal backers.

Both kinds of dispute resolution, however, contributed to European efforts to control these semi-autonomous communities. Colonist-led efforts to utilise non-violent dispute resolution were rarely out of a desire to listen to Maroon grievances. Rather, it was a way to placate aggrieved Maroons whilst still, far more often than not, coming to decisions which benefited the British. Similarly, violent acts of retribution were used to condemn Creeks to violent responses by Americans. When successful, these violent responses led to land loss either formally or informally. Indeed, Creeks were often provoked in order to react and set in motion the chain of events which would end in land gains for Americans. Ultimately, neither form of dispute resolution was altruistic, and both served only the wider aims and interests of the British and Americans in controlling Maroons and Creek communities.

Acknowledgements

Parts of this chapter have previously been published in Helen McKee, 'From Violence to Alliance: Maroons and White Settlers in Jamaica, 1739–1795,' *Slavery & Abolition*, 39, 1 (2018), 27–52.

Notes

1. Thomas Thistlewood, Folder 1, Box 1, Thomas Thistlewood Papers, James Marshall and Marie-Louise Osborn Collection, Beinecke Rare Book and Manuscript Library (BRBM), Yale University (YU), United States.
2. Thistlewood, Folder 2, Box 1, Thistlewood Papers, Osborn Collection, BRBM, YU.
3. Robert C. Dallas, *The History of the Maroons: From Their Origin to the Establishment of Their Chief Tribe at Sierra Leone: Including the Expedition to Cuba, for the Purpose of Procuring Spanish Chasseurs; and the State of the Island of Jamaica for the Last Ten Years: With a Succinct History of the Island Previous to That Period* (London: Printed by A. Strahan. . ., for T. N. Longman and O. Rees. . ., 1803), 116.
4. Kathleen Wilson, 'The Performance of Freedom: Maroons and the Colonial Order in Eighteenth-Century Jamaica and the Atlantic Sound,' *The William and Mary Quarterly*, 3rd Series, 66, 1 (Jan., 2009), 63.
5. Thistlewood, Folder 4, Box 1, Thistlewood Papers, Osborn Collection, BRBM, YU.
6. *Ibid.*
7. *Ibid.*
8. Thistlewood, Folder 11, Box 2, Thistlewood Papers, Osborn Collection, BRBM, YU.
9. Michael Mullin, *Africa in America: Slave Acculturation and Resistance in the American South and the British Caribbean, 1736–1831* (Urbana: University of Illinois Press, 1992), 48.
10. *Ibid.*, 54.
11. *Ibid.*, 48.
12. The Petition of Sundry Maroons Belonging to Trelawny Town, 9th May 1796, CO137/96, National Archives, Kew, United Kingdom (NA).
13. Carey Robinson, *The Iron Thorn: The Defeat of the British by the Jamaican Maroons* (Kingston: Kingston Publishers Limited, 1993), 121.
14. Mavis Campbell, *The Maroons of Jamaica, 1655–1796: A History of Resistance, Collaboration & Betrayal* (Trentin: Africa World Press, 1990), 255. There is a significant amount of literature on naming practices in the Americas. For example, Cheryll Ann Cody, 'There Was No "Absalom" on the Ball Plantations: Slave-Naming Practices in the South Carolina Low Country, 1720–1865,' in *The Slavery Reader*, eds. Gad Heuman and James Walvin (New York: Routledge, 2003), 331; Trevor Burnard, 'Slave-Naming Practices: Onomastics and the Taxonomy of Race in Eighteenth-Century Jamaica,' *Journal of Interdisciplinary History*, 31, 3 (2001), 325–346; Jerome S. Handler and JoAnn Jacoby, 'Slave Names and Naming in Barbados, 1650–1830,' *The William and Mary Quarterly*, 53, 4 (1996), 685–728.
15. Burnard, 'Slave Naming Practices,' 346.
16. *Ibid.*
17. Sabelo J. Ndlovu-Gatsheni, 'Re-thinking the Colonial Encounter in Zimbabwe in the Early Twentieth Century,' *Journal of South African Studies*, 33, 1 (2007), 173–191; David Richardson, 'Cultures of Exchange: Atlantic Africa in the Era of the Slave Trade,' *Transactions of the Royal Historical Society*, 6th Series, 19 (2009), 151–179; Abimbola O. Adesoji, 'Colonialism and Intercommunity Relations: The Ifon-Ilobu Example,' *History in Africa*, 32 (2005), 1–19; John Wood Sweet, 'The Subject of the Slave Trade: Recent Currents in the Histories of the Atlantic, Great Britain, and Western Africa,' *Early American Studies*, 7, 1 (Spring, 2009), 1–45; Ernst van Den Boogaart, 'The Trade Between Western Africa and the Atlantic World, 1600–90: Estimates of Trends in Composition and Value,' *The Journal of African History*, 33, 3 (1992), 369–385; David Richardson, 'Shipboard Revolts, African Authority, and the Atlantic Slave Trade,' *The William and Mary Quarterly*, 58, 1 (Jan., 2001), 69–92; Robin Law, 'Slave-Raiders and Middlemen, Monopolists and Free-Traders:

The Supply of Slaves for the Atlantic Trade in Dahomey, c. 1715–1850,' *The Journal of African History*, 30, 1 (1989), 45–68; Robin Law, 'Dahomey and the Slave Trade: Reflections on the Historiography of the Rise of Dahomey,' *The Journal of African History*, 27, 2 (1986), 237–267.

18. Thistlewood, Folder 5, Box 1, Thistlewood Papers, Osborn Collection, BRBM, YU.

19. Bryan Edwards to Mark Davis of Bristol, 18th April 1774, Add. Ms. 12431, BL; Keith to Dartmouth, 22nd April 1774, CO 137/69, NA.

20. Thistlewood, Folder 38, Box 7, Thistlewood Papers, Osborn Collection, BRBM, YU.

21. For example, Supplement to the *Royal Gazette*, 22nd May 1795, CO 137/94–7, NA.

22. Thistlewood, Folder 11, Box 2, Thistlewood Papers, Osborn Collection, BRBM, YU.

23. Supplement to the *Royal Gazette*, Vol. 2, No. 67 (29th July 1870–5th August 1780), 458; Supplement to the *Royal Gazette*, Vol. 3, No. 93 (27th January 1781–3rd February 1781), 79.

24. Dallas, *History of the Maroons*, Vol. I, 105.

25. *Ibid.*

26. *Acts of Assembly Passed in the Island of Jamaica from 1681 to 1733 Inclusive* (BL), CSF., 154/7, 480.

27. Bryan Edwards, *The Proceedings of the Governor and Assembly of Jamaica, in Regard to the Maroon Negroes: Published by Order of the Assembly. To Which Is Prefixed, an Introductory Account, Containing, Observations on the Disposition, Character, Manners, and Habits of Life, of the Maroons, and, a Detail of the Origin, Progress, and Termination of the Late War Between Those People and the White Inhabitants* (London: John Stockdale, 1796), 559.

28. Alexander Crawford Lindsay, *Lives of the Lindsays: Or a Memoir of the Houses of Crawford and Balcarres. . .* (Wigan: Privately Printed, 1840), Vol. III, 136.

29. Bev Carey, *Maroon Story: The Authentic and Original History of the Maroons in the History of Jamaica, 1490–1880* (St. Andrew, Jamaica: Agouti Press, 1997), 425.

30. Campbell, *The Maroons of Jamaica*, 195.

31. *Acts of Assembly Passed in the Island of Jamaica from 1681 to 1733 Inclusive* (BL), CSF., 154/7, 204.

32. *Journals of the House of Assembly* (JHA), 26th November 1773, Vol. XI, National Archives of Jamaica (NAJ).

33. *Votes of the House of Assembly of Jamaica*, Appendix (not numbered), 1st September 1835, (BL).

34. Diary of John Innerarity, 14th October 1812, Archivo Nacional de Cuba (ANC), Library of Congress, Washington, D.C., United States (LOC).

35. Grace M. Schwartzman and Susan K. Barnard, 'A Trail of Broken Promises: Georgians and Muscogee/Creek Treaties, 1796–1826,' *Georgia Historical Quarterly*, 75, 4 (Winter, 1991), 697–698.

36. Affidavit of David Shaw, 2nd June 1792, ANC, LOC.

37. Theda Perdue, *"Mixed Blood" Indians: Racial Construction in the Early South* (Athens: University of Georgia Press, 2003), 19.

38. Unknown, 'Old Age Respected by the Creek Indians,' GDAH.

39. Perdue, *"Mixed Blood" Indians*, 2.

40. Taylor Russell, "Kendall Lewis: Citizen of Four Nations—United States—Creek—Republic of Mexico—Republic of Texas" (typescript, University of Georgia Library, 15th March 1969).

41. *Journal of the House of Assembly of Jamaica (JHA)*, 6th November 1795, Vol. VI; 24th February 1801, Vol. X, National Archives of Jamaica, Spanish Town, Jamaica (NAJ).

42. Campbell, *The Maroons of Jamaica*, 186–187.

43. See, for example, E. Schmidt, *Peasants, Traders & Wives: Shona Women in the History of Zimbabwe, 1870–1939* (London: James Currey, 1992); Edward E. Baptist, '"Cuffy," "Fancy Maids," and "One-Eyed Men": Rape, Commodification, and the Domestic Slave Trade in the United States,' *The American Historical Review*, 106, 5 (Dec., 2001), 1619–1650; Samita Sen, '"Without his Consent?": Marriage and Women's Migration in Colonial India,' *International Labour and Working-Class History*, 65, Agriculture and Working-Class Formation (Spring, 2004), 77–104; Koni Benson and Joyce M. Chadya, 'Ukubhinya: Gender and Sexual Violence in Bulawayo, Colonial Zimbabwe, 1946–1956,' *Journal of Southern African Studies*, 31, 3 (Sep., 2005), 587–610; Astrid Cubano-Iguina, 'Legal Constructions of Gender and Violence against Women in Puerto Rico under Spanish Rule, 1860–1895,' *Law and History Review*, 22, 3 (Autumn, 2004), 531–564; Pamela Scully, 'Rape, Race, and Colonial Culture: The Sexual Politics of Identity in the Nineteenth-Century Cape Colony, South Africa,' *The American Historical Review*, 100, 2 (Apr., 1995), 335–359; Andrea Smith, *Conquest: Sexual Violence and American Indian Genocide* (Cambridge, MA: South End Press, 2005).
44. J. M. Allain, 'Sexual Relations Between Elite White Women and Enslaved Men in the Antebellum South: A Socio-Historical Analysis,' *Inquiries*, 5, 8 (2013).
45. Perdue, *"Mixed Blood" Indians*, 16–17.
46. Kathryn Holland Braund, *Deerskins and Duffels: The Creek Indian Trade with Anglo-America, 1685–1815* (Lincoln: University of Nebraska Press, 1996), 83.
47. Andrew Frank, *Creeks & Southerners: Biculturalism on the Early American Frontier* (Lincoln: University of Nebraska Press, 2005), 33.
48. Diary of Benjamin Hawkins, 3rd January 1797, in *The Collected Works of Benjamin Hawkins*, ed. H. Thomas Foster (Tuscaloosa: University of Alabama Press, 2003), 33–34.
49. Frank, *Creeks & Southerners*, 34.
50. Ibid.
51. Benjamin Hawkins, *Letters of Benjamin Hawkins, 1796–1806*, Vol. II (Savannah: Published by the Georgia Historical Society, 1916), 340.
52. Ibid.
53. Entry for 2nd May 1799, and Benjamin Hawkins to Samuel Alexander, 21st May 1799, Benjamin Hawkins' Letterbook, Independence National Historical Park, Philadelphia (INHP); Benjamin Hawkins to Edward Price, 19th November 1798, Entry No. 42, National Archives and Records Office, Washington, D.C., United States (NARO).
54. Benjamin Hawkins to S. Alexander, 21st January 1799, Benjamin Hawkins' Letterbook, INHP.
55. Dallas, *History of the Maroons*, Vol. I, 135; *JHA*, 29th November 1786, Vol. VIII, NAJ.
56. Dallas, *History of the Maroons*, Vol. I, 133–134.
57. *JHA*, 20th July 1795, Vol. IX, NAJ.
58. Deposition of James Merody, 11th May 1795, CO137/94, National Archives of Jamaica, Spanish Town, Jamaica (NAJ).
59. Ibid.
60. *JHA*, James Stewart magistrate of Trelawny, to Balcarres, 20th July 1795, Vo. IX, NAJ.
61. Examination of John Merody, late assistant to Trelawny Town before the Commander in Chief at Head Quarters Vaughansfield, 16th August 1795, CO 137/94, NAJ.
62. Dallas, *History of the Maroons*, Vol. I, 208.
63. George Stiggins, *Creek Indian History: A Historical Narrative of the Genealogy, Traditions, and Downfall of the Ispocoga or Creek Indian Tribe of Indians* (Birmingham: Birmingham Public Library Press, 1989), 74–75.
64. Ibid.
65. Robbie Franklyn Ethridge, *Creek Country: The Creek Indians and Their World* (Chapel Hill: University of North Carolina Press, 2003), 18.

66. *Ibid*, 74–75.
67. Ethridge, *Creek Country*, 32.
68. Hopoi Micco to Benjamin Hawkins, 3rd November 1804, Reel 12, ANC, LOC.
69. Bryan Edwards to Mark Davis of Bristol, 18th April 1774, Add. Ms. 12431, British Library, London, United Kingdom (BL); Keith to Dartmouth, 22nd April 1774, CO 137/69, NA.
70. Edward Long Papers, Add. Ms. 12413, BL.
71. *Ibid*.
72. *Ibid*.
73. Campbell, *The Maroons of Jamaica*, 171.
74. Letter from the Custos of Saint James to the Right Honourable Earl Balcarres, 25th July 1795, CO 137/95, NA.
75. Donald Campbell and John Parry to Earl Balcarres, 18th July 1795, WO 1/92, NA.
76. Examination of John Merody, late assistant to Trelawny Maroon Town before the Commander-in-chief at Vaughansfield, 16th August 1795, WO 1/92, NA.
77. JHA, 20th July 1795, Vol. IX, NAJ.
78. JHA, 2nd August 1795, Vol. IX, NAJ.
79. *Ibid*.
80. William Vaughan to the Right Honourable Henry Dundas, 7th November 1795, WO 1/92, NA.
81. Copy of a Letter from the Magistrates of the Parish of St. James to Earl Balcarres, 18th July 1795, WO 1/92, NA.
82. JHA, 18th July 1795, Vol. IX, NAJ.
83. *Ibid*.
84. Copy of a Letter Sent by Colonel Reid to the Maroons and Accompanying the 2nd Letter sent to them by the Commander-in-chief, 8th August 1795, CO 137/92, NA.
85. JHA, 23rd July 1795, Vol. IX, NAJ.
86. *Ibid*.
87. *Ibid*.
88. Balcarres to the Duke of Portland, 29th August 1795, WO 1/92, NA.
89. Lindsay, *Lives of the Lindsays*, 44.
90. JHA, 29th July 1795, Vol. IX, NAJ.
91. JHA, James Stewart magistrate of Trelawny, to Balcarres, 20th July 1795, Vol. IX; NAJ.
92. JHA, 21st July 1795, Vol. IX, NAJ.
93. Examination of John Merody, late Assistant to Trelawny Maroon Town, before the Commander-in-chief at Headquarters Vaughansfield, 16th August 1795, WO 1/92, NA.
94. Richard Hart, *Slaves Who Abolished Slavery: Blacks in Rebellion* (Kingston: University of the West Indies Press, 1985), 202.
95. Inventories, 1805, IB/11/3/104/33/, NAJ.
96. Balcarres to the Duke of Portland, 17th April 1796, CO 137/96, NA.
97. Scott V. Parris, 'Alliance and Competition: Four Case Studies of Maroon-European Relations,' *Nieuwe West-Indische Gids/New West Indian Guide*, 55ste Jaarg., 3/4 (Dec., 1981), 177.
98. Flávio dos Santos Gomes, 'Peasants, Maroons, and the Frontiers of Liberation in Maranhão,' *Review (Fernand Braudel Center)*, 31, 3, The Second Slavery: Mass Slavery, World Economy and Comparative Microhistories, Part II (2008), 373.
99. N. A. T. Hall, 'Maritime Maroons: "Grand Marronage" from the Danish West Indies,' *The William and Mary Quarterly*, 42, 4 (Oct., 1985), 476–498.
100. JHA, 7th July 1737, Vol. III, NAJ.
101. William Vaughan to Henry Dundas, 7th November 1795, WO1/92, NA.
102. Robinson, *The Iron Thorn*, 154.

103. Carey, *Maroon Story*, 472.

104. Balcarres to the Duke of Portland, 27th October 1795, CO 137/96, NA.

105. Richard B. Sheridan, 'The Jamaican Slave Insurrection Scare of 1776 and the American Revolution,' *The Journal of Negro History*, 61, 3 (July, 1976), 291.

106. Orlando Patterson, 'Slavery and Slave Revolts: A Socio-Historical Analysis of the First Maroon War, 1655–1740,' *Social and Economic Studies*, 19, 3 (Sept., 1970), 289–325.

107. Hart, *Slaves Who Abolished Slavery*, 130, 148, 158; Srinivas Aravamudan, ed. *Obi: Or, the History of Three-Fingered Jack* (Ontario: Broadview, 2005).

108. For more on this, see Roger N. Buckley, 'Slave or Freedman: The Question of the Legal Status of the British West India Soldier, 1795–1807,' *Caribbean Studies*, 17, 3/4 (Oct., 1977–Jan., 1978), 83–113.

109. *Ibid.*, 102.

110. Barry Higman, *Plantation Jamaica, 1750–1850: Capital and Control in a Colonial Economy* (Kingston: University of the West Indies Press, 2005), 4.

111. Trevor Burnard, 'European Migration to Jamaica, 1655–1780,' *The William and Mary Quarterly*, 53, 4 (Oct., 1996), 769–796.

112. Edward Long, *The History of Jamaica: Or, General Survey of the Ancient and Modern State of That Island: With Reflections on Its Situations, Settlements, Inhabitants, Climate, Products, Commerce, Laws, and Government* (London: F. Cass, 1970), 263.

113. George Metcalf, *Royal Government and Political Conflict in Jamaica, 1729–1783* (London: Longmans, Green & Co., 1965), 23.

114. Robert Nelson Anderson, 'The Quilombo of Palmares: A New Overview of a Maroon State in Seventeenth-Century Brazil,' *Journal of Latin American Studies*, 28, 3 (Oct., 1996), 552.

115. Aba Karama, 'The Origin of the West Indies Regiments,' *Science and Society*, 35, 1 (Spring, 1971), 59.

116. Barbara Klamon Kopytoff, 'The Development of Jamaican Maroon Ethnicity,' *Caribbean Quarterly*, 22, 2/3, Essays on Slavery (June–Sept., 1976), 43–50.

117. Petition of Sundry Maroons Belonging to Trelawny Town, 9th May 1796, CO137/96, NA.

118. Kenneth Bilby, 'Swearing by the Past, Swearing to the Future: Sacred Oaths, Alliances, and Treaties among the Guianese and Jamaican Maroons,' *Ethnohistory*, 44, 4 (Autumn, 1997), 655–689.

119. Barbara Klamon Kopytoff, 'Colonial Treaty as Sacred Charter of the Jamaican Maroons,' *Ethnohistory*, 26, 1 (Winter, 1979), 45–64.

120. Burnard, 'Slave-Naming Practices,' 342.

121. Robert Paul Hogg, '"A Hand Prepared to Be Red": Manliness and Racial Violence on Britain's Colonial Frontiers,' *Australasian Victorian Studies Journal*, 15, 1 (2010), 22–35; Wilbur R. Jacobs, 'The Fatal Confrontation: Early Native-White Relations on the Frontiers of Australia, New Guinea, and America—a Comparative Study,' *Pacific Historical Review*, 40, 3 (Aug., 1971), 283–309; Richard J. Reid, *Frontiers of Violence in North-East Africa: Genealogies of Conflict Since 1800* (Oxford: Oxford University Press, 2011); Karl Jacoby, *Shadows at Dawn: A Borderlands Massacre and the Violence of History* (New York: Penguin Press, 2008); Ned Blackhawk, *Violence over the Land: Indians and Empires in the Early American West* (Cambridge, MA: Harvard University Press, 2006); Benjamin Claude Brower, *A Desert Named Peace: The Violence of France's Empire in the Algerian Sahara, 1844–1902* (New York: Columbia University Press, 2009); A. Dirk Moses, ed., *Genocide and Settler Society: Frontier Violence and Stolen Indigenous Children in Australian History* (New York: Berghahn Books, 2004); Hal Langfur, *The Forbidden Lands: Colonial Identity, Frontier Violence, and the Persistence of Brazil's Eastern Indians, 1750–1830* (Stanford: Stanford University Press, 2006);

Nigel Penn, *The Forgotten Frontier: Colonist and Khoisan on the Cape's Northern Frontier in the 18th Century* (Athens: Ohio University Press, 2005).

122. David Murray, *Indian Giving: Economies of Power in Early Indian-White Exchanges* (Amherst: University of Massachusetts Press, 2000); Daniel H. Usner, *Indians, Settlers, and Slaves in a Frontier Exchange Economy: The Lower Mississippi Valley before 1783* (Chapel Hill: University of North Carolina Press, 1992); John Sutton Lutz, *Makúk: A New History of Aboriginal-White Relations* (Vancouver: University of British Columbia Press, 2008); Joseph M. Hall Jr., *Zamumo's Gifts: Indian-European Exchange in the Colonial Southeast* (Philadelphia: University of Pennsylvania Press, 2009); Lisa Ford, *Settler Sovereignty: Jurisdiction and Indigenous People in America and Australia, 1788–1836* (Cambridge, MA: Harvard University Press, 2010).

123. Michael Craton, *Testing the Chains: Resistance to Slavery in the British West Indies* (Ithaca: Cornell University Press, 1982), 99.

124. For more on the violent punishments inflicted upon enslaved peoples, see Diana Paton, 'Punishment, Crime, and the Bodies of Slaves in Eighteenth-Century Jamaica,' *Journal of Social History*, 34, 4 (Summer, 2001), 923–954; Jonathan Dalby, *Crime and Punishment in Jamaica: A Quantitative Analysis of the Assize Court Records, 1756–1856* (Mona: University of West Indies, 2000); Diana Paton, *No Bond but the Law: Punishment, Race and Gender in Jamaican State Formation, 1780–1870* (Durham: Duke University Press, 2004).

125. Christina Snyder, 'Conquered Enemies, Adopted Kin, and Owned People: The Creek Indians and Their Captives,' *The Journal of Southern History*, 73, 2 (May, 2007), 255.

126. Linder to Favrot, 13th November 1786, in *McGillivray of the Creeks*, ed. John Walton Caughey (Norman: University of Oklahoma Press, 1938), 137.

127. Timothy Barnard to James Seagrove, 2nd July 1793, LTB, 188, GDAH; *American State Papers, Class II: Indian Affairs* (Washington, DC, 1832), Vol. I, 400; Governor of Florida to Marqúes del Campo, 9th April 1793, East Florida Papers, NARO (microfilm, bnd., 46G4, 128, reel 18, PKY; James Seagrove to the Secretary of War, 19th April 1793; *ASPIA*, Vol. I, 378–789; James Seagrove to the Secretary of War, 31st July 1793, *ASPIA*, Vol. I, 399–400.

128. James Seagrove to Edward Telfair, 17th March 1793, CIL, Vol. I, 272–274, GDAH; Timothy Barnard to Henry Gaither, 10th April 1793, LTB, 145, GDAH; *ASPIA*, Vol. I, 419; James Seagrove to the Secretary of War, 19th April 1793, *ASPIA*, Vol. I, 378–379.

129. Richard Land to the Governor of Florida, 19th April 1793, EF, bnd. 123F10, doc. 1793–79, reel 48, PKY; James Seagrove to the Secretary of War, 19th April 1793, *ASPIA*, Vol. I, 378–9; John Forrester to the Governor of Florida, 20th April 1793, EF, bnd. 123F10, doc. 1793–84, reel 48, PKY.

130. Hawkins, *Letters*, Vol. I, 313; Timothy Barnard to James Seagrove, 18th December 1798, LTB, GDAH, 37.

131. Major Jacob Kingsberry to Governor John Milledge, 6th May 1803, CIL, GDAH, 672–673.

132. Benjamin Hawkins to the Upper Creek Chiefs, 25th March 1813, *Collected Works*, 631–632.

133. Rey Buen Hijo, Rey Mas Distante, Perro Ravioso to Juan Nepomuceno de Quesada, 8th January 1795, PC, leg. 1438, doc. 680, frame 1052, reel 26, PKY.

134. John Forrester to Juan Nepomuceno de Quesada, 18th February 1793, EF, bnd. 123F10, doc. 1793–25, reel 48; PKY; Timothy Barnard to Major Henry Gaither, 18th February 1793, LTB, 125 GDAH.

135. Juan Nepomuceno de Quesada to Luis de Las Casas, 26th April 1793, PC, leg. 1436, 5614, reel 158, PKY.

136. John Cannard to John Leslie, 12th March 1793, EF, bnd. 114J9, reel 43, PKY; Timothy Barnard to James Seagrove, 26th March 1793, LTB, 136, GDAH.

137. Timothy Barnard to James Seagrove, 2nd July 1793, LTB, 188, GDAH; Governor of Florida to Marqúes del Campo, 9th April 1793, EF, bnd. 46G4, 128, reel 18, PKY; James Seagrove to the Secretary of War, 19th April 1793, *ASPIA*, Vol. I, 378–789; James Seagrove to the Secretary of War, 31st July 1793, *ASPIA*, Vol. I, 399–400.

138. Richard Lang to the Governor of Florida, 19th April 1793, EF, bnd. 123F10, doc. 1793–79, reel 48, PKY; James Seagrove to the Secretary of War, 19th April 1793, *ASPIA*, Vol. I, 378–379; John Forrester to the Governor of Florida, 20th April 1793, EF, bnd. 123F10, doc. 1793–84, reel 48, PKY.

139. Alexander McGillivray to Francisco Luis Héctor, barón de Carondelet, 10th April 1792, ANC, LOC.

140. John Reed Swanton, *Early History of the Creek Indians and Their Neighbours* (Washington, DC: U.S. Govt. Print. Off., 1922), 339.

141. William Bartram, *Travels of William Bartram*, ed. Mark van Doren (New York: Dover Publications, 1955), 383.

142. John Philip Reid, *A Law of Blood: The Primitive Law of the Cherokee Nation* (New York: New York University Press, 1970), 155–157.

143. Robin F. A. Fabel and Robert R. Rea, 'Lieutenant Thomas Campbell's Sojourn Among the Creeks, November 1764–May 1765,' *Alabama Historical Quarterly*, 36 (Summer, 1974), 109.

144. *Ibid.*

145. James Adair, *History of the American Indians* (New York: Promontory Press, 1973), 156.

146. Alexander McGillivray to Manuel Vicente de Zéspedes, 6th October 1787, EF, bnd. 114J9, reel 43, PKY.

147. James Wright to the Earl of Dartmouth, 31st January 1774, CRG, Vol. 38, 1: 169, GDAH; James Wright to the Earl of Dartmouth, 12th March 1774, CRG, Vol. 38, 1: 188, GDAH.

148. Adair, *History of the American Indians*, 157.

149. Reid, *A Law of Blood*, 154.

150. Charles Hudson, *The Southeastern Indians* (Knoxville: University of Tennessee Press, 1978), 239–240.

151. Hawkins, *Letters*, 102.

152. Philip Henry Gosse, *Letters from Alabama (U.S.)*, *Chiefly Relating to Natural History*, 1859, Reprint (Tuscaloosa: University of Alabama Press, 1973), 250.

153. Joseph Phillips to E. Park, 8th December 1804, Creek Indian Letters, GDAH, 705.

154. *Ibid.*

155. John Galphin to George Matthews, 14th June 1797, *American State Papers*, 32.

156. Hoggarth to Alexander McGillivray, 25th May 1792, *McGillivray of the Creeks*, 324–325.

157. Alexander McGillivray to Arturo O'Neill, 20th June 1787, ANC, LOC.

158. Braund, *Deerskins*, 86.

159. Chiefs of Cussitah and Cowetahs to James Seagrove, 23rd August 1792, ANC, LOC.

160. Benjamin Hawkins to Henry Dearborn, 28th March 1798, *Collected Works*, 286.

161. Benjamin Hawkins to William Eustis, 8th August 1798, *Collected Works*, 297.

162. Caleb Swan, 'Position and State of Manners and Arts in the Creek, or Muscogee Nation in 1791,' in *Historical and Statistical Information Respecting the History, Condition and Prospects of the Indian Tribes of the United States*, ed. Henry Rowe Schoolcraft (Philadelphia: Lippincott, Grambo and Company, 1851), 281–282.

163. *Ibid.*
164. John Reed Swanton, *Social Organization and Social Usages of the Indians of the Creek Confederacy—Religious Beliefs and Medical Practices of the Creek Indians—Aboriginal Culture of the Southeast* (1928), 339.
165. Talk delivered by the Governor and Council of Georgia to the Tallassee King, 24th September 1784, "Indian Treaties: Cessions of Land in Georgia, 1705–1837," 164, GDAH.
166. Hallowing King and Fat King to George Mathews, 14th June 1787, *ASPIA*, Vol. I, 32.
167. George Mathews to the headmen and warriors of the Lower Creeks, 29th June 1787, *ASPIA*, Vol. I, 32–33.
168. Fat King to George Mathews, 27th July 1787, *ASPIA*, Vol. I, 33.
169. Claudio Saunt, *A New Order of Things: Property, Power, and the Transformation of the Creek Indians, 1733–1816* (Cambridge: Cambridge University Press, 1999), 90–110.

Bibliography

Primary Sources

Beinecke Rare Book and Manuscript Library, Yale University, New Haven, United States

Thomas Thistlewood Papers.

British Library, London, United Kingdom

Acts of Assembly Passed in the Island of Jamaica from 1681 to 1733 Inclusive.
Edward Long Manuscripts.

Galileo Online Digital Library of Georgia (website)

South-eastern Native American Documents, 1730–1842.

Georgia Department of Archives and History, Morrow, Georgia, United States

"Creek Indian Letters, Talks, and Treaties, 1705–1839."
"Creek Letters, 1800–1819."
"Indian Treaties: Cessions of Land in Georgia, 1705–1837."
"Letters of Benjamin Hawkins, 1797–1815."
Miscellaneous Creek Indian Documents.
South-eastern Native American Documents Database.
Treaty at Fort Wilkinson with the Creek Indians, 1802.

Library of Congress, Washington, D.C., United States

Archivo Nacional de Cuba Collection (microfilm).

National Archives, Kew, United Kingdom

Adm. 1/240	CO 137/18	CO 137/21
CO 137/32	CO 137/40	CO 137/42
CO 137/56	CO 137/69	CO 137/73
CO 137/90	CO 137/91	CO 137/92
CO 137/94	CO 137/95	CO 137/96
CO 137/97	CO 137/98	WO 1/92
WO 1/96		

National Archives of Jamaica, Spanish Town, Jamaica

Inventories.
Journals of the House of Assembly, Vols. I–X.

National Archives and Records Office, Washington, D.C., United States

Foreign Letters of the Continental Congress and the Department of State.
Records of the Bureau of Indian Affairs.

National Library of Jamaica, Kingston, Jamaica

Notes on Survey Diagram of Charles Town by William Frazier.

P. K. Yonge Library, University of Florida, Gainesville, United States

Archivo General de Indias (microfilm).
East Florida Papers (microfilm).
Papeles Procedentes de Cuba (microfilm).
Records of the Creek Trading House, Letter Book, 1795–1816.

Special Collections, University of Georgia, Athens, United States

Southeastern Native American Documents, 1730–1842.

University of North Carolina Special Collections, Chapel Hill, United States

Hawkins Family Papers.

Newspapers and Magazines

Royal Gazette.
Supplement to the Royal Gazette.

Published Sources

Adair, James, History of the American Indians (New York: Promontory Press, 1973).
Adesoji, Abimbola O., 'Colonialism and Intercommunity Relations: The Ifon-Ilobu Example,' History in Africa, 32 (2005), 1–19.

Allain, J. M., 'Sexual Relations Between Elite White Women and Enslaved Men in the Antebellum South: A Socio-Historical Analysis,' *Inquiries*, 5, 8 (2013).

Anderson, Robert Nelson, 'The Quilombo of Palmares: A New Overview of a Maroon State in Seventeenth-Century Brazil,' *Journal of Latin American Studies*, 28, 3 (Oct., 1996), 545–566.

Aravamudan, Srinivas, ed., *Obi: Or, the History of Three-Fingered Jack* (Ontario: Broadview, 2005).

Baptist, Edward E., "Cuffy," "Fancy Maids," and "One-Eyed Men": Rape, Commodification, and the Domestic Slave Trade in the United States,' *The American Historical Review*, 106, 5 (Dec., 2001), 1619–1650.

Benson, Koni, and Joyce M. Chadya, 'Ukubhinya: Gender and Sexual Violence in Bulawayo, Colonial Zimbabwe, 1946–1956,' *Journal of Southern African Studies*, 31, 3 (Sept., 2005), 587–610.

Bilby, Kenneth, 'Swearing by the Past, Swearing to the Future: Sacred Oaths, Alliances and Treaties Among the Guianese and Jamaican Maroons,' *Ethnohistory*, 44, 4 (Autumn, 1997), 655–689.

Blackhawk, Ned, *Violence over the Land: Indians and Empires in the Early American West* (Cambridge, MA: Harvard University Press, 2006).

Braund, Kathryn E. Holland, *Deerskins and Duffels: The Creek Indian Trade with Anglo-America, 1685–1815* (Lincoln: University of Nebraska Press, 1996).

Brower, Benjamin Claude, *A Desert Named Peace: The Violence of France's Empire in the Algerian Sahara, 1844–1902* (New York: Columbia University Press, 2009).

Buckley, Roger N., 'Slave or Freedman: The Question of the Legal Status of the British West India Soldier, 1795–1807,' *Caribbean Studies*, 17, 3/4 (Oct., 1977–Jan., 1978), 83–113.

Burnard, Trevor, 'European Migration to Jamaica, 1655–1780,' *The William and Mary Quarterly*, 53, 4 (Oct., 1996), 769–796.

Burnard, Trevor, 'Slave-Naming Practices: Onomastics and the Taxonomy of Race in Eighteenth-Century Jamaica,' *Journal of Interdisciplinary History*, 31, 3 (2001), 325–346.

Campbell, Mavis, *The Maroons of Jamaica, 1655–1796: A History of Resistance, Collaboration & Betrayal* (Trentin: Africa World Press, 1990).

Carey, Bev, *Maroon Story: The Authentic and Original History of the Maroons in the History of Jamaica, 1490–1880* (St. Andrew, Jamaica: Agouti Press, 1997).

Caughey, John Walton, *McGillivray of the Creeks* (Norman: University of Oklahoma Press, 1938).

Cochran, Thomas C., ed., *The New American State Papers, 1789–1860* (Wilmington: Scholarly Resources, 1972–81).

Cody, Cheryll Ann, 'There Was No "Absalom" on the Ball Plantations: Slave-Naming Practices in the South Carolina Low Country, 1720–1865,' in *The Slavery Reader*, eds. Gad Heuman and James Walvin (New York: Routledge, 2003), 328–351.

Craton, Michael, ed., *Testing the Chains: Resistance to Slavery in the British West Indies* (Ithaca: Cornell University Press, 1982).

Cubano-Iguina, Astrid, 'Legal Constructions of Gender and Violence Against Women in Puerto Rico Under Spanish Rule, 1860–1895,' *Law and History Review*, 22, 3 (Autumn, 2004), 531–564.

Dalby, Jonathan, *Crime and Punishment in Jamaica: A Quantitative Analysis of the Assize Court Records, 1756–1856* (Mona: University of West Indies, 2000).

Dallas, Robert C., *The History of the Maroons: From Their Origin to the Establishment of Their Chief Tribe at Sierra Leone: Including the Expedition to Cuba, for the Purpose of Procuring Spanish Chasseurs; and the State of the Island of Jamaica for the Last Ten*

Years: With a Succinct History of the Island Previous to That Period (London: Printed by A. Strahan . . . for T. N. Longman and O. Rees. . ., 1803).

dos Santos Gomes, Flavió, 'Peasants, Maroons, and the Frontiers of Liberation in Maranhão,' *Review (Fernand Braudel Center)*, 31, 3, The Second Slavery: Mass Slavery, World Economy and Comparative Microhistories, Part II (2008), 373–399.

Edwards, Bryan, *The Proceedings of the Governor and Assembly of Jamaica, in Regard to the Maroon Negroes: Published by Order of the Assembly. To Which Is Prefixed, an Introductory Account, Containing, Observations on the Disposition, Character, Manners, and Habits of Life, of the Maroons, and, a Detail of the Origin, Progress, and Termination of the Late War Between Those People and the White Inhabitants* (London: John Stockdale, 1796).

Ethridge, Robbie Franklyn, *Creek Country: The Creek Indians and Their World* (Chapel Hill: University of North Carolina Press, 2003).

Fabel, Robin F. A., and Robert R. Rea, 'Lieutenant Thomas Campbell's Sojourn Among the Creeks, November 1764–May 1765,' *Alabama Historical Quarterly*, 36 (Summer, 1974), 97–111.

Ford, Lisa, *Settler Sovereignty: Jurisdiction and Indigenous People in America and Australia, 1788–1836* (Cambridge, MA: Harvard University Press, 2010).

Foster, H. Thomas, ed., *The Collected Works of Benjamin Hawkins* (Tuscaloosa: University of Alabama Press, 2003).

Frank, Andrew, *Creeks & Southerners: Biculturalism on the Early American Frontier* (Lincoln: University of Nebraska Press, 2005).

Gosse, Philip Henry, *Letters from Alabama (U.S.), Chiefly Relating to Natural History*, 1859, reprint (Tuscaloosa: University of Alabama Press, 1973).

Hall, Joseph M., Jr., *Zamumo's Gifts: Indian-European Exchange in the Colonial Southeast* (Philadelphia: University of Pennsylvania Press, 2009).

Hall, N. A. T., 'Maritime Maroons: "Grand Marronage" from the Danish West Indies,' *The William and Mary Quarterly*, 42, 4 (Oct., 1985), 476–498.

Handler, Jerome S., and JoAnn Jacoby, 'Slave Names and Naming in Barbados, 1650–1830,' *The William and Mary Quarterly*, 53, 4 (1996), 685–728.

Hart, Richard, *Slaves Who Abolished Slavery* (Kingston: University of the West Indies, Institute of Social and Economic Research, 1985).

Higman, Barry, *Plantation Jamaica, 1750–1850* (Kingston: University of West Indies Press, 2008).

Hogg, Robert Paul, '"A Hand Prepared to Be Red": Manliness and Racial Violence on Britain's Colonial Frontiers,' *Australasian Victorian Studies Journal*, 15, 1 (2010), 22–35.

Hudson, Charles, *The Southeastern Indians* (Knoxville: University of Tennessee Press, 1978).

Jacobs, Wilbur R., 'The Fatal Confrontation: Early Native-White Relations on the Frontiers of Australia, New Guinea, and America—a Comparative Study,' *Pacific Historical Review*, 40, 3 (Aug., 1971), 283–309.

Jacoby, Karl, *Shadows at Dawn: A Borderlands Massacre and the Violence of History* (New York: Penguin Press, 2008).

Karama, Aba, 'The Origin of the West Indies Regiments,' *Science and Society*, 35, 1 (Spring, 1971), 47–69.

Kopytoff, Barbara Klamon, 'The Development of Jamaican Maroon Ethnicity,' *Caribbean Quarterly*, 22, 2/3, Essays on Slavery (June–Sept., 1976), 33–50.

Kopytoff, Barbara Klamon, 'Colonial Treaty as Sacred Charter of the Jamaican Maroons,' *Ethnohistory*, 26, 1 (Winter, 1979), 45–64.

Langfur, Hal, *The Forbidden Lands: Colonial Identity, Frontier Violence, and the Persistence of Brazil's Eastern Indians, 1750–1830* (Stanford: Stanford University Press, 2006).

Law, Robin, 'Dahomey and the Slave Trade: Reflections on the Historiography of the Rise of Dahomey,' *The Journal of African History*, 27, 2 (1986), 237–267.

Law, Robin, 'Slave-Raiders and Middlemen, Monopolists and Free-Traders: The Supply of Slaves for the Atlantic Trade in Dahomey, c. 1715–1850,' *The Journal of African History*, 30, 1 (1989), 45–68.

Lindsay, Alexander Crawford, *Lives of the Lindsays: Or a Memoir of the Houses of Crawford and Balcarres . . .* (Wigan: Privately Printed, 1840).

Long, Edward, *The History of Jamaica; or, General Survey of the Ancient and Modern State of That Island: With Reflections on Its Situations, Settlements, Inhabitants, Climate, Products, Commerce, Laws, and Government*, Vol. II (London: F. Cass, 1970).

Lutz, John Sutton, *Makúk: A New History of Aboriginal-White Relations* (Vancouver: University of British Columbia Press, 2008).

Metcalf, George, *Royal Government and Political Conflict in Jamaica, 1729–1783* (London: Longmans, Green & Co., 1965).

Moses, A. Dirk, ed., *Genocide and Settler Society: Frontier Violence and Stolen Indigenous Children in Australian History* (New York: Berghahn Books, 2004).

Mullin, Michael, *Africa in America: Slave Acculturation and Resistance in the American South and the British Caribbean, 1736–1831* (Urbana: University of Illinois Press, 1994).

Murray, David, *Indian Giving: Economies of Power in Early Indian-White Exchanges* (Amherst: University of Massachusetts Press, 2000).

Ndlovu-Gatsheni, Sabelo J., 'Re-thinking the Colonial Encounter in Zimbabwe in the Early Twentieth Century,' *Journal of South African Studies*, 33, 1 (2007), 173–191.

Parris, Scott V., 'Alliance and Competition: Four Case Studies of Maroon-European Relations,' *Nieuwe West-Indische Gids/New West Indian Guide*, 55ste Jaarg., 3/4 (Dec., 1981), 174–224.

Paton, Diana, 'Punishment, Crime, and the Bodies of Slaves in Eighteenth Century Jamaica,' *Journal of Social History*, 34, 4 (2001), 923–954.

Paton, Diana, *No Bond but the Law: Punishment, Race, and Gender in Jamaican State Formation, 1780–1870* (Durham: Duke University Press, 2004).

Patterson, Orlando, 'Slavery and Slave Revolts: A Socio-Historical Analysis of the First Maroon War, 1655–1740,' *Social and Economic Studies*, 19, 3 (Sept., 1970), 289–325.

Penn, Nigel, *The Forgotten Frontier: Colonist and Khoisan on the Cape's Northern Frontier in the 18th Century* (Athens: Ohio University Press, 2005).

Perdue, Theda, *"Mixed Blood" Indians: Racial Construction in the Early South* (Athens: University of Georgia Press, 2003).

Reid, John Philip, *A Law of Blood: The Primitive Law of the Cherokee Nation* (New York: New York University Press, 1970).

Reid, Richard J., *Frontiers of Violence in North-East Africa: Genealogies of Conflict Since 1800* (Oxford: Oxford University Press, 2011).

Richardson, David, 'Shipboard Revolts, African Authority, and the Atlantic Slave Trade,' *The William and Mary Quarterly*, 58, 1 (Jan., 2001), 69–92.

Richardson, David, 'Cultures of Exchange: Atlantic Africa in the Era of the Slave Trade,' *Transactions of the Royal Historical Society*, 6th Series, 19 (2009), 151–179.

Robinson, Carey, *The Iron Thorn: The Defeat of the British by the Jamaican Maroons* (Kingston: Kingston Publishers Limited, 1993).

Saunt, Claudio, *A New Order of Things: Property, Power, and the Transformation of the Creek Indians, 1733–1816* (Cambridge: Cambridge University Press, 1999).

Schmidt, E., *Peasants, Traders & Wives: Shona Women in the History of Zimbabwe, 1870–1939* (London: James Currey, 1992).

Schwartzman, Grace M., and Susan K. Barnard, 'A Trail of Broken Promises: Georgians and Muscogee/Creek Treaties, 1796–1826,' *Georgia Historical Quarterly*, 75, 4 (Winter, 1991), 697–718.

Scully, Pamela, 'Rape, Race, and Colonial Culture: The Sexual Politics of Identity in the Nineteenth-Century Cape Colony, South Africa,' *The American Historical Review*, 100, 2 (Apr., 1995), 335–359.

Sen, Samita, ' "Without His Consent?": Marriage and Women's Migration in Colonial India,' *International Labour and Working-Class History*, 65, Agriculture and Working-Class Formation (Spring, 2004), 77–104.

Sheridan, Richard B., 'The Jamaican Slave Insurrection Scare of 1776 and the American Revolution,' *The Journal of Negro History*, 61, 3 (July, 1976), 291.

Smith, Andrea, *Conquest: Sexual Violence and American Indian Genocide* (Cambridge, MA: South End Press, 2005).

Snyder, Christina, 'Conquered Enemies, Adopted Kin, and Owned People: The Creek Indians and Their Captives,' *The Journal of Southern History*, 73, 2 (May, 2007), 255–288.

Stiggins, George, *Creek Indian History: A Historical Narrative of the Genealogy, Traditions, and Downfall of the Ispocoga or Creek Indian Tribe of Indians* (Birmingham: Birmingham Public Library Press, 1989).

Swan, Caleb, "Position and State of Manners and Arts in the Creek, or Muscogee Nation in 1791," in *Historical and Statistical Information Respecting the History, Condition and Prospects of the Indian Tribes of the United States*, ed. Henry Rowe Schoolcraft (Philadelphia: Lippincott, Grambo and Company, 1851).

Swanton, John Reed, *Early History of the Creek Indians and Their Neighbours* (Washington, DC: U.S. Govt. Print. Off., 1922).

Swanton, John Reed, *Social Organization and Social Usages of the Indians of the Creek Confederacy—Religious Beliefs and Medical Practices of the Creek Indians—Aboriginal Culture of the Southeast* (Washington D.C.: Smithsonian Institue, 1928).

Sweet, John Wood, 'The Subject of the Slave Trade: Recent Currents in the Histories of the Atlantic, Great Britain, and Western Africa,' *Early American Studies*, 7, 1 (Spring, 2009), 1–45.

Usner, Daniel H., *Indians, Settlers, and Slaves in a Frontier Exchange Economy: The Lower Mississippi Valley before 1783* (Chapel Hill: University of North Carolina Press, 1992).

van Den Boogaart, Ernst, 'The Trade Between Western Africa and the Atlantic World, 1600–90: Estimates of Trends in Composition and Value,' *The Journal of African History*, 33, 3 (1992), 369–385.

van Doren, Mark, ed., *Travels of William Bartram* (New York: Dover Publications, 1955).

Wilson, Kathleen, 'The Performance of Freedom: Maroons and the Colonial Order in Eighteenth-Century Jamaica and the Atlantic Sound,' *The William and Mary Quarterly*, 3rd Series, 66 (Jan., 2009), 45–86.

Epilogue

For both the Maroons and Creeks, their decision to sign peace treaties ultimately led to further warfare in the form of the Second Maroon War and the Creek War of 1813. Their allegiance allowed Jamaica and the United States to grow economically, to unite divided societies and to advance the system of slavery. This enabled both countries to transform from under-developed territories to formidable powers in the region. The subsequent refusal of Maroons and Creeks to bow to the demands of federal and colonial officials, especially in light of external events such as the Haitian Revolution, led to both governments moving to destroy these semi-autonomous, free communities.

However, it was the aftermath of the war which shocked both the Maroons and Creeks. In Jamaica, a treaty was put forward by the colonial government which required the Maroons to beg for forgiveness on their knees, return all runaway slaves and be relocated elsewhere in Jamaica. The most devious part of the proposal was that the colonial government gave the Maroons only three days to turn themselves in, an impossible feat given the Maroons' location. The colonial government then used their lack of surrender as a pretext for deporting the Trelawny Maroons. The Trelawnys were invited to a friendship feast with representatives of the government where the Maroons were thrown into chains, boarded on ships and sent from the island.[1] Thus, the Trelawny Town Maroons, the largest and most influential of the Maroon towns, ceased to exist in Jamaica.

The remaining Maroon towns were subject to further restrictions and reductions in their autonomy. In particular, the glut of laws introduced in 1791 was finally enforced. The colonial government specifically focused on those which curtailed Maroon movements outside the boundaries of their settlements and their opportunities to secure income through putting down slave rebellions.[2] On the eve of the nineteenth century, colonial officials also began the process of registration for all Maroon communities. By 1805, missionary work was taking hold and the baptism of Maroons was in full swing. Despite all of these measures, however, Maroon communities still persist in Jamaica to the present day.

Likewise, the outcomes of the Creek War of 1813 stunned the Creek Nation. The majority of the Redsticks had fled to Spanish Pensacola, where they continued their fight against the United States on the side of the British in the War of 1812. The rest of the Nation, mainly those who had sided with the Americans, was forced to sign the Treaty of Fort Jackson, which compelled the Creeks to cede 21,086,793 acres—half of present-day Alabama and parts of Georgia—to the United States.[3] The treaty made no distinction between the Creek allies of the United States, belonging to largely Lower Creek towns, and the Redsticks, who had fought against the federal government. The effects of this were devastating and set in motion the events leading to the removal of all Creeks from the south-east during the Trail of Tears. However, much like the Maroons of Jamaica, the Creek Nation still endures to this day.

Therefore, we have a situation in both cases where initial peace terms were agreed, followed by a period of uneasy alliance, which in turn led to increasing restrictions being implemented. Those restrictions ultimately led to war and the alteration, but not complete destruction, of both communities. Such a tentative model allows us to consider Maroons and Creeks as part of a similar framework, rather than as different ends of the racial spectrum. Of course, that is not to say that their experiences were completely uniform—important differences could, and did, occur. However, this would be true of any communities under comparison. Whilst it is important to acknowledge such differences, it is equally important to recognise the similarities in order to deduce that Maroons can be considered within an indigenous framework.

Some things were, of course, unique to the Maroon experience—for example, the act of slave-catching was particularly controversial because of the shared background on the plantations of many Maroons and the enslaved population. Whilst Creeks also hunted slaves in return for financial reward, few Creeks, in this period, had been enslaved and, therefore, they were less expected to have an affinity with enslaved people. The other differences that did occur, such as the lack of violence between Maroons and settlers or the use of debt to force Creek land cession, were largely a result of the type of borderland on which each community lived. A worthwhile future comparison, therefore, would be between the Jamaican Maroons and another semi-autonomous community, although indigenous, surrounded by one nation, or colonial power. Such a comparison would allow us to further explore the similarities between Maroons and indigenous people, without such a focus on race—an issue which, whilst should never be ignored, needs to be analysed alongside other critical factors. Overall, therefore, this work should be considered as the first step in a process which requires more comparative analysis of other communities.

Notes

1. Kenneth Bilby, 'The Treacherous Feast: A Jamaican Maroon Historical Myth,' *Bijdragen tot de Taal-, Land- en Volkenkunde*, 140, 1 (1984), 1–31.
2. Bev Carey, *Maroon Society: The Authentic and Original History of the Maroons in the History of Jamaica, 1490–1880* (St. Andrew, Jamaica: Agouti Press, 1997), 493.
3. Daniel Walker Howe, *What Hath God Wrought: The Transformation of America, 1815–1848* (Oxford: Oxford University Press, 2009), 75.

Bibliography

Bilby, Kenneth, 'The Treacherous Feast: A Jamaican Maroon Historical Myth,' *Bijdragen tot de Taal-, Land- en Volkenkunde*, 140, 1 (1984), 1–31.

Carey, Bev, *Maroon Society: The Authentic and Original History of the Maroons in the History of Jamaica, 1490–1880* (St Andrew: Agouti Press, 1997).

Howe, Daniel Walker, *What Hath God Wrought: The Transformation of America, 1815–1848* (Oxford: Oxford University Press, 2009).

Index